Glenway Wescott Personally

Glenway Wescott Personally

A BIOGRAPHY

Jerry Rosco

The University of Wisconsin Press

The University of Wisconsin Press
1930 Monroe Street, 3rd Floor
Madison, Wisconsin 53711-2059
uwpress.wisc.edu

3 Henrietta Street
London WC2E 8LU, England
eurospanbookstore.com

5 4 3 2

Printed in the United States of America

Library of Congress Cataloging-in-Publication Data
Rosco, Jerry.
Glenway Wescott personally : a biography / Jerry Rosco.
pp. cm.
Includes bibliographical references and index.
ISBN 0-299-17730-0 (cloth: alk. paper)
1. Wescott, Glenway, 1901– 2. Authors, American—20th century—Biography. 3. Americans—France—Paris—History—20th century. 4. New York (N.Y.)—Intellectual life—20th century. 5. Paris (France)—Intellectual life—20th century. 6. Gay men—United States—Biography. 7. Wisconsin—Biography. I. Title.
PS3545.E827 Z84 2002
813'.52—dc21 2001005410

ISBN 978-0-299-17734-8 (pbk. : alk. paper)

To my great friend Peter Adelman.
Also in thanks to John Stevenson and Ian Young.
And in memory of Glenway's editor, Robert Phelps (1923–89),
and my companion, Jack Bissell (1962–95).

Contents

Illustrations ix
Preface xi
Acknowledgments xiii
Introduction xv

1. Wisconsin Farm Boy to Midwest Prodigy 3
2. The Next Step: New York and Europe 21
3. The Expatriate Twenties 32
4. Paris and a New Family 47
5. Lost in America: The Thirties 62
6. The Little Masterpiece and Willie Maugham 89
7. The Bestseller 108
8. Dr. Kinsey and the Institute for Sex Research 126
9. Inside the Circle: Farewell to George 152
10. Beyond Fiction: The Valley Submerged 164
11. The Great Divide and Images of Truth 191
12. "Quail and Strawberries" 217
13. Golden Leaves and the Birthday Book 244

Epilogue: Other Voices and Continual Lessons 260

Notes 271
Index 297

Illustrations

Glenway Wescott in Paris, 1925 81
Glenway Wescott, Paris, 1930 82
Glenway and Lloyd Wescott with Monroe Wheeler, 1934 83
"Acteon," advertisement 83
Monroe Wheeler, W. Somerset Maugham, and Wescott at Stone-blossom 84
Nelson Lansdale 85
Baroness Pauline de Rothschild 85
Ralph Pomeroy with Wescott 86
Raymond Mortimer visits Wescott at Stone-blossom 86
Wescott with Alfred C. Kinsey at the Institute for Sex Research, 1952 87
Wescott and his mother at Stone-blossom, 1959 87
Wescott and John Connolly in the farmhouse kitchen 88
Wescott's elegant script, from "The Valley Submerged" 88
Wescott and Wheeler at Stone-blossom, 1959 181
"Luncheon at Haymeadows," painting by Harold Bruder 181
Katherine Anne Porter with Wheeler and Wescott, Summer 1960 182
Anatole Pohorilenko, 1977 182
Wescott with attentive barn cat at Haymeadows 183
Dinner conversation with Wescott 184
At home on the farm, Wescott in denim overall 185
Wescott and Marianne Moore at the artists' colony, August 20, 1967 186

Tennessee Williams with Wheeler and Wescott 186
Barbara Harrison Wescott 187
John Stevenson and Wescott, January 8, 1979 187
Tigers at Haymeadows 188
Wescott siblings: Lloyd, Beulah, Glenway, Katherine, and Elizabeth, 1978 188
Monroe Wheeler at 81, 1980 189
Wescott with a branch of blossoms at Haymeadows, 1980 190

Preface

BEYOND the standard resources of biography, this rendering of Glenway Wescott's life is illuminated by his own words. From the mid-1970s to the early 1980s, he granted a generous number of interviews, first with the devoted editor of his journals, Robert Phelps, and then with myself. We are fortunate to have these interviews on audio tape because Wescott was one of the great speakers and storytellers. In addition, while his archives are massive, they are typically weighted toward his middle and late years, so the interviews filled in important parts of the early story and added rich detail in other areas. Robert Phelps let him speak expansively without interruption. I tended to be more journalistic and kept him on specific topics, or tried. Both methods worked.

After Robert Phelps died in 1989, Rosemarie Beck Phelps gave me her late husband's interview tapes and I took over his project of editing Wescott's journals. (They were published the following year under the title *Continual Lessons.*) Along with my own tapes, they were helpful with the journals but they held far greater value. Many scholars have written about Wescott from a literary perspective, but that is only part of his story. A true biography should reveal the subject personally, and the interviews do capture Wescott's voice and his heart. He was a complex, extraordinary, deeply humanistic, and compassionate man. His personal perspectives on the joys and mysteries of life tell us as much as his writings do. Like his writing, his spoken words convey more than the topic at hand. In *Glenway Wescott Personally* his comments are used more in some places, such as the first chapter, less in others, but I believe the emphasis is well positioned.

Of course, the facts and dates are supported by years of research and interviews with others. But perhaps the greater truths can be found in Wescott's storytelling.

Anyone who knew Glenway Wescott invariably says that he or she can hear his voice still. I hope that voice will now speak directly to you.

Acknowledgments

I KNEW Glenway Wescott for thirteen years, but I came to know him better through interviews with those who knew him longer and who invited me into their homes, especially Paul Cadmus, John Connolly, Charles Henri Ford, Ruth Ford, Carl Malouf, Bernard Perlin, Rosemarie Beck Phelps, Anatole Pohorilenko, and Ralph Pomeroy. And I appreciate Mr. Pohorilenko's help as executor of the estates of Glenway Wescott and Monroe Wheeler.

I thank editor Raphael Kadushin for his perspective, and the writers who offered valuable advice, especially Sargent Bush Jr. for his help and encouragement, as well as David Bergman, Daniel Curzon, Fielding Dawson, Edward Field, Jonathan Gathorne-Hardy, John Gilgun, Paul Reed, and Thomas Waugh. I'm also grateful for the help of graphic artist Kim Kasow, the staff of the University of Wisconsin Press, and the support of longtime friends David Orbach, Jennifer Pader, James R. Rosenfield, and Daniel Rossicone.

Thanks also to the research libraries, curators, and staff who were very helpful during many visits over ten years—the Beinecke Rare Book and Manuscript Library, Yale University (Patricia Willis, Elizabeth Wakeman Dwight Curator of American Literature; Timothy Young, archivist; and Stephen Jones of Library Services) and the Henry W. and Albert A. Berg Collection of English and American Literature, New York Public Library (Rodney Phillips, then curator; Stephen Crook, librarian; and Philip Milito, technical assistant).

Grateful acknowledgment is made for the use of illustrations to Harold

Bruder, Jill Krementz, the Estate of George Platt Lynes, the Kinsey Institute for Research in Sex, Gender, and Reproduction, Inc., Gerard Malanga, and John Stevenson. For the greater number of photos, thanks and acknowledgment go to Anatole Pohorilenko for the estates of Glenway Wescott and Monroe Wheeler, and to John Connolly, Ralph Pomeroy, and the Beinecke Library.

I also offer acknowledgment and thanks to the following people and agencies for permission to quote from unpublished letters: A. P. Watt, Ltd., on behalf of the Royal Literary Fund, and Kay Collyer & Boose, with permission of the Estate of Elizabeth Lady Glendevon, for William Somerset Maugham; Don Bachardy, for Christopher Isherwood; Edward Burns, for Alice B. Toklas; Deborah Wescott Clark, for Barbara Harrison Wescott; David Higham Associates, Ltd., for Edith Sitwell, Osbert Sitwell, and Sacheverell Sitwell, Higham reference Sitwell\5.9.00; Barbara Thompson Davis, for Katherine Anne Porter; Marianne Ehrlich, for Elizabeth Ames; Ruth Ford; Stuart M. Rosen, for the Edna Ferber Literary Trust; Richard Hawkes, for John Hawkes; The Kinsey Institute for Research in Sex, Gender, and Reproduction, Inc., for Alfred C. Kinsey; Lescher & Lescher, Ltd., and A.M. Heath & Company, Ltd., for Isaac Bashevis Singer; Ruth Limmer, for Louise Bogan; Mary Anita Loos, for Anita Loos; George Platt Lynes II, for George Platt Lynes; Marianne Craig Moore, for her aunt, Marianne Moore; David Rockefeller; Baroness Philippine de Rothschild, for Baroness Pauline and Baron Philippe de Rothschild; The Society of Authors as agent for the Provost and Scholars of King's College Cambridge, for E. M. Forster; A. J. Szold, for Bernadine Szold; Nancy Tate Wood, for Caroline Gordon Tate.

Thanks also to Edward Field for use of the Ralph Pomeroy poem, "The Novelist at Home in New Jersey." Some Wescott interview material was used previously in articles in *Chicago Review, The Guide, James White Review, Literary Review, Lost Generation Journal,* and *Sequoia.*

Introduction

A WISCONSIN farm boy, Glenway Wescott made his way to Paris in the 1920s where he became one of the major expatriate writers of those years. When his early celebrity faded, he became a New York literary figure, with another period of success and a bestseller in the forties. Afterward he turned to his other talents as an essayist and critic. Like E. M. Forster, he is criticized for not producing novels after midlife. Yet two of his four novels, *The Grandmothers* and *The Pilgrim Hawk,* stand as classic works of their kind. He is also respected as a prose stylist of unsurpassed skill, intelligence, and subtlety.

Wescott's place in literature is a matter of debate. His first two novels and a book of stories, *Good-bye, Wisconsin,* are memorable regional works of the Midwest. Remembering his friend, the novelist William Maxwell said, "He was at home in France and New York, in a certain part of New Jersey, and I suppose in many other places. But when he reached for a comparison it came, like him, out of rural Wisconsin." After the expatriate years, Wescott returned an urbane writer with a New York home. But by good fortune his Wisconsin family went east to a lavish farm in western New Jersey. His writing took him in many directions, but he always wrote beautifully of nature and farm life.

It is worth remembering that Wescott was one of the outstanding speakers and readers of his time. Even at sixteen, as a freshman at the University of Chicago, he was chosen president of the prestigious Poetry Club because of his reading voice. When the poet Margaret Anderson first met twenty-year-old Wescott in the office of *Poetry* magazine, she asked him about his distinguished speech. He said he loved the English language and had trained himself to speak it well. Later in life, he was a popular lecturer, storyteller, and conversationalist.

As a longtime member, and once president, of the American Academy-Institute of Arts and Letters, he gained the reputation of being a part of the literary establishment. Yet his considerable work for the arts in many areas was helpful, not hurtful, and over the decades he secured grants and awards for many new writers, as well as established ones.

Through much of his century, his circle of friends and acquaintances included many of America's and Europe's great creative people, as well as others in public life. A gay man, he was always "out," and his lifelong companion was Monroe Wheeler, a curator for New York's Museum of Modern Art who revolutionized museum publications. Wheeler arranged art exhibits around the world and was awarded France's Legion of Honor. For seventeen years, Wescott and Wheeler lived with the photographer George Platt Lynes, and their connection to many notable gay figures has been widely recounted.

Because Wescott cared passionately about sexual freedom for all people, it was fitting that he befriended and worked for Dr. Alfred Kinsey and the Institute for Sex Research. In this biography, the chapter on the Kinsey years necessarily steps away from some chronological detail for the sake of clarity. Those details are easily caught up in the following chapter. But the impact of Kinsey on Wescott personally is essential to the larger story. In light of contemporary biographies of Kinsey—as well as society's ongoing battles over individual and sexual freedom—I know that Wescott would strongly emphasize this topic.

An agnostic, he said the gods he believed in were "Time . . . Memory, Sex, Language." Yet he was a moralist, both in everyday life and in his belief in moral fiction. No doubt, he was a complex man. Though a lover of classical music, especially Bach, he attended a Rolling Stones concert in his sixties. In his seventies, he laughingly admitted to dancing alone to David Bowie's songs "Fame" and "Young Americans" because the lyrics reminded him of his youth in the Paris years. And while it's true his fame came early, it may also be true that his middle and late years were richer and more interesting. The rural bus or Trenton train connected his country and city homes and a busy world of literature, art, society, farm, and family. Once, he delighted in sharing a bus trip with chef Julia Child and discussing his specialties, soups and salads.

Perhaps love of life crowded Wescott's time and production, but he never stopped writing, and his late journals and essays keep the promise of his youth. Certainly, no one was ever more devoted to literature. In one of his last interviews, Wescott reflected, "Maybe because I myself was incapable of greatness, I have preferred middle-sized writers and my-sized writers, and smaller books. I don't think that's an acknowledgment of inferiority exactly because there are two families in literature: the gigantic poseur with colossal powers of invention, preaching . . . and there are writers who write as human beings for human beings. And they last."

Glenway Wescott Personally

1

Wisconsin Farm Boy to Midwest Prodigy

GLENWAY GORDON WESCOTT was born in Wisconsin farm country, near Kewaskum in Washington County, at 5 P.M. on April 11, 1901. He was the oldest of six children. The others were his brother, Lloyd, who was the youngest, and four sisters: Beulah, Marjorie, Katherine, and Elizabeth. Their father, Bruce Wescott, was proud of the land. The bees in his hives were descended from those his own father had owned during the Civil War. But Bruce struggled with his hundred-acre farm, breeding pigs because he couldn't afford horses or cows, and unable to use some of his fields because of runoff from the hills. His older son was little help. While still a boy Glenway would make his way to Chicago, then as a young man to Santa Fe, New York, and Europe. But the earliest steps in his journey were the most difficult. Many years later, Wescott remembered, "I couldn't work for my father on the farm. He was so sorry for himself because he had more work than he could do, and I was sickly and irritable. Most of the time he was exhausted and had difficulty feeding us all."[1]

Bright and precocious, Glenway was a puzzle to his parents. Even as a child he seemed determined to escape from the farm, yet he developed a love of nature and country life that would be reflected lifelong in his writing. He attended the local one-room red schoolhouse, Orchard Grove Country School, from 1906 to 1912, but it was the weekly journey to church that gave him his first impression of an outside world. "When we went to Sunday school," he recalled, "we children would lie in the back of the wagon in the straw with a buffalo rug over us. It took us an hour to travel the six miles to the church in West Bend."[2] Early memories of long-time residents gave him a rich sense of the previous century. There was an Indian reservation nearby, and an elderly neighbor told him a story from her youth, when she sat up all night with a rifle, anticipating an Indian attack.[3]

Two incidents scarred his early childhood. Glenway was traumatized when he accidentally knocked his baby brother against a hot stove, although the infant wasn't seriously burned and their parents were forgiving. The other incident occurred when Bruce Wescott encouraged his son to climb a tree, in the presence of several men and boys, including a cousin Glenway admired. When a rotted branch snapped and dropped him to the hard ground, the boy believed his father knew this would happen and wanted to humiliate him. Later, when his devout Christian parents learned of his suspicion they were shocked, and his father fell to his knees in prayer.

Of the reading materials available to Glenway, the only ones that stirred his imagination were the books of Leviticus and Deuteronomy in the Old Testament and serialized Hall Caine novels.[4] He had a good soprano voice, took lessons, and earned a few dollars singing at funerals. But the rough, sometimes brutal, work on the farm upset him. Even peaceful moments could turn with the whim of wild nature. He recalled once driving a neighbor's cows in a straight line at sunset for a few hundred yards when "suddenly a nighthawk that was flying just above the backs of the cows crashed right into my face with a thump!"[5]

At age twelve Glenway found an excuse to leave the farm. He was ready for high school and was obliged to live near the school in West Bend, although he would return home for weekends. "I was prepared to go to high school a year ahead of time," he said, "and I boarded with the Methodist clergyman. We weren't Methodists but in those days you had to go to whatever Protestant church you had in your town; there'd be a Protestant church and a Catholic one. I lived one year with this English clergyman who had a handsome wife who tyrannized over him, and they had a terrible little boy. I was so unhappy there in this churchy household with this ghastly nine-year-old boy whom, for part of my board, I was supposed to mind. So, I complained to my parents and in the second year of high school I went to live with my maternal grandparents, and that was very pleasant."[6]

Glenway attended West Bend High School from 1913 to 1915, and in his second year he published a little essay, "King David and His Court," in the school periodical, *The Tatler.* Now that more books were available to him, the youngster read widely and at a pace and level far beyond his years.

In 1914, Glenway began a relationship with a fifteen-year-old boy named Earl who "relieved me of my virginity." He recalled, "My grandparents couldn't feed me and I took my meals at a boarding house run by a woman who was a second cousin to my family. And there I fell in love with Earl Rix Kuelthau. In the second year of high school I didn't eat dinner: I gave it up to deliver a newspaper route with Earl. It was terrible food anyway, as well as terrible company. And in May of that second year I lost my virginity." That first experience took place during a sleepover, in a large bed in which a third boy was fast asleep. "I always believed that set the course for the triangularity of my relationships," he said, referring to many love triangles over the decades.[7]

To the older boy, the relationship was one of friendship and experimentation. To thirteen-year-old Glenway, discovering his sexuality in the puritanical atmosphere of the Midwest, it meant far more. Many years later he recalled in a journal note, "My first kiss (except for my mother's kisses in infancy) took place beside a very tall and wide-spreading syringa bush in full bloom; a cool, kindly, thin-lipped, cigarette-flavored kiss, in a rocking chair swing on a lawn in the county seat of my native county in Wisconsin, in the gloaming, while the Lutheran Church choir next door practiced the following Sunday's anthems. I was thirteen years old and my then beloved, fifteen."[8]

The secret romance with Earl, or "Carl," as Wescott would later fictionalize him in a story, lasted more than a year, and then Earl discovered girls. Afterward, Glenway painfully shut off all thoughts of affection with another male for five long years.

By his third year of high school he had yet another home—this time with his mother's brother, Will Gordon about thirty miles downstate. "My grandparents didn't really want me anymore," he said, "but my parson uncle by this time had a church in Waukesha. They had a nice house and I think he was rather lonesome because his wife was always visiting her rich mother in Chicago. I think it embarrassed him to have a wife who wouldn't stay with him. He was terribly good looking, in the most corny way in the world—you know, like all clergymen and preachers; a Greek profile with a little hair floating over his forehead, a beautiful voice, and women were mad about him. I went there to live with him and go to a better school, and stayed there two years."[9]

Glenway's short story "The Dare" appeared in the Waukesha High School *Megaphone* in 1915. As he recalled, he wasn't planning to be a writer, but his creative spirit was greatly influenced by a schoolmate with a notorious reputation: "Virginia Bugbee was a very mannish girl from a distinguished family, and she was liberated, mysterious, and obscure—and smoked cigarettes! Night after night she'd drive at the speed of light out to the lakes and we would sit on steep hillsides looking out at Lake Oconomowoc. I would read aloud out of Whitman. The first thing that I ever wrote that I took any pains with were a series of love letters in the style of Walt Whitman that I wrote to her when I was fifteen or sixteen."[10] His friendship with Virginia not only encouraged his reading and writing but also strengthened the rebelliousness and tenacity he needed to survive.

Wescott excelled in high school and earned a scholarship to the University of Chicago at sixteen. He also had earned a reputation as a great talker. In the high school yearbook, the student editors captioned his photo, "Have I said enough? Shall I say more?"

Uncle Will helped once more by asking his mother-in-law in Chicago and her two other daughters to provide Wescott with room and board. Wescott remembered, "I got a scholarship from the University of Chicago and went down there in the fall of '17. Out of great condescension toward the dutiful, devoted, though dubious son-in-law, I was allowed to room at this home and have my evening meal there. They were on the West Side, halfway to Oak Park where Hemingway was, and it was a pretty grand red brick house on a great big tree-lined square. Naturally, it would seem grand to me anyway."[11]

Even before he found his footing in the complex caste system of the vast university, the child-freshman had to learn the rules of the strange, provincial household of delicate ladies, various guests, and a staff of Belgian servants. As he described it:

> The house was well furnished and everything was brass and shiny. The bookcases were built-in and made of curly maple, but the cases were locked! I never forgave them for that. I think it was assumed that my hands weren't clean enough. It enraged me because I was the only person in the world who wanted to read a book!
>
> At the evening meal the food wasn't anything to brag about but the dishes and silver were absolutely fantastic. There was another poor relative who shared the attic with me, and who never spoke above a whisper. He worked at a department store.
>
> I had an allowance from them of fifty cents a day. And I think that was the only money I had. Out of that I got my food, and my fare on the elevated train. It took almost an hour to get out to the campus—this way into the loop, and then out that way. And I had to buy my own textbooks. It doesn't seem possible: three dollars and fifty cents a week! And sometimes I went to the symphony. If I went with the relatives I sat in the third row, but if I went alone I sat way up on top.[12]

Chicago was as alluring as it was daunting to the sixteen-year-old. He was not afraid. Poverty in Wisconsin and years of boarding had made him resilient. He felt there was no turning back to the family farm, but his first weeks at the large university were intimidating. "Looking around that campus I couldn't see how I could make contact with anyone or have any fun at all," he said. "I lived all the way on the West Side. I was small. I was bad tempered. I was homosexual. I was poor. And I had a very bad tongue, if you provoked me. I was not afraid of anybody. There were about twenty thousand people there and I didn't fit in any category. I couldn't go in for sports. I couldn't go in for girls. I couldn't go to ordinary clubs around there because I had to go on out to the West Side after classes. No one would speak with me."[13]

Luckily, he met Arthur Yvor Winters, a talented student and a rebel of a different sort who would become a central figure among the Imagist poets of the late teens and twenties. The meeting came about when Wescott "noticed on the bulletin board that something called the Poetry Club was having a competition to fill two or three vacancies. The first poems I ever wrote were two I sent in. I don't have them. They weren't very good. One was about Cleopatra and the asp, and I can't remember the other one at all. It was just a trick. I'd never done anything like it before. I never had any notion to be a writer. I wanted to be a singer. Then I wanted to be an actor. And then in high school, to buck up my homosexual love for a bisexual girl who wouldn't let me touch her, I wrote those letters."[14] Nevertheless, the poems impressed the Poetry Club members—which included Winters—and Wescott quickly joined this exceptional group. It was the practical and generous Yvor Winters who helped Wescott get on as a student and an artist, led him to other creative young people, and opened the way to literature.

"Yvor, who had a rich stockbroker for a father," said Wescott, "was a socialist and vowed that he would take not one cent more from his father than was absolutely necessary. So he budgeted himself and found a place where we could lunch for fifteen cents a day. And that's where my education began with a vengeance. Because Yvor decided that I was bright as a whip and could be taught anything. And he decided to teach me to be a poet."[15]

Winters himself recalled the Poetry Club of the late teens: "This was a very intelligent group, worth more than most courses in literature; among the new members were Glenway Wescott, a year younger than myself, who, like myself, had discovered most of the unknown moderns in high school, and Elizabeth Madox Roberts, about twenty years our elder."[16] Like Wescott, Roberts went on to make her reputation as a novelist, as did another member of the Poetry Club, Janet Lewis, who eventually married Winters. The club met in a small first-floor room near the main entrance of Ida Noyes Hall on the university campus. Wescott, the best reader, became its president, yet the real leader was Winters, whose precise, elegant poems set an example for the others.

Although illness and circumstances would limit Wescott to a year and a half at the university, the experience of the Chicago poetry crowd and his vast self-education made the matter of a degree secondary. At sixteen, he was not aware that his literary skills were far beyond those of most graduate students. His memory of his freshman year is illustrative:

You had to consult your instructor and make a plan and write something rather important which would take you a couple of months. I said I'd thought about it and would like to write a piece tracing the dramatic technique of Maurice Maeterlinck in the thirty-seven plays he'd written to that date. And the professor said, "My God, my poor young man. You're not going to have time to read thirty-seven plays, much less write about them! What ails you?"

And I said, "Oh, I read them year before last." I had a passion for contemporary drama; I'd read all the playwrights. I'd read Johan Strindberg and Leonid Andreyev and Anton Chekov, of course, and Henrik Ibsen and all the rest. All of them—I forget what I *didn't* read! I even read Harley Granville-Barker, Jean Giraudoux, Lottie Blair Parker, people like that. And I was crazy about Maeterlinck. The professor said, "In that case, we'll just excuse you from it."

So, then I applied for Mrs. Edith Foster Flint's creative writing class. She was a celebrity out there. She was a woman of extraordinary beauty, as tall as a door, just about as wide as a door—she was sort of a giantess—sparkling eyes, lovely laughter. She was a first cousin of the playwright Edward Sheldon. And her son became a grand professor at Yale.[17]

While he was learning to master the precise, rigid form of Imagist poetry, Wescott's greater talent as a prose writer was coming to life. For an assignment in Edith Foster Flint's class, he chose as his subject a tragic young woman he had known in Wisconsin, a woman shunned by the townspeople but kindly received by Wescott's mother, Josephine. He said, "Mrs. Flint asked me to write a remembrance of my youth, a little character sketch. I chose this woman who had had a disastrous love affair, and later broken her hip, the way it is in the novel. I think I wrote a short story about her. Mrs. Flint wrote in red ink up the side of it with the highest praise you can imagine. I don't think she called me a genius, but she used the word somehow, saying, 'I suppose it's really ridiculous to call somebody a genius at your age, but you write like one.'"[18] Later he would develop the story into his first novel.

More of his prose of that time appeared in a hodgepodge journal, a notebook that he called his earliest sequential writing aside from letters and poems. "On such a night one can feel the distance between the stars," the sixteen-year-old wrote on the first page.[19] In several Wisconsin sketches, he described an Indian campground near the schoolhouse and a lynching in West Bend. He included several first drafts of poems with midwestern themes. Like the schoolboy notebook of F. Scott Fitzgerald's fictional character Gatsby, Wescott's reveals early evidence of ambition, such as the studied development of his strikingly beautiful handwriting and a Gatsby-esque list of words-to-learn, many of them beyond the vocabulary of most adults.

Wescott grew from rich relationships as well. In addition to Yvor Winters, Janet Lewis, and Elizabeth Madox Roberts, members of the Poetry Club who affected him deeply were Kathleen Foster, Maurine Smith, Paul

Humphrey, and Maurice Lesemann. He remembered, "Kathleen Foster was an extraordinarily beautiful girl with a lovely voice and a dusky-rose complexion, very dark hair, red lips, and flushed cheeks. In 1917 when I met her she had just lost her fiancé—he had been killed in the war—and she was grief stricken and very Irish about all that; emotional and frank and beautiful in her grief. I got myself engaged to her. I should think I must have written fifty poems to her, and daily letters over long periods of time, and was very much in love with her—in fancy."[20] The engagement was a platonic, sympathetic friendship that nevertheless lasted several years. Wescott realized it was also a way of deferring his suppressed homosexual feelings. "I was trying to put my life in order. But I think an analyst would certainly force me into saying that I picked her out because I knew there was the taboo of her grief. I wouldn't be expected to be passionate. Certainly, if I hadn't proposed marriage to her, the issue might never have come up."[21]

Nevertheless, his homosexuality was a reality he could not escape. By his second year at the university, his world began to tilt and sway. Later he recalled:

> Paul Humphrey was a student who was decisive and important because he was one of the elements that jarred me. He was very attractive physically, blond and tawny, a big strong boy. One day he took me for a walk and told me that I wouldn't be accepted by his fraternity, and that in fact he had blackballed me. He said he did it for my own good because he knew I wouldn't fit in. I remember that instead of being angry, I took it as a kind of token of love, because Paul was taking responsibility for me, in a way. But then he went on to say that it would be better if he, not I, had a love affair with Kathleen Foster, and that he was going to have her long before I did. Then I suddenly realized he was the end. He was going to kill both sides of me, the true and the false. He was going to block me on the fantasy side, and just frustrate me on his own side. I simply couldn't stand it. Who else could I turn to in the world? I turned to Maurice Lesemann.[22]

A member of the Poetry Club, Lesemann listened to Wescott's confessed version of his high school affair—in which Wescott was the young innocent—and he began to offer his amateur Freudian analysis of his dreams. "Maurice told me that people made fun of me, and he always told me that I was ridiculous. He got me to smoke cigarettes, for example, because he said it was effeminate not to smoke. So I went and got long cigarettes with gold tips and black paper and smoked about five a day, like this, puffing, which couldn't have improved my image very much! Ha!"[23]

During this same time period Wescott recognized two members of the Poetry Club as homosexual, and each caused a bit of trouble. Neither seemed very open about his sexuality but they were strongly interested in Wescott. His disinterest seemed to anger them. "Of course, those times weren't like now," he reflected. "There were an awful lot of people who knew they were homosexual and knew what they wanted, but were shy with each other."[24] As young as he was, Wescott was probably more shy and confused than most. The first student to make advances to him was Paul Gennes. He became frustrated with Wescott's disinterest and fear, then quit the club and started a rival student literary group.

More troublesome was Clement Auer. "One of the members of the Poetry Club fell in love with me," Wescott recalled. "Clement was a rather handsome but sinister boy. He carried around Oscar Wilde poems bound in velvet leather in the side pocket of his coat, and he was absolutely in love with me. He proposed going to bed with me several times, and I just brushed it off, thinking that the fact I wasn't attracted to him would discourage him. But it didn't; it just excited him. One day we went for a walk, after I'd declined his advances, and he put a pistol at the small of my back. And we walked for half a mile with that gun at my back, while I tried not to overstimulate him, but not take him too seriously, counting on his not really meaning it. But he was a dangerous fellow."[25] Shortly after the incident with the pistol, Clement Auer forged some checks and got arrested. The Poetry Club members expelled him, not for the alleged forgeries, they said, but for the poor quality of his poetry.

To complicate matters, another of the poets, a talented but tragic young woman, was drawn to the handsome teenager from Wisconsin. "At about that time," Wescott recalled, "Maurine Smith fell in love with me and began writing me these desperate poems."[26] That was in 1918. By the following year, the frail Maurine would die at the age of twenty-three. Many years later, Janet Lewis remembered being struck by Wescott's reading of one of Maurine's poems: "He read it, as he read each of the poems which we dropped on the table, without giving the name of the writer." Of the Poetry Club members she said, "The whole group, not large, was warm, lively and in some way devoted not only to the art of poetry but to its individual members."[27]

Wescott remained close to Maurine in her last year. One of her last poems to him was "I Am As Fair As I Would Be": "I am as fair as I would be, / Joyous as I dream; / Since I am hastening to thee / I must be all I seem."[28]

Wescott's own health failed in late 1918, ending his days as a student. The deadly influenza known as Spanish flu was at its height and had struck especially hard in the Chicago area. Possibly the worst pandemic in human history, the Spanish flu claimed 675,000 lives in the United States and between thirty and forty million worldwide, with the greatest losses in India. It was believed to have started at a military base in the Midwest, then spread to Europe by soldiers. Once advanced, the flu caused rapid lung congestion and death. Parts of the United States ran short of coffins. Victims who survived usually suffered secondary infections. Nearly seventy years later, researchers discovered that Spanish flu was a form of the swine fever virus and called for research into a vaccine in case of a future outbreak.[29]

Wescott remembered 1918 vividly: "I was alone in the house on the west side; the relatives were away. The Sunday paper came and I read about the terrible plague. I was feeling like hell and there the symptoms were in the paper, and I had them all! I had ringing in my ears, throbbing in my temples, a swollen throat, and so on, worse and worse." Finally, the house servants returned from church, found him, and got a doctor. For more than a week he remained in bed with chest and stomach pains, unable to eat, and suffering from fevered dreams. One was a recurring dream of his father's disappointment and condemnation: "For the first time the bad dream of father came out of the night and stalked me in the day." In another hallucinatory dream, probably triggered by the church steeple outside his window and the noise of streetcars and the steam radiator, Wescott heard the voice of God condemning him: "I'd wake up, almost able to understand what the damnation was."[30]

Although he recovered to some extent, he was still distressed psychologically with guilt and confusion about his sexuality. "The doctor thought it would be good for me to get up and get a little exercise," he said. "But on two nights I tried to kill myself by running as fast and as far as I could, into the night, until I fell down in a faint in the gutter."[31] The depression and poor health continued.

Wescott's outlook changed in January of 1919 when Maurice Lesemann introduced him to Monroe Wheeler. Born in 1899 to Fred and Ana Wheeler, Monroe was a handsome, dark-eyed young man with a short sturdy build and a winning smile. Very ambitious and a lover of the arts, he had chosen to work rather than attend college. He had a younger brother, Richard, and sister, Doris. An older sister, Helen, had died of appendicitis. His father was an artist and bibliophile, with a talent for bookbinding. When Monroe hoped for a motorcycle on his eighteenth birthday, his father instead gave him a small Gordon printing press. Like his father, he developed a love of typography and fine printing.

Wescott recalled, "I don't know when I first heard of Monroe but he was god for Maurice and all these people who came down to the university from Evanston. After high school he'd refused college, lied about his age, and got a job in the most prestigious advertising agency in the Midwest, and wrote for the Pierce-Arrow automobile account and so on—not twenty years old! He dressed very snappily, with striped red and white socks and a straw hat turned to one side, you know—ravishing looking he was, in a gypsy sort of way. He came from a very aristocratic middle-class family and Maurice hesitated to introduce me. Finally I was brought to Evanston to meet him. And Monroe was more beautiful than the sun, you can't imagine, and radiantly joyous. His personality expressed that everything was the best it could possibly be and everything was just around the corner, and the arts were the only thing that mattered on earth."[32]

Wescott returned to Chicago with that glowing first impression of Wheeler, but Lesemann perversely dampened his hopes of a new friendship. "Maurice, the carrion crow, the stick I picked up to beat myself with," recalled Wescott, "said Monroe had laughed at me afterward, and that I'd better wait awhile before I saw him again."[33]

Though discouraged, Wescott had learned to rely on himself. Courageously, he decided to face the problem of his sexuality—though he now suspected the problem was with others, not himself. He remembered, "I was told there was a famous psychotherapist named Holmes in Chicago who had had a homosexual son who killed himself, and he was specializing in homosexual cases. I applied and got an appointment, and told him my story. And he got up and marched around and told me it was all rubbish, that I was just talking myself into depravity, and that I was a perfectly healthy boy who just needed to go to a cat house and fuck a whore. I got up and said, 'I came to you because I understood that you had a son who killed himself. And I think it's no wonder.' And I left the room."[34]

Shortly afterward, Wescott was stunned by the news that Maurine Smith had died at her family's home. Then he had a relapse of Spanish flu, including hyperthyroidism, colitis, and painful inflammation of the large intestine, and he returned home to Wisconsin. "I went up to the country and stayed for weeks and the doctors thought I was getting worse instead of better. They wanted to send me to the Mayo Clinic for an operation to remove my thyroid. But my mother wouldn't allow it; she felt it would harm me—she had an instinct, like mine. Finally I returned to Presbyterian Hospital in the west side of Chicago and lived in the ward. And then, instead of laughing at me, the great Monroe Wheeler arrived with a limited edition of the homosexual essays of John Addington Symonds—the most mixed-up homosexual who ever lived—and three bright red roses. He came every other day with a book and red roses, the two weeks I was there."[35]

At that point, neither the sick and unemployed former student nor the successful nineteen-year-old copywriter from Evanston knew what direction their new friendship might take, but the connection was made. Wescott felt there was a bond but not sexual energy between them; besides, Wheeler was dating several young women. But the two saw in each other an oasis of sharp intelligence, humor, and love for the arts. Wescott's condition stabilized, and he returned again to Wisconsin farm country. "All during the spring of 1919, I lay under the apple trees," he said. "I was only allowed to eat white meat of chicken, cream of wheat, and no fruit, no salad."[36] In his rough schoolboy notebook, he wrote a one-line entry on July 5: "Yesterday I was separated from my body when the pain was greatest."[37] But slowly he recovered, and there was an added benefit from the time with his family. "The one thing that came out of that summer was that the idea for what would be my second novel [*The Grandmothers*] was born there, because my grandmother was dying slowly. Since I slept enough during the day, I stayed within call of her at night."[38] His paternal grandmother's storytelling left an impression he would later use in his family-chronicle fiction.

"At the end of the summer I went back to Chicago because I thought I would die if I didn't. I went to the university employment service and found that Hart, Schaffner and Marx needed young people."[39] But the work as a department store shipping clerk, the only conventional job Wescott would ever know, lasted only a few weeks. He was an almost comically poor worker and still in poor health. Once again, Yvor Winters came to his rescue. Winters himself had left the university and was living in Santa Fe, recuperating from tuberculosis. When a friend told him of Wescott's troubles, Yvor wrote to his father, saying he himself was not doing well and that his doctor thought it was because he was bored and lonely. Then he mentioned his talented friend Glenway, who was poor and forced to work instead of write. The plan worked. "His father and mother called me to their home in Evanston," said Wescott, "and wept and asked if I could possibly be persuaded to go to Santa Fe. Of course, I knew I was going to get fired from my job the following Friday, and I hadn't another bean."[40]

Accepting the offer of room and board and a small allowance in Santa Fe, Wescott agreed to be secretary and companion to Winters. In truth, Winters was more interested in continuing his friend's development as a poet, and in fact Wescott had been writing poetry all along. Before leaving Chicago for the Southwest in November of 1919, he gave Monroe Wheeler a gift of seven poems in a hand-stitched booklet.[41] Although Wescott and Wheeler would not clarify their relationship until late the next year, one poem, "Black Art," seemed to foretell their early struggle as an artistic male couple in a hostile, homophobic world:

> You did not know how brave you were.
> And I, like a starving wolf,
> Followed the shadow of your fire,
> Sorted your secrets from the dust
> To satisfy my hunger.
>
> You did not know,
> I was a coward . . .
> Now we can shift the skies.
> We can endure
> The hoof-beats of the wind upon our heads.
> Why, we would dare to climb
> Out of a withering world
> Into a new star!

But let us laugh carelessly like other men.
Let us be timid, even among fools.
Let us knot silence round our throats.
For they would surely kill us.

While the nature of his friendship with Wheeler remained unresolved, Wescott was still writing to Kathleen Foster. Ten months in Santa Fe gave him a chance to reflect on these relationships. The landscape was beautiful, the climate ideal for his health, and there was a thriving arts community. Wescott remembered,

It was an amazing place to arrive at, because it was a very spread-out city of low adobe houses. In the center of the town were a church and a nunnery, and the nuns rented rooms—there was no hotel. It's a very different place today, with great hotels and everything under the sun.

Up the hill from the town was the sanatorium. They had a big barn of a place with little houses all along it, and Yvor Winters was in a little house at the end of the row. They found a place for me to live on Canyon Road, the road that goes up into the mountains. I had two rooms on the ground floor of a Mexican row house. It was two or three miles up to the sanatorium and I presently had to run errands for everyone, as well as for Yvor. I was the only healthy person around who everybody liked, all the poor sick ladies and so on. I would buy them things and go to the post office. I had this feisty little Mexican horse with a long mane, which was supposed to have been one of Pancho Villa's cavalry horses. I would pull and pull on the reins, and he would just set his teeth on it and run away with me. He ran away with me every day for months, and the amazing thing is he never threw me off. Those Mexican saddles are like an armchair; it's hard to be thrown off. But he ran up onto the hills on these miserable stony roads. I just barely stayed alive. But I liked him very much.[42]

At an altitude of five thousand feet, Santa Fe was cold at night during the winter months but the environment was invigorating. The unique beauty of the landscape would be captured in some of Wescott's poetry. He sensed a mystical quality to his surroundings. One night he woke in a startled fright and realized a cat had jumped through his window and pounced on him with a howl. "It was sort of spooky for me out there but I liked it. I'd been ill, you see, and I was getting well. This was all wonderful for my health."[43]

A variety of interesting people were recuperating at the sanatorium. Wescott recalled a stout twenty-four-year-old man from New York—a Wall Street genius with a photographic memory—who arrived with servants. Another tuberculosis patient, Alice Corbin Henderson, became friends with Wescott and Winters and was a connection to the emerging poetry scene in Chicago. Until her illness, Henderson had been associate editor of *Poetry,* the Chicago magazine founded in 1912 by Harriet Monroe. Wescott was also exposed to painters for the first time, as Henderson introduced him to a number of artists, including Marsden Hartley. "Meanwhile," he said, "Yvor Winters was making me write; I was writing masses of poetry. He'd told his father and everybody else that I had a great poetical gift. That February [1920], Vachel Lindsay came and stayed with me and gave a reading. I arranged all that."[44] In thanks, Lindsay gave him a gift of cuff links for his first dress shirt. Later that year, Wescott met Carl Sandburg and Edgar Lee Masters.

During that summer, some of his new friends took Wescott to nearby Abiquiu to see the Pentecostals, a sect whose fanaticism was frowned upon by legal authorities and may have involved the use of peyote. "It was very beautiful with the snow falling in the mountains," he recalled. "There was a triangular canyon and these men came out marching and singing, with their wives all huddled up, watching. The men whipped themselves with hemp with bits of glass and barbed wire woven in. Twelve of them in a row would take a step and you'd hear the slashing sound as they hit one side, then another step, and they'd hit the other side. We tried to keep a respectful distance and of course it was very awe-inspiring—it was as far back as you could get into early Christian European nonsense."[45]

During the summer, he saw Indian dances—buffalo dances at Santa Domingo and corn dances at Santa Clara. Wescott remembered a corn dance that began at dawn: "They danced all day and it was very, very moving because the chorus—women with flat shoes and men pounding the earth—went on and on. They had huge palaces of carved wood with fox fur hanging at the end, and the chorus pretended to be corn, you know, dancing like corn, swaying, and shaking pollen down to the ground. I had to run behind one of the buildings and weep; I got so overwrought I couldn't watch them anymore."[46]

Overall, the rich experience of Santa Fe was a time of healing and development for Wescott, and the presence of Winters kept him on the path of literature. He also befriended a thirty-nine-year-old writer he called Elsie, Elizabeth Shepley Sergeant, who would later write a biography of Willa Cather. But by spring and summer of 1920 the problems and contradictions he had left in Chicago began to catch up to him. Monroe Wheeler had already promised to visit in midsummer. Yvor Winters's parents were coming for the entire season, along with their daughter, Faith, who secretly dated Wheeler. "Also," said Wescott, "the Winters family knew I was lonesome for my family and invited my sister Elizabeth to visit. Suddenly, I got a letter from Maurice Lesemann asking me to invite him out for the summer. He said he'd lost his mistress and didn't have much money and was lonely and bored, and that I couldn't abandon him, a Poetry Club friend in need. I read the letter aloud in front of Yvor and burst out sobbing. And I never saw Yvor become so angry. He wanted me to refuse to let Maurice come, but I simply couldn't. I did have a home, I did have two rooms. But I hoped he wouldn't come and tried to discourage him."[47]

Before summer and the guests arrived, the plot thickened. Although Wescott insisted that he had completely avoided any sex life since his high school romance, his repressed homosexuality nevertheless became a lightning rod for trouble. In the community were two middle-aged brothers named Thorpe, British nationals who had lived most of their lives in America. The men admitted to Wescott that they had been intimate with Oscar Wilde in their late teens, when Wilde in his late twenties visited New Mexico, during his American tour of 1881–82. Wescott remembered, "The older brother, Charley Thorpe, had a mustache, cowboy clothes and high boots, and he was as gay as a barber pole! Charley took a great liking to me and one day said, 'You know, there is an awfully nice Scandinavian boy who is living in the most miserable situation up on Canyon Road.'"[48]

Fredrick Nyquist was a very attractive youth who had studied at the Art Institute of Chicago and then gone to Santa Fe as an artist's apprentice. He was working at house construction and living in the basement of a half-built house. Thorpe talked Wescott into giving Nyquist temporary lodging. "This must have been April or May and there were a couple of months before the Chicago people came," said Wescott. "So Fredrick worked up the road during the day and they fed him, then he came to my home and we slept in the same bed. But the moment he moved in, he told me that his best friend in Chicago had made a pass at him, and it upset him and that's why he moved to Santa Fe. Ha! Well, I just resolved this was typical Wescott booby trap—I just had to put up with it." Innocent and timid, Wescott accepted this masochistic situation for months. "Nyquist had a body like a Danish dirty book," he recalled, "with soft but formed muscles, and a great loose sex with blond pubic hair—and he took three quarters of the bed. I really think he was so straight that he didn't realize. . . . And I wasn't combustible; I was just pitiful, that was all I was."[49]

The situation worsened, of course, when Maurice Lesemann arrived in early summer. Wescott got a bed for his second room, but Lesemann was quick to pass judgment on Wescott's living arrangement with Nyquist. Wescott recalled that "he just sat there and gloated at my deterioration. He would take me for walks and bawl me out, and I would say, 'Now look, this boy is afraid of homosexuality, and I'm not going to bother him, or put him out.' Of course, it makes me laugh to think of this because it became a kind of pattern in my life—always thinking I was the cock in the roost, when really I was everybody's patsy. Yvor Winters was furious with me. Then Monroe was coming, and the idea of Monroe finding me in all this—this triangle with Nyquist and Maurice! And Yvor fulminating upon the hill."[50]

Wescott explained that Winters was not concerned about any appearance of homosexuality. "Yvor didn't care a damn about that. He wasn't the least bit prudish. But he wanted Maurice out and he sensed—more than I—a good deal of tension building." Wescott recalled, in fact, that some of the artists in the community were pleased to assume the worst of him. "I really was a very heady brew—I was too good looking, too pretty, with a pout like Rimbaud, and very flamboyant. I talked and talked and some people adored me, and others got irritated."[51]

Trouble broke out when Wescott went off to greet Wheeler at the railroad station in Lamy. Maurice Lesemann was supposed to move to a rented room, but some problem brought him back to Wescott's apartment during a rainstorm, and Nyquist refused to let him return. Angry, Lesemann turned to some of the artists in the community and started the rumor of homosexual scandal. "When Monroe and I got there," Wescott recalled, "the town was all agog—it hadn't taken more than twenty-four hours. And it went on for several weeks. We were constantly being informed that something terrible was going to happen. There was a meeting where they considered tar-and-feathering me and driving me out of town. Of course, Yvor Winters was so mad, he insulted them all. Finally, Monroe rented two horses and we set off up the Blood of Christ Mountains and rode all the way to Taos and back. So we were out of the way for about two weeks. When we returned, my sister had arrived and we managed to keep peace."[52]

By the fall, Winters's parents, their daughter, Faith, and Wheeler had all returned to the Midwest. A number of people in the arts community remained hostile to Wescott. Winters perhaps kept the issue alive by defending Wescott so indignantly. "Yvor and his friends were so angry with the others, they insulted them every time they saw them," Wescott recalled. "If only they'd have shut up!"[53]

Finally, in September, Wescott left for the Midwest, with every intention of returning to his new life in Santa Fe. "Yvor told his family that I was homesick," said Wescott, "and that I would have to come back to Wisconsin. So they treated me to a trip back to Chicago, and Wisconsin to see my parents."[54] Unfortunately, shortly before Wescott paid a visit to the Winters family in Waukesha, Mrs. Winters discovered love letters from Wheeler to Faith in her daughter's room. Wheeler's friendship with Wescott and the recent rumors of scandal in Santa Fe made matters worse. Wescott recalled:

> The Winterses summoned me to pay a visit, and as I approached the house I saw Faith up on a second floor balcony, weeping and saying "Sshhh!" and making terrible gestures to warn me. And when I opened the door, there was Mr. Winters, the stockbroker, all red and shivering and shuddering in a rage. And his wife was raging that I'd corrupted her children and turned her son against her and that my friend had taken her daughter's virginity. I'd never been so excoriated before. I

shriveled and shrank away. All that autumn, people would come up to me and report that Mrs. Winters was saying, "Glenway Wescott is the anti-Christ."

Well, they wouldn't let me go back to Santa Fe. If I had gone back, I probably could have civilized the whole place and calmed the artists down. I had a good many friends. I didn't have any place to live, and Monroe and his family took me in, and I stayed with them from October of 1920 until January or February of 1921.[55]

Meanwhile, late in 1920, Wheeler published Wescott's first work, *The Bitterns,* a dozen poems in the elegant, formal style of Winters and other Imagist poets such as Janet Lewis, HD (Hilda Doolittle), Mina Loy, and even T. S. Eliot. It was dedicated to Winters, and the striking cover on black stock was designed by Wescott's former roommate, Fredrick Nyquist. Wheeler had created the chapbook on his home press, and planned to publish more for his poet friends. In launching Wescott's career, he had launched his own. Two hundred copies of *The Bitterns* were printed and a number were sent to established poets. Wallace Stevens read it and wrote to Wescott, "It is difficult to make poetry as sophisticated as this fly. But you certainly make it tremble and shake. I will watch your work with the greatest interest."[56]

Publication of the poems coincided with Wescott's first weeks at the Wheelers' home at 639 Forest Avenue in Evanston. He recalled that "Monroe's father painted, and he printed and bound books. I've got an Emerson bound by him. That's where Monroe got all that. In Monroe's room there was a clothes closet and a chest of drawers, and on top of it was a picture of writer Rupert Brooke in an exquisite little silver frame. I looked at it and thought, there's something here."[57] Even then, Wheeler's true nature was a mystery to Wescott. Since his youth, Wheeler had had a dignified reserve. He had sexual power, but it was cool and controlled. Although Wescott had spoken to him in Santa Fe about homosexuality, Wheeler had not been candid about his own bisexuality. Wescott did know that Wheeler was so sexual that he had been seduced by a woman friend of his mother at the age of eleven! And before Faith, there had been a steady girlfriend named Elva. While Wheeler and Wescott had not been completely innocent, it hadn't gone beyond a certain schoolboy level. Finally, something more happened. "It was in his house and in his mother's guest bed," said Wescott. "I was intimidated by the whole thing and I didn't feel I understood him well enough."[58]

By the end of 1920, Wheeler and Wescott began to form the bond that would produce one of the great relationships of the century. "We were walking on the campus of Northwestern University and we stopped to sit on the grass," Wescott recalled of a day in Evanston. "By that time, we'd had a few episodes of love. I said I really took a dark view of my future and I didn't have any vocation. And Monroe said, 'I don't know how I know this but I feel very strongly that in the American culture artists have privileges of freedom that are recognized. Most artists are eccentric. If you will be a poet and make a life of writing, they will let you alone.' So, I proceeded to become a writer and work at it. Because Monroe, who seemed to know everything, said that if I did it, I could live my life without disaster or drama."[59]

Clearly, they delighted in each other's intelligence, wit, social skills, and love of the arts. As for their private relationship, Wescott volunteered, "You'd probably like to know what I really can't tell you: what our sexual relationship was like. It wasn't very highly charged ever. There wasn't any great elaboration or eroticism. Monroe was incapable of it, really, and I hadn't learned it. But he was like a father figure for me, or an older brother, a savior. I was so grateful."[60]

Early in 1921, Wescott was reminded once again that he didn't have a home of his own when "Monroe's mother came to me and said it wasn't really fair to her or myself or Monroe for me to just move in and stay, and that I shouldn't complain to Monroe, who was full of affection, but that I should get a job and move out. And then I moved into the most sordid house I've ever lived anywhere in the world, a boarding house in the north end of Chicago, really in the very slums." Luckily, there were supportive people in Chicago. Harriet Moody, widow of the poet and playwright William Vaughn Moody, lived near the campus and owned a restaurant where young poets could find a free meal. Her home often served as a literary salon where esteemed visiting poets met the youngsters and where Wescott was something of a beautiful teacher's pet. There was also Harriet Monroe, who published *Poetry* magazine. Wescott recalled, "There wasn't a very good relationship between the two Harriets."[61]

While living for several months in a dingy room of plywood partitions in the boarding house at 1033 North Dearborn Street, Wescott worked as an office boy at *Poetry.* He recorded one memory on a loose page of late journals entitled, "Oscar Williams on the Doorstep":

> I was office boy for *Poetry* magazine briefly in the spring of 1921. One morning, upon my arrival at the office to take in and sort out the mail and to empty the wastebaskets and to dust the desks, before the editoress arrived, I found a lean teenager on the doorstep, with poor poems clutched in his hand; and I was good-natured toward him, polite to him. That is, I mean polite about his poems. His name was Oscar Williams. I did not happen to see him again for many years. But when he edited a best-selling anthology, *The Little Treasury of Modern Poetry,* he repaid me for my slight kindness by putting one of my youthful poems in it. And you know what a writer really wants more than anything is to have his work kept in print . . . and that is harder to bring about than being favorably reviewed in the *New York Times* or to be selected and circulated by the Book-of-the-Month Club.[62]

At the *Poetry* office and at the University of Chicago's Harper Library, Wescott copied out the work of his favorite contemporary, Marianne Moore. He also continued to endear himself to the Chicago literary set, including Margaret Anderson and Jane Heap. There was one exception: "Carl Sandburg talked terribly against me because I was a homosexual. He thought it disgraceful."[63]

Wheeler, meanwhile, published two more chapbooks of verse, including Yvor Winters's *The Immobile Wind.* By the end of spring he was ready to quit his job and spend his savings on passage for two to Europe. Wescott explained, "He decided that if I was going to be a poet I should meet the poets abroad, not just the Chicago group. I don't know what he was thinking, because the Chicago group really was very glamorous and extraordinary."[64]

The creation of *The Bitterns* in 1920 had marked the start of Wescott and Wheeler as a team. Glenway would prove one of the most talented of the emerging midwestern writers, but Wheeler's instinct about Europe revealed more about how their dynamic worked. Soon enough, the phenomenon of the expatriate twenties would prove Wheeler right.

Before their first trip abroad, the young friends enjoyed an idyllic summer of 1921 in Massachusetts, thanks to Harriet Moody. In addition to her Chicago home and restaurant, Mrs. Moody owned a house and property in the Berkshires, and she encouraged Wescott and Wheeler to spend months there. When they left for the East Coast, they didn't know they were saying good-bye to the Midwest as their home.

2

The Next Step
New York and Europe

ACCEPTING Harriet Moody's offer, Wescott and Wheeler spent the summer of 1921 at her retreat in the Berkshires of western Massachusetts. They found themselves in West Cummington, a town of fewer than one hundred people, set in a landscape of rich overgrown valleys and pine-covered mountains. There Wescott turned to the fiction piece that Edith Foster Flint had praised in her creative writing class and began work on his first novel. "Mrs. Moody lent us the house," he remembered, "a big log cabin that she'd had built for her husband in his last years, up on top of a hill. And she'd bought the William Cullen Bryant birthplace, which was a small two-room frame house that had been moved down the hill. She bought it and moved it back up. And I used it as a studio and wrote the first part of *The Apple of the Eye* in it."[1]

The quiet summer months were ideal for work and health. Wheeler's doctor had found him anemic and suggested that he build up his strength before traveling abroad. Wescott's sisters gave him a cookbook that had photos showing how to prepare food, and he developed a talent for cooking. At one point, he remembered, their peaceful routine was interrupted when "Yvor Winters sent a telegram saying his father had left with a gun to shoot us! And for a week or ten days we kept the front door locked and the back door open. We slept near the back door, ready to run out and hide in the woods. It was too nerve-wracking for me and one day I ran off and Monroe ran after me. He knocked me down and sat on my chest and slapped me in the face until I came to my senses."[2]

When a gun-toting Mr. Winters never appeared, the question of commitment emerged. Until recently Wheeler had dated girls, and Wescott was still writing to Kathleen Foster. He questioned himself. "Right smack in the middle of the summer I was tormented by thoughts of Kathleen Foster," he recalled. "I wasn't willing at any point to end it and I suppose it was because the relationship with Monroe wasn't sexual enough to pull my roots up, you know. And I thought of him as being straight in the first place. He didn't interfere in any way. There was only one thing he would do, at all stages—right up to the day before yesterday! If I showed any signs of being unfaithful he would promptly be unfaithful himself in a much stronger, decisive way. It made me squirm like mad. Then he'd say, 'My poor dear, you're giving every sign of running away and leaving me, I've got to look after my own interests. If you're going to write poetry every day to Kathleen Foster, and try to raise money to go home to Chicago, I'm going to have a love affair of my own.'"[3] Their relationship survived the conflicts, as it would for many years.

Late that summer, Harriet Moody asked Wescott to travel to the MacDowell Colony, a working retreat for creative artists, in Peterborough, New Hampshire, to deliver messages to poets Edwin Arlington Robinson and Robert Frost. "Robinson was a man of bad luck in many respects, famous but unsuccessful, which is often the fate of poets," he said. "Frost didn't like me, but that didn't trouble him, given the purpose of our meeting. What a diplomat he would have made! I didn't like him either, and I remember priding myself just a little on the fact that, though I was young, it didn't spoil the occasion for me either."[4] Later in life, they would have better meetings. At the MacDowell Colony, he also met the bohemian and tragic poet Maxwell Bodenheim.

While he had met a number of famous poets in Chicago, in Santa Fe, and at the MacDowell Colony, Wescott's greatest thrill up to this time was in meeting Marianne Moore. He and Wheeler were in New York in the autumn of 1921, visiting friends and preparing for their trip abroad. Wescott took the opportunity to call on Moore, then thirty-four, at her apartment in Greenwich Village. The building at 14 Saint Luke's Place was—and still is—just across the narrow tree-lined street from the small public library where she worked. He remembered that first meeting: "I especially admired her softly blond hair, braided and put up in a crown, but not a tight crown. Her mother, Mary Warner Moore, coresided with her and was present that afternoon."[5] At that time, Moore didn't have a book of poetry in America but she showed him a paperbound collection that London's Egoist Press had just printed. She also spoke of her interest in species and plumage of songbirds and showed him her shoe box full of colorful feathers. The visit led to her lifelong polite friendship with Wescott, and a closer one with Wheeler.

Meanwhile, the September issue of *Poetry* contained "Still Hunt," a grouping of six new Wescott poems. One of them, "The Poet at Nightfall," would later appear in several anthologies. Another, "The Chaste Lovers," evoked Wescott's lingering relationship with Kathleen Foster. At that very point, Wescott had to choose between his feelings for Kathleen and the approaching trip to Europe with Wheeler. Suddenly he decided to return to Kathleen in Chicago, with the intention of marrying. Yet the men believed their own relationship would survive. In a diary note, Wheeler wrote: "Today Glenway and I decided that I should go on to London alone, and let him return to Chicago. It is certain that he will be happier there with Kathleen. He will plan to come abroad as soon as he is married. He will take a room on the north side, and Harriet [Moody] will let him take his meals at Le Petit Gourmet. It is not easy to do—for a long while we have sat with tears in the eyes of both of us—but we are exceptionally happy."[6]

Wescott described the climactic decision and what happened next. "Monroe said that I had to meet all the great poets in England, and actually I think he wanted to meet them more than I did. At any rate, I panicked just before we were to leave, said good-bye to him in New York and went back to Chicago, and tried to make love to Kathleen. I took her in my arms and kissed her and—I almost jumped out the window. It was a very extraordinary panic—not disgust but an experience so foreign, the physical sensation so foreign, that it really was the limit. I knew it was the end of it. A friend lent me enough money to go back to New York."[7]

Wescott made plans to meet Wheeler in England. In November he boarded a small ocean liner bound from Hoboken, New Jersey, to Plymouth, England. Rough weather and a heavy swell followed the ship across the Atlantic. Worse, he could afford only a third-class "steerage" bunk, where sleeping spaces were separated only by partitions. The mattresses were really sacks stuffed with cornhusks, each with only one blanket and no sheets or pillows. He remembered, "The accommodations were on both sides of the propeller, which shook us until our teeth rattled. . . . The stern went up and down, up and down, as though it were a bad dream about an elevator."[8] Despite the gloomy weather, he stayed on deck from morning until night, reading and writing and looking forward to England.

His first impressions were powerful. "The first time I arrived in Europe," he wrote, "I disembarked at Plymouth an hour or two earlier than scheduled, and sped up to London on a small train; my nose pressed to the window, marveling at Devon—where Wescotts originated, I believe—and Dorset and perhaps Hampshire, in the late afternoon light. Monroe was already in London. It was a Saturday evening." At the Paddington station, he waited at the raised wooden platform where horse cabs stopped at regular intervals. "There was an unimaginable yellow fog, of a density that I have been told doesn't happen nowadays. I waited there in it, sitting on my carpetbag and wrapped in my Civil War cape—both purchased at an auction in Massachusetts that summer. The cab horse's hooves sounded, *clonk, clonk,* in the strange atmosphere; somehow hell-like. I imagined that I felt as though I had died and arrived neither in heaven nor hell, but in a wonderful limbo—and a part of the wonder was literary; for at that age I unrealistically believed that I was going to be able to commemorate in good prose everything or almost everything that I experienced. . . . And at last Monroe materialized out of the golden-black twilight, with his jaunty step. I love the way of walking of those I love."[9]

After their happy reunion they followed a plan. Aside from Wheeler's small savings, they had valuable letters of introduction from Harriet Monroe of *Poetry.* One was to a Chicago woman who had married a successful London portrait painter, Sir John Lavery. Tea with the Laverys was well timed. Among the guests was a popular novelist whom Wescott had hoped to meet, R. B. Cunninghame-Graham. Also present was writer Osbert Sitwell, the tart-tongued brother of poet Edith. At one point, the distinguished gathering turned silent when Wescott mentioned that he hoped to visit novelist Ford Madox Ford. Although Ford was popular with American expatriates, the British considered the man and his writing scandalous. After a pregnant pause, Osbert Sitwell said, "We call him Freud Madox Fraud."[10]

Cunninghame-Graham, a Socialist member of Parliament and a writer of travel and adventure books, generously showed Wescott around London. The young man was impressed by Graham's storytelling and especially by his long, red-lined, nineteenth-century black cape, which he wore with a flourish. Wescott wore an even older cape and later acquired several more.

The highlight of that first London trip was Wescott and Wheeler's stay in Sussex with Ford Madox Ford. Ford lived in a small cottage with his third wife, actress Stella Bowen, and their baby. While Stella politely carried the crying baby outdoors for a stroll on a cool, windy day, the forty-eight-year-old writer read to the young men in front of his large fireplace. Wheeler later admitted to Wescott that, between the dense prose and Ford's singsong reading voice, he barely understood a word. But Wescott was enthralled by every word. Though Ford was a controversial figure, his work fascinated Wescott. He later wrote, "I believe he was somewhat blameworthy in many ways but I have never known a man of letters to be so continuously opposed and punished for shortcomings and misfortunes having nothing to do with his literary ability and career."[11] Ford himself was deeply moved by their conversations, and later wrote in his memoir, *It Was the Nightingale,* that "if Mr. Wescott had not paid me a visit of some duration, I do not think I should have taken seriously again to writing."[12]

Wescott and Wheeler struck up other friendships with English writers, including Raymond Mortimer and Edward Sackville-West. Meanwhile,

Wescott's own name was now familiar in the little magazines. He had reviews in the October and December 1921 issues of *Poetry,* and the December issue of the *Dial* contained his "Natives of Rock," a model of an Imagist poem. Though homesick, he continued writing because, he said, Wheeler made sure of it. "I mourned the whole time I was abroad, and still went on writing poetry," he recalled. "And Monroe instinctively decided something I think he's resolved more than once in his life: he would take my stance and my account of myself for matter of fact, and then pin me to the reality of it."[13] When their money ran low, Wheeler decided they should stretch their funds in poverty-ridden Germany, and it was Wheeler who told the German consulate that his poet friend wanted to learn the language so he could translate Heinrich Heine. Suddenly they were in Wiesbaden. There Wescott saw the aftermath of war and later recalled that "the countryside was beautiful, but what was shocking in the cities was the amount of poverty. I remember once we were in a sort of lunch room and outside the windows there were people looking in, moving their mouths as they watched the diners eat."[14]

During the lean months in Germany, one of their strongest supporters was Harriet Moody in Chicago. She helped calm Wescott's worried mother, though she didn't know the truth about his private life: "I feel secure that in the end he will manifest himself as one of the chief poets of his time . . . and Glenway has found, it seems to me, just the right woman for him in dear Kathleen."[15] Mrs. Moody and others helped Wescott meet Elly Ney, a German concert pianist who was world renowned as an interpreter of Beethoven. Ney's first marriage was ending and she welcomed the new friendships. Wescott recalled what followed:

> I was weeping to come home, we ran out of money, and then some friends in America sent this famous female pianist with a letter of introduction to us. Elly fell in love with both of us at first, and lent us her house on the same street in which Beethoven was born. Then we made a tour of Germany with her.
>
> We went to one of those castles in Germany where people go for vacations, sort of cultural centers, in the mountains. . . . The second night in the mountains we slept in one of those hay houses, the three of us lying in the hay side by side. Monroe and Elly had intercourse while I lay there, presumably asleep. I was in absolute torment of coming out of my chrysalis, you know, breaking my pupa, my idea of myself. Actually it was very extraordinary because Monroe realized when he took one look at me in the morning that I'd been awake. He took me right up onto the top of the mountain and made love to me then and there, which I hated because I'm always afraid of the sky. And he said, "Now, don't play the fool. You know perfectly well we can go right down there and say good-bye to Elly and leave at once. But we'll have to send home for money, and you can't go back to Chicago."[16]

Before they returned to the states in the spring of 1922, Wheeler got enough money from home to take advantage of low printing costs in

Germany. He followed up his earlier chapbooks of work by Wescott, Yvor Winters, and Mark Turbyfill with *The Keen Edge* by Maurine Smith and *Poems* by Janet Lewis. Each title demonstrated his talent for creating beautiful books.

Back in New York, they settled in a basement studio at Lexington Avenue and East Eighteenth Street. Marianne Moore would visit, bringing homemade soup, and for the first time they saw the city as their home. During the summer, they visited their families in the Midwest. The Wescotts were now living in Ripon, Wisconsin, and there Glenway was surprised to see Virginia Bugbee, the great friend of his high school years in Waukesha. Once again Virginia influenced him for the good. Years earlier she had shown him the importance of self-reliance. Now, he said, she gave him the example of a successful homosexual relationship. "It was the only time I saw her with her female co-resident friend," he recalled. "They were teaching school, the two of them, in the town where my family lived when I went to see them in 1922. They looked wonderfully happy and serene, and she was like a beautiful youngish boy in tweeds and her beloved was all lace and curls and little delicate movements. They looked so happy, so happy together, and so pleased to see me. I was very joyous for them."[17]

Wescott contributed to his own home with Wheeler by selling reviews that appeared in the *New Republic* and in Chicago newspapers that fall.[18] Late in the year he was hired as personal secretary to the financier, art collector, and philanthropist Henry Goldman. He accompanied his employer's family to Europe and read to Goldman, who was losing his sight. In return, Goldman taught him a good deal about modern art and in Berlin gave him a gift of an alchemist-enhanced sapphire. Wescott, who wrote Wheeler every day, had the stone set in a silver ring and sent home. Wheeler would wear it for the rest of his life.

The Goldmans returned to New York for several months, then took Glenway abroad again, visiting England, France, Italy, and Germany from February through August 1923. Marianne Moore and her mother commiserated with Wheeler: "We often deplore the loneliness that Mr. Wescott's going has made for you."[19] But the experience was rich for Wescott. The Goldmans introduced him to a new friend, thirty-nine-year-old Elena Gerhardt, a renowned German mezzo-soprano. And in April they arrived in Paris. Wescott captured the memory in a story: "It was my first trip to Paris, I was young. I had never loved a city, of course I loved it. The famous festive style and modest proportions of its architecture surprised me as much as they pleased me; all so pale, with a rosy tinge early in the day and a blue tinge later. . . . The weather that week was enchanting; the sunshine rippled over everything and at the same time the moisture in the air veiled it."[20]

Wescott saw the Louvre and the Tuileries and strolled at night in Montparnasse. He called on Gertrude Stein and Alice B. Toklas at 27, rue de Fleurus and was impressed by the continuous stream of guests and the paintings by Pablo Picasso, Juan Gris, and others.

On his first visit to the south of France, Wescott met novelist Mary Butts and her younger brother, Anthony. He remembered, "Mary was an astonishing girl who wrote very talented stories. She was a great beauty, with carrot-red hair and green-blue eyes. The Butts family had been patrons of Blake. It's in Blake's letters. At any rate, a friend introduced us and more or less maneuvered me into seducing Anthony. Tony was maybe twenty and I was twenty-two. He was the most effete person I've ever known in my life. He was quite large and pale with a sort of rabbity mouth and pink cheeks. Tony and I met probably two or three times and a lot of letters were exchanged. Then Mary wrote to me, reproaching me." Wescott mended fences somewhat with a positive review of Mary's first book of stories in the *Dial*.[21]

Before returning to America, Wescott wrote a story about two American boys he had visited at Oxford. He didn't attempt to publish it, but the fifteen-page "Sacre de Printemps," about wise and jaded young Valentine and Hamilton, is sharp, gripping, homophilic, and wildly surrealistic. On the last page, he wrote, "Influence of Mary Butts."[22] The work Wescott did publish, reviews and poetry, appeared throughout 1923 in numerous issues of the *New Republic, Broom,* the *Dial, Poetry,* and *Contact.* Of Wescott's poem "Men Like Birds," *Contact* co-editor William Carlos Williams told Wheeler, "I cannot believe that Wescott realizes what he has written," and called the poem "about the best piece of work that I have on hand."[23] At the same time, Wheeler created more beautiful chapbooks, of Williams's poems, *Go Go,* and of Marianne Moore's famous long poem *Marriage.*

Greenwich Village society included *Broom* editor Lola Ridge's Thursday gatherings on East Ninth Street, where Wescott met with Williams, Moore, Kay Boyle, Elinor Wylie, Edgar Arlington Robinson, and Babette Deutsch. Mina Loy arranged a meeting between Wescott and the eccentric Ezra Pound. Wescott later wrote, "He seemed unable to sit still, jumping from chair to chair, from chair to couch, throwing himself down flat on his back and kicking his legs in the air; and all these extraordinary acrobatics were going on in the middle of sentences. Ezra never seemed to finish what he was saying, splintering his syntax into fragments. He was decidedly a man who did not appear to be normal."[24]

Along with the literary personalities, Wescott and Wheeler experienced the bohemia of Greenwich Village when they moved to the two-room apartment where Wescott would complete his first novel, on the second floor of 17 Christopher Street. Neighbor Marianne Moore approved:

"Christopher Street is not a very exposed street and I should think the gas radiators will be enough."[25] The little three-story building still stands, its lower-right shop housing the Oscar Wilde Bookstore. The liberated Village residents in the twenties included poets, artists, actors, and students, in a pleasant confusion of homosexuals, bisexuals, and heterosexuals who were modern. For example, Wescott remembered, three men who were attracted to his blond androgynous beauty were all heterosexual:

> That year, 1924, I had sex with three people not Monroe. My closest friends in Greenwich Village were Tony Salemme, a sculptor, and his beautiful blonde wife Betty. When we lived on Christopher Street, they lived on the top floor of a building next to that church on Washington Square South. Tony was not handsome but a very sexy and attractive Southern Italian, and he seduced me eventually.
>
> One night there was a party with lots of people at their home. I was propped up on the bed and a married woman friend came and nestled inside my arm. Then Tony came and nestled on the other side of me. His wife, Betty, was near us, playing guitar and singing. Suddenly I realized that charges of sexuality were going through me, from one of them to the other, and I was amused by this. I must say it was more or less the way I felt about myself at the time: I didn't very much expect to be the bride or even the bridesmaid, but I realized that people grew sexy around me. Suddenly they sprang up and went into another room and made love, and Betty was angry but went on singing. But it was Betty who had an affair with Paul Robeson. That's been written. One time she had spent the night with Paul and he'd bitten her so that she was afraid Tony would come home and beat her. So she sent me to Mulberry Street to get a jar of leeches, so that she should get the blood blisters out of her skin before Tony got home.[26]

Robeson was friendly to Wescott, who liked the intellectual actor, singer, and future activist. They first met at the Salemmes' Greenwich Village apartment and in a few years they would meet again in the south of France.

Wescott's adventure with Tony Salemme occurred when the sculptor was creating a bust of him in bronze. Salemme began recalling youthful experiences he'd had with other boys, and one thing led to another. "It didn't amuse me," Wescott said, "he was one of these rough, jumpy fellows." Other unlikely flings that year included a man named Witt Verner and a young German immigrant named George Van Erring, who played the cello. "George lived in a tiny room before he met his mistress, and he used to come on Sunday mornings to our Christopher Street apartment and ask if he could practice the cello. It used to drive Monroe mad! . . . It was so funny, all that Greenwich Village life, and we were all nudists. We would go out to one of the unknown parts of Fire Island, staying at a hotel in Bellport and getting ourselves rowed across. We'd spend days together."[27]

The happy freedoms of New York did not keep Wescott from his prolific writing. During 1924, his work appeared in Margaret Anderson's

Little Review, the Dial Press newsletter *Cupid and the Lion, Transatlantic Review,* and the *Dial.* His early reviews showed great self-confidence. At just twenty-three, he didn't hesitate to criticize an author of fifty-four books, Arnold Bennett: "His massive novels have a certain curious dignity, though it is threatened on every page by sly innuendoes, by self-conscious crudity, by mingled echoes of cynicism and sentimentality."[28]

Most of Wescott's writing time was now devoted to fiction. A midwestern story, "In a Thicket," appeared in the June issue of *Dial,* was later included in *The Best Short Stories of 1924,* and was translated into French for *La revue europèene VI.* More important, the fifty-page story "Bad Han" had been serialized in *Dial* in the crimson-covered issues of January and February 1924. This was the material started in Edith Foster Flint's writing class and developed during the summer of 1921. Wescott said, "Bad Han was a real woman whom my mother was very fond of. It amused me that my very puritanical mother should be so fond of a woman who had a rather bad reputation. My story is pretty close to the truth. She'd had this disastrous love affair, and had broken her hip, the way it is in the book. She appealed to my imagination, this whole earth-mother business, this woman with a bad reputation who would become a sort of saint."[29]

Wescott completed a three-part novel, *The Apple of the Eye,* and the magazine's new book division, Dial Press, agreed to publish it. Before turning it in, Wescott said, "I myself had removed a good many sexy paragraphs, including one or two rather daring episodes of a bull and a cow in intercourse that I had described very voluptuously and a rather long erotic dream that went on for two or three pages."[30] He also cut, he said, overblown or overly romantic prose. When the final galleys arrived that fall, Wescott was sick in bed in his Christopher Street apartment, using ice packs to bring down his fever. He had just been released from the hospital where a case of the mumps and a high temperature, possibly related to the Spanish flu, had resulted in the removal of a testicle. In this condition, he discovered that his publisher's lawyer had made fifty-two small deletions of words and phrases. He recalled, "The one chapter I had been worried about, which had a theme of definite but latent homosexuality, my expurgator evidently had not noticed."[31] But words such as "naked" and "breast" were removed, as were a few sentences, such as one suggesting a boy and girl making love in a wheat field. Wescott put most of the deletions back, and Dial relented. *The Apple of the Eye* was released in December.

A novel of the Midwest, the story is about the land and region as much as its characters. Dialogue is minimal, and the elegant lyrical prose includes stark descriptions of nature and the harsh realities of a poor farming community. The decade of the teens, and even the previous century, are captured in the farmers' conversation, the work, and such detail as the many kinds of horse-drawn vehicles: democrats, drop-seats, wagons, buggies, carts, and cutters. The characters are torn between the stifling puritanism of the region and unsanctioned love and passion.

The first part, "Bad Han," is the story of Hannah Murdoc—inspired by the woman whom Wescott's mother knew. Her lover, Jules, marries a woman respected by the community, leaving Hannah an outcast. Eventually she becomes a hermit, living in the shadow of her youthful love, roaming the fields and marshes. When she sees cattle resting on a hillside, she lies down beside them. She serves as a midwife, a nurse, a healer of people and animals. After an accident she dies, a saintlike figure. By any standard, Hannah is a strong and fascinating female character.

The tragic cost of morality without humanity is driven home in the two other parts of the novel, "Rosalia" and "Dan Alone." Jules's daughter Rosalia falls in love with a young farmhand named Mike. Their summer love affair deeply affects her fifteen-year-old cousin, Dan, a sensitive farm boy who clearly is Wescott's fictional self.[32] Dan idolizes Mike, but Rosalia is terrified of their "sin." Jules is ready to approve the relationship, but his religious wife rejects it. Finally, Mike leaves, kissing tearful Dan goodbye. But the girl, abandoned and imagining herself pregnant, runs off to the marshes during a winter storm. Her body is not found until spring.

The writing includes poetic but not sentimental descriptions of the Wisconsin countryside: "The April spring being an illusion of light, the setting sun left the farms clasped in a hand of darkness and wet ominous air." There is the dignity of outcast Hannah: "To her simple eye nothing was degrading, nothing evil; everything formed a single difficult pure coil—moralless and pure." And there are surprising moments for a novel of this era which Dial's lawyer missed, such as timid Dan discovering a circle of schoolboys in a woodshed, obviously masturbating—which Wescott had witnessed in high school. In contrast to the tragic love of Rosalia and Mike is the subtle love between older boy and younger. "'In my opinion,'" Mike tells Dan, "'everything is pure, everything is good that doesn't hurt somebody else. Life is dull enough if we have all the fun there is.'" And: "He took Dan's hand and pressed it, and picked out an unbroken dried clover leaf, and laid it on the boy's palm, and closed the hand."[33] Young Dan eventually has a confrontation with his father, and goes off to a university and the hope of a freer life.

Novelist Sinclair Lewis offered the book jacket comment, "I have finished with the greatest delight *The Apple of the Eye*. It seems to me that it has something curiously like genius." Dozens of excellent reviews followed. Kenneth Burke in the *Dial* praised the book's "keen emotional appeal and stylistic vigor," and the *Boston Evening Transcript* called it "one of the most interesting and one of the ablest of the season." "He has perfected a prose of extraordinary suppleness, strength and beauty," noted

Vanity Fair, and the *New York Evening Post* remarked, "It has something in it of the modern painters." Of the character Dan Strane, the *Brooklyn Eagle* stated, "There is nothing in recent novel writing quite so poignant as this boy's struggle. It is moving and grips the imagination."[34]

Suddenly Wescott had made the step from the literary journals to the wider reading public. Wheeler's dream of living among the expatriates in France was within their grasp. Ford Madox Ford, now living outside Paris, sent his compliments on the book and invited them to visit.[35] But money was the question. Wescott had drafts of new stories and an outline of a second novel, and Dial Press offered a modest advance of $1,000. Then Wescott met Frances Lamont Robbins at a party in the Greenwich Village apartment of Tony and Betty Salemme. A wealthy New Yorker and a lover of the arts, Robbins told him she had read *The Apple of the Eye* and liked it very much. The next day she sent him a check for $3,000 in an envelope, with a note telling him she didn't want to be a patron, but she did want him to go to France and write his new novel. Wescott never forgot Robbins's crucial and timely gift, and over the years she offered helpful advice about his writing, and true friendship.

3

The Expatriate Twenties

Some of Wescott's earliest impressions of the move to France were captured in a series of letters to an older friend, Caroline Newton of Gramercy Park in New York. At the Halifax mail drop, he sent a letter from the British ocean liner *Orduna*. "So far the trip has been quiet and pleasant," he wrote, "with the tragic exception of the end of a young Austrian Jew. After behaving so abnormally that the ship's officers intended to put him off in Halifax, he committed himself and his troubles to the sea."[1] Years later that mysterious incident would appear in a Wescott manuscript. At the moment, he wrote his friend, he was completing a new story, preparing a book of poetry for publication, and looking forward to Paris.

In mid-February, he reported: "We are established impermanently but very comfortably in a little hotel across from the Senate. Paris is no longer very cheap and we are thinking of going to the country as soon as it gets warm. . . . I have begun to write." A week later, on Hotel Savoy stationery, he wrote, "I'm at work on a story called 'Fire and Water.' . . . I find my writing mind a little slow and mannered and am glad to limber it up on a small piece before I set myself, for better or worse, at the perfectly terrifying *The Grandmothers*. Something in me, I suppose, is always whimpering to be let off writing altogether." Those words reveal more than worry about his new novel. Although success, when it came, never surprised him, Wescott keenly felt a need not to fail. On April 9, he wrote Newton to say "Fire and Water" had been sold to *Collier's* magazine for an "immense" sum, which they needed. "We're established in a miserably inconvenient little flat on the Boulevard Raspail—a most likeable place withal—unfortunately only for three months. Then we hope to get to the sea shore. . . . *The Grandmothers* begins to live, slowly, painfully; with—I suppose—the inevitable mortification and sense of weakness rising in me to stop its progress altogether . . . and then it stirs anew."[2]

A month later, they were visiting Villefranche-sur-Mer in the south. "This fishing town is practically heaven. . . . We expect to come back to stay for the rest of the summer." *The Grandmothers* was going well, he noted. As for "Fire and Water," he didn't mind that she and Frances Robbins disliked the story. "Yet the *Collier's* check rounds out our budget for the rest of the year."[3] The story that appeared in *Collier's National Weekly* on July 4, 1925, may have displeased his women friends because of its dark humor. Like his first novel, and the earlier story "In a Thicket," it is an antiromantic depiction of the Midwest. Its main characters are an unpleasant young couple who set fire to a farm they inherited but fail to convince the insurance company, then run away with a traveling carnival. Versions of the story appeared in *The Best Short Stories of 1925* and, as "The Runaways," in his 1928 story collection and a later anthology.

Wescott knew he should get away from the expense and distractions of Paris. "We were being very sociable and it was a very good time," he remembered, "except that I wanted and needed to get to work." Several friends, including Ford Madox Ford, suggested Villefranche, and Wescott was pleased. "Villefranche is a small town, actually a suburb of Nice, where the American Navy has been going since the Civil War. It's an almost circular port, very beautiful, very deep, and the ships come in quite close. The Alps come right down to the water, which means the town gets protected from the north winds. It's an extraordinary climate." He and Wheeler stayed at a quiet hotel at first but soon moved to the nearby Hotel Welcome, a four-story waterfront building popular with artists, including the French writer and artist Jean Cocteau. "Monroe and I took two great rooms one flight up and facing Italy," he said. "Cocteau had a large room and a little room at the other end, facing the harbor." Within days Wescott met Cocteau, then thirty-five and a celebrity. The hotel had a bar, popular with sailors, which had windows facing the harbor. Wescott was having a drink with an American friend, Katherine Harvey, who suddenly pointed to the water. "She said, 'See that rowboat coming? That's Cocteau.' And there was a fairly good-sized seagoing rowboat with a ragamuffin of a boy sitting in the prow, and Cocteau in his eternal Terrycloth robe rowing very deftly."[4]

A 1925 photo shows a somewhat awed Wescott in his midtwenties with his arm self-consciously around a dapper-looking Jean Cocteau. "He had a long French face," Wescott recalled, "with eyes high and a long nose. He was very tall and very inclined to be like a dancer, with extraordinarily elegant sharp movements. We made friends very rapidly. He got up early every morning to write and dictate letters. He would hold his writing tablet out with one hand, with his pencil in the other, and write as if he were drawing, and very fast, even putting in little drawings, and all the time talking. I never heard anyone talk so beguilingly and passionately, all showing off—not vain, but just like Fourth of July, just fireworks! Underneath it all there was a great deal of sorrow, and never being quite satisfied with his work, or with the people who held back on him in their admiration."[5]

Other residents at the hotel included Christian Bérard, Mary Butts, Georges Hugnet, and Philip Lassell. Some of the hotel's visitors were Isadora Duncan, Paul Robeson, Francis Rose, Rebecca West, Igor Stravinski, Pablo Picasso, and Allen Tate and his wife, Caroline Gordon. "We lived as the Victorians wrote!" Wescott said with a laugh. "What should have taken months we did in weeks."[6] Despite the lively atmosphere, he was working on his novel and, in 1925, released his second book of poems.

Natives of Rock appeared in a deluxe edition of 550 copies, published by Francesco Bianco and illustrated by Bianco's wife, Pamela. Boxed and printed on lavish stock, it was dedicated to Bernadine Szold, a writer from the Chicago days who was then living in Paris. Wescott's foreword acknowledges Ezra Pound and HD. Noting that the twenty poems were written in Evanston, Illinois, and Germany, he adds, "Since that time I have come to think of myself as a narrator, and unless I am mistaken, each of these poems represents an intense moment in an unwritten narrative."[7] Poems such as "The Penitent in the Snow" and "Gifts of the River" evoke Santa Fe, as do lines such as these from the title poem: "The fires cut away / the soft forest / down to the rose-pink rock / harder than light." Marianne Moore's review in the *Dial* noted, "The New Mexico country—a heightened, poetic equivalent of the literal—is here. Verbal harmony and cadence are here, and a veritable Scheherazade's rainbow-garmented, many-ply tissue of color." The *Chicago Evening Post* agreed: "The most striking of these poems were written in and of New Mexico and their stripped line and sharp cadences are themselves a faithful transcription of the landscape." According to Wescott scholar William Rueckert, "It is with *Natives of Rock* that Wescott makes his contribution to Imagist poetry and becomes significant, in a minor way, in the history of poetry in the 1920's."[8]

Though disciplined in his work, Wescott took short trips with Wheeler to northern France and Italy, and was drawn deeper into the world of Jean Cocteau. He soon realized that Cocteau was addicted to opium, a habit that started with the death of the young novelist Raymond Radiguet. Wescott learned the whole story. In 1919, the poet Max Jacob had sent sixteen-year-old Radiguet to Cocteau. Wescott described him as "a sturdy little boy with a pretty face and a walking stick who knocked on Cocteau's door and offered him some manuscript, and the manuscript was brilliant.

And, in fact, a great many people think Radiguet was the more brilliant of the two. This boy, with only an ordinary education, was able to indict Cocteau for affectation and mannerism and repetition and poetical fantasy, and made him try to write short sentences with impact, as he himself did. His first novel, *The Devil in the Flesh,* is one of the most beautiful books you can imagine. Cocteau taught him everything he knew and learned everything he could learn, and was very happy for a while."[9]

In December of 1923, Radiguet contracted typhoid fever and died at the age of twenty. The proofs of his second novel, *Count d'Orgel,* had just been corrected. Cocteau was shattered, Wescott said:

> He'd devoted himself so intensively to the work of Radiguet, and he built him up into a very famous young writer, and meanwhile he'd learned a kind of humility about his own work. And when Radiguet died Cocteau completely went to pieces. He stumbled along and one day met a boy carrying opium pipes. Opium is a curious drug. The Egyptians call it *kif,* which means peace. It gradually disables you in physical ways but it also relieves you of all your anxiety and ambition and jealousy. Presently you lie on the floor a great deal too much, daydreaming, and it gradually undermines the sexual intimacies. When the addiction gets bad it becomes impossible to sweat, to ejaculate, to urinate. And then the person has to be carried off to a sanatorium and dried out. The best way to do it is cold turkey and it's a grueling experience. I decided that opium addiction varied with the reason for taking it. Elizabeth Barrett Browning took it for pain and became addicted, but without the psychological effects one gets when he takes it for escape. Cocteau went headlong into it and became extremely intoxicated. But he wasn't sick enough not to fall in love or not to care.[10]

Cocteau's lover after Radiguet was Jean Bourgoint, or "Jeannot." He and his sister Jeanne were a strange pair whom Cocteau had met in Paris. Wescott recalled Jean and Jeanne as "very eccentric middle-class Parisians. Jean looked like Greek sculpture, pale, very handsome, with broad shoulders, large and blond. They lived in a small house and shared the same cluttered double room, beds side by side, and they quarreled and had strange hobbies and games. She presently got into a tragic marriage. When Jean became involved with Cocteau, she hated it and hated him and blamed him. Cocteau later went on and wrote the novel *Les Enfants terribles,* about them both living together. And Jeanne didn't like it at all."[11]

Wescott remembered when Cocteau's opium habit led to a sanatorium stay and a cold-turkey treatment. "They did it the hard way and the days were terrible. Jean Bourgoint would come into the adjacent park and wave to him and Cocteau would come out and wave, so that they didn't touch during the whole time. But Cocteau said to me afterward that the most shocking experience of his entire life was when we met him when he first came out—with all his senses intact, fresh and anxious to get back to work—and he saw Jean and felt as if he'd never seen him before, as if he'd seen a postcard of him, or somebody else's snapshot; it was no one he knew. And it was then that he told me about his suicidal influence on people. He told me that five boys he'd known had killed themselves and he had then on his hands a sixth one who he was very worried about. It was the theme of his life. Of course, he had this magic, especially with young people—as a poet, and doomed, comparing himself to Dante and Petrarch, feeling that he worked as hard as that."[12]

Cocteau was no longer attracted to Bourgoint, but he was worried about him. Wescott continued:

> Of course, Cocteau saw at once that I was enchanted by Jean, and I thought he encouraged me to take him under my wing. Perhaps I was wrong about that. But he obviously didn't want him anymore. I immediately pounced. Jean and I spent one night on the beach, on the stones, right on the water in one another's arms. And every time I made a move for the center of his body or to his mouth, he pushed me away with his great hands and great strength. Then we'd talk again and that went on through the night. He had an erection, but no reaction. I was allowed to touch him, but then he'd roll over onto the stones again. It was hopeless. Perhaps he still loved Cocteau. Anyway, he didn't respond to me. I was very fond of him.
>
> No, I haven't had a great deal of sex appeal in my life. I've been loved more than anyone I've ever known but I haven't had the power to suddenly seduce someone. There are all sorts of reasons for it and it doesn't really matter. I wasn't awfully surprised, only I was embarrassed and grief stricken, because I'd entered into the magic of this whole thing. Jeannot was very, very close to me for a year or so. Then he went away to military service in the summer of 1926. I went over to Montpellier to see him and tried everything I knew about seduction, with no luck. But we remained friends. I didn't see him again until 1938, just before the war, and by then he was very intoxicated himself with opium.[13]

Among Wescott's unpublished poems is a four-stanza poem about unrequited love called "Venus on the Shore," later inscribed, "Villefranche-sur-Mer, 1927. A poem about Jean Bourgoint; not for him—he knew only a few words of English."[14]

The drama around him did not keep Wescott from his work. In March 1926, his agent, Lloyd Morris, arrived from New York with a contract from Harper and Brothers, which had obtained rights to *The Grandmothers* from Dial Press. Harper also released a new edition of *The Apple of the Eye,* as did Butterworth in London. A Wescott story, "Sisters of Hunters," appeared in the March issue of the *Dial,* and Monroe Wheeler published another, as the last of his series of deluxe books. Printed on creamy white stock in Mâcon, France, *Like a Lover* was another portrayal of a midwestern farm community with an ominous undercurrent, in this case a man predestined to homicide, despite his romantic intentions.

There was a growing feeling of security about Wescott's career, and that summer he and Wheeler took a trip to Venice and Vienna. They had a scare when Wheeler suffered a perforated appendix and needed emergency surgery. He recovered at Aix-les-Bains, near the border of Switzerland. When they returned to Villefranche, they moved out of the Hotel Welcome to a house with an olive garden on a hillside above the town. They called their small villa La Cabane, hired a housekeeper, and were able to invite friends for the first time.

Among the first to visit was the expatriate Bernadine Szold. Wescott recalled, "In 1918 in Chicago I met Bernadine Szold, whose cousin Henrietta founded Hadassah and whose cousin David Lilienthal presided over the Tennessee Valley Authority in the early days. Without really meaning to, I cast a spell on her."[15] Well known in Paris society, Szold wrote for the *Manchester Guardian* and had written for the *New Yorker* before Janet Flanner began her "Paris Notebook" column. Other visitors included the writer Kay Boyle, whom Wescott considered "more abroad" than the other expatriates, and his New York patron, Frances Robbins. Over the next six months the guests included the sculptor Arthur Lee, Paul Robeson, now one of America's top recording artists, and Essie Robeson. There were also Wheeler's handsome young friends from Chicago, David Halliday, who late in life would marry actress Mary Martin, and Paul Soutter.

One of their more colorful friends was red-haired Mary Butts, a friend of Cocteau who was working on her second novel, *Armed with Madness.* Influenced by the writer and prophet of the occult, Aleister Crowley, Mary became carried away with mysticism and magic. The poet Oswell Blakeston said that even Crowley called Mary "very dangerous." Wescott recalled one incident: "Mary had been up on a hill and came back all puffing and sweating, tears in her eyes, and sat down and said she'd had one of the great experiences of her life. She said she'd sat on a hill and found that she was surrounded by all the weeds and flowers that are in *The Bacchae* of Euripides, and she believed it meant she was going to die. And Monroe said, 'But what exactly did you see? What were the names of these flowers? Were they really all there?' Mary finally burst into tears and ran upstairs to her room."[16]

Distractions didn't stop Wescott from completing *The Grandmothers* by November. Surely one reason for his writing facility at this time was the influence of so many creative people in Villefranche—far different from the world of socialites he would later know in Paris and New York. Most significantly, Jean Cocteau had insisted that he read the works of Marcel Proust, among other French literature. Wescott scholar Sy M. Kahn points out that Wescott was reading Proust's *In Remembrance of Things Past* while he was writing *The Grandmothers.*[17] His personal vision of the Midwest, fictionalized accounts of his ancestors, and a strong retrospective voice influenced by Proust carried the work smoothly through its final drafts.

In December, Wescott and Wheeler traveled to New York where he presented the manuscript to Harper and Brothers personally. Another significant event on that trip was his first meeting with George Platt Lynes, an attractive and ambitious twenty-year-old from New Jersey. Lynes had already visited Paris and met all the right people, including Bernadine Szold, who suggested that they meet.

Wescott and Wheeler never really shared boyfriends simultaneously, but they were both interested in meeting Lynes. They were staying at the Hotel Lafayette on University Place, and Wheeler happened to be out when Lynes called. He was attractive, fair, slender, and precocious. "That first time we met," Wescott recalled, "he picked up a photo of Monroe that was in our room and gave a whistle. And I thought, 'Uh, oh.'"[18] Despite that premonition, Wescott promised Lynes he would write, and Lynes promised to visit them in France.

After seeing friends in London and Paris in early 1927, Wescott returned to Villefranche with Wheeler. When *The Grandmothers* was released in August, their world changed. By luck of timing, he had written an innovative, breakthrough novel in a period when the novel was at the center of American culture. Suddenly he was the author of a popular and critical success that put him among the major expatriate writers.

Reviewer Burton Rascoe wrote, "I find it difficult to remain calm. Its appearance at this time is comparable to the occasion when *Spoon River Anthology* and *Winesburg, Ohio* were first given to the public. It is a novel with its roots in the American soil. It is a novel that gives new significance to American life." The *Nation* recognized the book as a regional classic: "Mr. Wescott's very beautiful and moving chronicle is possibly the first artistically satisfying rendition of the soul of an American pioneer community and its decedents." A featured interview in the *New York Herald Tribune* of December 18 was entitled, "A Celebrity at Twenty-seven."[19]

While *The Apple of the Eye* had been praised for the haunting beauty of its prose and its sensitively drawn characters, *The Grandmothers* showed major development. The story is presented as a family chronicle, narrated by Wescott's fictional self, Alwyn Tower. Looking back on it, Wescott said, "*The Grandmothers* was an important book and an influential book, but a great many other people could have written it, if they thought of it. They wrote it afterward, right down to Alex Haley. I invented the family tree and everyone has been doing it ever since."[20]

Nearly every chapter of *The Grandmothers* is devoted to a different character. A page-long listing of twenty-seven people spanning three generations precedes chapter 1. Alwyn Tower looks back on these people and on his own life as well, and his voice is clear right from the opening paragraphs: "Until Alwyn Tower grew to manhood he never forgot that everyone was older than he. People remembered things not in existence now, and many of them had been born in houses which had vanished long ago. A cabin which had stood in the melon patch had been his father's birthplace; and as a child, jumping over the heavy, downy vines, he tried in vain to find a trace of its foundations."[21]

Sometimes the young Alwyn is part of the story, more often he is not, but the reader quickly learns that the adult Alwyn, an expatriate in Europe, is speaking. Gradually, his perspective brings a deeper level of meaning and understanding: "Indeed, it was an instinctive law for Americans, the one he had broken. Never be infatuated with nor try to interpret as an omen the poverty, the desperation, of the past; whoever remembers it will be punished, or punish himself; never remember. Upon pain of loneliness, upon pain of a sort of expatriation though at home. At home in a land of the future where all wish to be young; a land of duties well done, irresponsibly, of evil done without immorality, and good without virtue."[22]

At the same time, Alwyn's compassionate voice brings the characters to life. Chapter by chapter, they are unveiled: Alwyn's grandparents and parents; his great-aunt Nancy, who escapes from an unhappy marriage; his great-uncle Leander, who lost his beloved younger brother Hilary when they both served in the Civil War and decades later adopted Nancy's son, Timothy; Uncle Jim, a minister; Uncle Evan, the deserter; tragic Aunt Flora; and more. Many of the characters were drawn from family stories Wescott's grandmother had told him in the summer of 1919, when he was recovering from the Spanish flu. Uncle Jim the minister recalled his parson uncle in Waukesha. Chapter 6, "His Great-Aunt Nancy Tower's Unhappiness," repeated a family tale he had sketched out years earlier in a long, unpublished poem entitled "Flight and a Victory."[23] A subtle homosexual undercurrent exists between Leander and Hilary, and several other characters.

Some characters, Wescott recalled, were more fictional or drawn from people outside the family: "That great-aunt had no child. I brought in Timothy in order to introduce the physical description of one of the people I desired most in the entire world and couldn't have, Jean Bourgoint. And I brought in the character who went to the Spanish war, Uncle Evan, because I thought *The Grandmothers* was a little too goody-goody and there ought to be more life in it, and a way to end it. I knew there was a man in the family who had gone AWOL from the war and married a European. And he came to see my grandmother on her deathbed."[24] When the runaway uncle comes to bid farewell to his dying mother, he brings along his son, Orfeo. Instantly, Orfeo and Alwyn become friends. At the grandmother's death at the very end, the two boys walk through the countryside toward town, to spread the word and to buy as many flowers as possible. In fact, Orfeo was drawn completely from Wheeler, and Alwyn and

Orfeo's leaving the farm represents Wescott and Wheeler's leaving the Midwest.

"I knew early on that Monroe had taken me over and was going to save me," Wescott said of his true-life story. "He did come to see my grandmother and then we went for a walk, and I described him exactly as I saw him." In the book, Orfeo "was not like a member of the family nor even like an American; he had no appearance either of the country or the sort of city Alwyn knew. He was exceedingly dark, with strange variations of the same dark, burned rose without pinkness in his mouth and skin. His eyes were heavy-lidded, dark, and bright. He seemed never to have a sharp or clever look under any circumstances."[25]

Harper and Brothers expected *The Grandmothers* to be a success. Wescott was obliged to autograph a specially bound and encased announcement edition of 250 copies. The standard first edition went through twenty-six printings in its first six months and won the publisher's Harper Prize Novel Award, which brought a bonus of $10,000. Wescott accepted the award that fall when he and Wheeler visited New York. Butterworth in London published an edition under the alternate title *A Family Portrait.*

In France, the American expatriates were well aware of each other's new releases. Only one writer seemed to resent Wescott's good fortune. While being interviewed by a reporter for the *Herald Tribune* in Shakespeare and Company, Sylvia Beach's Paris bookstore, Ernest Hemingway picked up a copy of *The Grandmothers.* "Would you like to know what's wrong with this book?" he asked. "In the first place, every sentence was written with the intention of making Glenway Wescott immortal. And in the second place—but what's the use of telling you what's in the second place. You work for a kind of family newspaper and you couldn't print it. Your editor wouldn't let you."[26]

At first Wescott wondered if Hemingway was accusing him of being part of Cocteau's opium-smoking circle. "But I was never tempted to smoke opium," he said, "and I'd seen Cocteau when he was as sick as a dog."[27] Then he realized Hemingway was referring to Wescott's homosexuality. After all, he'd done it before. *The Sun Also Rises,* Hemingway's popular action-and-dialogue novel of late 1926, contained the first public expression of his dislike for Wescott. In chapter 3, protagonist Jake Barnes is irritated by the presence of a group of gay men in a club. He becomes more angry when his would-be lover, Brett Ashley, introduces him to one of the group, Roger Prentiss, who "was from New York by way of Chicago and was a rising new novelist." In a letter to Scribner editor Maxwell Perkins, Hemingway had admitted that the character in his manuscript was Wescott and he agreed to the request to change the name from Prescott to Prentiss.[28] The fictional exchange of Jake and Roger poked fun at Wescott's speech and manners:

"You're from Kansas they tell me," [Roger] said.
"Yes."
"Do you find Paris amusing?"
"Yes."
"Really?"
I was a little drunk. Not drunk in any positive sense but just enough to be careless.
"For God's sake," I said, "yes. Don't you?"
"Oh, how charmingly you get angry," he said, "I wish I had that faculty."[29]

While Wescott didn't remember his exact conversations with Hemingway, it's likely that Hemingway, with his brilliant ear for dialogue, captured one exchange in his novel. More annoying to Hemingway may have been Wescott's friendship with the real-world model for Brett Ashley, the young British woman Jake Barnes could not make love to in the novel, the woman Hemingway could not seduce in real life. Wescott said, "I was on the English side of the fence when he had that romance with Lady Duff Twysden. She was a marvelous woman. I remember her perfectly well, and she was the one who refused to go to bed with him."[30]

There was also the fact that Hemingway resented literary rivals, and he disliked Wescott's prose—so different from his own. Just months after Wescott's first novel was released, Hemingway had met with publisher Alfred Harcourt, who happened to praise *The Apple of the Eye*. Young Hemingway replied that he found Wescott's work "fundamentally unsound."[31] The distinguished Harcourt raised his eyebrows and changed the subject. Yet homophobia may have affected Hemingway as much as competition, as his work suggests. An early unpublished story, "Crime and Punishment," expresses shock at discovering homosexuals of all types in New York.[32] Among his published stories, "A Simple Inquiry" is about an Italian officer in World War I who makes a pass at a young orderly. "Mother of a Queen" is a tirade against a homosexual bullfighter, probably modeled after a real life matador named Ortiz. "The Sea Change" and the posthumous novel *The Garden of Eden* dwell obsessively on lesbianism. Early nonfiction writing that eventually appeared as *A Moveable Feast* expressed shock at discovering Gertrude Stein's lesbianism—surely suggesting that Hemingway was the last to know. *Death in the Afternoon* (1932), about bullfighting, contained a number of homophobic remarks, including references to Cocteau, André Gide, Oscar Wilde, Walt Whitman, and even El Greco. And Hemingway was probably expressing more than competitive jealousy when he complained to Max Perkins about three popular writers who were also homosexual: "Glenway Wescott, Thornton Wilder and Julian Green have all gotten rich in a year in which I made less than I made as a newspaper correspondent—and I'm the only one with wives and children to support."[33]

In 1986 biographer Peter Griffin volunteered another reason for Hemingway's dislike of Wescott: "As you know, Ernest's mother loved Mr. Wescott's work, and she suggested to Ernest that if he wished to please her, he should write like that gentleman. Naturally Ernest who, despite what he said, always hoped to please his mother, took it out on Mr. Wescott." Much earlier, biographer Carlos Baker noted Hemingway's response when his mother criticized his own work: "No doubt, Ernest said sourly, Grace wished that her son Ernie were Glenway Wescott or some other highly respectable Fairy Prince with an English accent and a taste for grandmothers."[34]

Wescott didn't remember feeling particularly threatened by Hemingway. Wheeler recalled that they first met him in 1925, before they left Paris for Villefranche, when Ford Madox Ford arranged a game of bridge. Otherwise, they saw each other fleetingly in the clubs and cafes. Hemingway socialized mostly with other Americans. Wescott and Wheeler preferred the British expatriates, as well as the French. Late in life, Wescott sometimes said, "I didn't suffer for my homosexuality." And the fact was that in France he could avoid Americans of Hemingway's type. In later years, he and Wheeler were able to choose their company even more exclusively.

What Wescott did remember was that he didn't share others' enthusiasm for Hemingway. He recalled a day in 1925 when F. Scott Fitzgerald approached him in the south of France. Fitzgerald said their own books had inflated market value, and that an up-and-coming writer, Ernest Hemingway, deserved their help. He shook Wescott's elbow and asked him to write an essay praising Hemingway's early stories. It didn't occur to Fitzgerald that Wescott had no intention of doing so. Even at that early date, Wescott sensed something destructive about Hemingway's influence on Fitzgerald.[35]

Reflecting on Hemingway the man and the artist, Wescott had both scorn and praise. He said, "You see, he was the kind of person who would go to a party and think the hostess was a lesbian, whereas the hostess was sleeping every night with the black butler. He got everything wrong, he wouldn't know what was going on, ever. And he knew perfectly well that if you couldn't understand characters you had to compensate for it in your writing.

"His really first rate writing is where there is no motivation: in the middle of a battle, in bed in Venice, out fishing somewhere, or in bullfights or drinking bouts; situations in which the normal cause and effect of human behavior in real life can be avoided. And the fact that his stories are like that makes them unique. I think he's one of the greatest storytellers who ever lived. Better than Maupassant. Better than Willie [Maugham]."[36]

The competition between the writers would end soon enough, when Hemingway achieved greater popularity with his World War I classic, *A*

Farewell to Arms (1929). But for a time Wescott's reputation was unsurpassed among the expatriates. He would experience success again, but it was in 1927 that he enjoyed his greatest fame.

Only one thing marred the breakthrough year, and that was the dramatic death of Isadora Duncan. He recalled, "When we knew Isadora of course she was fifty and didn't dance exactly but moved with that extraordinary grace. She had students. And she was concerned about her autobiography." In early September, he visited Duncan in nearby Nice and she was worried about the autobiography she had written for money already spent. She did not expect it to be literary but was afraid the manuscript was filled with misspellings and bad grammar. "She wept and said that some people had objected to her dancing but at least there'd been no bad grammar in it," Wescott said. Reluctantly, he promised to return in a week and look at her manuscript. But on September 14 Duncan was strangled when her scarf became caught in the steering wheel of her car. "That night, Monroe and I sat up with her body all night, along with her good friend Marie Destri, who told us stories of Isadora's great days."[37] Wescott recalled that the body continued to bleed and, without being too obvious in front of the tearful Destri, he and Monroe placed towels around it. They did not leave Duncan's side until her brother Raymond arrived from Paris. Wescott told his American friend Zena Naylor, "I've never known so beautiful a place as it was that night, in that great bare room, in the midst of the flowerbed fenced with the church candles she had such a weakness for, under a veil and the famous old purple cloak, the beautiful worn-out old body with the hands folded on its belly. Whenever I think of it as long as I live, a heartbreaking scent and a sort of smoke will rise from the bottom of my heart."[38] Duncan's *My Life* was published months later.

Change came with the new year and the arrival of George Platt Lynes in Villefranche. Since their first meeting in New York, Wescott had kept in close contact with the young man who seemed so intent on joining their world. By the time Lynes arrived in March 1928, he was almost like a member of the family.

Born in 1907 in Englewood, New Jersey, George Platt Lynes was influenced by a friend from prep school, Lincoln Kirstein, the arts patron and publisher of *Hound and Horn*. Lynes had his own ambitions in the arts. He had visited Paris at eighteen in 1925 and met writers Carl Van Vechten, André Gide, René Crevel, Gertrude Stein, and Alice B. Toklas, as well as the Russian painter Pavel Tchelitchew (pronounced *chelitchev*). When he returned to the States, he published several literary chapbooks, with the help of his friend Edith Finch. Although it lasted only a year, his As Stable Publications printed Gertrude Stein's *Descriptions of Literature*, René Crevel's *1830*, and Ernest Hemingway's play *Today Is Friday*. In October 1927, he opened a little bookstore called Park Place in Englewood and managed it for six months. But he was anxious to return to France, and Wescott in particular encouraged him to come abroad.

Wescott's letters to Lynes had addressed him intimately, as "Dear Boy," "Sweet Boy," "Dear Little George," and "Child New York." And when Wescott's handsome and blond twenty-year-old brother arrived in New York the previous spring, Lynes quickly befriended him. Lloyd Wescott, like his four sisters and older brother, was resourceful and ambitious, and Wisconsin seemed hopelessly poor. He followed a girlfriend to New York and took a job at Harper, his brother's publisher. Although voraciously heterosexual, Lloyd was seduced by Lynes at least once, an unimportant event. Glenway's letters to George were discreet, but one made a clear reference to the incident: "I expected Monroe to call my displeasure with your intimacy with Lloyd jealousy; he calls it instead 'innate pitilessness,' and defies me to reproach you for what he maintains to be my own fault."[39]

When Lynes finally arrived in Villefranche, Wescott's year of fawning letters backfired. The real chemistry was between Lynes and Wheeler. Eight years older, Wheeler liked Lynes's boyish figure, sense of fun, and interest in creating deluxe books. While Lynes had something of a relationship with French novelist René Crevel, he was quickly swept away by Wheeler's social charm, art world wisdom, and Hollywood good looks. That spring and summer, Wheeler introduced Lynes to friends as a writer who was working on a novel. Lynes did compile a small manuscript but soon discarded it. Soon enough he would find his true talent, photography. As for those first months with Wheeler and Wescott, Lynes was enchanted with them and their success, but his youth and charm gave him equal power in the dynamic. His intimacy was mostly with Wheeler, and occasionally with Wescott. Lynes never left America completely, however, visiting France only several months at a time. From the start, their threesome was daring, original, and unpredictable.

By now, Wescott's private life often became secondary to social obligations he had never known before. He preferred writer friends such as Ford, Osbert Sitwell, the *Sunday Times* of London art critic Raymond Mortimer, and Cocteau. But he was obliged to meet other major authors of the day, including William Somerset Maugham. The renowned British novelist and playwright had purchased the Villa Mauresque, a Moorish-style house with eight acres on the narrow Cap Ferrat peninsula, near the Villefranche harbor. All of Cap Ferrat had previously belonged to King Leopold II of Bulgaria. Maugham refurbished the house and settled there in 1927. When they first met in 1928, Wescott found the fifty-four-year-old author cold and stuffy. He would never have guessed that a dozen years later they would become close friends.

The invitation to formal dinner at Villa Mauresque came not from Maugham but from an American writer who wanted an escort. The music critic Katherine Lane (Mrs. Sigmund Spaeth) had first met Wescott at the captain's table of an ocean liner. The night of the Maugham dinner, Wescott remembered, got off on the wrong foot: "Before we even left for Cap Ferrat, she told me that she'd learned I was a homosexual and said she was horrified by that. I said, 'Well, I'll cancel out if that's how you feel. I'm as shocked by your attitude as you are by me.' She backed down and we left together."[40]

They made the short trip from Villefranche by boat. Lights along the harbor led the way. With its fortresslike walls, grand entrance, marble staircase, and large drawing room, Mauresque was Maugham's reward to himself for becoming one of the most successful writers in the world. With seven bedrooms and a large swimming pool, Mauresque would attract his famous friends for four decades. But Wescott's first visit was less than pleasant. "Maugham was in a bad temper," he said, "harping at everyone, his eyes blazing at his assistant and lover, Gerald Haxton. It was one of his tense days when, to control his stammer, he would pull his mouth down like a snapping turtle's."[41] Over dinner, the host congratulated Wescott on *The Grandmothers,* but when Wescott mentioned his new love for Proust, Maugham frowned and made a remark to the whole company. "Willie said, 'Mr. Wescott, who is our youngest guest, is one of these American writers who come to France and don't know anything else but Proust, and haven't even heard of the journals of Marcel Jouhandeau or Jules Renard.'"[42] While Wescott hadn't read them yet, he would later believe Jouhandeau's journals to be among the greatest ever written. But he considered Maugham's comments rude.

More pleasant was an extended visit by Thornton Wilder in the summer of 1928. Wilder had first met Wescott three years earlier, when he praised *The Apple of the Eye,* but warned him that an author must keep himself before the public. Now, at thirty, Wilder had been awarded the Pulitzer Prize for *The Bridge of San Luis Rey.* In Villefranche for several days, he took long walks with Wescott, from the harbor to the foothills outside town. Wilder again warned him about the fleeting nature of fame. It was fine that *The Grandmothers* had excellent reviews and sold well, he said, but on a recent trip to Texas he had found the locals didn't know of the book. No doubt, Wilder said, most of the book sales were in New York, Boston, and Chicago. And book reviews didn't matter much in the long run, he cautioned. Front-page publicity, some mention on a page devoted to news, was far more important to one's career.[43] Future meetings with Wilder would involve the same kind of straightforward talk.

Wescott's success continued with the publication of *Good-bye, Wisconsin* in the fall of 1928. The title essay, first published in *New York Herald Tribune Books,* describes the impressions of an expatriate who makes a return visit to the Midwest. Most of the ten short stories that follow had been published in magazines, and all describe the Midwest as a place of repression and frustration. One of the new stories, "The Sailor," is about a young, worldly-wise sailor who returns from Europe to visit his family's Wisconsin farm, but not to stay. He remembers Villefranche: "A little half-moon of stone-and-plaster town in a narrow-necked harbor, all the buildings facing the sea, flesh-pink and yellow like a faded canary-bird and different shades of white and blue shutters. . . ."[44] F. Scott Fitzgerald would compare that passage to his own description of the town in his novel *Tender Is the Night* (1934). Fitzgerald later admitted that Hemingway had warned him to read Wescott's story first to avoid duplication, but he thought he should write first. "There are unavoidably certain resemblances," he wrote to Wescott, "but I think I will let it stand."[45]

Another new story, "Adolescence," is one of Wescott's best. It is a portrait of adolescence mysteriously in league with James Joyce's "Araby." In Wescott's story, however, his character's emerging sexuality is different from Joyce's. Thirteen-year-old Philip goes to a Halloween party dressed as a girl, at the suggestion of his fifteen-year-old friend Carl. Philip's disguise fools the other youngsters at the party, and he is thrown into confusion when a boy dressed as a soldier tries to kiss him. The characters are based on Wescott and his boyhood lover, Earl. Wescott once inscribed a copy of *Good-bye, Wisconsin* on the blank page next to "Adolescence": "The earliest communication in my big wild archive . . . is a postcard dated September 1914, addressed to my mother, telling her that I wanted to stay in West Bend that weekend—in order to go to this party disguised as a girl. I was thirteen, 'Carl' was fifteen."[46]

A favorable review in the *Boston Evening Transcript* was entitled, "Glenway Wescott, Prophet of a New America." Theodore Purdy in *Saturday Review of Literature* wrote, "It is a continuous pleasure to read his prose, fresh, unstrained, unaffected in description, sensitive and direct in narrative." The *New York Times* predicted, "It marks, judging from the external evidence, the end of a phase in the author's progression; he has had his say about the people, the characteristics, of the region of his birth, and is ready for other things."[47] Some of the stories appeared in *Harper's Magazine, Bookman, Century,* and the anthologies *Contemporary Trends* and *The Best Short Stories of 1928*. That year he also had poems in the anthologies *The Turquoise Trail* and *Voici les rhythmes subtils*. The German publisher F. G. Spiedel released an edition of *The Grandmothers* entitled *Die Towers,* translated by Georg Terramare. All these publications marked the end of Wescott's most productive period, the Villefranche years, which he now left behind.

4

Paris and a New Family

WESCOTT, Wheeler, and Lynes moved to Paris in the fall of 1928. Thereafter, Wescott's expatriate years centered on the new and complex relationships in his life. At first he and Wheeler stayed at the apartment of Jean Guérin, a friend of Jean Cocteau, and then they took a flat on rue des Eaux. Lynes took a room at an inexpensive hotel, which gave him the freedom to see the novelist René Crevel, while staying close to Wescott and Wheeler.

At about the same time, Bernadine Szold returned from a trip around the world with her friend Barbara Harrison. Only twenty-four, Harrison was beautiful and independent, a British and French citizen, and an heiress. Her mother was Virginia Crocker of the banking and railroad Crockers of California. Her father was Francis Burton Harrison, a former United States congressman who was governor general of the Philippines under President Woodrow Wilson. Barbara had experienced an unstable childhood after her parents separated. A notorious character, her father traveled continually and eventually married six times. After three years of study at Oxford, Barbara moved to Paris in 1925. As adventurous as her friend Bernadine Szold, she loved horseback riding, fast cars, outdoor sports, and travel. She was attracted to Wescott's charm and fame, Wheeler's artistic sensibility, and Lynes's wit and fun. In turn, they were intrigued and charmed by her, and they learned that despite her youth she understood the arts well. They quickly became friends and spent Christmas 1928 together.

Their unorthodox family continued to grow. Wescott was closer to

Wheeler than ever, but after nearly a decade together he understood that their relationship was changing. Wheeler wanted a secondary lover and a protégé, and Lynes was filling those roles. Lynes was becoming a serious photographer, accumulating travel photos as well as portraits of Gertrude Stein, Crevel, Cocteau, and others. Though married in a real sense to Wheeler, Wescott realized that he too needed a secondary lover. He had a brief affair with a Parisian named Gustov Levin, who owned concessions at the Eiffel Tower. Then he turned to someone he already knew, the brother of Jean Guérin, a sophisticated young Frenchman his own age named Jacques.

Tall, aristocratic, and sensual, Jacques Guérin greatly influenced Wescott's self-education, helping him develop his knowledge of French literature and art. They were well matched. Wescott would write and see friends during the day while Guérin was working. At night they would meet at the Guérin household. Not only was Guérin a good lover, but he was adorned with the aroma of fine perfumes manufactured by his family's business. "It was heaven for me," Wescott said. Afterward, he would walk more than a mile through the quiet nighttime streets of Paris, back to his home with Wheeler in the Left Bank.

Jacques Guérin, however, insisted that Wescott stop seeing Cocteau, because he considered the opium-smoking artist a bad influence on his brother. Wescott, while sympathetic to Guérin's concerns, had a weakness for Cocteau's mystic nature and later remembered "being in the back seat of an open motor car with Cocteau when a carriage horse was startled by a backfire and got out of control. The horse rose up on its hind legs, and its front legs came down in our car, kicking and thrashing, nearly striking our driver. I was frightened but Cocteau loved it. That's how he was." But trouble followed Cocteau. When he and his new lover, Jean Desbordes, were living in Toulon, "there was a wealthy Parisian boy named Rich who had sent Cocteau money and visited him several times. When Rich met Desbordes he fell in love with him. Once, to avoid him, Desbordes went out the back door of the house, and Rich saw him leave. Then Rich went back to Paris and cut off the end of his finger and sent it to Cocteau in a package. It was that kind of violence—well, I got tired of it. It seems to me I wasn't very worried about the opium. I don't think I saw him much in 1927 and 1928. I saw his films."[1]

Wescott explained his choice. "Jacques Guérin came into my life in 1928. He just wouldn't tolerate my seeing Cocteau at all. He and his younger brother were the love children of a great industrialist, the man who started the first chain store in France. A Jewish family, a gentile mistress, and the boys were brought up in Versailles. And the younger one, Jean, took opium and broke his mother's heart. And Jacques loved his mother, Jeanne-Louise, more, and felt he was loved less than his brother.

It was a tragic household. I indulged them and I understood them, and they didn't want me in Cocteau's circle. And they were more important to me than Cocteau was at the time, so I didn't see him for quite a long time."[2]

Life in Paris seemed ideal at first. Wescott was working on a novel, and his private life was happy. He and Wheeler took a trip to Spain and Morocco in March 1929, and Lynes returned to America. They met the writer Cyril Connolly in Tangiers and saw exotic desert landscapes, ceremonial Arabic dances, and a Bedouin horse race. But there was bad news upon their return. Lynes had suffered a dangerous ruptured appendix in New Jersey and undergone surgery. Lynes wrote to reassure Wheeler as he recuperated. Then Wescott suffered his own health problem, a bout of anal gonorrhea, which was difficult to treat in those days. The experience, he said, was more upsetting psychologically than physically.

Another sort of trouble followed when, unexpectedly, Barbara Harrison and Jacques Guérin became interested in each other. Wescott and Wheeler enjoyed Harrison's company, but they didn't anticipate her needs. She was worldly-wise for her age, but with little positive experience of men. Now she was close to this new circle of friends and welcomed the possibility of love. Wescott felt a sense of betrayal. "I'd had a superb relationship with Jacques and he taught me a great deal and made a Frenchman of me," he said. "But I spent much of 1929 in America because that was the year Barbara decided that she wanted to go to bed with Jacques Guérin, and Jacques decided that he didn't want to go to bed with her particularly but he wanted to marry her. Marry her and keep me—something like that. Well, I was just disgusted. I had a great theory, still do, that dog doesn't bite bitch. I never entered into competition with a woman. And I got out. Monroe and I went to America. Jacques wanted to become her fiancé before going to bed with her; she wanted to go to bed with him, fiancé or not. She was attracted to him because he was exotic and had lots of art and books and so on."[3]

Glenway and Monroe arrived in New York on the *President Harding* on June 28 and were met by Lloyd Wescott. During the Paris years, Glenway's supportive letters to Lloyd were sometimes headed, "My poor little brother" and "Dear small brother."[4] It is unlikely that either could imagine how their relationship would change in Lloyd's favor over the years.

In New York, Wescott visited Harper and Brothers, talking hopefully of his novel-in-progress, "The Dream of Mrs. Cleveland." Then, while Wheeler stayed with Lynes, Wescott began a long visit with his family in Ripon, Wisconsin. The luxuries of Paris were suddenly far away. This was the year of the stock market crash and the beginning of the Depression. It was coincidental but symbolic that the physical dimensions of American paper money were reduced that year by twenty-five percent. No longer a farmer, Bruce Wescott now took occasional work where he could find it.

He and Glenway's mother lived in a small, cold-water house. Glenway's sister Elizabeth was still living with her parents, along with her young, unemployed husband and their infant son. Although *Good-bye, Wisconsin* had marked an end to his Midwest fiction, Wescott made a last exception. Inspired by his Wisconsin summer, *The Babe's Bed* is a long story that describes expatriate Alwyn Tower's visit to his family home in poor farm country. The opening paragraph is an example of Glenway's elegant poetic-prose at its best:

> All summer long that country and the sky over it, if any one gaze could have embraced it all at once, would have been seen to be silken, Roman-striped with rainbows. Hard-looking clouds and hard rains were interspersed with choking sunshine. Prodigal breezes brought the needed moisture, and then perversely burned the oats and the immature corn. The continual lightning had much in common with the wild lilies, the grass snakes. The heat smelled like wine. Flowerbeds, green fruits, and pools, shone in abundance in the landscape—false jewels upon plaques of wind-engraved light. None of it, alas, was worth as much as it looked. Never were penury and extravagance so softly fused.[5]

As in *The Grandmothers,* Alwyn Tower is the third-person protagonist, and like Wescott, his attractive expatriate lifestyle was largely about appearances: "He felt poor: luxury went with his way of earning a living—by his wits—there was nothing left over," the story reveals.[6] But Alwyn recognizes the difference between his false wealth abroad and his family's authentic poverty. The tension in the Wisconsin household builds with the summer heat. The unemployed young husband is uncomfortable in his dependent position among his in-laws. Alwyn's sister is in poor health and unable to care for her demanding one-year-old. Their mother cares for the baby and the household; their father is resentful. Finally the situation climaxes with a family argument and the father's threatening to ask the young couple to leave. Alwyn, in a passage strongly evocative of Wescott's boyhood problems with his father, sees the present argument as a throwback to his childhood.

> Oh, indeed the past had come back—all of it in disorder. A moment ago it was with his infant nephew that he had identified himself; now as he spoke he was confusing himself with himself as he had been years before, a small boy. Thus his father had provoked him; then, too, there had been talk of youngsters' deserving to be driven from home, of whether or not a father was master in his own house—the poor great-hearted man! Then, as now, unhesitatingly he had replied, the most logically insulting phrase after phrase. He remembered vividly how he had been: slight and pallid, detestably afraid, fighting back in barking tones like some small animal instinctively inspired.[7]

Tempers cool, harsh words are soothed, as the father and son realize the quarrel this time is not between them. As the story ends, Alwyn and his father are in a car, shoulder to shoulder in the Wisconsin night. The real life story, Wescott said, ended with a letter from Jacques Guérin. "Finally, at the end of the summer, which is the summer I describe in *The Babe's Bed,* I got a letter from him saying, 'I finally got punished. Barbara got me to bed and it was no good.' And he said, 'Forgive me, come back.' And I did go back."[8] Wheeler was visiting his parents in Evanston and they discussed their return to Paris.

Wescott also got a letter from Barbara Harrison, who had gone off to Scotland to visit her father. She was hoping they could be together again: "But anyhow, do come back. I'd like you and Monie to be nearer to me, I mean geographically. Glenway dear, you are so extraordinary—with all your strength (I mean the essence of you) and your comprehension and the proud grace with which you move through life—you allow so many people and things and circumstances to touch you so profoundly. They all come to you for help. They make demands on your power, your goodness. It is because they know you to be understanding and moral."[9]

Thereafter, Harrison became more important in their lives. Wescott and Wheeler had a number of wealthy friends, but Harrison was close enough to be generous unself-consciously. Even before 1929, she invited them to stay at her small city house while she lived in her large house in suburban Rambouillet. Wescott described the building at 32, rue de Vaugirard to his brother as "two stories, tiny enough, in a court across from the Senate."[10] Sometimes they stayed at a nearby apartment, but Harrison's address put them on the fashionable side of the longest street in the Left Bank. Adding to the beauty of the location were the seventeenth-century Luxembourg Palace and the sixty-acre Luxembourg Gardens.

They also spent weekends at Harrison's Rambouillet home, which her architect had created from two small houses and a large horse stable. The former stable was turned into a grand living room with white walls and peaked chestnut rafters thirty feet high. There were paintings by Courbet, Gauguin, Derain, and Picasso and antique French furniture. A third of the rear wall was replaced by two great panes of glass for a view of the gardens and pond. At twenty-five, Harrison wasn't just wealthy but also sophisticated and free spirited, with intelligence and humor that matched their own. Their friendship seemed fated for something deeper, and as the year ended she and Wheeler made plans to launch the deluxe press they had envisioned.

Letters to and from 32, rue de Vaugirard show that Wescott and Wheeler kept close ties with their families in the Midwest.[11] Bruce Wescott sent a few friendly, if formal, notes. Glenway's mother, his sisters Elizabeth and Beulah, and Lloyd sent enthusiastic letters. Clearly, they admired his life. Wheeler's father, Fred, who had inspired his son's love of bookmaking, was pleased with the deluxe book venture.

By the spring of 1930, Wheeler and Harrison released a lavish-looking prospectus, introducing Harrison of Paris, which would publish limited-edition books in the finest French tradition, using superior typography, paper, and the work of renowned illustrators. Paris in the twenties was rich in small presses, including Robert McAlmon's Contact Editions, Jack Kahane's notorious Obelisk Press, and Bill Bird's Three Mountain Press, which in 1928 he sold to Wescott's friend Nancy Cunard, who renamed it Hours Press. But Harrison of Paris would be in a class of its own, producing beautiful editions at reasonable prices.

The first four Harrison of Paris books were released in the fall of 1930. They included *Venus and Adonis,* the long Shakespeare poem suggested by Wescott; seven Bret Harte stories entitled *The Wild West;* and Thomas Mann's long essay *A Sketch of My Life.* The fourth was *The Babe's Bed,* Wescott's long story about Alwyn Tower's visit to his midwestern home. Printed in Holland, set in a brand-new typeface, Lutetia, and dedicated "To Barbara," it was a thin red volume in a gold slipcase. The edition numbered just under four hundred copies. London's *Times Literary Supplement* noted that *The Babe's Bed* was really about Alwyn Tower's inner crisis and added, "It is a delicately drawn picture, drawn so delicately, indeed, that one cannot always be sure of its outlines." The *New York Times* found the prose "amazingly sensitive" but not consistently strong, and remarked, "In an enigmatic way Wescott promises us he may round out his testimony."[12] Although *The Babe's Bed* was Wescott's last midwestern work, its quality suggests that he left behind some of his promise when he abandoned his regional themes.

Harrison and Wheeler released five books the following fall that were just as impressive. They included *Fables of Aesop* with Alexander Calder illustrations, *The Death of Madame* by Madame de La Fayette, Fyodor Dostoyevsky's long story *A Gentle Spirit* with drawings by Christian Bérard, and Lord Byron's *Childe Harold's Pilgrimage*—a big handsome volume published at Wescott's request—illustrated by Sir Francis Rose. Most notable was Prosper Mérimée's *Carmen* and *Letters from Spain,* with illustrations by the Swiss artist Maurice Barraud. The book's new translation was uncredited at publication, but it was largely Wescott's work, with contributions from Wheeler and Harrison. Years later Wescott said, "I translated *Carmen.* I've often said I could have been perfectly happy being a translator."[13] The books were praised by the *Times* of London, the *New Yorker,* and the *New York Times.* London's *Times* said of the anonymous translation of *Carmen:* "a translation worthy of the elegant frame in which it appears."[14]

Translating a major work is time consuming, and no doubt Wescott contributed far more than translation to Harrison of Paris books. His dedication to his friends' venture is just one example of why his life changed in Paris, with his own writing becoming almost secondary. In addition, his datebook listed lunches, dinners, and concerts with Barbara Harrison, Bernadine Szold, Jacques Guérin, and others. Clearly, his social world consisted of mostly French and English artists and friends. In contrast, Hemingway and other Americans kept close contact with each other. Possibly, Wescott missed the kind of creative interaction he had enjoyed with writers in Chicago and New York. "I knew a lot of Americans," he said, "but Hemingway despised me, Fitzgerald was a drinker with a miserable wife, and the Americans who hung around the cafes bored me to death."[15]

Looking back, the American artist, poet, and novelist Charles Henri Ford recalled seeing Wescott only occasionally in the early thirties. "I'd see him in the popular cafes once in a while," Ford said, "but not often. We knew each other through Tchelitchew. And Monroe and Glenway were supportive of my novel. But we really became friends later, after they returned to the States."[16] Ford, who had earlier published the avant-garde magazine *Blues,* coauthored with Parker Tyler *The Young and Evil,* the notorious novel of Greenwich Village gays and their friends. In Europe, Ford had become the lover of the Russian surrealist artist Pavel Tchelitchew.

As a public figure, Wescott was unchanged. Recalling the expatriates of that time, Janet Flanner wrote about "Glenway Wescott, who always seemed fresh from his Harper Prize for *The Grandmothers,* and was already regarded as a handsome, formal literary figure, and his friend Monroe Wheeler, who set up the private bibliophile press called Harrison of Paris, which brought out a *rarissime* edition of Aesop's *Fables,* with original drawings by Alexander Calder."[17]

What had changed was Wescott's productivity. A British edition *of Good-bye, Wisconsin* appeared, and some of his stories were reprinted in Germany, America, and France.[18] But he was writing only small pieces, such as an essay for Poetry Club friend Elizabeth Madox Roberts. Roberts had written to say that her next novel, *The Great Meadow,* was set back one hundred years in time.[19] Because *The Great Meadow* was dedicated to him, Wescott didn't review it but wrote of their early friendship. And in writing about her southern, historical fiction, he referred to her as "a poet," then added, "Needless to say, I use the word 'poet' in the sense which may include a writer of prose and excludes most versifiers."[20] He himself fell into that category, of course, as *The Babe's Bed* proved. But what was missing was a major new work, and he explained why.

"I tried to write a novel," he said, "at which I failed entirely, called 'The Dream of Mrs. Cleveland,' a story about rich people, Long Island people, and I simply couldn't make it come alive."[21] What remains of Wescott's typescript includes his notation: "All that I have kept of one of my weakest attempts at novel writing, weakest and soonest given up as a bad job.

It was prompted or prophesied in the first part of *Good-bye, Wisconsin,* pp. 42–43."[22] The lines he refers to are in the title essay and begin: "I should like to write a novel about ideal people under ideal conditions." The plot wouldn't involve poverty or hunger or the problems of Wisconsin, he explained. Instead he would stress the inner workings of the human spirit, which, he believed, would pass for tragedy.

The failed novel's first chapter, "The Storm," describes the thunderstorm outside Mrs. Cleveland's home, as well as the emotional storm within the woman. She is an introspective character worthy of Virginia Woolf. Alwyn Tower is present but on the sidelines, not as the central narrator as in Wescott's best fiction. Some autobiographical background about Tower seems promising, but does not connect to Mrs. Cleveland's story. And though Mrs. Cleveland's reflections promise an interesting plot, they don't pay off. Any lingering hope Wescott held for "The Dream of Mrs. Cleveland" may have ended with a letter from his trusted friend Frances Robbins. Among her keen observations about the manuscript, Robbins wrote, "The chapters can't stand alone, as in *The Grandmothers*. . . . There is more of the thinker and less of the poet in this book."[23] What Robbins identified was the loss of narrative voice and a plot too complex for good storytelling. While this aborted work was a setback, Wescott put it aside and began outlining another novel.

His ambition was as practical as it was artistic. His income was dwindling, and he was concerned about his parents. The Depression in America had hit the Midwest hard. His mother wrote, "The next week is Old Settlers' Day and unless the weather is bad or uncertain we may go to town and stay over a day. For Dad wants to spend some time . . . looking over the possibility for work." A letter from Wescott's father, apparently mailed in the same envelope, mentions money and worries about the financial dependence of daughter Elizabeth, son-in-law Tom Hotchkiss, and baby Bruce—the models for the characters in *The Babe's Bed.* "I do not know how much work there will be in the spring," Bruce Wescott wrote. "These are anxious days and hard to take when you are so helpless."[24] Glenway sent what money he could, but the truth was that, while living among luxury, he seldom had much money of his own. His financial situation would be the same for much of the rest of his life.

Wheeler's prospects were rosier. Harrison of Paris was successful in its first few years, and his own parents needed no help. His younger lover, George Platt Lynes, returned to Paris for six months in 1930, renting his own rooms, and his lively humor and charisma won over Harrison and everyone else. That fall, Wheeler returned to the States with Lynes and promptly fell ill. He had gall bladder surgery and recuperated in Englewood with Lynes before returning to Paris by Christmas. Afterward, Wheeler and Lynes were never separated for long. Lynes was building his reputation as a photographer in New York, including gallery shows, but he was often in Paris. More than once, Harrison sent him round-trip fare. On one visit, he was commissioned to take advertising photos for Jacque Guérin's Parfum d'Orsay.

Clearly, Wescott's new family was now a complex web of relationships: Lynes and Wheeler, Wheeler and Harrison, himself and Guérin—and each with the others. There was also an unexpected and powerful new friendship. This time it was not a man but one of the great female friends of his life.

Pauline Fairfax Potter, a distant cousin of Barbara Harrison, had already lived a very interesting life. She was born in Paris in 1908 to Francis and Gwendolyn Potter of Baltimore. The family's name was respected but its wealth was mostly depleted. Francis abandoned his wife in 1909, and for eleven years sickly Pauline lived with her mother in cheap Parisian hotels, then for four years with her father in Biarritz. At seventeen she was sent to Baltimore relatives. Not a natural beauty, Pauline was tall, with large eyes, a beautiful voice, and a powerful sense of style. Her mother left her a small trust and at eighteen Pauline turned a tiny house in downtown Baltimore into a social salon. The photographer Cecil Beaton said that Pauline created her own style. She changed the color of her hair from brunette to a golden hue and the lashes of one eye to black and the other white. She began to design her own clothes. Pauline left Baltimore by marrying a gay man who was an art restorer for New York's Frick Collection. Later they moved to the Spanish island of Majorca, and Pauline opened a craft and art shop. When her husband's drinking became too much, she moved to Paris. There she established herself as a fashion designer. She and Wescott loved each other's company and became fast friends. Over the years, her celebrity grew, and eventually she would marry a Rothschild and become one of the most famous women in the world.

During the Paris years, Wescott spent so much time with Wheeler, Lynes, and Harrison, it is not surprising that their travels together inspired his next book. At Harrison's suggestion they took a motor trip through Austria and Germany in late August and September 1931. Traveling through Europe by chauffeured car was a common practice, even practical, in those days. But there was nothing routine about driving through the increasingly tense cities and towns of prewar Germany. Several of Lynes's photos and negatives from the trip show Wescott and Wheeler standing uneasily beside Harrison's car. Wescott had witnessed the post–World War I hunger and poverty in Germany and now things seemed even worse. He decided to write about the danger he saw in the high unemployment and political extremism. He put aside his novel-in-progress, "The Deadly Friend," and alerted Harper and Brothers that a new book of essays, *Fear and Trembling*, would be ready in several months.

In fact, the potential of *Fear and Trembling* was great. Wescott had a strong sense of what was coming, and the idea of capturing that sense of urgency through the experiences and words of four people driving through Germany promised a suspenseful book. It would be hard to find four more interesting narrators than Wescott, Wheeler, Harrison, and Lynes. Their personal impressions, with news accounts and background, would give American readers a clear sense of what was happening in Europe. Unfortunately, that was not the book Wescott wrote.

The appearance of the original manuscript, written between mid-October 1931 and March 1932, is uncharacteristic: neat script in pencil on white paper, without Wescott's usual amount of revision and insertion.[25] The final work had some historical overview, too little direct narrative, and too much subjective theorizing. The prose had the intelligence but not the beauty of his fiction. His editors at Harper might have but did not offer suggestions for changes. In fact, lack of editorial advice might have had a negative effect on Wescott's career overall. In contrast, Maxwell Perkins at Scribner's was diplomatic but bold in editing such authors as Ernest Hemingway, F. Scott Fitzgerald, and Thomas Wolfe. At Harper, Wescott had been signed by the esteemed editor Eugene Saxton and publisher Henry Hoyns, and *The Grandmothers* and *Good-bye, Wisconsin* were successful without editorial help. Editors such as William Briggs and Frank MacGregor were reluctant to edit Wescott, and by the time Saxton died, the great Harper editor Cass Canfield was already involved in executive duties. In any case, without editorial direction, *Fear and Trembling* was released immediately, in May 1932.

The book was dedicated to Wescott's three fellow travelers, who are identified only by their initials; their names never appear in its pages. There are chilling prophesies: "When supposedly self-governing men fail to govern, or give it up as a bad job, there is bound to be hunger, raging fever in the fields and the streets, bloodshed—worse than bloodshed, with our wonderful inventions." But eight short chapters of background essays pass before the car trip is mentioned! Despite Wescott's intelligence and self-education, he was no historian and the unscholarly theories and opinions of a youthful novelist did not have the weight he imagined. Interest is stirred when the group sees a communist poster in a small town, and when they see a group of Germans in uniform at a town on the Rhine—"Solemn concentrated fellows: very grave issues might have been at stake, wherever they were going." But at every turn Wescott turns away from personal experiences and returns to historic overview and didactic theorizing. There are some good passages with a strong sense of foreboding: "We are faced with a ridiculous prospect of group-suicide for us all together, an epic blunder." Even a reassuring line is filled with threat: "We met a brilliant and well-informed journalist who, when he realized how anxious we were, reassured us, saying that there could not possibly be any sort of world war for two years."[26] The prophecies are on target, about the coming war, the rise of Russia and communism, and such future issues as birth control and especially the place of the artist in society. But the clear voice of the Midwest is muted by the tone of Paris high society. *Fear and Trembling,* written quickly and with great anticipation about its importance, was a disappointment. Wescott reflected sadly, "I tried in a much too soft and elegant way to alarm the United States about the intentions of Germany. I bitterly regret the way it was written."[27]

Ernest Hemingway, now living in Key West, got early word of the book through a Harper press release. In a letter to John Dos Passos, he mocked, "Glenway Wescott, this is no kidding, is issuing a Call to Action. He feels things are in A BAD WAY."[28] A neutral review in the *Herald Tribune* was outweighed by others that focused on the book's problems: "clever, witty, often highly intelligent, [but] its conclusions are pitifully inadequate" in the *New York Times;* "Good-bye, Wisconsin, Hello Economics" in the *New York Sun;* and "Wescott Worries in Fine Words About Us" in the *New York Journal.* The *Nation* decided, "Mr. Wescott has used his culture not to enrich his understanding but to embellish a drawing-room brilliance." And the *Boston Transcript* felt that the book's impersonal tone was the key mistake: "Indeed, the author's very attempt to keep his own personal feelings out of the picture discounts considerably its strength."[29]

The gentlest words came from Marianne Moore, in a letter to Wheeler: "Considered impersonally, the content is not Glenway at his best. . . . But the thing that matters is that one should have a best. Glenway has a gift for seeing things in an unusual way and of expressing what he sees in an unusual way."[30]

Book sales were poor and after the first few months there was only silence. Years later, Wescott noted in his journal that even his friends and usual readers saw no sense in the hastily written book, and he added, "My sense of its failure had a depressing effect on my talent, never very well assured anyway. . . . It was to compensate for the failure of *Fear and Trembling* that I wrote A *Calendar of Saints for Unbelievers.*"[31]

Researched from a half dozen sources and written in six weeks, *A Calendar of Saints for Unbelievers* is his witty portrayal of Catholic saints, one or more for each day of the year. The descriptions range from long, respectful entries for Thomas Aquinas and Joan of Arc to brief, tongue-in-cheek items, such as Cassian (August 13): "A schoolmaster whose pupils stabbed him to death with their pens." Or Edward the Martyr (March 18): "Edward, King of the West Saxons, was murdered by his step-mother's servants. His half-brother's grief, and popular horror of the crime, appear to have dictated his saintly reputation; so he may be said to have been canonized more or less to make amends."[32] Published by Harrison of Paris in

1932 and illustrated with original signs of the zodiac by Pavel Tchelitchew, *Calendar* is attractive and pleasing to read, but its small success didn't add to the reputation of the man who wrote *The Grandmothers*. Wescott scholar William Rueckert remarks, "It is the work of a self no longer in search of truth but settled into a kind of self-satisfied urbanity where the sheer play of the mind is all that is wanted."[33]

Yet Wescott was not self-satisfied. He was simply following his instincts in quickly publishing an amusing and well-executed small work that would help dispel the failure of *Fear and Trembling*. The following year, Harper and Brothers published its own edition of *Calendar,* though not on the elegant stock of Harrison of Paris. And, while the book was handsome in its silver dust jacket, Harper omitted Tchelitchew's drawings for the signs of the zodiac. The problem was clearly the artist's renderings of Aquarius, a naked youth pouring a bucket of water over himself, and of the Gemini, two naked boys lying head to toe. America was not, and never would be, as liberal as Paris. While few critics saw how the strange book fit among Wescott's other works, a number admitted they liked it. The *New York Herald Tribune* remarked that its charm was in being read aloud: "One can go on quoting from this Calendar indefinitely." The *Nation* couldn't see why a novelist would attempt a book in an area where scholars have dedicated their life's work, but said, "One can at least take off one's hat to this American youngster's pluck." The *New York Times* reviewer wrote, "It must be admitted that this book is extremely funny. Only a stuffy person would deny that these little thumbnail caricatures are smartly and shrewdly drawn." And the *Saturday Review of Books* avoided overanalysis and simply admired a rare talent: "Mr. Wescott's flexible style was never more entirely at his command than in this book. He has written a thoroughly delightful book."[34]

Still, Wescott felt the pressure to produce a new novel. In 1932, Dawn Powell's *Tenth Moon* featured a character supposedly modeled after Wescott, Star Donnell, a writer famous for only one big novel. That September, Wescott published a story called "Hurt Feelings" in the *North American Review.* The story's main character, Mrs. Cleveland, discovers during her father's last days how an old jealousy involving his wife had led him to acts of vengeance over the years. She is left awaiting her father's passing, so that she can right the wrongs created by his long ago hurt feelings. The story has Wescott's familiar quality of seeking and telling truth, and is his first piece of non-Wisconsin fiction. And it is all that was salvaged from the abandoned novel, "The Dream of Mrs. Cleveland."

Wescott managed to secure a Guggenheim grant from New York toward his next effort, "The Deadly Friend." At first called "The Blind Beloved," it was a complex story about a respected doctor who disappears mysteriously, with hints of sexual scandal. In April, he sent sample chapters to his Harper editor, Eugene Saxton, and even suggested publicity for the book, which he hoped to complete and deliver personally by midyear. It could be promoted as a kind of crime or detective novel, he wrote, but he thought his regular readers wouldn't like that. "Much could be made of it also as a contribution to modern sex-psychology. . . . Anyway, the public loves a good yarn and this ought to suffice: love and death and landscape; a novel in the sense that *The Apple* was, more so and a great deal more shapely, pure fiction."[35]

But only weeks later Wescott confessed to his German American friend Caroline Newton his overlapping worries about the book, his career, and the all-encompassing German problem: "I will never get it done in time to set sail before August. . . . What a comfort it must be to have some real subject matter in this day of bad dreams and disgust. . . . Goethe said, did he not, that Germany was nothing and any German a great deal; and regretted that the Germans, otherwise much like the Jews, had not been persecuted and dispersed, as the Jews were, for the world's benefit. . . . I begin to want to live in Sicily or New Zealand or Wisconsin; and, perhaps, never have to talk about the world again."[36]

By now, Wescott was ready to leave Paris. He said it had become a "trap" for the expatriates, and he knew other Americans had already left. But Wheeler was still very involved with Harrison of Paris. One of Wheeler's favorite projects ever was the 1932 release *A Typographical Commonplace Book,* which contained his selections of literary anecdotes from all eras, each set in a different typeface. A proud achievement, it was Wheeler's way of showcasing the great European faces. Harrison of Paris also led to a long friendship with Katherine Anne Porter.

At forty-one, Porter had lived in New Orleans, New York, and Mexico and had published *Flowering Judas and Other Stories.* She was visiting Paris for the first time, and Ford Madox Ford put her in touch with Harrison and Wheeler. A matchmaker, Ford knew that his friends hoped to publish a book of historical French songs, and he suggested that Porter make the selections and translations. When the time came, Wescott helped oversee the production of the *French Song Book* in Germany and Holland—printing in France was becoming expensive. For her part, Porter soon came to trust and like Harrison and—despite some homophobia—the trio of Wescott, Wheeler, and Lynes. In Wescott's case, there began a sometimes close, sometimes contentious relationship that was to last nearly fifty years.

Aside from the Harrison press, love kept Wescott from making a decision about his future. They had become a very close-knit, complex, extended family. When he was visiting Edward Sackville-West in London, Harrison wrote: "Glenway dear—I feel quite forlorn, as though Paris were a great vacuum now that you're away." When Wheeler was visiting his family in Evanston, he sent Wescott a birthday note: "How far away you seem from this home where we spent so many days together, and now the home has changed, and likewise everyone in it, and our love is still the same."[37]

At one point, Wescott and Wheeler experienced the longest separation they had ever known. Harrison planned a long visit to Shanghai where their friend Bernadine Szold was living with a man she met and married named Chester Fritz. Wescott preferred staying in Paris, but Wheeler couldn't resist such an exotic trip, though it would mean five months apart. Furthermore, Wheeler and Harrison had grown very close in their work and friendship. Whether they were ever intimate was not discussed with friends. For a short time, there was actually some thought of marriage—not surprising, considering the times, their determination to stay together as a family, and Wheeler's somewhat pliable sexuality. However seriously it was considered, this trip together had some significance.

Wheeler and Harrison sailed from Venice on November 10, 1932. They arrived in the harbor of Shanghai at night to find the city lit up spectacularly all around them. After nearly two months with Bernadine and Chester Fritz, they traveled to Peking and Tokyo and made several stops in Europe before returning to Paris in the spring of 1933.

Wescott wrote a letter to Sackville-West that captured his life at that moment. He mentioned his lover Jacques Guérin, a visit to the popular Café Boeuf sur le Toit, the appearance there of Christian Bérard and others, and the fact that Wheeler and Harrison were returning from their long trip: "Last night J. G. and I, immensely unoccupied after dinner, wandered into the Boeuf. . . . Bérard made a triumphant entrance. . . . And there were women with pearls enough; and journalists, and the sort of new lovers people have nowadays. I am sorry to say that Paris is as petty as that for me, for the moment. . . . Everyone's absence has annoyed me and I myself have been absent-minded. I should have worked; and now when the family gets back, I shall automatically go into harness, and drudge for six weeks."[38] The words reveal his lack of inspiration for the new novel.

Wescott revealed other candid feelings when he made a false start at keeping a journal. He wrote: "This is my thirty-second birthday. I have loved and lived with Monroe for fourteen years. I have been Jacques's love for exactly five years. I'd met him on April 8, went to bed with him in that miserable hotel in Antibes on April 12. No powerful work done during those five years. For a long time I wanted to keep a journal and shall take this occasion to make a trial of it."[39] The journal attempt ended the following day when his morning writing was interrupted by a visit from Tony Butts, but he would pick it up again several years later.

Finally, the logic of returning to New York became clear. George Platt Lynes was living and working there, and so was Lloyd Wescott. Another Harrison of Paris title was being planned, but Wheeler and Harrison agreed that it could be published in New York. Wescott's relationship with Guérin was waning, and he was ready to let it end when he left Paris. Harrison was less sure about leaving France, but the possibility of war forced her to consider the move.

As they moved closer to a decision, they made the most of their time together. Harrison invited Lynes back to Paris and gave him a new camera, the Rolleiflex, which he used for travel photos during their trips to Frankfurt, Holland, and Spain. A bout with tuberculosis then separated Harrison from her friends for fall and winter. They remained close through letters and visits as she recuperated in Davos Platz, Switzerland. At the end of the year, Wheeler visited Lynes in New York, and Wescott wrote to Lloyd, suggesting he search for a large Manhattan apartment.

In the spring of 1934, Lynes joined Harrison and Wheeler for a final trip to Spain and Austria. Then Wescott and Wheeler, who had arrived in Europe with almost nothing, packed their belongings for the ocean voyage home. The Paris years had ended, but a long and amazing life in New York was just beginning.

5

Lost in America
The Thirties

When Wescott and Wheeler arrived in New York in the spring of 1934, it was George Platt Lynes who made the return easier. Their younger friend put them up at his East Fiftieth Street apartment until they found their own flat at 228 Madison Avenue, near the Morgan Library. Attractive, outgoing, and the life of any party, Lynes also reintroduced them to the city. He was now a successful fashion photographer and was known for his striking portraits.

It was an exciting time for the arts in New York, and Lynes brought Wescott and Wheeler together with an old friend from prep school who was now an important figure, Lincoln Kirstein. When Kirstein was still a student at Harvard he founded the literary journal *Hound and Horn.* His father, Lewis, president of the Boston Public Library, gave him a graduation gift of millions of dollars, and with it Kirstein became not just a patron but a force for the arts. In 1933, at twenty-six, he brought Russian choreographer George Balanchine from London to New York to start the School of American Ballet and a performing company. Kirstein was also involved in the new Museum of Modern Art, and Wheeler was interested in working for a museum.

Wescott, on the other hand, did not share Wheeler's enthusiasm for the creative opportunities in New York. Most of his writer friends were abroad, particularly in England, and he found that his two incomplete novels worked no better on the American side of the Atlantic than they had in France. Part of the problem was where to go as a novelist, after leaving behind his stories of the Midwest. The critic Bruce Bawer suggested that

Wescott's slump in the thirties was largely due to his sexuality. A few renegades of the day wrote candid homosexual novels, such as Charles Henri Ford and Parker Tyler's *The Young and Evil* and Radclyffe Hall's *Well of Loneliness.* But major authors who happened to be homosexual made their reputations in the mainstream. Gertrude Stein, W. Somerset Maugham, E. M. Forster, Thornton Wilder, Wescott, and others wrote about homosexuality only in indirect ways. This would begin to change in midcentury. "But in the 1930s," Bawer wrote, "Wescott could hardly write about the life he was leading with Monroe Wheeler. In *The Grandmothers* he had written a book about a family, a book that almost anyone could identify with; but few readers, at that time anyway, would have regarded an equally sensitive and candid novel based upon Wescott's adult domestic life with anything but horror."[1] There was truth to this, but Wescott understood the boundaries well. Both of his Midwest novels had included some homosexual undercurrent, as did his manuscript for "The Deadly Friend." A bigger part of his problem of the thirties, he realized, was that of the returning expatriate: his deep involvement with French language and culture. "I felt I had stayed abroad for too long," he said. "I had spoken French for too long. I came back not only thinking but *dreaming* in French. And I'd had all that success with my Wisconsin material and with Paris and the luxury of Paris. That's when I decided it was the fault of my language. And I wasn't able to write. I wrote book reviews and lectures. My [new] short stories were written in France."[2]

Wescott complained to Caroline Newton that his writing frustrations were not helped by the social world of New York City where "weekends are half a week long. . . . I have grave wants and worries and am in no state to shine. . . . I often wish I were a recluse but certainly am not."[3]

Wescott carefully studied his manuscript for "The Deadly Friend." The idea had come on his 1925 ocean voyage to France, when a mysterious passenger on the *Orduna* took his life by jumping overboard. The trouble was that "The Deadly Friend" became overly complicated as it grew to hundreds of pages. Wescott outlined dozens of chapters and a plot with surprising twists and turns. A renowned surgeon, Dr. Aaron Smart, mysteriously disappears. Earlier he had confronted an emergency of a teenage boy with a ruptured appendix. Unwilling to perform the surgery, Dr. Smart admits to his young associate his emotional attachment to the teenager and persuades him to take over while he feigns illness. Unfortunately, through no one's fault, the boy dies. Dr. Smart disappears. On the run, he treats a dangerous criminal. A farmer discovers a burned body. An abandoned house catches fire, and an unknown man rescues a boy. Beyond the manuscript pages, notes outline an ocean suicide that appeared to be Dr. Smart but may have been his father, the exiled doctor's life in Paris, his reappearance in disguise in Florida, involvement with a woman, her suicide, a court trial, and more. There are enough story lines for a shelf of mysteries, but not enough purpose for a novel worthy of Wescott.[4]

In view of time invested and some chapters of fine writing, Wescott would not completely abandon "The Deadly Friend" for years. At one point, he tried to restructure some of the material into a more cohesive novel called "The Little Ocean Liner," even incorporating Alwyn Tower as a part-time narrator, to no avail.

Finally, as a courtesy to his publisher and as an escape from his writer's block, Wescott walked into the Harper and Brothers office and told one of his editors to remove the book from the "forthcoming" list. On a card entitled "The Dummy Book," he captured the moment: "My failure to finish 'The Deadly Friend,' and having to explain this to old Mr. Henry Hoyns—and lo and behold, there amid other books behind his desk, I saw it as if it were already published—a dummy! Nightmarish."[5]

On a positive note, Wescott published an essay in an issue of *Hound and Horn* devoted to Henry James.[6] Both personal and scholarly, "A Sentimental Contribution" describes the childhood emotion he and one of his sisters felt in reading James's works together. Then he offers his adult opinion that James compromises and sublimates truths and that contemporary writers must be more truthful, even explicit. William Rueckert praised the piece: "The lyric essay is ideally suited to Wescott's needs, just as it is to those of E. B. White," adding that the essay would prove the most consistent form of Wescott's lifelong work.[7] It is true that he mastered critical essays, then remembrances, and, eventually, rich multilayered personal essays. Later in 1934, Wescott wrote the catalog text for the exhibit "Fifty Photographs of George Platt Lynes" at the Julian Levy Gallery.

Busy with photo assignments from *Harper's Bazaar, Town and Country,* and *Vogue,* Lynes took a larger studio at 214 East Fifty-eighth Street. Wheeler got himself a small office at 175 Fifth Avenue for Harrison of Paris, and Katherine Anne Porter wrote from Paris, "With an office on Fifth Avenue, and your address on your letter paper, how enviably settled you seem."[8] Porter was writing a new, longer version of her story "Hacienda" for Harrison of Paris, and Wescott admitted to her that "'Hacienda' did make me ashamed of my sloth, even of the chilliness of my talent at its most active."[9] When the book appeared on deluxe white rag stock in an apple-green slipcover, Marianne Moore complimented Wheeler: "'Hacienda' is one of the finest looking—perhaps the most consistent—of the books that you have done."[10] Wheeler hired a distributor for all their titles, but he knew the press would end. American printers could not match the workmanship, or the prices, of the Europeans.

Nevertheless, New York was once again their home. That did not please Bernadine Szold, who was back in Paris. Complaining of Wescott's absence, she mentioned "The Deadly Friend" and said, "I know that I am the deadly friend—and feel that somehow the sweetest part of my life is over forever." When Wescott didn't write often enough, she said of her recent surgery, "I went under the anesthesia thinking, well, it doesn't matter after all; nothing matters since Glenway ceased to need me."[11] But Paris was suddenly far away. That fall Wescott , Wheeler, and Lynes took a large apartment at 48 East Eighty-ninth Street, their first permanent home as a trio. Yet there was some convention to their unconventional arrangement: Wheeler and Lynes took one of the bedrooms as their own. As Wescott admitted, "Monroe and I stopped having sex with each other about 1930."[12] Still, no one ever doubted the permanence of their relationship.

Barbara Harrison arrived in New York late in the year, and she saw how quickly they were building a life in the city. Lincoln Kirstein was a frequent guest. George Lynes's brother, Russell, and his wife, Mildred, were friends. Pavel Tchelitchew ("Pavlik" to his friends) and Charles Henri Ford had returned from Europe. Ford's sister, actress Ruth Ford, was now in town. Wescott's sister Beulah was starting a job with her brother's editors at Harper. Wescott himself was beginning to give lectures, at Bryn Mawr and other colleges. And the city's atmosphere was lively. Lynes had already taken Wheeler and Wescott to the Cotton Club in Harlem.

What surprised everyone was the instant attraction between Lloyd Wescott and Barbara. After meeting during the holidays, they were dating seriously by early 1935. But it wasn't a complete surprise. While Barbara was a sophisticated and beautiful woman at thirty, and the boyishly handsome Lloyd was only twenty-eight, he had lived in New York for several years and learned a few things about style, manners, and dress from his older brother. He was also a natural connection to the bond Barbara felt with Wheeler, Lynes, and Wescott—especially Wescott.

That winter their mother, Josephine, wrote Glenway, "It makes me so happy to know that you and Monroe are pleased over Lloyd's and Barbara's love. You have been good big 'brothers.'" The Wescott parents were living in a very different world, unable to find work in the Midwest or even to fix a broken heater, and were dependent on their children. When she wrote again, she said she understood his need to stay in New York to write. "I love and admire you most for the hidden power which controls you," Josephine allowed, adding the classic mother's twist, "even though it means a sacrifice on the part of those who love you."[13]

On April 4, Lloyd proposed to Barbara and they decided to marry immediately, waiting only four days until Wheeler returned from a trip to Bermuda. After the wedding Lloyd, Barbara, Glenway, and Monroe drove to Wisconsin to visit the parents. It can be assumed that Barbara toned down the amount of jewelry she wore while in farm country, and that Josephine and Bruce Wescott were quietly taken aback by their new daughter-in-law. Next, the four visited Wheeler's parents in Evanston.

When they stopped in Milwaukee, Wescott looked up Earl Kuelthau and met for dinner with his high school lover, who was now a married man.

Back in New York in May, Glenway suddenly fell ill with pneumonia and was hospitalized at Saint Luke's Hospital uptown. Although he recovered quickly, it was a reminder of his youthful battle with the Spanish flu. It didn't help that he, like most men he knew, was a cigarette smoker. In mid-June, he recuperated in upstate Milbrook, New York, at the home of Frances Robbins, who gave him a gift of a signed volume of Lord Byron.

Barbara and Lloyd insisted that Glenway accompany them on their long honeymoon through Italy. On June 29, 1935, they embarked on the Italian ocean liner *Conte di Savoia,* and Glenway left Lloyd and Barbara alone for much of each day. He remembered that when their ship passed the southern coast of Spain, out of sight of land, a powerful scent of the herb rosemary descended from the Iberian mountain slopes and out to sea, reaching the deck where he stood: "It seemed the very soul and ghost of divine Earth; and it transfixed itself in my mind as a metaphor for the good fortune of my existence overall and of the entire human species, relatively speaking. More fortunate, more blissful, than any other animal's existence!"[14]

Before Italy, they visited Villefranche for several days, arriving on July 7. Wescott was delighted to find Cocteau there. His previous lover, Jean Desbordes, had been replaced by a young actor named Marcel Khill. Wescott recalled, "We went to Villefranche and there was Cocteau with Marcel Khill. When I first saw Marcel, they were in bed. He had a ravishing, slim body. He was so full of life and had such charm! I was very fond of Marcel—and I delighted him. He once told me that Cocteau wanted sex from him so much that he had to go off to a ski resort to get his energy back. He was like that; he talked like that."[15]

After that happy reminder of the Villefranche days, Wescott led the way into Italy. "We took a little car and drove all over Italy," he recalled. "They wanted me to run the trip, they wanted to be chaperoned by me really. They were so in love and so antithetical; neither of them had had any of the other's experience."[16] Over the next three weeks, they stopped at the Grand Hotel in Florence and the Hotel Continental in Siena, but also visited many small towns, some twice. By August they were in Paris, and Wheeler and Lynes came over to meet them. They visited with Katherine Anne Porter, Janet Flanner, Jacques Guérin, and others. Finally on August 11, they boarded the SS *Columbus* for home.

During the voyage, Wheeler met with Alfred Barr, director of the six-year-old Museum of Modern Art, and spoke about his ideas for museum publications. Once back in New York, he joined the staff of the museum. In fact, Wheeler's creation of catalogs and other publications was invaluable to MoMA. He was also helpful as a curator because in France he had become acquainted with Renoir, Picasso, Chagall, and other European artists. And his impressive apartment on East Eighty-ninth Street served as an important meeting place for the young museum's business.

Wheeler's work seemed to influence Wescott. Like Hemingway, Wescott saw a link between the creative processes of painters and writers. But unlike Hemingway, he wrote serious essays about artists. In a piece about the French artist Jean-Baptiste Greuze, he said he saw the man's tragic, shameful marriage in the emotion of his work. Such mysteries of the soul are the secret to works of art, he wrote, "one picture, just adequate pictorially, will appeal in a wonderful way to almost everyone's imagination for years or centuries, while another, which with reason artists may admire and art historians esteem, will not only displease but disappoint, and go briskly out of fashion, and never come back."[17]

Wescott published no other work in 1935, but a new edition of *The Apple of the Eye* was released by Grosset and Dunlap. That year he also met the great French writer Colette, now sixty-two, who was visiting New York with her third husband, Maurice Goudeket. Wescott acted as a translator at her publisher's reception and recalled, "I remember her strong hands—serious writing is a manual labor!—and her fine feet in sandals, perhaps larger than most, rather like the feet of Greek goddesses."[18] Years later they would meet again and he would write of her life and work. Such admiration for other writers reflected the decline in Wescott's own fame. Cyril Connolly's satiric novel of expatriate France, *The Rock Pool,* referred to Wescott, Gertrude Stein, and Cocteau as part of the charmingly dated Paris of the Select and the Bal Musette, and described parties on Île Saint-Louis.

A figure from that recent past, Jean Cocteau, arrived in the United States in June 1936. *Paris-Soir* was celebrating the centenary of Jules Verne by sending Cocteau around the world in eighty days, in return for his travel pieces. After his ocean voyage to California, Cocteau took a plane for the first time, flying to New York. He asked Wescott to show him Coney Island—a lifelong dream, after seeing it in a film as a child. At the Brooklyn amusement park, they posed for a comical group photo, Wescott with Cocteau, Marcel Khill, Cecil Beaton, and George Platt Lynes.

At Wheeler's apartment, Wescott recalled, Cocteau's opium pipe reappeared. "I remember a reporter from the *Times* doing an interview that went on forever. Cocteau excused himself to make a phone call—and presently a strange smell came from the other room. The reporter sniffed and I began telling stories, bringing out more and more secrets of Cocteau."[19] Before Cocteau left New York, Wescott and Lynes took him to Minsky's burlesque club and to Harlem. The well-heeled homosexual crowd of the thirties found a free and open atmosphere at the stylish uptown nightclubs, but Wescott and Lynes also had true friends among the black actors, singers, and dancers of that time. One was singer and club owner Jimmie Daniels, who slept with Wescott and was a model for Lynes's nude portraits. When Wescott began to keep a journal, one entry recorded a dinner party in Harlem with Jimmie Daniels and others.[20]

During 1936, Wescott's relative silence as a writer continued. Two minor stories appeared, "The Sight of a Dead Body" in *Signatures* and "The Rescuer" in the London periodical *Life and Letters Today.* Both were fragments from the abandoned novel "The Deadly Friend" and had little importance among his other works.[21]

The big news among the Wescott clan that year was Barbara and Lloyd's purchase of a farm. They had been living at 77 Park Avenue, but Barbara had no patience for living in a big city, or in an apartment, or with a husband who worked in an office. They bought a five-hundred-acre farm in Hampton, in Hunterdon County, western New Jersey, alongside the Mulhocaway River. Soon afterward, they added more than a hundred acres on the other side of the Mulhocaway. On land that had been largely used for dairy farming were ten houses, mostly for workers, and nine small barns. Lloyd ordered construction of a large, modern aluminum barn. Barbara was an expert equestrian, and a friend from England, Sir Victor Sassoon, sent them a belated wedding gift of two Suffolk horses. Architect William Hunt refurbished the farm's eighteenth-century mill into a main house with glass and stucco and named it the Mill. At great expense, Barbara had the seventeenth-century parquet flooring from her Rambouillet house taken up, shipped to America, and installed in the Mill. Part of one wall was replaced with a giant sheet of thick glass, as in Rambouillet, and outdoors a low stone wall enabled cows to graze near the huge picture window. Wescott, Monroe, and Lynes kept their Manhattan apartment but visited the farm on weekends and holidays. At first they took just three rooms in one of the farmhand houses, but Lynes insisted that they take over the entire house, refurbish it, and put in a lawn and garden. He was earning the money to make it happen, with fashion accounts from Henri Bendel, Saks Fifth Avenue, Hattie Carnegie, and Bergdorf Goodman. That year, one of his best photos, "The Sleepwalker," was included in the Museum of Modern Art's exhibit "Fantastic Art, Dada, Surrealism."

Wescott named their corner of the farm Stone-blossom, for the limestone on the grounds. Although he and Wheeler would always keep an apartment in the city, the farm images of his childhood had returned, this time in luxury, not poverty. There was a full mile of farmland between Barbara and Lloyd's main house and Stone-blossom, but the country home created a stronger bond among the five friends. They spent their first Christmas together at the Mulhocaway farm.

In the city, Wescott's current interest continued to be the art world. He wrote a piece for the February 1937 exhibit of Kristian Tonny, a Dutch-born artist he had known in France. As always, his essay was subjective, and poetic: "In the background of most of his new drawings is some florid Nordic architecture—as it were windmills with their wings clipped; fussy burgomasters' mansions striving to be mystic cathedrals, and half succeeding."[22]

Artists who joined their circle that year were Paul Cadmus and Jared French. Cadmus, thirty-two, had done his first pencil sketch at age four, and his parents and sister, Fidelma, were artists. After art school and work as a commercial illustrator, he had lived for two years with French in Majorca, Spain. They remained close long after bisexual French married. Many years later, Cadmus recalled, "I came back from Europe in October of 1933. I didn't meet Glenway and Monroe until after I met Lincoln Kirstein, in 1937. Shortly after that, he got me into the circle of George and Glenway and Monroe, when they were living on Eighty-ninth Street. It may have been that I was invited to a party there. I began seeing them regularly, all the time practically. I became very good friends with George, more than the others. People are usually quite surprised that I never went to bed with Glenway, Monroe, or George. Or Lincoln, as a matter of fact."[23]

Cadmus remembered his 5 Saint Luke's Place brownstone, which became the Greenwich Village headquarters for their crowd for thirty-five years. "We had one floor, a walk-through. But later on Margaret and Jerry [Jared French] went to one of the other floors. And eventually they owned the whole building. . . . And Glenway came there often." The first year they knew each other, Cadmus did an ink sketch of Wescott, who later wrote of the picture: "A good likeness, I think, at least psychologically like—my sweet-sour expression, spoiled but virtuous, voluptuous but tough, heartbroken but happy." Cadmus remembered, "I did quite a few drawings of Glenway, quite a few of Monroe, and of George. More of George than anybody. We didn't have any pact about photographs and drawings. It just turned out that way. I gave presents because I was their guest so often. I certainly accepted every invitation of Glenway and Monroe and George's. And they loved to pose, all three of them."[24]

Also bringing new life to the New York art scene were Pavlik Tchelitchew and Charles Henri Ford. They were a unique couple, both surrealists, though Ford worked in collage, cutouts, and photography and was also a poet. The older, more accomplished Tchelitchew worked mostly on canvas, often large scale. Their unusual relationship, as artists and lovers, led to amusing moments. Ford remembered once being struck by a revelation and saying aloud, "Matisse can't draw!" Tchelitchew rolled his eyes with impatience and shouted, "I know!"[25] When Barbara and Wescott were visiting Tchelitchew's studio in 1937, Wescott fell in love with an erotic male nude painting called "The Lion Boy," and Barbara immediately bought it for him.

While artists seemed to dominate the landscape, Wescott remembered meeting the writer Jean Toomer, the Harlem Renaissance author of *Cane.* "I visited Toomer's apartment on Christopher Street in the thirties," he said. "He was a beautiful man, and a ladies' man. He told me, 'As a young boy in the South I used to jump and dance for joy. But, you know, since then, each day, I grow sadder and sadder.'"[26]

More significant to Wescott's story, Katherine Anne Porter returned to the States in 1937, living for months in nearby Bucks County, Pennsylvania, then at an apartment at 67 Perry Street in Manhattan. Porter's third marriage was ending, and she became very close to both Barbara and Wheeler. She enjoyed Lynes and liked his portraits of her. And with Wescott she developed a relationship that would run hot and cold over many years. On the positive side, they could speak to each other about writing and their work as few writers can. Porter agreed that part of Wescott's 1930s writing problem was that he had lost himself in French language and literature. One day she asked him if he had read E. M. Forster, and he admitted he hadn't. "What," said Porter, "you've not read Forster!"[27] And Wescott began to read as voraciously as he had in his teens and twenties.

"This is what I did to get the French out of my system," Wescott said. "I reread all of the writers that I cared about. I reread all of Ford Madox Ford. I reread every last one of Maugham's stories. I read Forster. Katherine Anne had told me to read him and I'd happened not to. And it was funny because, later, Maugham disliked Forster and it was because Christopher Isherwood and I thought he was a greater artist than Maugham was, and he knew that we thought it."[28] Notably, the writers Wescott chose to read were British, not American, perhaps because they better suited his own style of prose.

Wescott also recalled, "I remember that George and Jared French were creating the design for a love seat, a divan, out at Stone-blossom. Jared was choosing the pattern and colors and George was sewing it together, and I read Maugham stories aloud as they worked."[29] The antique French divan remained in the household for the rest of their lives. French's design was of a life-size nude man and woman lying side by side. Years later, Paul Cadmus remembered, Wescott's cook Anna Brakke used to complain, "It's like living in Dante's Inferno!"[30]

Now that the farm was settled and fully staffed, Barbara and Lloyd moved the Wescott parents east from Wisconsin. Bruce and Josephine Wescott brought everything, even the beehives that had belonged to Bruce's father. Barbara found the parents a small house in nearby Clinton, and now daughters Elizabeth and Beulah were living in the area. For the parents, who had struggled with poverty for so many years, it was an emotional time. They would never worry about money again, and they were reunited with their children. Bruce repaid Lloyd and Barbara in small ways. Never a successful farmer, he was nevertheless a real one and was helpful at Mulhocaway.

At Christmas, Wheeler asked Wescott to write a short holiday piece that could be printed on fine paper and sent to all their friends and relatives. Wescott's "New Jersey Farm—Christmas Images" includes the humor, subtleties, optimism, and philosophy often found in his prose. It read in part:

> This is the season of the barn-born god. Our New Jersey barn is two stories high, all of silvered metal. Milking-machines with pink tentacles murmurously are clasped to the long bosoms of a hundred high-born cows. The setting of the sun intensifies fragrances; now it sets early in the afternoon, and the shadowy yards around the barn reek of milk.
>
> The setting of the year intensifies the affections. Heart-ache and gaiety, generosity and the sense of poverty, meet, casting light upon each other, seasonally, like stars. . . .
>
> Parked in a muddy lane a mistreated old Ford sings carols to itself: there must be a brand-new radio in it, probably a Christmas present. Human beings are often like that—a poor old thing with a little new thing holidaily installed in it—and at their best then perhaps.
>
> Up the rocky hill somewhere the snakes in secret sleep, in family knots. In a few months they will untie and individually, lonesomely, adorn the grass. There is a great rock shaped like a bed. In a few months it will be cushioned with shadows of the leaves of the half-wrecked cherry-tree beside it, and it will drip with the blossoming blood of wild columbines.
>
> How the human fancy works, running ahead, anti-wintry! Somehow winter implies spring; bitterness seems to promise revolution or recompense; and for those too old or weary to wait, even as interest in life abates, interest in some sort of holiday or some sort of immortality takes its place.[31]

The little holiday piece was a reminder of Wescott's unique writing voice. That year eight of his early poems were reprinted in the anthology *Poetry Out of Wisconsin,* and he began writing the lifelong journal that would bring important perspective to his career.[32]

Early in 1938, Wescott experienced one of those strange, timeless moments that creative people sometimes share. Thornton Wilder's play *Our Town* opened at New York's Henry Miller Theater on February 4. Wescott had asked Wilder to put an actress friend in the play, and afterward he went backstage to congratulate her. The play had not been well received in a short Boston run, but he found it wonderful. As he left, he saw Wilder standing alone in a little alleyway; he had been too nervous to watch the opening night. Wescott wrote later that Wilder was shaking and said, "How did it go? Was it worth doing? You didn't feel, I hope, that I had disgraced myself?"[33] Wescott told him it was powerful, beautiful, and important, even if it might not do well at the box office. That moment of Wilder's lost confidence and Wescott's caution was a metaphor for the despair and courage of the serious artist. Of course, *Our Town* went on to win the Pulitzer Prize in drama and become one of the most successful plays of all time.

Wescott's lack of success in recent years added to a growing discomfort between him and his brother. More than a gentleman farmer, Lloyd shared Barbara's interest in collecting art and publicly supporting culture and the community. In his new role as head of the family, he surprised Glenway with the offer of a trip to Europe. Wescott said, "My brother thought I was stir crazy and gave me two thousand dollars to go abroad—before devouring me entirely. That's really the way I look upon it now. I think he felt I was lonesome for Europe. I really wasn't. But I was very much interested in having a vacation." Marianne Moore revealed her concern for Wescott to Wheeler: "We hope Glenway will have a beneficial, nutritious, exhilarating time in Paris. It sounds very 'elegant' to be departing for Paris; but elegance is ipecac unless one is at peace, and we do want him to be."[34]

Wheeler was planning his own trip to Mexico for the museum but he saw Wescott off with roses on the *President Harding* on March 16. As the ship put out to sea, Wescott began a letter to him: "My own: Except for the cinders I didn't shed tears until I opened your roses. . . . The best of our secret is too sentimental and too true for anyone else to believe in."[35]

During his first few days in Paris, Wescott saw his ex-lover Jacques Guérin, who had visited New York in recent years. Now a major bibliophile, Jacques had a younger lover with whom he spent weekends in a rented house. Wescott also saw old friends Nancy Cunard, Julian Green, and Janet Flanner and her lover Solita Solano. But for nearly two weeks he had no word of Cocteau. "I wanted to see Jean and couldn't find him," he said. "Jacques Guérin told me that no one knew where he was and that he wasn't important anymore. Then one day I was walking along the Left Bank and saw a little sports store with a poster saying there was to be a performance of *Oedipus Rex* with a 'Jacques' Cocteau. It was an indication of his being out of fashion just then."[36] The performance on April 2, in an auditorium at the Sorbonne, was for a conference of boy scouts from all over Europe. Cocteau praised the good sense of youth—like any writer, trying to win over a new generation, Wescott thought. Afterward, they met backstage.

Cocteau's new lover was a young actor named Jean Marais, but former lovers were still in the circle, including Jean Desbordes, Marcel Khill, and Jean Bourgoint. Wescott worried about these young men and opium: "One problem about opium is that the good kind is very expensive and the other kind is very bad for your health." Cocteau smoked only the good kind, but his ex-lovers were reduced to smoking poor quality street opium, when they could get it. Khill took advantage of Wescott's arrival to visit Cocteau's hotel. "Unfortunately," said Wescott, "as soon as Marcel got near Cocteau he got drugs. He was very, very drugged by the end of ten days."[37]

Despite Cocteau's own bad habits, he had rehabilitated an American boxer, a former world featherweight champion. Wescott recalled being dragged along to a prizefight: "One of Cocteau's lovers was this broken down black fighter called Al Brown who had taken to opium in France. He was a very popular sort of figure but was thought hopeless, but Cocteau took him up and wrote great pieces about boxing. I went with the owner of a newspaper and Marcel and sat in front to see this boxer—who had overcome opium and gotten back into condition—manage to beat this little Alsatian boy. It was very tawdry."[38]

Observing Cocteau's lovers and friends, Wescott was impressed by Jean Marais. "I saw that Desbordes was somehow not in Cocteau's good graces. While I was there in 1938 the great figure in Cocteau's life appeared as a boy. I didn't know him but I knew all about him. Jean Marais was the extremely good-looking movie star, who played in all his big movies and went on to become the matinee idol of France." It was Marais who began to pressure Cocteau to give up opium. "It was terrible how ill Cocteau was," said Wescott. "I remember one day I went out to Orgeval in the suburbs to see Janet Flanner and a couple of other friends, and during the day there were messages from everyone! That morning the boys couldn't wake him up. Finally they lit up a pipe of opium and Jean Marais, despite his own horror of drugs, drew it in and blew it into Cocteau's mouth and woke him. That's when he told him, 'You've got to stop it.'"[39] Eventually, Marais's good influence prevailed.

As always, Cocteau was productive. Wescott said, "I remember one night in his hotel, Cocteau propped up in his bed with pillows, the boys sitting around on the floor, and I at the bottom of the bed. And Cocteau read to us the manuscript of his play, *The Terrible Parents*. Later, the kids all went to sleep—and Cocteau and I stayed up, and talked our age."[40]

One highlight of the springtime trip was Wescott's fling with a young actor named Tito Valdez, who was a distant nephew of Barbara—distant because her father had married so many times. Tito, who had a fiancée, hosted a large birthday party for Wescott, and the legendary cabaret star Mistinguett appeared. Though over sixty, she was sexy in a split skirt and was escorted by a young man. Wescott recalled that she said, "Ah, Monsieur Waistcoat! I have heard much of you, and not only from Tito. You are Cocteau's American friend, are you not? *Pauvre* Jean! Is he all right? Does he speak of me?" Then she whispered in his ear, "Has he told you? I was his first, when we were very young."[41]

There was sadness about leaving France again, partly because of the impending war. Jean Bourgoint, the attractive blond who had frustrated Wescott ten years earlier in Villefranche, was now sick from street opium, and nostalgic for Wheeler and Wescott. "He said to me, 'Oh, Glenway, where did I go wrong? When did you despair of me?' And I said, 'My dear, I didn't despair of you. I just went home to America. And there were all the stalemates and frustrations in our relationship.'" Bourgoint went into military service but would survive the war. "After the army," Wescott said, "he was employed as a gardener in the south of France. Then he decided he had a vocation and took vows with the Trappist monks—who don't speak except with permission—and ended up working in a leprosarium in Africa, where he died."[42] Wescott heard that theologist Thomas Merton actually considered Jean—Brother Pascal—a candidate for sainthood.

Another young friend, Michel Girard, was wearing a uniform much too small for his large frame when Wescott saw him off on a train filled with French soldiers. Girard would inspire a Wescott story, "The Frenchman Six-Foot-Three." Jean Desbordes, who had helped Cocteau recover from the loss of Raymond Radiguet, would die a hero in 1944, under torture by the Nazis during the Paris Occupation.

Most emotional for Wescott was his parting with Marcel Khill. During this trip, they were intimate, and Wescott was concerned about him. When Khill heard that Wheeler's close friend from the Museum of Modern Art, Alan Porter, kept a collection of erotic art, he foolishly made bad tracings of some of Cocteau's erotic drawings. Wescott politely gave him something for the drawings but left them rolled up behind the radiator of his hotel room. "He was on his way to the gutter, phased out. He wanted to get married. He wanted me. And he was the only true intimate of mine who was killed in the war." The last night they spent together, in Khill's modest hotel room, Wescott had a chilling premonition: "I saw it in the light in Marcel's eyes. He would become a martyr. That was the farewell. I came away in great anxiety and grief."[43] Khill died in the battle of Sudan two years later.

Late in April, before returning to the United States, Wescott visited in London for a week with friends Osbert Sitwell, Raymond Mortimer, and the writer Robert Gathorne-Hardy. At least for a time, the atmosphere in London seemed lighter than that of Paris. Upon arriving in New York, he was interviewed by the *New York Times* and the *New York Herald Tribune,* as had happened after previous trips abroad, and he spoke vaguely about an upcoming book. "In those days," Wescott said, "arrival by ship was an event and there were always reporters at dockside waiting to do interviews. When he was still a little-known artist Salvador Dali got the attention of reporters by arriving in America in a great big cape with red lining."[44] While no book was on the horizon, Wescott had found his writing voice again, perhaps because of the trip abroad, as well as rereading his favorite writers. Also, Wheeler suggested that Wescott write about himself—good advice because the failed novels were based largely on invented material. That spring and summer, he wrote excellent drafts for an essay and two very long stories. The first was "The Stallions," a full binder of material about some of the horses there and at neighboring farms. In later years, Wescott would try to develop "The Stallions" into a novel, but the best of the material is what he wrote in June 1938, inspired by Stoneblossom.[45]

In the manuscript, Alwyn Tower sees a horse fair in the country and remembers seeing a horse fair in Antwerp years earlier, when the threat of war was beginning. Now in America he sees the symbolic dread of war in the local fair's closing ceremony. A cowboy dressed in red, white, and blue, "so vainly seated on his great curtseying golden stallion, surrounded with escort of nervous tough cowboys on other gaudy showy mounts." In connecting segments, the Alwyn Tower character mentions to his brother Tim that he has never seen horses breed. He is invited to see the Suffolk stallion Beauboy mate with a young mare named Sapphire. Beautiful descriptions of the whole ritual follow, from the stallion's dance steps to his love bite. After the mating, the stallion, in a kind of swoon, holds on to the female: "With his disheveled locks shaken above his old eyes of folly he reminded me of King Lear." The male takes several minutes to recover: "This look of weakness impressed me as truly a look of strength, greater than I have ever seen before."[46]

Later, Alwyn Tower contrasts that mating with a very different one by an expensive Arab stallion named Ibn Nafa. At orgasm, the horses sway together, "as if in a far-away waltz." Tower says: "It is the wonderful, or wondrous, which seems to me divine. And this extremity of sex, this epilepsy, this so-called 'little death,' no doubt is wonderful, even as great death itself." When the female, Winona, is returned to her stall, her two-month-old colt Mecca becomes excited by the scent, jumping about, erect but harmless. Tower reflects: "I suppose that in general, where sex appears greatest, in ostentatious embodiment or personification, it is not the strongest. Idea and ideal and affection are the great hormones."[47] The subject matter was perhaps risqué but intriguing.

Next, Wescott wrote "An Example of Suicide," a sixteen-page polished typescript about a true incident of that summer. A young man climbs onto a ledge of the Hotel Gotham at Fifth Avenue and Fifty-fifth Street and threatens to jump. Three hundred police and ten thousand spectators gather. Wescott/Tower sees him from the street: "His name was Wards. I took a good look at him. He was young, slight, handsome. He wore a white shirt, and no coat. He was smoking a cigarette, and moved restlessly; and to every move the crowd responded with its immense and confused, if not altogether stupid, sympathy." The drama continues into the night, until the narrator hears from friends arriving at his apartment that it is over: "Down from the seventeenth-story ledge like a falling star in a quick whitish streak he had slipped, or, possibly, leapt. Down into West Fifty-fifth Street, paved, like hell, with good intentions."[48]

The suspense and commentary of "An Example of Suicide" make it excellent as a story or essay, but somehow Wescott didn't publish it at the time and put it aside. In a binder with the same material, he added a fifteen-page typescript, "Long Island—August 7–10, 1938." These were amusing anecdotes and thoughtful reflections, centered on a visit to socialite friends Paul Ferragut and his sister, Anne. The best of this was eventually published with his edited journals.[49]

Most impressive among Wescott's new writing was "A Visit to Priapus," though it was kept from publication during his lifetime because of its sexual theme.[50] The fourteen-thousand-word story reveals something about his private life with Wheeler and Lynes and also raises a question: could an unhappy love life have stifled Wescott's creativity for several years? He and Wheeler were devoted to each other in a lifelong relationship that was the centerpiece of many lives. But it was also true that Wheeler and Lynes were a couple in ways that left Wescott as a third wheel. Instead, he managed only occasional minor affairs. The previous year, there had been a fling with one of Balanchine's ballet stars, Eugene Loring, a handsome twenty-three-year-old who had modeled nude for Lynes. Loring later become an accomplished choreographer. Through the first half of 1938, at Wheeler's suggestion, Wescott dated a tall, attractive young artist from the Midwest named Charles Rain. The weekly dates with the discreet, good-natured Rain suited Wescott in a way, because his life was very busy, but by midyear they naturally drifted apart.

As autobiographical as anything Wescott ever wrote, "A Visit to Priapus" involves the two-day rendezvous of Alwyn Tower and a painter from Maine named Jaris Hawthorn. Most of the background characters have familiar names: Monroe, George, an artist named Pavlik, and his friend Charles. There is an Alan Porter—the same name as Wheeler's real-life friend from the museum—who first tells Tower of an artist in Maine better known for his endowment than his canvases. Tower visits a friend named Frances in Sorrento, Maine, and arranges a side-trip to meet Jaris Hawthorn. In fact, the story is based on an actual trip to Maine that August, when Wescott visited his friend Frances Robbins, who had a summer home in Sorrento.

As the Tower character waits at the meeting place, he thinks about his current relationship with George and Monroe: "Naturally, bitter regret for my great days as a lover assailed me. Also a fresh and terrible kind of sense of devotion to the two whom I love, who love me, who cannot keep me happy, whom I torment and disappoint year in and year out, ached in my grotesque heart. With which my pride also started up, at its worst. To think that I should have come to this: sex-starved, in a cheap provincial hotel humbly waiting for a total stranger; and it should be so soon, at thirty-eight!"

But Tower catches himself and looks at the situation with humor, especially because he normally avoids any sort of undignified ventures. When Hawthorn arrives, we are reminded that the Tower character represents Wescott's fictional self: "There he was, and naturally he recognized me at once: I had forgotten that I am somewhat a celebrity." They visit a maritime museum, take lunch at an inn, and then stop by the seashore. The descriptive writing of New England landscape and seascape, architecture, and townspeople is classic Wescott prose—beauty and clarity that had been missing from the two abandoned novels. The story continues with a long and awkward night of lovemaking. Erotic but never pornographic, the narrative includes Tower's reflections on the psychology of Hawthorn and the problems of sex, in this case the explorative nature of first-time sex between two males, "the worry of what to do and what not to do, and why not and what next and what else." Throughout the story there is an honesty about sexual topics that most writers would not attempt.

The following day, Tower reflects on his friends back home and their own questionable affairs. He takes a fresh look at his needs and his true loves. On the bus, Tower notices that the middle-aged bus driver is driving carelessly because he keeps turning his head and flirting with a young woman. This helps Alwyn realize that sexual escapades can sometimes be foolish or reckless, but they are also remedial. For example, during long periods without sex he loses confidence in himself and becomes ungrateful for his lucky life: "But now, as a result of just a little bout of disgraceful fornication, for the time being I felt willing to call myself happy, willing to be myself, glad to be myself, able to face my maker without grimacing—that is, in a fit state to die. How fantastic and wonderful! And readiness to die is equivalent to courage: therefore I did not mind how foolishly the bus driver flirted, how damnably he drove, all the way to Sorrento."

At his best, even in a story about sex and sexuality, Wescott is a moralist, an agnostic with a strong sense of right and wrong, good and evil in the world. Though he never saw it published, "A Visit to Priapus" is one of his best stories.

At this time, Wescott also collaborated with George Platt Lynes on a book of photos and text based on classical myths. He wrote one- and two-page descriptions of more than twenty mythological figures, which Lynes matched with photos of young models dressed, or undressed, as Orpheus and Eros, Pan, Actaeon, Cyclops, Ascalaphus (using Bruce Wescott's stuffed owl as a prop), and others. A book wasn't published then, but *U.S.*

Camera used some of the material the following year for a piece called "Images of Mythology."[51]

Artist friends such as Paul Cadmus no doubt encouraged Lynes in his nude photography. "I was considered controversial," Cadmus reflected with a smile. "I never thought I was." It was Cadmus who reintroduced Wescott to Fire Island, though the location was different from Wescott's nude sunbathing trips of the early twenties. Cadmus remembered that Jerry and Margaret French and he rented at Fire Island for about six or seven full summers, beginning in 1937: "Jerry and Margaret rented a house each summer at Saltaire, which is about four or five miles from Ocean Beach, almost eleven miles from Cherry Grove. . . . I had my own room and we all painted there, we worked quite hard. So, you see I wasn't just sunbathing. After we'd been working most of the day, we'd go out late afternoons and take photographs when the light was best. They were just playthings. We would hand out these little photographs when we went to dinner parties, like playing cards." When Wescott and Lynes came out, Cadmus remembered, "George brought his Rolleiflex, he didn't bring his big camera. He took quite a few photographs there."[52] Though he called them playthings, the small black and white photos by Paul, Jerry, and Margaret became known as the Pa-Ja-Ma photos, a history of the time and their famous friends. In the city, Wescott's and Wheeler's friends now included a wider variety, including Porter, Christopher Isherwood, Mark Van Doren, illustrator Clement Hurd, mythology scholar Joseph Campbell, novelist Frederick Prokosch, composer Samuel Barber, and fashion critic Diana Vreeland.

The threat of war hung over those years in New York. On September 3, 1939, two days after the Nazis invaded Poland, France was forced to declare war on Germany. Wescott knew his friends in Paris were in great danger. That very evening he kept a date to hear Rachmaninoff's Concerto no. 2, but during the performance he remembered, and he covered his eyes and wept for France.

Grateful for his own good fortune, Wescott did what he could, which was to make the most of his talent. William Rueckert notes, "In 1939 the creative springs began to flow again, and in the five years that followed, Wescott produced, with all the rapidity of the earlier creative period (1924–28), one excellent work after another in a variety of modes."[53] He began work on "The Dream of Audubon," a libretto for a ballet in three scenes that was unlike anything he had attempted before. He published a long essay on Katherine Anne Porter's *Pale Horse, Pale Rider: Three Short Novels* in the summer issue of *Southern Review.* Another of his unique art essays describes the murals of Jared French, but also reveals what Wescott saw in all sorts of American art: "You can always tell that we are a people very empirical and sportive, not over-educated and not really religious, not maniacal, not even logical; and that our continent is not narrow, our atmosphere not opalescent or shadowy."[54]

In connection with the Jared French exhibit, Wescott was interviewed by a twenty-four-year-old critic for *Newsweek,* Nelson Lansdale, and the meeting developed into a surprising relationship. In his journal, however, he wrote about his bedrock relationship with Wheeler, and how much Wheeler's support and encouragement had meant to him. In fact, he realized, Wheeler had the same powerful effect on other creative friends: "In any case, he immediately intensifies, he exaggerates, he amplifies, he multiplies by ten, whomever or whatever it is. If you are a low number, a 2 or a 3, he will make 20 or 30 of you; but if you fortunately are 9 in some way, the combination with him is the way to become 90. His happening to meet me when we were young, and my happening to have a little knowledge and talent for literature, in which he saw a correspondence to his love of art and a compensation for his lack of talent and an opportunity for us both to get on in the world—this gave his life the shape it has had."[55]

On the other hand, Wescott's new poem, "The Summer Ending," used farm and summer storm imagery to describe the rocky, changed relationship of longtime lovers. It ends with this stanza:

> What was all of a piece, now our intellects acutely part.
> Through the pink of each cheek, the form loosely voluminous,
> Each beholds the bone of the other's beloved head.
> The healing concupiscent fit may not occur again in us.
> I hiss in disappointment, your discipline of me is blunder—
> As lightning lets fly in sensitive tree its golden witticism
> And laggard along after it comes the thunder:
> Nagging or warning, domestic, like a palpitating heart.
> The hot sod under us creaks, reminiscent of the laborious bed
> On which our young characters grew as in a cradle.
> Now our kiss grows brotherly but love remains fatal.
> Now lover hits lover, in loathing, in fright of
> criticism.[56]

Wheeler did not know what he had unlocked when he suggested that Wescott write more forcefully about his own life. The following year, within only a few months, Wescott would write *The Pilgrim Hawk,* one of the most highly acclaimed short novels in English.

Wescott in Paris, 1925. Publicity photo by James Abee Studio.

Glenway Wescott, Paris, 1930, by George Platt Lynes. With the permission of the Estate of George Platt Lynes.

Glenway and Lloyd Wescott (in car) with Monroe Wheeler on Midwest car trip, 1934.

"Acteon," advertisement of Sonnabend Gallery, from mythology series by George Platt Lynes.

Monroe Wheeler, W. Somerset Maugham, and Wescott at Stoneblossom.

Nelson Lansdale, to whom Wescott dedicated *The Pilgrim Hawk*. "He was trouble, terrible trouble," said Paul Cadmus.

One of Wescott's favorite longtime friends, Baroness Pauline de Rothschild.

The poet and artist Ralph Pomeroy with Wescott.

Sunday Times of London art critic Raymond Mortimer visits Wescott at Stone-blossom.

Wescott in conversation with Alfred C. Kinsey at the Institute for Sex Research, 1952. Photo by William Dellenback. With permission from the Kinsey Institute for Research in Sex, Gender, and Reproduction, Inc.

Wescott and his mother share a laugh on the front steps at Stone-blossom, 1959.

Wescott and John Connolly in the farmhouse kitchen.

Some mornings the sun seemed to fall back to sleep, once or twice before it actually got its stride and started up the sky.

Wescott's elegant script, from "The Valley Submerged." Edmund Wilson said, "The handwriting of Glenway Wescott is unusual and rather arresting . . . elegant and rigorous."

6

The Little Masterpiece and Willie Maugham

EARLY in 1940, Glenway Wescott began writing a long story about a hawk, based on an incident he remembered from the Paris years. "When I began to write my journal I looked back and found three letter references to the hawk," he said. "I had been using it as a symbol of the aging process and sexual frustration, and as an image, a metaphor, for everything bestial and instinct-ridden."[1] The image of the hawk, he realized, arose from an afternoon and evening in the late twenties in France, when he had been visiting Barbara Harrison at her home in Rambouillet. A limousine arrived unexpectedly, carrying a wealthy Irish couple named McLain, their young chauffeur, and their trained hawk. The McLains were friends of Barbara's mother and were traveling through Europe by car. They were invited to stay for dinner, and the trained hawk on Mrs. McLain's arm made a fantastic conversation piece.

Remembering all this, Wescott realized he had the makings of a vivid story set in expatriate Paris. The McLains became the Cullens. The hostess, Barbara Harrison, became Alexandra Henry. And Wescott naturally became Alwyn Tower, the familiar narrator who could both recall events and comment on them for the reader. "From a technical point of view," he said, "that was an extraordinary afternoon. Mrs. McLain threatened to sue me for years!"[2]

The opening pages include a rare glimpse of Barbara Harrison in Paris when Wescott and Wheeler first knew her. His first draft mentioned Orfeo Craig (his fictional name for Wheeler) but he changed it to "my cousin" because the story needed few characters.[3] But the Alexandra Henry character is very much Barbara in her twenties: "I was much impressed by Alex's enthusiasm during the first part of the Cullens' visit. It reminded me that she must be lonely here in France with only myself and my cousin and a few other friends rather like us. She had spent a number of years in Scotland with her father, and in Morocco, and journeying around the Orient; and in London also the acquaintances of her girlhood had been outdoor people like these two, self-centered but without any introspection, strenuous but emotionally idle. It was a type of humanity that she no longer quite respected or trusted, but evidently still enjoyed."[4]

Wescott knew he had the plot he needed to develop Alwyn Tower's reflections about love and lust and creativity, but there was one problem, and that was the character Larry Cullen. "Barbara and I and the McLains were all becalmed personages," he said. "Mrs. McLain was happy with her husband and loved that bird. But Mr. McLain was just a gentle little man tagging after this great lady. I learned from Willie [Maugham] that if you were going to make a short novel, you had to tighten it up in such a way that the beginning would lead on to the next part, so that the reader would turn over the pages. You couldn't just say 'this' and then 'that' and who was there. You had to get it to move a bit and get your characters to do something. I suddenly realized that Nelson Lansdale was the key to the whole thing because that was the major act of fiction. The rest of it was the extraordinary experience of that bird."[5]

Nelson Lansdale was the young reviewer whom Wescott had met in early 1939. They began a steady relationship, though Wescott admitted that Lansdale was hardly a suitable companion. "He was a drunkard, the worst drunkard in the world. He got to be drama and literary editor of *Newsweek* at the age of about twenty-three—the magazine was quite new then—and he came one rainy afternoon to interview me. He had a wild, doomed face. He was just as precocious as I was, in much the same way, except that he was accursed and I was blessed."[6]

When Lansdale interviewed Wescott at the city apartment, he saw Tchelitchew's erotic painting "The Lion Boy" in Wescott's room and it ignited a spark between them. Wescott explained, "Monroe and George had a big room in the Eighty-ninth Street apartment and there was a big piano. I had a front room with a double bed and over it was 'The Lion Boy.' I once said how wonderful it was that I could hang that painting over my bed in New York and everyone would be coming and going and no one objected to it. And Monroe said, 'What! No one objected to it? Everyone who came in the apartment had a fit!' Well, I asked, why didn't they say so? Monroe said, 'They were frightened that you would give them hell.' I really was a fearsome fellow by this time. And frustrated."[7]

Nelson Lansdale was more than just an important influence on *The*

Pilgrim Hawk. His larger story may be a lesson about the connection between sexual power and creativity. Wescott said:

> He was an extraordinarily sexual man, with the most marvelous skin you can imagine, and an enormous cock, and a wild lust. He didn't have it solved in any way. He told me afterward that the whole time he interviewed me he looked at "The Lion Boy" and rejoiced because he knew his cock was bigger than that. He asked me to lunch and I saw what he'd written about the exhibit, and then he asked me to dine. And he gave me sensations that I'd never felt before, just never felt before! I'd never before had anybody who just got me at the bottom of my . . .
>
> But he was wicked on every point and he was wicked to me. I could go on for hours about the miserable things he said and did. He once said something anti-Semitic and I said, "If you're going to talk like that you can get out of my house. Anti-Semitism is just out; it doesn't exist in my world." But he was also shocked by me; he'd never known anyone who was so shameless. And he adored me, and thought he was doomed to die of alcohol.
>
> He was very agreeable to know in New York because he had all the concert tickets there were. I remember one day he took me to see an Ethel Merman musical at Yale; he was going to write a review. We stayed at the Hotel Taft, and between teatime when we got up there and one in the morning he had eighteen double-Scotches! He didn't know anything that he said, there was no truth in what he said; it was like being with an animal that had learned to talk! Alcoholism is the important part of the Cullen character and furthermore it made a murderer of him, a potential murderer.[8]

The novel was dedicated "To Nelson," which some misunderstood. "It was dedicated to him because I couldn't see any way of making a plot or any kind of story without his character. But everyone thought the dedication was to Nelson Rockefeller."[9] Museum of Modern Art trustee Rockefeller and Wheeler were friends. In *The Pilgrim Hawk,* the Cullen character is in his forties and wealthy, while Lansdale was in his twenties and middle class. But Wescott's description of the alcoholic personality is one of the more successful in literature, and it helped underscore the sober voice of the narrator, Alwyn Tower.

The novel opens with the simple line: "The Cullens were Irish; but it was in France that I met them and was able to form an impression of their love and their trouble." Alwyn Tower is visiting his friend Alexandra Henry, or Alex, at her home in a Paris suburb he calls Chancellet. He says the time is 1928 or 1929, "before we all returned to America, and she met my brother and married him."[10] The Cullens arrive in a long Daimler limousine driven by a handsome young chauffeur, and Alwyn is surprised when Mrs. Cullen emerges with a full-grown, hooded hawk on her arm. Alex's home is described much as Barbara's had been, with a grand living room, polished wood and white walls, a thirty-foot-high ceiling with chestnut beams, and a large window looking out to the garden. As most of the story takes place in this setting, the novella seems ideal for conversion to a play. Decades later Wescott said, "I have a feeling that one of these days Edward Albee, for example, who likes it, will do a play of it. The fact of the matter is that it would be perfectly possible. You can teach a hawk to do all its tricks in six weeks."[11]

The hawk, named Lucy, is unhooded and becomes the center of attention. Then the conversation alternates between the hawk and more conventional topics. Alwyn Tower narrates the whole story from the present time, recalling not only what happened that afternoon but what was going through his mind, and how the hawk symbolized so much of it—thoughts about love, marriage, sexual desire, alcoholism, religion, and artistic freedom. William Rueckert comments, "The whole novel moves forward then in a very dense and complex (but never confusing) way as Alwyn Tower shuttles around from external to internal, from present to various points in the past, and from one kind of comment to another." For example, when Mrs. Cullen compares a hawk's hunger with that of humans, Alwyn's mind wanders: "And I thought—as the relatively well-fed do think—of the other human hungers, mental and sentimental and so on. For example, my own undertaking in early manhood to become a literary artist. No one warned me that I really did not have talent enough. Therefore my hope of becoming a very good artist turned bitter, hot and nerve-wracking. The unsuccessful artist also ends in apathy, too proud and vexed to fly again, waiting upon withheld inspiration, bored to death . . . ." Then, when the self-criticism becomes too sharp, Alwyn thinks instead of the universal hunger of love: "Life goes on and on, after one's luck has run out. Youthfulness persists, alas, long after one has ceased to be young. Love-life goes on indefinitely, with less and less likelihood of being loved, less and less ability to love, and the stomach-ache of love still as sharp as ever. The old bachelor is like an old hawk."[12]

At thirty-nine, Wescott was clearly drawing from his own artistic frustrations of the thirties, and from the frustrations of his present love life. The Wescott scholar Ira Johnson says of *The Pilgrim Hawk:* "Wescott's talent for the carefully turned aphorism and the memorably stated generality reaches a new level of achievement."[13]

The novel takes a turn when the hawk is tethered in the garden and Mrs. Cullen and Alex withdraw to another room. Alwyn offers Cullen a drink, then another, and slowly notices the mood swings of the problem drinker. Alwyn coolly observes how Cullen is soon revealing all his jealousies and fears: about the handsome boy chauffeur who sometimes flirts with Mrs. Cullen, about all women in general, and about his wife's excesses—especially her trained hawk which shames and frightens him. Alwyn: "All alcoholism in a nutshell, I foolishly mused. And while he, poor man, counted his sports and his travels on his fingers, I meanly ticked off the drunkard's faults and pitfalls of drink as it were on my fingers—indiscretion and boastfulness and snobbism; and sentimentality so nervous that it may switch any minute to the exact opposite; and the sexual note and the sadistic note, undesirable desire, improbable murder. All of it of course a bit unreal and unrealizable in fact."[14]

Wescott, who endured a two-year relationship with Nelson Lansdale, said years later, "Since Dionysus came over from India, half the world has been drunk." Alwyn Tower in *The Pilgrim Hawk* remarks: "For alcohol is a god, as the Greeks decided when it was first introduced from the East, although a god of vengeance. The drinker becomes the drunkard. Everyone is to blame."[15]

Larry Cullen foolishly releases the hawk. Angry but composed, Mrs. Cullen retrieves it. They change their mind about staying for dinner but before their limousine can pull away Cullen takes out a handgun, perhaps to threaten the young chauffeur. Mrs. Cullen gets the gun away from him, leaves the men in the car, and throws the gun into Alex's pond. After her apology they leave. But the Maugham-like movement of plot is not the real story.

The novel is subtitled "A Love Story," and there are reflections about marriage and love throughout. Not only the Cullens have problems—Alex's young newlywed servants have a tearful fight in the kitchen, and Alwyn worries about his young unmarried host and reflects on his own romantic life. Again with the hawk as a powerful symbol, his thoughts are revealed in some of Wescott's finest writing:

> Then, I lamented to myself, if your judgment is poor you fall in love with those who could not possibly love you. If romance of the past has done you any harm, you will not be able to hold on to love when you do attain it; your grasp of it will be out of alignment. Or pity or self-pity may have blunted your hand so that it makes no mark. Back you fly to your perch, ashamed as well as frustrated. Life is almost all perch. There is no nest; and no one is with you, on exactly the same rock or out on the same limb. The circumstances of passion are all too petty to be companionable. So there you sit, and you try to sit still, and doze and dream to save trouble. It is the kind of thing you have to keep quiet about for others' sake, for politeness's sake: itching palm and ugly tongue and unsighted eye and empty flatulent physiology as a whole; and your cry of desire, ache, ache, ringing in your own ears. No one else hears it; and you get so tired of it yourself that you can't wait to grow old. [16]

Throughout the novel Alwyn's memories of what happened ten years earlier shift to his feelings in the present moment, for another level of understanding and insight: "Unrequited passion; romance put asunder by circumstances or mistakes; sexuality pretending to be love—all that is a matter of little consequence, a mere voluntary temporary uneasiness, compared with the long course of true love, especially marriage. In marriage, insult arises again and again and again; and pain has to be not only endured, but consented to; and the amount of forgiveness that it necessitates is incredible and exhausting. When love has given satisfaction, then you discover how large a part of the rest of life is only payment for it, installment after installment."[17]

The story ends gently, optimistically, with humorous words between Alex and Alywn. Rueckert concludes, "Whatever one says of *The Pilgrim Hawk,* the excellence of it, especially the great formal beauty of it as a particular kind of prose fiction, cannot be denied."[18]

The first draft was completed quickly in two small notebooks, and by early summer a few typescripts on crimson paper were marked up and polished. On a draft Wescott read to friends, Tower reflects on how the suburban Paris countryside is now probably equipped with antiaircraft guns for the defense of the city. Wescott crossed out those lines and wrote on the back: "When I began to write this, France was ready to defend itself, we supposed. Before I was able to finish it, the Germans were able to make their ghastly dubious conquest. The changes on this page, as I have marked them, show the haste of history."[19]

In midsummer, Wescott gave a series of lectures in Michigan with Katherine Anne Porter, Sherwood Anderson, Isabel Bishop, and others. He also had a reunion with Janet Flanner at the Algonquin Hotel in New York—she had been one of the last Americans to leave Paris. During those few weeks, George Davis, the literary editor of *Harper's Bazaar,* wanted *The Pilgrim Hawk,* but the senior editor Carmel Snow wanted the story shortened. Wescott refused. That same year, Snow, whom he referred to as "Mrs. Cold Caramel," had asked Porter to cut her story "Leaning Tower" in half, and Porter withdrew it. "Finally," he said, "Harper's rapped on the table and said, 'We want it and we'll publish it right away.'" The senior editor Eugene Saxton informed Wescott of its acceptance on August 19. Harper president Cass Canfield wrote, "I was so pleased to learn about the story you have written. It is grand to have you on our list again."[20] It was agreed that the book would be released that fall and also serialized in the November and December issues of *Harper's Magazine.*

The publisher asked for an autobiographical sketch for the book jacket, and printed it below a handsome portrait of Wescott by George Platt Lynes:

> I am a farmer's son, descendant of pilgrims and pioneers; an idealizing, nervous, migratory type of man. In war time (the other war) I attended the University of Chicago for a year and a half, when my health went a little wrong. Then I lived in New Mexico a year, horse-back. Then a great lady, William Vaughn Moody's widow, lent me William Cullen Bryant's birthplace for the summer; and I got started at *The Apple of the Eye.* Europe was my real education: Ford Madox Ford

and Cocteau, Elly Ney, Isadora Duncan and Rebecca West, for example, were my teachers. I went abroad at twenty, almost by accident: first to London, and then tragic Germany. I stayed in great delectable France for many years because I could live there on what I could earn by writing. At the start of the thirties I saw that Europe had become a rat-trap, so I came back where I belong. My Wisconsin family meanwhile had moved and resumed its ancestral farming in the New Jersey hills; and two life-long friends kindly constitute for me another home in New York.

Advance copies were sent out in the fall. Wescott's sister Marjorie reacted the way many did who read a story they had heard Wescott read aloud: "It is a great pleasure to hear it all as I read it now; like having a present of a record as well as a book." Thomas Mann's son, the novelist Klaus Mann, took him out to celebrate. Loyal friend Frances Robbins wrote: "We do hope it will be good luck to you. We are so proud of you, dear." Caroline Gordon Tate—she and her husband, Allen, were southern writers and poets who had known Wescott since the twenties—wrote: "You are fortunate in your symbols. Of course you did not choose them haphazard. I imagine they picked you."[21]

The book reviews were all that a writer might hope for. The *New York Herald Tribune:* "Brilliant. . . . The writing is beautiful, cut to the bare bones." Sterling North wrote in the *Chicago News,* "Glenway Wescott's short novel is the sort Henry James would have written, if he had that much talent." Mark Schorer in *Kenyon Review:* "*The Pilgrim Hawk* is at least as special in its point of view as *The Turn of the Screw,* but it is not ambiguous." The *New York Times* added, "The product of an intensely individual mind." Wescott told *Time* magazine, "If this simple story is as good as I hope, it will be a fresh start."[22] While not a popular success at first, *The Pilgrim Hawk* would be critically acclaimed, reprinted, translated for foreign editions, and included in anthologies of great modern short novels.

At the end of the year, Wescott's most unusual work, "The Dream of Audubon," appeared in *Dance* magazine and later in the anthology *The Best One-Act Plays of 1940.*[23] A libretto for a ballet in three parts, it was written for the Ballet Guild and Lincoln Kirstein. Later, composer David Diamond wrote a musical score for it. Wildly imaginative and original, "The Dream of Audubon" centers on the life and legend of naturalist Jean-Jacques Audubon. Part of the legend is that Audubon was the lost Dauphin, the son of Louis XVI and Marie Antoinette. The text explains the story, describes the characters and costumes, and suggests the choreography. In the first scene, in a Louisiana setting at evening, Audubon shows off all his skills for a group of country boys and girls. Audubon in fact could paint portraits ambidextrously, was a taxidermist, gave fencing lessons and dancing lessons, and performed sleight-of-hand tricks. In the second scene, at night, he dreams of the execution of Louis XVI and Marie

Antoinette, and his own coronation as king. The third scene, at night back in Louisiana, is a pure fantasy of colorful dancing birds and Indians. William Rueckert called the closing scene "fantastic and brilliant" and concluded, "'The Dream of Audubon' is a joyful work; it is the creation of an imagination which feels at home with itself and its material."[24]

Wescott next wrote an important remembrance of F. Scott Fitzgerald. After Fitzgerald died at forty-four on December 21, 1940, some critics wrote harsh, judgmental pieces. Both Wescott and John Dos Passos wrote more balanced essays for the *New Republic.* In "The Moral of F. Scott Fitzgerald" Wescott admonished him for his spell of hack writing but praised his novels, his best stories, and essays. He said of his fellow expatriates: "In any case we are the ones who know about Fitzgerald. He was our darling, our genius, our fool. . . . He was young to the bitter end. He loved and he wrote at last as a scapegoat, and now he has departed as one. As you might say, he was Gatsby, a greater Gatsby." Dos Passos sent a handwritten note to Wescott complimenting him for saying many things that needed to be said, while his own piece, he said, was just an effort to put a few punches into the critics. Dos Passos added that he was fond of Scott, but that he was a man who never understood anything of the world except writing.[25]

Wescott worried that his own writing was at a crossroad. He told Caroline Newton: "I do believe, you see, that mine is the most precious or most interesting talent in this country today; and that it is entirely in jeopardy at this point, touch-and-go whether or not I get anywhere." Some writers friends sent reassuring words. E. M. Forster commented on *The Pilgrim Hawk* and its symbolic center, Lucy the hawk: "Being a great deal older than you must be, I followed with anxiety your prophecies about sex, and asked my own experience to what extent they were true. On the whole, my report is a less gloomy one. Anyway, I have never had such a bad time as Lucy. Poor Lucy . . . going off with those terrible people!"[26]

In April 1941, a week after Wescott's fortieth birthday, Katherine Anne Porter offered some of her kindest words during the half century of their hot-and-cold friendship. While she was closer to Barbara and Monroe, she knew that no one appreciated her writing more than Wescott. Her deeply personal note revealed mutual respect: "Your letters always make me feel that I have not said what I meant to about your writing. For I admire and believe in and hang on your next paragraphs, and go back to them for reassurance, and love them. It is perhaps that you are all that I am not: and I do not love me any more than you love you, it appears. How often I have read *The Pilgrim Hawk,* thinking to myself, 'This time I shall certainly find out his trick,' but I don't, and of course I know all along that I can't find it because there is no trick."[27]

Later that month, Porter and Wescott met for lectures and readings at the Yaddo writers' retreat in Saratoga Springs, New York. To the author and critic Mark Schorer, Wescott revealed, "I am working with great force and high hopes and perilous lapses of confidence on another short novel, 'A Fortune in Jewels.'"[28]

In the city, he had a surprise reunion with W. Somerset Maugham. In a restaurant he had recognized Lady Emerald Cunard, whom he once met at the Russian Ballet, and greeted her saying, "'Lady Cunard, I must reintroduce myself, I'm an old friend of your daughter's.' She said, 'Do you know Somerset Maugham? He's the most unhappy man in the world. He doesn't know anybody here. He had to leave his house, the Germans seized it, and they took his boat and everything under the sun, and the British sent him here. He's at my hotel, the Ritz. If you can give a kind word to him, you'll be doing him and me a great favor.'"[29]

Wescott remembered how Maugham had criticized him and all young expatriates at the Villa Mauresque in 1928, but he agreed to a meeting at Emerald Cunard's suite at the Ritz. "So I went to tea, knocked on the door, and this marvelous Lady Cunard answered. She was the most attractive woman who ever lived, she was like a little parrot, and witty beyond belief. She was not naturally in society but she dominated it." (American born, Cunard had married into the London social scene.) She went off to get the tea, telling him to wait for Maugham to arrive. "Then the door opened and there was Maugham, saying, 'Oh, Glenway Wescott, I'm so glad to meet you. I've wondered all these years what you're like. And if you'll remember I praised *The Grandmothers* to the skies.'" It irritated Wescott that Maugham seemed to forget their brusque meeting in the late twenties. "Later, when his lover Gerald Haxton came over here during the war, Gerald and I talked about that twenties luncheon and the people who were there—and Willie just gave us the fish-eye, as if he didn't know what we were talking about."[30]

Despite Maugham's quirks, they became friends. Wescott said,

> The first time he took me to dinner, at that same restaurant, I told him the story of how I lost my virginity. And I said, "I hope I haven't bored you with an old story." "Bored me?" said he, "I was thrilled. And you must write things like that—in the same way that you talk!" But then he said to me, "Now look, I've got to warn you. You haven't any business writing things like *The Pilgrim Hawk*. You've got to write the great fiction of America. You've got to choose right now. You can either be the American Cocteau, or you can be the American Trollope, and what you ought to do is be Trollope."
>
> Well, I'd read Trollope, but I'd read him to go to sleep! And as to Cocteau, I said I never liked his writing, I never praised a word of it. It was the bane of Cocteau's life: he asked me to translate him, he asked me to do anything collaborative, because he loved me dearly. He was a fascinating man, but I just didn't like his novels.

> Willie was forgetting entirely that both he and Arnold Bennett went over to France and learned from the French. Then they came back and were middle-class English, you see, and had a middle-class audience to the end. And I didn't dare tell him, because he wouldn't believe it, that as to the form of *The Pilgrim Hawk* and the workmanship, it was influenced by him, by his stories.[31]

Still, Wescott and Maugham enjoyed each other. Maugham appreciated the formal elegance of Wescott's prose and thought him first and foremost an essayist. He was also grateful for the younger writer's friendship during his war years in America. As a friend, he gently expressed his opinion about Nelson Lansdale. Wescott remembered, "Maugham said to me one day, 'I must say, I hope you won't be offended, but I was not impressed with your young man. He doesn't seem suitable to you, neither in looks nor manner.' And I replied that Nelson was good for me in some basic, sexual way. Willie said, kindly, 'Well, that's the important thing.'"[32]

Paul Cadmus drew a portrait of Lansdale, which Wescott said captured his "accursed or haunted expression." But Cadmus admitted, "I did the drawing for Glenway, or else I would have never drawn him. I never could understand Glenway's fascination with him. Nelson did an article about me one time. I was friendly with him, but he didn't interest me terribly much. He was trouble, terrible trouble. A drunk."[33] Lynes photographed Lansdale, but he and Wheeler disliked him. Needless to say, Lloyd and Barbara were aghast.

"I saw myself really in a ludicrous light," Wescott said. "And all the time my family was perfectly appalled, but they knew very well that I'd had miserable luck and boring lovers and no fun at all. I was more grateful to Monroe and Barbara than I ever was before, because they really saw me through this thing. Nelson came out to the farm all the time. George wouldn't come out from the city when Nelson came. And you can't imagine how Monroe loathed him. But Monroe remembered how I'd supported him when George became a part of our lives. And he loved me more than he'd ever loved me before."[34]

In April 1941, Wescott traveled to Frederick, Maryland, to visit Lansdale's adoptive parents, who were worried about the young man's drinking and had no clue that Wescott was anything but a well-meaning, and somewhat famous, friend. "I went down there and saw his parents, and Nelson and I had sex in the bathroom right under his father's nose!" he said. "They were proud of him but they saw he was right at the edge."[35] When they got back to New York, Lansdale made things worse by pursuing a younger man. Finally, the breakup was completed in late spring when he was inducted into the military service and sent abroad. Wescott's letters and journals show the experience was an emotional milestone from which he emerged for the better.

The other news around Wescott included some family drama at the Mulhocaway farm. Bruce Wescott had been kicked by the horse Mecca and was briefly hospitalized. Barbara announced that she was pregnant, which was a surprise and perhaps a concern, because she was such an independent, free spirit. Wheeler had his own romantic problems, because George Lynes had developed a crush on his handsome studio assistant and model, George Tichenor. Otherwise, Wheeler was proud of Lynes, whose gallery exhibition, "Two Hundred Portraits by George Platt Lynes," included portraits of Gertrude Stein, Orson Welles, Jimmie Daniels, Lloyd and Barbara, Wescott and Wheeler, Ruth Ford, Somerset Maugham, and Salvador Dali. Wheeler's own career blossomed as the Museum of Modern Art named him director of publications and exhibitions. It opened the way to decades of beautiful museum publications, world travel, acquisitions, and exhibit planning with great artists.

Wescott's writing seemed on track and he now seemed completely at home in New York. Klaus Mann wrote in his 1941 memoir, *The Turning Point:* "As for Glenway Wescott, he now appears almost as conspicuously European in America as he used to be conspicuously American in Europe. As a writer and a character, he is just as suave and subtle. Being highly fond of civilized people, I always relished his company." Wescott was working on a novel about wartime France, and he published an important essay on the theme of war in the *Chicago Sun.* "The Writer's Problem in the World Today" suggests that novelists should avoid ordinary human sentiments during times of crises and concentrate on truth telling and healing. The essay recalled his youthful visit to Morocco, when he saw storytellers in the marketplace of Marrakech: "The one I liked best narrated very loud and never laughed at his own jokes or put on airs of virtuosity or vanity, but scowled a great deal, flashing his eyes, then shutting them tight, and sitting in silence for a while to consider the next development of his plot. He made me think of blind Homer, and reminded me of the fact that, for a storyteller, a sort of blindness to everything except the story is a good thing." He read the *Chicago Sun* essay in patron Josephine Crane's "Monday Class," an ongoing literary gathering. Years later he would develop and republish it.[36]

In February 1942, Somerset Maugham invited Wescott for a long visit at his new home in Yemassee, South Carolina. Maugham's American publisher, Nelson Doubleday of Oyster Bay, Long Island, had a large vacation property there that included a mansion called Bonny Hill and a cottage built for Maugham called Parker's Ferry. At sixty-eight, Maugham was lonely because his hard-drinking lover, Gerald Haxton, was staying in Florida. Haxton, fifty, had been with Maugham for three decades but was becoming increasingly difficult. Maugham's ex-wife, Syrie Wellcome, and many others saw only the worst in Haxton, and there was plenty of cause.

But Gerald Haxton had been Willie's companion and the major inspiration of his fiction.

Wescott spent more than three weeks at Parker's Ferry and learned a good deal. He said, "Maugham's story 'The Treasure' was really about Gerald. Gerald once went to jail for Willie, who was nearly in trouble for molesting a minor in Italy. Some said that was Gerald's hold on Willie: guilt, fear, and moral blackmail."[37] Whatever their secrets, Haxton's absence now allowed for a peaceful visit, including long walks and horseback riding. Wescott remembered, "Willie was a born teacher. I went down there for three weeks, and he told me everything that he knew about writing. We were there all alone and we'd walk along the swamps and amid the snakes, and we'd go on to dinner. The whole of the Doubleday staff was there, and Nelson would do anything for him, his wife adored Willie. He was their great money maker." At the time, Maugham was completing *The Razor's Edge,* in which his main characters are based on Emerald Cunard and Christopher Isherwood. Maugham told Wescott, "Not only did you tell me more about Isherwood than anyone, but you posed for me as much as he did." Maugham also revealed his first rule of fiction writing: "I never begin a story or novel until I have all five parts that go into it: scenes, places, characters, events, and the ending."[38]

Wescott also began to understand the dark side of Maugham's personality. He said, "Ford Madox Ford and Alan Searle [Maugham's last lover] both said that Maugham lived his whole life in fear. He'd lost his faith as a medical student when he saw a child die of spinal meningitis."[39] And while some criticized Maugham for hiding his homosexuality, Wescott pointed out that men like Maugham and E. M. Forster could actually remember the trials of Oscar Wilde.

During his stay in South Carolina, Wescott received two bits of dramatic news. One was that Barbara had given birth to a girl, Deborah, on March 9. The other, about a week later, was that his divorced sister Elizabeth Hotchkiss had undergone a double mastectomy. It was Elizabeth and her baby, Bruce, who had inspired *The Babe's Bed.* He sent his sister a long letter of support, praising her for all she had done for the family and the farm, and reminding her how much she was needed.

Before leaving Parker's Ferry, Wescott admitted to Maugham that he was thinking of abandoning his novel-in-progress, "A Fortune in Jewels." Exasperated, Maugham was the first to admit that some of his many works were not first-rate, but the idea of abandoning large manuscripts horrified him. Of course, many quality writers give up on some novels. But as Maugham's friend, Wescott suffered doubly from this, because of the older man's spectacular productivity. Several times during their long friendship he was stung by Maugham's scolding criticism.

Sometime later, Maugham complained to playwright Edward Sheldon that Wescott was unduly influenced by the French: "It was a misfortune for him that by spending his most impressionable years in their company he should have attached an exaggerated value to things of small consequence, and I have tried to suggest to him that the proper material of the novelist is the primary emotions of normal man." Wescott heard of the criticism and had a response: "Isn't it the job of the novelist to make the biggest bubble out of the smallest piece of soap?"[40]

Unfortunately, Wescott's good effort at an ambitious, moral novel ran aground. Finally, he would confess to Caroline Newton, "I must explain to my agent that 'A Fortune in Jewels' will not be ready to submit for serialization upon the date they fixed." Harper and Brothers had already typeset and bound sample pages. The abandoned manuscript of "A Fortune in Jewels" includes a note by Wescott explaining that it was the predecessor to his World War II novel *Apartment in Athens*.[41] Enclosed is a *Time* magazine article, "Five Years of Dates," annotating major events of the war. The manuscript numbers hundreds of pages, including some second draft pages. There is an outline for nineteen chapters, with the story of wartime France told by characters in New York, especially by a woman, Mademoiselle Lully, whom Alwyn Tower had known in Paris.

Early in the story, novelist Tower is arguing with journalists and other friends about the importance of fiction as a vehicle for truth telling, as opposed to the limited language of journalism. Regarding the war in Europe, Tower says that a literary man, not a journalist, should be sent to France to write a magazine feature. Articulating Wescott's feelings, Tower tells the journalists: "The novel is a form which permits us to tell things truly, without knowing all the facts. Indeed, that is my own notion of fiction now: that there shall be scarcely anything fictitious about it, only the necessary conventions—transportation and synthesis and alias—to enable us to reveal certain truths while they are still current, still vital, helpful or harmful as the case may be; truths which the journalist can only hint at and which history has not yet come to."

Alwyn Tower discusses Ernest Hemingway's novel about Spain and his own recent novel about a hawk and his "brother's wife, Alex"—clearly making this a sequel to *The Pilgrim Hawk*. When the conversation turns to jewelry, Alwyn tells what jewels represent to most people. The prose recalls the high standard of Wescott's previous novel: "I remarked at last that the best excuse for wanting diamonds and the like, useless petty expensive objects, must be simply this: They serve as a nucleus for one's memory, a stimulant of it, a convenient portable key to it. The same is true of a work of art; and certain accessories of religion such as crucifix and rosary; and other things we unreasonably delight in, even beautiful human features. It is a part of what we mean when we say they are beautiful—they make the memory flash and flash, with the spectrum of all it has known all at once, all it has enjoyed and endured and wanted and lost; light and dark together; irrespective of sadness or happiness."

Later in the story, when Mademoiselle Lully mentions that her young cousin was taken away by the Germans, she falls silent, turning the diamond ring on her finger. Another of Alwyn's observations, about the end of a love relationship, suggests Wescott's final breakup with Nelson Lansdale: "We are always quite prepared to fall out of love when the time comes, we have only to recall all that marginal observation which we have never ceased making, which we have kept to ourselves, filed away in a compartment of our heads or our hearts. And I think as a rule we take what we discover at the end, the last straw, the little intolerable final trouble, only as an excuse; a pretext; and a simplification of farewell."

Wescott's notes show that the character of a French politician named Jean Ravoux is drawn from Jean Cocteau, a Mary Born is modeled on Mary Butts, and another character's death resembles the unhappy fate of Isadora Duncan. While the novel is promising and begins well, it fails to keep Alwyn Tower in the foreground and bogs down with too many plots and characters. Still, his next attempt at a war novel would succeed.

In early May 1942, Wescott was hospitalized with pneumonia for ten days at Saint Luke's Hospital—just as he had been exactly seven years earlier. This time he had an allergic reaction to a drug with sulfur, and his dreams were filled with hallucinations of the war. Years later he remembered it vividly:

> I was delirious for three days. Day and night the same, for my nightmares had the daytime background, the ward, the patients on either side of me, the same nurses; and all the while I was overpowered by the thought that the Germans were winning the war, and the fear of their invading the country. Very late one night when everyone else had fallen asleep, I was visited by a young man from Washington, a soldier, but not in uniform. He told me what was happening—to be kept secret, lest it set off a nationwide panic—and assigned my part in the underground after the invasion, with instructions and contacts. He came again the next night. It was all quite realistic. "Now listen," I said, "how do I know that your coming here is not all delirium?" He said, "I'll give you a button from my coat." He brought out a pocket knife, removed a button and gave it to me. Next morning, a button lay on the floor between my bed and the adjacent bed on the left. Had I seen it before the delusion began? I got out of bed and weakly shuffled to the window, followed by a worried nurse. My soldier had entered through that window and I wanted to see if there was a fire escape. There was.[42]

According to a letter from friend Elsie Arden, Wescott recovered normally and returned to Stone-blossom on May 15. The dream revealed his preoccupation with the war, as did two excellent stories he published in *Harper's Magazine* that spring.

"Mr. Auerbach in Paris" recalls Alwyn Tower's first trip to Paris in

1923 and his foreboding of war. Mr. Auerbach is based on Henry Goldman, the retired German Jewish investment banker who hired young Wescott in 1923 to accompany him and his family through Europe, collecting art and donating and fundraising for the benefit of German universities. A good-hearted man who believes Germany must be strengthened after the indignity of World War I, Auerbach/Goldman introduces his young assistant to the art, architecture, and atmosphere of Paris. But he also shocks the young man when he says that, while Paris is the most beautiful city in the world, it would be the greatest if only the Germans ruled it. Alwyn Tower of the forties reflects, "The point of it was the incredible lack of foresight of so many well-meaning Germans and German-Jews, caring for nothing in the world so much as the recovery of that injured, invalid Reich which was to grow too strong for them, so soon."[43]

The other new story, "The Frenchman Six-Foot-Three," describes Alwyn Tower's return to Paris in 1938. Tower sees a friend, Roger Gaumond, dressed in a too-small French uniform, a symbol of his ill-prepared nation. The character is based on Cocteau's friend Michel Girard. Tower says, "He told me the officers were severe with the men, but ruefully, like doctors keeping some secret." Another character, an American journalist named Linda Brewer, is really Janet Flanner. To Wescott she was "a really old and fond friend of mine, one of my generation, a fellow writer; not a novelist but a journalist in the great way, personal, unpretentious, and scrupulous." Together, the stories showed Wescott's writing voice in fine form. An old story, "The Sailor," with the description of Villefranche that Fitzgerald had liked, was reprinted in a new anthology, *American Harvest*.[44]

As always, family issues crowded in, claiming much of Wescott's energy. In particular, he was worried about Wheeler and his loss of George Platt Lynes. Lynes had been in love with his studio assistant, George Tichenor, who in 1943 went off to serve as an ambulance driver for the British military. In June, a telegram announced that he died in combat. The news affected Lynes profoundly. In his grief he developed a compulsive attachment for Tichenor's younger brother, Jonathan, who also worked and modeled in the studio. George Tichenor had been sexually straight but flexible, and a good boy. Jonathan, who had first worked on Lloyd's farm, was bisexual, flamboyant, and trouble. Some of Lynes's best work was included in the Museum of Modern Art exhibit "Twentieth Century Portraits," but it was not a happy time. Lynes began to spend less and less time at Stone-blossom, less time with Wheeler, and in a number of ways behaved badly.

One of Lynes's best friends, Paul Cadmus, had done paintings of the Tichenor brothers. "Aviator" showed George Tichenor holding a kite, and a later one, "Survivor," depicted a somber Jonathan. Cadmus remembered the whole story and how it affected Lynes, Wescott, and Wheeler: "That was the breaking point. Jonathan, the second brother, caused their breakup as a threesome. And I remember the day when Jonathan first appeared. I was out at Stone-blossom and Jonathan and his older brother drove up for a visit. We were out on the lawn and the car was in the distance at the other side of the house. And when Jonathan got out of the car, Glenway said, 'I saw him first!' We laughed. But it didn't work out that way. His brother had already been working with George. They were beautiful. Jonathan was a bit more mysterious and sly. I never quite understood him."[45] One of Lynes's Fire Island photos captured his fascination with Jonathan Tichenor, a close-up of the youth's shoulders, arms, and strikingly handsome face.

Finally, Lynes decided to make a break, to leave Stone-blossom and the East Eighty-ninth Street apartment. On February 24, 1943, he sent Wheeler a two-page letter from his 540 Madison Avenue studio, saying in part: "You have been hurt so much and I've been hurt too and I feel I cannot face any more of my own double-dealing and you shouldn't have to. It's so hellish because I'll never love anybody as I've loved you, perhaps not as much as I love you still. . . . But I've got to get my life simplified, even for the worse, heartbreaking as it is, sick as it makes me to write it." Six hours later, he sent a one-page letter that concluded: "The thing I cannot understand, the thing I've been asking myself all afternoon, is how I who have loved you so much could have behaved so abominably and so brutally. I've done something to myself I'll never get over. I wish to god I could know that you will be all right."[46]

Like most people, Wescott gained an inner strength over the years. He showed it by acting as the go-between for Lynes and speaking to all parties. Two days after the breakup, Wescott in New York sent the stunning news to Barbara and Lloyd by letter, announcing that Lynes was leaving them. He said: "Monroe knows as well as I how fond you are of George, and twice this evening he has talked of that, thinking how you may miss him, because he is younger and gayer than we; wishing that his intimate misfortune did not have to keep George away from Mulhocaway. But it cannot be helped." Barbara, whose life had become more isolated and domestic, cherished the memory of their happy years in Paris. She answered: "You don't know how strongly and deeply I am concerned for the harmony of your menage—for the three of you and myself because I selfishly don't want to lose even a fraction of any one of you."[47]

Wescott sympathized with Lynes but admonished him, reminding him that Wheeler had suffered silently for months and never considered giving Lynes an ultimatum, "given his natural nobility, gentleness, and scorn of extreme emotions, even his own." As for the shock of the sudden breakup, "At first, I must say, I could not think or feel anything much except a great fear of Monroe's dying of a broken heart. I have taken care in all my letters not to dwell on his shock and extreme sadness, and I do not want to now. He loves me, and that will serve for the present; and he will be happy again in due time."[48]

Monroe Wheeler was hard to fathom. He was a man who could not raise his voice in anger or be vindictive. He was extremely formal, as befit the no-nonsense world of museum bureaucracies, art dealers, and patrons. What passion he expressed was in support of his creative friends. Some complained that he was stuffy and conservative, but he was much more than that. His importance to Wescott's early career cannot be exaggerated, and he had a similar good effect on many writers and artists he believed in, including Lynes. On the other hand, detaching oneself from Wheeler, one might suggest, did not bode well.

After about six months, relations with Lynes became friendly again but things were never really the same. It wasn't long before the hard-drinking Jonathan Tichenor met a woman named Bridget Bate, left Lynes, and married. Many years later, Wescott looked back with emotion on the whole experience, believing in his romantic way that Lynes's behavior contributed to his early death in the fifties. "Everyone felt sorry for George," he said. "It was young love, and so on. George was so beautiful . . . and that boy destroyed him! Nelson Lansdale couldn't destroy me. Poor George. I knew he was doomed. That determination to destroy one brother because he couldn't have the other one. And then getting what happens to people who do that sort of thing, you know, back and forth. It's evil subject matter."[49] Though more mystical than logical, those were his feelings.

Wheeler recovered. He found a new apartment, at 812 Park Avenue, and resumed giving parties, with such guests as the artists Marsden Hartley and Alexander Calder, young actor Yul Brynner—whom Lynes photographed nude—and budding writer Gordon Merrick. He and Wescott were sustained all their lives by their work, their friends, and each other. Professionally, Wheeler made a major decision. Offered a position at the Library of Congress, he decided to remain loyal to the Museum of Modern Art.

On September 30, 1943, Wescott's friend and early patron Frances Robbins died. She left behind a large sealed packet of her unpublished writing, with handwritten instructions that it was to be destroyed, unless Wescott wanted it. After the funeral, he took her writing and kept it. It contained intelligent but unlively stories and some good, original verse.[50]

The loss of Robbins underscored how important women friends were to Wescott, not only women writers but also many other woman who understood him and remained devoted to him throughout his life. Wescott once said, "A woman scorned is absolutely frightful; it's as if she had snakes wound round her neck! Yet women have been kinder to me than men ever were. And I think generally women *are* kinder than men."[51]

Perhaps most important was Pauline Potter, the fashion designer. Pauline had moved from Paris to New York in the late thirties because of the war, leaving behind everything but a set of china and two small Jean Vuillard paintings. Before long she was designing clothes for Hattie Carnegie. By the forties she was known as one of the highest paid women in the United States. Her townhouse was elaborately designed and furnished with museum-quality pieces. There she entertained such close friends as Wescott and Wheeler, Cecil Beaton, fashion editor Diana Vreeland, and film director John Huston. Unpretentious, brilliant, refined, witty, she was the ideal female counterpart to Wescott. If he had been heterosexually inclined, she might have been the great woman of his life. Along with Barbara, that is. Between them, nothing changed when Pauline later became a Rothschild and a celebrity.

Peace returned to Stone-blossom. One day an amused Wescott saw Marsden Hartley and Wheeler luxuriating naked at a sunlit brook near Mulhocaway Creek. He noted in his journal that the scene made him want to write a story called "The Love of Money," possibly referring to Wheeler's nickname, Monie, or a double-meaning. A nude photo of Wescott, his long body reflected in the water, made the rounds, and was mentioned in Tennessee Williams's *Memoirs.*[52]

Wescott published no major work in 1943 but several pieces expressed his complexity. In his journal he wrote about the poet A. E. Housman and about honesty in sexuality: "Having read all of the poems of A. E. Housman this morning, I thought a good deal of sexual frustration. He makes it seem simple in his case: because the objects of his passion cannot by their nature requite it; and perhaps in any case a moral scruple would have kept him from the physical satisfaction. Passive in any case; there was nothing to be done about it except to rock the spirit asleep for its eventual bed, the grave, and what a lullaby he made of it. But I was thinking about my own case. And this is what I thought: If I were asked what I want more than anything else on earth to do, there would not be a moment's hesitation in my answer: a certain sort of fornication. And in my case there is no reason why I should not have it. . . . I am not ashamed of this, nothing so deep-seated and impulsive can be shameful."[53]

Another aspect of Wescott was revealed in an art essay he wrote at the request of Erich Maria Remarque, author of the World War I classic *All Quiet on the Western Front.* Wescott had known Remarque, a German immigrant, in France. In the forties, Remarque was living in America and exhibited his personal collection of nineteenth-century paintings by Van Gogh, Cezanne, Utrillo, Daumier, Delacroix, Pissaro, Renoir, Degas, and others. In the essay Wescott spoke of Remarque's literary fame and pointed out the importance of the writer's showing his art collection during the war: "There is grandeur in war, even in its evil," Wescott warned, and in such times art can be overlooked, even belittled. With special insight, he wrote about Utrillo's "White House." A decade earlier he had seen the painting in a small circular museum in France, a building with only skylights, not windows. He was sure he was alone in the room when suddenly he jumped at the sensation that someone was behind him. There was no one. He looked back at the painting and felt the same sensation again. Then he realized what had happened. Through the skylight, a cloud was passing under the sun and casting a different light on Utrillo's painting. Wescott, so astute in articulating the subtleties of art, wrote, "This is a quality which is the same in Utrillo's early work as in that of his predecessors, Cezanne, Pissaro, Corot, especially Corot; so great a sensitivity to light that the canvas seems to breathe as the weather changes."[54]

Far more accessible to most readers was a Wescott essay in *Harper's Bazaar.* "The Love of New York" is a long, good-humored piece that captures not only Manhattan as it was in the forties but Wescott as he really was for most of his life in New York. A man who never learned to drive a car, he describes himself strolling through midtown Manhattan in late December and recalls how his sullen mood and discouragement turned to a sort of mystic trance, filled with thoughts and impressions of the city he loved. He realized that if he had a choice he would prefer to live the rest of his life in New York, despite its discomforts and shortcomings, rather than in Paris or Rome or London. Optimism, hope, possibility, and talent were part of the reason, but so was charm: "I think it is the only great city with all the importance and activity and amusement of city life, which nevertheless appeals to the imagination like wild country. Its charm depends on the weather, the light and the dark, and the time of day, and the momentary emotion of the beholder." From East Fifty-ninth Street he walked down Madison Avenue, past the men's store where he bought shirts, and the shop where he bought British periodicals, past friends on the street, all the way to Thirty-fourth Street. There he saw a crowd of Christmas shoppers gathered in front of Kress Department Store, admiring not a reproduction of a work of art but a world famous original, Giorgione's "Adoration of the Shepherds." The store owner recently had made a gift of it to the nation, a sign noted. "Characteristic of our good cultivated old merchant princes," Wescott wrote. Realizing he would be late for dinner, forgetting his errands, he turned and began the walk uptown, describing the crowds, shops, the changing weather, the feeling of New York.[55]

The way Wescott saw himself in that essay was appropriate, because for much of his life, he loved walking in midtown Manhattan: "I saw myself there in the street very small, with objectivity and subjectivity mixed in a dream."[56]

7

The Bestseller

A GREEK resistance hero named Alex Melas inspired Wescott to change his idea for a World War II novel. On an abandoned draft of "A Fortune in Jewels" Wescott noted: "In the autumn of 1943 a Greek friend suggested I take the fate and symbol of his country instead of France; and with a little anecdote of a Greek family which he mentioned in passing, I began again, to far better purpose."[1]

Wescott salvaged nothing from the manuscript of "A Fortune in Jewels," except the idea of a World War II novel set in Europe. Like *The Pilgrim Hawk,* the book that became *Apartment in Athens* was written quickly, despite a busy schedule. All his life, he did most of his writing between dawn and midmorning. After that he was off to a long day and night of activity.

The working title was "The Change of Heart," and drafts of the novel show how Wescott worked when he was working well.[2] Handwritten pages were on rose-colored paper, and typescript was on white. His working drafts always show several choices of wording within sentences, with none crossed out. His clean final drafts show the choices made (newspaper reporters often write the same way). The first draft of *Apartment in Athens* reveals ease and decisiveness. Even crossed-out pages were quickly replaced by fresh text, clearer and simpler.

At first Wescott began the novel with his narrator, Alwyn Tower, explaining that a Greek resistance hero was in New York to see a specialist about his injured arm and to raise money for the war effort. In one of the early, crossed-out pages, Tower says, "Therefore one afternoon I invited a half dozen trustworthy friends and one or two important charitable personages to meet him." Upon hearing terrible stories of the German occupation, one guest says that she believes old-fashioned, culture-loving Germans still exist. The Greek hero replies, "Well, yes, Madam, Germany changes every so often. They get tired of war, they love culture, they are sorry for those of us whom they have made unhappy. But I think this good mood is dangerous for us." The Greek hero tells the story of a middle-class family in Athens that became servants to a Nazi officer who takes over their apartment.

Wescott realized, however, that Alwyn Tower could not narrate another narrator's story, and that a story about wartime Europe cannot be told from New York. He removed Alwyn Tower, dropped the introductory pages, and used the traditional, omnipresent voice, as he had done in his first novel, *The Apple of the Eye.* His youthful fiction's greatest strength had been its poetic prose. Twenty years after *Apple,* Wescott was a master narrator with a fine-honed edge, thanks in part to the direct influence of Maugham. In fact, he was visiting Maugham throughout February 1944, and Wescott told Barbara that his host was as tough as ever: "William, seeing me close my manuscript book with a sigh of relief at bedtime, inquired blithely, 'Oh, have you finished your story? What, not yet?'"[3] But Wescott worked quickly and found the simple, clear voice he wanted. The novel's first sentence reads: "All this happened to a Greek family named Helianos."

Among his manuscript drafts is a large photo from a 1944 Sunday supplement to the *New York Times* captioned "The Lost Children of Paris." Above the picture of a ragged boy and girl he wrote, "Alex and Leda," the names of the Greek children in his novel. The photo image helped him create the Helianos children, and the boy's name is a tribute to Alex Melas.

Chapter 1 explains that Nikolas Helianos is a publisher who lost his business when Greece fell. He and his wife lost their adored son Cimon in the Battle of Olympus. They have abandoned their home in the suburbs for a four-room apartment in Athens, living in dignified poverty with frail twelve-year-old Alex and backward ten-year-old Leda. Their hardship worsens in 1942 when they are forced to take in a Nazi officer. Captain Ernst Kalter takes the best room for himself and makes the Helianoses his servants. The officer likes the apartment's proximity to his headquarters, and "they soon found, their waiting on him meant more to him than comfort or luxury, and his power over them in little ways day in and day out more than vanity."[4] A haunting story of psychological domination and physical dread follows.

Amid terror in the streets and domestic worry for the safety of their children, the couple tries to deal with the aristocratic but demanding and short-tempered Nazi. Meanwhile, the well-educated Nikolas holds his tongue while he studies this German officer: "The unnerving thing was the great Prussian manner, serene and abstract, almost a mannerism; with insincerity in it somehow, but combined with absolute conviction."[5]

Heart-broken and humbled, the middle-aged couple sleeps chaste on a cot in their own kitchen, and there find their only comfort: "It was the autumn of their love no longer, but suddenly winter, when in fact, with illness and starvation and decrepitude, the coldest husbands and the bitterest wives often do find each other kinder than other people, kinder than nature, kinder than God." Similar moral aphorisms, typical of Wescott, heighten the narrative: "It is never too late for a little happiness even in the shadow of death; and death itself may come and go with fascination like a spell."[6]

After long months, the Nazi officer takes a two-week trip to Germany and returns, greatly changed. Promoted to major, he now seems sad and distracted, yet kinder. Nikolas Helianos's undoing comes when he trusts that apparent change of heart. Kalter begins to invite him into his room after dinner for long talks. Chapter 9 is largely an extended monologue by Kalter that reveals his education and intelligence, as well as his total faith in the destiny of Germany. In the next chapter, Helianos hears a terrible story from Kalter. On his visit to Germany the officer learned that both his sons had been killed in battle, and his home was destroyed in the Allied bombing. Kalter spent several days beside his badly burned wife in the hospital, until she too died. In tears he admits that he is putting his affairs in order and means to commit suicide.

Fooled by this apparent humanity, Helianos makes the fatal mistake of saying that he too had lost a son, and that two men, Hitler and Mussolini, had caused all this tragedy. Kalter explodes in fury, beats him, and has him arrested. The suspense only continues, because Kalter eventually commits suicide and leaves behind a letter condemning Helianos, who does in fact have relatives in the underground.

While other German officers debate her jailed husband's fate, Mrs. Helianos receives a smuggled letter from him. This is the second extended monologue in the book, and it is a very effective one. Written on scraps of paper, Helianos's letter admits that his wife was right not to trust the Germans at all. He says, "In fact the likeable and virtuous ones are far worse than the others as it works out, because they mislead us. They bait the trap. . . . For every few years the Germans mean to come back, to bludgeon our new generation into a psychotic stupor, to set up their slaughterhouses all anew."[7] Word comes that Helianos has been executed. In the end, Mrs. Helianos is determined to send young Alex to her relatives in the underground.

By spring of 1944, the manuscript was nearly finished. Wescott gave a reading on June 6 and remembered, "During the reading I glanced up and saw one of my editors from Harper, and he looked at me with his arms wrapped around himself in an embrace, you know, rocking back and forth and smiling. They wanted it right away. They were afraid that the war might end before it got in print. The trouble was I'd never written anything for a deadline, and they wanted me to write the final chapters and have it all ready within six weeks. Well, I went to my doctor and asked for Benzedrine. I said, 'I won't abuse it and if you don't give it to me I can get it somewhere else.' He did, and it was a help."[8] Wescott admitted that he did use Benzedrine afterward, only a few times a year when he found it useful. He didn't give it up completely, he said, until the early sixties.

Actually, he wrote past the close of the novel. Among his manuscripts is a folder on which he inscribed "The imaginary last chapter" with material that could have been an afterword, as well as several pages he'd deleted from chapter 12 with the notation, "Omitted at Pauline's suggestion." Pauline Potter was close enough to read his work and advise him, and she obviously had his trust.

Wescott turned his novel over to Harper at the July deadline, then took a vacation at Josephine Crane's summer home in Woods Hole, Massachusetts. The publisher was excited—by the mid-forties, publicity and advance sales methods gave an established author a major advantage. But several mishaps threw the book off schedule. He recalled, "My original title was 'The Change of Heart.' Just at the last minute a magazine novelist named Faith Baldwin used it, and I hit upon 'The Children of Wrath,' which no one liked."[9] No one liked it, but no one offered a better title. Among Wescott's papers is his own list of dozens of possible replacement titles, including "The Dead of Night," "The Blind Alley," "The Death Watch," and "The Land of Misgiving."[10] Finally, Harper released a flyer to bookstores for "The Children of Wrath," with a publication date of October 25. A bound proof edition in a gold cover was prepared for reviewers. Suddenly, Wheeler thought of a better title: "Apartment in Athens."

"Too late! No, not too late," Wescott said.[11] Wheeler and Willie Maugham, whose clout was never stronger, approached Harry Scherman of the Book-of-the-Month Club. The company had been interested but unsure about the new novel. Scherman liked the new title, and Wheeler and Maugham suggested diplomatically that he approach the publisher about going back to press, in order to get Book-of-the-Month Club sponsorship. While Wescott remained silent, Cass Canfield at Harper made the obvious choice. As a Book-of-the-Month Club selection, the first edition run would be boosted to four hundred thousand. A bulletin was sent to bookstores, renaming the book and moving publication to early 1945. Even though low-grade paper stock was used in wartime; the publisher must have felt sheepish about pulping the "Children of Wrath" press sheets.

Nevertheless, *Apartment in Athens* contains a notice that the book was "manufactured in strict conformity with Government regulations for saving paper."

There was still pressure to get the book out as fast as possible. In August, Maugham learned that U.S. Marines in France had taken his beloved Villa Mauresque from retreating Germans and were using it for a headquarters. The war was indeed ending. Wescott's agent, Helen Straus of the William Morris Agency, and the publisher made good use of the delay. Auxiliary editions were already being planned, and the book would be serialized in *McCall's* magazine. After years of earning only pocket money for his writing and lecturing, Wescott was assured a successful year ahead. He dedicated the book, "To my brother's wife."

Expectations grew. Old friend Bernadine Szold wanted to show bound galleys to David Selznick and other movie people. Still an odd mix of writer and social butterfly, Szold was now settled in Hollywood. She wrote, "Lillie [Lillian Hellman] had promised me your galleys the minute she was finished with them and by mistake they were returned to New York. I had already spoken to one of my favorite producers at Warners about it, and he asked for it as quickly as possible. Can you possibly have it rushed back to me?" Talk of a movie and some efforts at a play adaptation never went far, but during early 1945 Wescott experienced a kind of publishing roller coaster he'd never known before. "I remember opening a bottle of champagne with Barbara, Lloyd, Monroe, and George, and we were betting how well the book would sell."[12] Harper held a launch party on February 27 and the book was released the next day.

In his usual self-deprecating way, Wescott would later say *Apartment in Athens* wasn't a true bestseller, but by any measure it was. It sold well over half a million copies in its first year alone. The serialized version appeared in the January and February issues of *McCall's*. The Harper edition had a George Platt Lynes portrait of a serious-looking Wescott on the back cover with a call to buy war bonds. It was the Book-of-the-Month cochoice with Richard Wright's *Black Boy*. There was a sturdy, blue-covered Editions for the Armed Services printing, which was the size of a British pack of cigarettes and could fit in a back pocket. Other editions included an anthologized version by *Omnibook;* a Canadian edition by Musson Books, Ltd.; a London edition published by Hamish Hamilton as *Household in Athens,* with a cover illustration of a window looking out to the Acropolis; a translation by Maria Rosa Oliver published in Buenos Aires (Editorial Lautaro) as *En un departamento en Atenas;* and a French edition by the Robert LaFont press. Unlike most World War II novels, postwar editions would appear.

The novelist Edna Ferber wrote: "It seems to me, dear Glenway, that you've written the book of these last ten years. It came last Monday and I didn't put it down until I had finished it. Then I couldn't sleep for thinking of it. . . . Of course, one of its strengths lies in the under-writing. . . . A superb book. Deadly, compassionate, civilized." Willie Maugham wrote: "The beginning is beautifully done and when next you give a course of lectures on the writing of fiction you might very well give it to your students as an example of how a novel should begin. I have a very definite notion that our friend Monsieur Stendhal would have entirely approved of it."[13]

There were dozens of reviews, mostly favorable. "An unforgettable, searing picture," noted *Kirkus*. "It holds you spellbound as you see into the hearts of the Greeks in their efforts to fathom the character of the German," said *Library Journal*. Diana Trilling in the *Nation* praised Wescott's "distinction of prose," but disapproved his using his talent for a war novel, calling it "propaganda." Edmund Wilson in the *New Yorker* noted that all Wescott's novels end gently and that stronger endings would drive home the theme. But Wilson praised the psychological power of the new work: "I have not read any other book—either of fiction or of direct dramatization—which has given me the feeling of starving and stifling, of falling back on interior positions, constructing interior defenses, reorganized and redirecting, behind a mask of submission, the whole direction and aim of one's life, as *Apartment in Athens*." Eudora Welty, in the *New York Times:* "Its moderateness, lack of exaggeration, serenity are as admirable as the Greek ideal they reflect and honor." A. C. Spectorsky in the *Chicago Sun Book Week:* "Wescott's writing here has the leisureliness and compelling force, the calmness and inexorability of a rising tide. It is understated, unadorned. Yet it has the radiating warmth of a great love, and the love for humanity that comes with understanding. . . . It may be remembered, twenty years hence, as the finest book whose roots were in World War II."[14]

Among the fan mail was a letter from someone who turned out to be a bonus for Wheeler. "Herbert Kauffman was a beautiful, handsome man," recalled a friend of Wescott. "He was an officer in the army and loved *Apartment in Athens*, and sent a letter to Glenway with a photo. Glenway gave him to Monroe, and he became one of Monroe's lovers. Glenway used to say, 'I *invented* Herbie Kauffman!'"[15]

What Wescott called his contribution to the war effort included a spring 1945 tour with other writers to sell war bonds, and he was among the first to see films of the camps at Buchenwald, Auschwitz, and elsewhere. "Those of us who had done anything for the Writers' War Board briefly barnstormed in Texas with Louis Bromfield, S. J. Perlman and Kathleen Winsor, helping patriotic ladies to sell war bonds. We were privileged to see our Americans' pitiful triumphant entry into the concentration camps." What he saw of the dead and the near-dead compelled him to bear witness to the films a second time. "Both times I encountered Margaret Case, *Vogue*'s prestigious and somewhat comical fashion editor, no fool, silly but simple. 'Glenway, here again, you ghoul?' she cried in her softly rasping soprano. But she had no explanation for her own so-called ghoulishness." Shocked as he was by the films, Wescott understood their importance, on a level beyond his personal emotion: "My not finding them sickening was horror transcended by tragic imagery, and by ghastly and mysterious historic interest—and wanting to remember, to clear my memory of the useless pathos and animal fright."[16]

The publisher's publicity tour of interviews, broadcast appearances, and bookstore signings continued until spring. Wescott, who had taken his first plane trip in December, felt bullied by the process, what he called "the acting like a success in order to be success," and answering the same questions over and over.[17] One photo shows him in jacket and tie before stacks of his book in a Chicago bookstore, signing copies for a line of customers. It was different from the expatriate years when writers enjoyed success from a distance. Aside from publicity appearances for Harper, he used the agency of W. Colston Leigh to set up lectures. Part of his windfall of income went into refurbishing his and Wheeler's house at Stone-blossom, and that meant he lived for months at the city apartment, when he wasn't traveling.

Finally, in late May the hectic pace suddenly came to a halt. That spring, he enjoyed the quiet of the New Jersey farm as never before. He bought himself a painting by Yves Tanguy and enjoyed the revival of his celebrity. In September, he made a studio recording of the book. Katherine Anne Porter humorously wrote to Wheeler, "I picked up an astrology magazine idly the other day at a newsstand and saw Glenway's fortune in it, so I sent it on. I consider this as being real fame. His name must be a household word for an astrologer to have heard of him."[18]

During the mid-forties, Wescott remained close to W. Somerset Maugham. Wescott was among the first to know when Maugham's favorite nephew, Robin, was wounded in battle, and that the Nazis had taken his large boat *Sarah* from the Villa Mauresque. At seventy, Maugham had his greatest success when *The Razor's Edge* sold a million copies, and Hollywood bought the movie rights. But fame only made his secrets more troubling. Maugham indulged his fondness for very young men with a seventeen-year-old college student, an aspiring poet named David Posner. Later, at legal age, the self-possessed Posner moved on to intimacies with other luminaries—he teased, though he never pleased, Wescott.

Amid his success, Maugham was struck by tragic news when Gerald Haxton fell mortally ill with a virulent form of tuberculosis. Despite their bitter fights of recent years, Maugham rushed to Haxton's side and supported him through six painful months of clinics and hospitals. At the funeral, Wescott later told Maugham biographer Ted Morgan, those who had known Haxton were disturbed to see Maugham sobbing uncontrollably. Afterward, Maugham's nephew Robin came over from London to spend several months with him. Young Robin had fond memories of Haxton, who had led him astray nine years earlier.

Maugham admitted that he was in no rush to return to liberated France. Wescott wrote in a notebook: "In a very matter of fact tone, as the first of his reasons for not wanting to return to Villa Mauresque, Willie gave the fear of ghosts. I understood what he meant, but felt—if this is putting it clearly—that he meant something more than that. A mysterious man." Robin suggested that his uncle write about the flight of the residents of Cap Ferrat when the Germans invaded. Maugham said the British and American consuls ought to have been shot for not warning people sooner, but he thought no one would be interested in the story and that in any case it was all over. To that, Wescott noted, "The punches of literature, always being pulled."[19]

Finally, Maugham's companion-in-waiting, Alan Searle, arrived from London for Maugham's last months in America. Wescott made last visits to Parker's Ferry, for two weeks in January 1946 and two weeks in February. He decided that Searle was not the dynamic and clever man Gerald Haxton had been, but he was gentle, domestic, and loyal. That spring, they were surprised when Edmund Wilson savaged Maugham's new historical novel, *Then and Now,* in the *New Yorker,* turning a review into a personal attack. It was strange because Wilson, whom Maugham respected, secretly admitted to friends that he had never read the novelist's masterpieces, *Of Human Bondage, Cakes and Ale,* and *The Razor's Edge.*[20] Nevertheless, the book sold nearly a million copies in America, and Hollywood bought the movie rights.

Maugham made a last visit to Stone-blossom in April, then departed after a farewell party at the River Club on May 21. Even from France, however, he made his presence felt. The next time Wescott confessed that he was losing confidence in a new novel, Willie lashed out: "Don't tell me that you have fallen back into your old, neurasthenic, detestable habit of leaving a work unfinished just because what you have written doesn't come up to what you saw in your mind's eye before you began to write. It never does. I wouldn't mind betting that even Tolstoy was never quite satisfied with *War and Peace,* nor Flaubert with *Madame Bovary.*"[21]

Wescott didn't let such criticism dim his respect for Maugham. He had written a fine review for *The Razor's Edge.* In a *Harper's Magazine* piece, "Somerset Maugham and Posterity," he presented an overview of Maugham's work and a broadside against his critics. He gave special praise to the little World War II novel *A Christmas Holiday,* explaining that the simple story of an English boy vacationing in Paris and falling in love with a doomed unlucky girl is really about prewar Europe: "It is a political allegory as plain as *Candide;* though far tougher and less pleasant, less cocksure. . . . The last line in *A Christmas Holiday* is: 'The bottom has fallen out of the world,' that is, the holidaying English boy's. Now naturally almost all Europeans say as much; and Americans echo it."[22]

Privately, Maugham shared his deepest feelings with Wescott. After finishing his novel *Catalina,* he admitted, "I cannot tell you what a relief it is to think that I have written my last, my very last novel." Recalling Emerald Cunard, he said: "Yes, Emerald's death was a great grief to me and London will never be the same to me without her."[23] When Nelson Doubleday was dying in December 1948, Maugham returned to New York, stopped the company executives from taking power against Doubleday's wishes, and visited him in Oyster Bay. At Doubleday's funeral in January, Maugham spoke of his publisher's kindness during the war.

Of course, Maugham could just as easily be harsh to his friends. During his New York trips, he and Alan Searle would stay at the Plaza Hotel and visit Stone-blossom. At seventy-five, Maugham had another outburst about Wescott's not finishing a new novel. Wescott recalled Maugham's saying "'Whatever gave you the idea, whatever made you think, that you had the talent to be a novelist?' I was stung for a moment, and I said I'd need to think about that and answer him later. The next day, I said to him that all my life, everywhere I've gone, doors seem to swing wide, windows open, and I hear and understand the lives of the people around me. Willie looked at me and said, quietly, 'Well, that's a very good answer.'"[24]

Wheeler and Wescott's latest apartment was in a very grand building at 410 Park Avenue, and they gave a large party for their friend. Maugham enjoyed the gathering, but when their upstairs neighbor Marlene Dietrich appeared, he felt upstaged and left. Before returning to France, Maugham asked for Wheeler's assistance in buying paintings. Wheeler directed him to just the right galleries and dealers, and Maugham went home with a Renoir, a Rouault, a Monet, and an Utrillo. Months later, Wheeler saw them framed and hanging when he visited Villa Mauresque.

By this time, Wescott was giving more literary lectures, for both income and development of essay material. Two longstanding forums were the City College classes of Professor Henry Leffert and the so-called Monday Classes of Josephine Crane at her 820 Fifth Avenue home. Crane hosted decades of social evenings in which Wescott and many others gave lectures and readings. She also invited Wescott and Wheeler to late summer vacations at her home in Woods Hole, Massachusetts, where they would see such friends as the scholar Jacques Barzun and the playwright Padraic Colum. Wescott also made at least eleven appearances on the radio program *Invitation to Learning,* discussing current books with Columbia University professor Lyman Bryson.

Among Wescott's writings was an art essay for a Camille Pissarro exhibition. He also published reviews of Katherine Anne Porter's *Leaning Tower and Other Stories* and Elizabeth Bowen's *Heat of the Day.* For a journal he wrote about the civilized countryside as he knew it: "The country is essentially poetry, while the city is good prose." His essay "The Moral of F. Scott Fitzgerald" was reprinted in *The Crackup,* Edmund Wilson's popular anthology about Fitzgerald.[25]

While his new novel-in-progress, "Children of This World," was stymied, reprintings of Wescott's books were impressive throughout the forties. First, *The Pilgrim Hawk* appeared in a Chilean anthology as *El Halcón Errante.* Its reputation as a modern classic grew in 1946 as it appeared in a new edition by Hamish Hamilton in London, and was included in *Great American Modern Short Novels,* alongside works by Herman Melville, Henry James, Stephen Crane, Edith Wharton, F. Scott Fitzgerald, Gertrude Stein, and Porter. A Swedish edition followed, *Pilgrimsfalken,* two new editions of *Apartment in Athens* were released, and a translation appeared in *Omnilibro* of Buenos Aires. The next year, three more foreign translations appeared, in Italy, France, and Czechoslovakia. A Bantam paperback came out that carried a banner, in America's new style of sensationalized covers on pocket editions, that read: "A Novel of Revenge after Death!"[26] At the same time, Bantam marked the twentieth anniversary of *The Grandmothers* with a pocket paperback, as did Somerset Books in New York and Ambassador Books, Ltd., in Toronto. The Bantam cover offered a responsible headline, "The Story of a Midwest Pioneer Family," but also an unusually big-breasted farm girl as a cover illustration.

Wescott had a few offers to write stage versions of *Apartment in Athens* but he turned them down and tried one of his own.[27] He cut up copies of the Bantam edition, glued key pages to sheets of paper, outlined six scenes, and typed about fifty pages of dialogue in screenplay format.[28] He even sketched a blueprint for a stage set of the apartment. This attempt at a play, however, went unfinished.

As for his journal, Wescott seemed worried about scandal, often using code names for dozens of people in his world, including Wheeler, Barbara, and Lloyd. But he also wrote candid passages with real names: "Lunch with Gore Vidal. After certain discursive talk about books and book-criticism, and in answer to my inquiry as to Tennessee Williams, he mentioned the baths in Rome as one of the great advantages of living there: 'So wonderfully convenient. Both of us are highly-sexed, so we go to the baths every afternoon, just before dinner. We often have the same boy, and usually it takes no more than fifteen minutes. Sometimes Tennessee gets a little involved. He's sentimental. Physical beauty means a lot to him, and when he gets someone beautiful, he wants to give pleasure. I have a much happier nature. I'm not actually very susceptible to beauty. My needs are so much simpler. I am only interested in orgasm. I can't be bothered with my partner's pleasure or whether he has a good time or not.'"[29] Wescott added that Vidal also told of being invited to bed by Noel Coward and his current young lover, and he found Coward fit and energetic for a man of his age (by then about fifty). In most cases, Wescott's secrets and confessions were his own, but he didn't consider publishing his journals for many years, and much of his reticence was concern for Wheeler.

Wescott was also meeting public figures. In 1948 he met the recently elected senator from Minnesota, Hubert H. Humphrey, at a fundraiser at novelist Laura Z. Hobson's home. A few years earlier Wescott had befriended one of President Franklin Delano Roosevelt's top advisors, Harry Hopkins, and his wife, Louise. About six months after they first met, Wescott, Wheeler, Barbara, and Lloyd learned Hopkins was seriously ill. After he was hospitalized, Hopkins admitted that he and the president had kept his poor health a secret from the public. Knowing their friend loved art, Barbara sent a small Renoir painting, on loan, to cheer Harry during his illness. Six weeks later Hopkins died, and it was up to Wheeler to rush to the hospital and get through the confusion of doctors, friends, and the press to retrieve the Renoir.

Being in the public eye, Wescott received mail from aspiring writers and tried to help the talented. One example was young Charles Miller, whom he invited to Stone-blossom and helped get a Eugene F. Saxton Award from Harper. A charismatic ladies' man, Miller later published several volumes of poetry and a memoir of W. H. Auden, for whom he was a secretary for years. Wescott's interest in helping writers soon became part of his life's work. He had been a member of the Authors Guild for two years when, in 1947, he was elected to the National Institute of Arts and Letters. The Institute was the larger body of an organization that included the American Academy of Arts and Letters. Felicia Geffen, the salaried director at the time, remembered that Wescott hesitated. "He wanted to know if it was a purely honorary distinction or whether it served the arts," she said. "I told him of our programs and activities for supporting artists."[30] Wescott joined and began four decades of devoted work for the organization.

Though he was sometimes naive about literary politics, Wescott's intentions as a member of the Institute were good, and objective. He even considered nominating Hemingway, who had previously refused the honor, until Wheeler dissuaded him.[31] When the novelist Djuna Barnes was in financial need, but was ineligible because of a previous Institute award, he helped her get a Guggenheim grant. Over time, Wescott was drawn into the committee and administrative work of the Academy-Institute, the Authors Guild, and PEN. In addition, Institute president Archibald MacLeish persuaded him to take on the chairmanship of the National Commission for UNESCO.[32] During the forties, his most important work was on matters of international copyright and censorship.

By the late forties, Wheeler himself was a high profile New Yorker. His full-page portrait appeared in the November 1948 issue of *Vogue*. At his parties at 410 Park Avenue were such celebrities as Cecil Beaton, Francis Bacon, Ben Shahn, Gore Vidal, and Christopher Isherwood. Among the regulars were Paul Cadmus, Marianne Moore, Katherine Anne Porter, Tchelitchew and Charles Henri Ford, Diana and Reed Vreeland, Joseph Campbell, the Kirsteins, E.E. Cummings, and others. Wheeler's most amusing annual guests were Osbert and Edith Sitwell, the brother and sister poets famous for their double wit and set-up dry humor. In October 1948, they began their American tour in New York and posed for *Life* magazine's famous photo of a gathering of poets, which is still on display in the back room of the legendary Gotham Book Mart. Poet Charles Henri Ford recalled with a smile, "It was supposed to be a photo of all poets, but somehow Gore Vidal got himself in there." Ford remembered Tchelitchew's clashes with Edith Sitwell. They had been very close in Paris during the early thirties, and she blamed the boyish, blue-eyed Ford for Pavlik's move to America. They made peace through letters but, Ford said, "When the Sitwells came, Pavlik was in all his states. He said of Edith, 'I wish she would go back where she has been!' It was a totally explosive situation that never quite exploded."[33] Wescott sided with Edith, diplomatically. After all, he'd had his own fights with Tchelitchew, who could be excessive and insulting. Paul Cadmus remarked, "I'm sure they had run-ins. Tchelitchew didn't have much use for other artists, really. He was lots of fun to be with, but he was so exaggerated!"[34] After the Sitwells' national tour, Wescott helped Edith get a foreign honorary membership in the Institute of Arts and Letters.

As a public literary figure, Wescott also defended Elizabeth Ames, the director of the Yaddo writers and artists retreat in Saratoga Springs, New York. Robert Lowell and other writers wanted Ames dismissed because one of the Yaddo residents was a Communist. After Wescott wrote the board of directors at Yaddo, the charges were dropped. Elizabeth Ames wrote: "I wish I could really thank you for undertaking to defend me. During these six weeks I continually felt myself to be in a situation similar to Kafka's in *The Trial*."[35]

More than a literary politician and spokesperson, Wescott was also something of a literary thinker or theorist. About this time, he met Thornton Wilder for a night of drink and talk at the Gotham Hotel (today called the Peninsula). They sat in facing armchairs, each with his own bottle of whiskey in an ice bucket, and talked half the night about theories of literature. Wescott followed up the conversation with a sixteen-page letter.[36]

Behind the scenes, Wescott's private life was far more complex than his public persona. At Stone-blossom, matriarch Barbara had become increasingly unhappy and needy. Once, after Maugham and Alan Searle visited the farm, Wescott joked, "P.S. to Alan: He mightily impressed our jailoress and she asks to see him again." Yet, Wescott felt sympathy for the lost carefree friend of his Paris years. Publicly, Barbara had become a major patron of the arts, while Lloyd was a respected Guernsey breeder and gentleman farmer. Privately, she had tried to devote herself to motherhood and raising Deborah, but shied away from the work with a deep sense of failure. When Barbara had a breakdown in 1945, Katherine Anne Porter told Wheeler: "Barbara simply has too many people too close to her all the time, not enough change of pace, not enough freedom. And when you think what a hypersensitive she is, you wonder with real dismay how she can stand her life at all. She needs so many things she doesn't have, it must result in a kind of starvation."[37]

Barbara was treated for depression at Silver Hill Hospital in New Canaan, Connecticut, and saw psychoanalysts for several years. She became emotionally attached to one of them and became estranged from Lloyd although she remained with him. Finally, in May 1947, she confessed all to Glenway in a letter, and included a copy of a very long letter to the psychiatrist she had seen the year before. This was a terrible confidence to share with her husband's brother. She had known Glenway for twenty years, she said, and continued, "Love and faith tower above us, yet we do rise, most gloriously, within them, and I am asking for a chance to draw mine square with yours for the next twenty years."[38] Apparently Glenway's relationship with, and importance to, Barbara was greater than most people realized. Barbara soon turned to world famous therapist Karen Horney, who was known for her feminist and anti-Freud positions. Lloyd turned to mistresses. And their life together continued.

Away from the Wescott clan, 410 Park Avenue was home to all the dynamics of Wheeler and Wescott's larger family. Marianne Moore praised Wescott for his remarks at a memorial service for her mother and said to her dearer friend: "Monroe, how can I help saying that your heroism—and don't belittle it—steadied us and affected a safety that I can never forget." Another old friend, Jean Cocteau, visited New York for one of his film openings and reported that Wescott's lover of the Paris years, Jacques Guérin, was a patron of controversial new novelist Jean Genet. Wescott disliked Genet's violent themes, and in his journals wrote, "Jean Genet, a kleptomaniac assassinophilic pornographic writer, is the great celebrity in Paris now."[39] Cocteau's own news was of his new companion, Edouard Dermit, whom he made his adopted son and heir.

George Platt Lynes was now living in Hollywood. After Jon Tichenor left him, he took a job with the Los Angeles office of *Vogue* in May 1946 and stayed for three years. Bernadine Szold introduced him to the movie industry crowd, including actress Janet Gaynor and her husband, Adrian, and George produced some of his best portraits of actors, artists, and writers, including Katherine Anne Porter. Lynes continued photographing male nudes, often sharing pictures with Lincoln Kirstein in New York. Kirstein was married to Paul Cadmus's sister, Fidelma, and kept his interest in males hidden behind a gruff public image. But his letters to Lynes about the California models revealed the youthful fawning and admiration they must have shared in their school days.[40] In Hollywood, Lynes's undoing was a boyfriend who redecorated his lavish house, then presented him with a huge bill. On top of his other extravagances, it led to bankruptcy. No one was surprised.

Wheeler and Wescott's friends included a number of younger lovers. One, Christian William Miller, or Bill Miller, had been one of the most strikingly beautiful of George's models. Miller was a lover of Wheeler's and a family friend for many years. A later Wheeler intimate, Ralph Pomeroy, remembered, "Bill would go to a gallery and all the women and all the men would faint!" Wescott's young friend Bernard Perlin said, "Bill Miller was ga-ga-gorgeous!" Charles Kaiser's gay history of New York, *The Gay Metropolis,* states, "Bill Miller is also famous among his contemporaries as one of the most gorgeous men in 1940s Manhattan. Paul Cadmus drew him, George Platt Lynes photographed him, and everyone wanted him."[41]

One of Wescott's minor flings was a young man named Yuri, who had briefly been lovers with Klaus Mann. Lynes had photographed Yuri, and Mann promised that he was "heaven in bed." Wescott remembered, "A marvelously beautiful boy. A big blond Russian with tremendous muscles and a face rather like Nijinski. Wheat-colored hair and lovely skin and lovely fragrance. It was like going to bed with sweet butter and toast. He was a truck driver in New Jersey, and later married and had lots of children."[42] Yuri told Wescott that he wasn't very interested in homosexual sex, but liked it because "it's the path of least resistance." Another interesting character was Patrick O'Higgins, a red-haired, handsome veteran of the Irish Guards whom George met in California and sent to Wescott. Talented and charming, O'Higgins became popular among Wescott's peers. There was also John Yeon, a young architect from Portland who became known for his buildings in the Northwest. This affair was sporadic but held some potential for Wescott, and they met occasionally in Portland, Seattle, and San Francisco.

Far more meaningful was the artist Bernard Perlin. Lean, sensual, and smart—and captured that way in a Lynes portrait—Perlin was a worthy intimate of Wescott's in the early forties. After Perlin became involved with another young artist, Robert Drew, he remained a lifelong friend. He was a World War II photographer for *Life* magazine, received Guggenheim grants and other art awards, often worked in Rome, and was known for his silverpoint portraits. When Wescott found a new love, he wrote to Perlin about the importance of love in anyone's life. He titled his copy of the letter "Best Foot Forward in Love" and it reads in part, "Do you know, dear, one of the noble inconveniences of love is the need or desire to keep putting one's best foot forward. It is wondrous when it works; sometimes even if no one else is persuaded except oneself."[43]

Handsome and sensual, Mark Pagano was the new young love. Beginning in 1946, Wescott enjoyed what he called "a year of love," the most ideal relationship he had ever known. Pagano was a designer, wrote poetry, and made a fine companion in Wescott's world of museums, ballet, and concerts. But once again Wescott was disappointed. Early in 1947, Pagano broke off their relationship. Soon he resumed it, but on a less intense and exclusive basis. Wescott keenly felt the difference. He complained to Thornton Wilder, "My life itself has been exceedingly painful, in a deprivation of love, in a cessation of hope. . . . I have found it practically impossible not to grieve for what I cannot have."[44]

Finally, Wescott found a way to fill the needs that Wheeler could not. Carl Malouf, thirty-one and an Army veteran, was an artist who designed department store windows, and he liked to host parties for gay friends. Malouf remembered how they met in 1947: "I was staying at Ocean Beach, Fire Island, early in the spring and it was lonely and cold, too cold to paint. I saw smoke coming from the chimney of a nearby house and knocked on the door. There was Glenway in a chair, reading to Bernard Perlin and his friend Bob Drew. I said I was desperate for something to read and Glenway gave me something." They exchanged phone numbers, and Malouf knew a publishing house editor who encouraged the friendship. "My friend Hal Vursell wanted the man who wrote *The Pilgrim Hawk,* because he thought it was the best piece of writing in English that had ever been done," he recalled. Stocky, sensual, and a loyal friend, Malouf was a born storyteller, Wescott decided. Malouf told Wescott that he had recently picked up a boy who seemed a runaway, perhaps dangerous. When he noticed the young man looking at his books, he asked him if he had any favorite authors. The boy replied, "Scott Fitzgerald. Glenway Wescott."[45]

Malouf's youthful parties were an oasis for Wescott. At first Malouf lived in a cold-water flat at East Fifth-sixth Street with a young Navy veteran, Tommy Sullivan. Then Malouf found a bigger apartment on East Fortieth Street. "Glenway loved it," he remembered. "He said, 'It's perfect for my purposes.'" Some of the parties were wild, some were tame. Before one party, Wescott asked Malouf if there was anyone special he would like to attend. Malouf recalled asking, "'Anyone?' and Glenway said, 'Anyone.' So I said that young man Capote. I think he's the best of the southern writers." The party ran late into the night, but there was no sign of Capote. Finally, there was a knock on the door and Capote came in. Amid the uncleared table and boys asleep on the floor, he politely sat and talked with Wescott and Malouf. "When he went to the door to leave," Malouf said, "Truman held out his hand and said, 'I want to thank you for opening up your lovely home to me.'"[46]

Malouf and Tommy Sullivan, who was also an artist, loved Wescott and the three met almost weekly. Wheeler did not approve, but Wescott's new circle of young friends brought an important balance to his life over the next several years.

What cannot be overstated is the permanent bond between Wescott and Wheeler, whatever their other relationships. Their letters over the years say it best. Wescott once boarded a plane to California at La Guardia Airport, with plans to visit Isherwood and William Caskey, George Platt Lynes, Katherine Anne Porter, and John Yeon. He feared flying, and began a letter to Wheeler, who was with Willie Maugham in France: "In this little moment of reputed danger only my mind ever feels the slightest fear; my heart takes command of me and it has no concern except of love of you. If I were to meet with disaster, it would mean very little except farewell, and such is the habit of our lifetime, so good, that even the word farewell seems to suggest finding you again somewhere after awhile—and that (here we go, up, with a terrible buzz) and that is all I need to know of immortality."[47]

Wescott shared with Wheeler a transcendent experience in May 1949, one that linked their public and private lives in a profound way. Good timing made it possible for Wescott to bring together E. M. Forster, Joseph Campbell, and Dr. Alfred C. Kinsey of the Institute for Sex Research. He recalled, "I was very active in the Academy and Institute and it was time for the annual Blashfield address, for which there's plenty of money. Archie MacLeish was president of the Academy and I invited Forster. When he wrote back and said he would like to bring his friend Bob Buckingham, a policeman, we managed to get money enough for both of them."[48]

At the same time, Wheeler, just returned from France and Italy where he met with Picasso, Braque, and other artists, was planning to see Alfred Kinsey. Wescott explained, "Kinsey had been coming around to the Museum of Modern Art. He discovered it was great fun to interview painters, and of course he came to Monroe. When I first met him he had five hundred [sexual] histories of painters and sculptors, both sexes and all types. Monroe had helped him get them, from one to another and recommending him to other people. He took Monroe's history, and it was very amusing because he was fascinated by Monroe. And when Kinsey was done with him, he said, 'Mr. Wheeler, you're not unique, you wouldn't want to be unique. There are hundreds like you, but not thousands.' Ha! And Monroe said he'd never been so vain in his life. He could scarcely get his hat on all week, he said, because it was exactly true. He didn't want to be unique, but he didn't want to be everyman."[49]

Kinsey was still in town when Forster arrived, said Wescott, "so when they were going to be here at the same time and I hadn't met either of them, Monroe said, 'Well, we'll have a little dinner party.'" At the dinner, their interests made for great conversation. Forster, author of *A Passage to India,* and Joseph Campbell, mythologist and Sanskrit scholar, discussed with Kinsey the erotic sculpture of Kajaraho and other temples, and the sexual legends of gods and goddesses. Bob Buckingham talked about his police work and the sex laws of England, and Kinsey mentioned some of the research on the different reactions of males and females to pornography. Wescott was fascinated. "Forster was enchanted with Kinsey," he said. "Only about 15 percent of women like indecency and enjoy it. They pretend to, to please their men, but it doesn't do anything for them, as they say. It actually turned out to be one of Kinsey's discoveries; he found that the arousal patterns were very, very different. It happened that young zoologists, animal biologists in laboratories all over the country, just at that point had found a difference in the cerebral cortex of male and female animals, including the human. And the upshot of that meant that most men are aroused by imagination, and fantasy, and books and pictures. And women for the most part are aroused by the presence of the partner, and caresses, physical touch, and memories of past sexual experiences."[50] Before leaving, Kinsey asked Wescott to visit the Institute for Sex Research in Bloomington, Indiana, in July.

Forster made his appearance at the Academy of Arts and Letters. "Morgan—that's what his friends called him—had written a piece for us called 'Art for Art's Sake,' which is in his best nonfiction book, *Two Cheers for Democracy,*" recalled Wescott. "It was a great success, the most successful address we've ever had. And I was allowed to pick all the Blashfield speakers for years after that. I never got anybody as good, and we got some awful stinkers."[51]

After the speech at the Academy, Wescott's sister Elizabeth drove them all to Stone-blossom for the weekend. During his stay at the farm, and with his friend Paul Cadmus in Greenwich Village, Forster, then seventy, was encouraged about his unpublished novel *Maurice,* a story about love between Englishmen of different classes. There were antigay laws in England, but he began to consider a posthumous edition in America. "Actually it was very important for Forster," Wescott said, "because at that point he still did not think he could ever publish his homosexual novel *Maurice* in England."[52]

Forster had a copy of the manuscript with him during the 1949 trip. Cadmus recalled drawing a portrait of Forster while they were visiting Harvard: "I was sitting on the ledge of the window at his room in Cambridge and he was a little below me, and he read *Maurice* while I was drawing him. Morgan [Forster] didn't want it published in Bob Buckingham's lifetime, because it would have ruined Buckingham's life as a policeman, his mates and all that sort of thing, and he was married. Morgan was very fond of Buckingham's wife."[53] Over the years, however, Cadmus would encourage Forster, Wheeler would transport a revised manuscript of *Maurice* from London, and eventually Christopher Isherwood and Wescott would be involved directly in the book's publication.

The issue of gay civil rights was not lost on Wescott and Wheeler, though they were more privileged than most gay Americans in midcentury. But even they learned that they were protected to only a certain extent. In 1947 they had been burglarized at gunpoint at the Park Avenue apartment.[54] To their surprise, the doormen told the police that they had a number of young male friends. A detective visited Wheeler for two hours at his office in the museum, trying to get the names and addresses of their male friends. Wheeler refused, furious that the investigation was turning to their private lives. Luckily the police found the burglar and the matter was dropped, but they remembered the incident and learned a lesson. Now Kinsey's work and Forster's novel spoke to them of a different possibility, a freer society.

Less inspiring was Wescott's summer at Stone-blossom. He cared for his parents when both had health problems. Worse, his boyfriend Mark Pagano fell into a sexual relationship with his divorced sister, Elizabeth! Pagano was doing odd jobs for Lloyd at the farm. One day he and Elizabeth were sunbathing and Mark found himself attracted—partly, he admitted, because Elizabeth's double mastectomy of years earlier had left her with a boyish figure. The five- or six-month affair infuriated Wescott. Wheeler summed it up in a note to Forster: "Poor Glenway has had a rather sticky summer." Both his parents had operations, in different hospitals, he explained, and Barbara's visiting father, Francis Harrison, in a third. "And Glenway has been looking after them all. At the same time his sister fell in love with one of his boyfriends, which didn't please him much, to put it mildly."[55]

At least Wescott kept his sense of humor. When Katherine Anne Porter gave up her job and home at Stanford University—the latest in a long string—Wescott wrote in his journal: "She is as bad about her real estate as I have been about my love affairs; with some abler operator always coming along and foreclosing on us."[56]

Most important, Wescott had found something exciting, new, and different from the expectations of his career and demands of his family. The liberating work of Alfred Kinsey would involve him for years and affect him for the rest of his life.

8

Dr. Kinsey and the Institute for Sex Research

GLENWAY WESCOTT and Alfred Kinsey became friends almost immediately. For one thing, Wescott saw past the researcher's serious manner and appearance. Others could not, and misread him completely. "My brother Lloyd didn't like him at all," Wescott remembered. "Lloyd said he was 'the kind of person who could spit in your eye from ten feet distance.' You know, he had this churchy sort of moralistic, melancholy face, an impassive, sorrowful sort of face, with a marvelous grin every now and then. I think he had the most infectious smile—but he only laughed about once a month! And his sense of humor was really irresistible. When you got to know him you loved his eyes. You could amuse him. He never would stop taking notes and he never would crack a smile, until once in a blue moon. The picture that I have of him in a little frame is laughing."[1]

When Wescott first visited the Institute for Sex Research in Bloomington, Indiana, Alfred was in California interviewing men at San Quentin Prison. He recalled, "We first met in May 1949, and then in July I went out there. I was going to a writers' conference, and I called at the house and got Mrs. Kinsey. He was away. But I got used to the campus and worked very hard. Then he came to New York in the autumn and asked me to give my sexual history."[2]

Because Wescott had read *Sexual Behavior in the Human Male,* which the Institute published in 1948, he knew what to expect. "We both laughed because it went so fast. I knew the *Male* volume almost as well as he did, I knew it by heart, so that I was able to guess the questions from the material. I would answer three or four of his questions in a row. I was being naturally candid and he was following an absolute routine, taking things down in code on three-by-five cards and moving as fast as he could. And it took less than two hours. He was a very easy man to talk to, of course that was a large part of it."[3]

Although the interview went well and Kinsey found him an interesting case, Wescott's history wasn't included in the Institute's overall statistics because he fell into one of the extremes on the male sexuality scale. "I wasn't put in his statistics. When he told me I was in the 4 percent group, he said the odd thing is that at the other extreme about 4 percent of men are so exclusively geared to the female that in no circumstances—their closest friend, or in an emergency, or God knows what—could they have any kind of erection, any kind of sexual response whatever, with another male. And they throw them out of the big statistics. So I was never counted, and neither were these great big studs who couldn't respond to males. But you see, what that means is that 96 percent of men, in some circumstance, could be aroused, they figure."[4]

Even with a subject as prepared and candid as Wescott, Kinsey knew how to change the pace during uncomfortable moments. Wescott said, "I'd get nervous about something or I'd get tired. The questions would become harder, or he'd get tired. Then he'd light a cigarette and shuffle his cards, and change the subject, ask something different. He did that with everybody, when you were not answering questions freely, or he was touching a nerve. Then he'd start some other angle, shift the whole order of question. The questions were always the same and arranged in an order, but there were certain questions for writers, certain questions for painters, whatever odd was in your history. There was an extra set of questions for people who had experience with children, or had extraordinary circumstances in their youth. But he said to me, this was perhaps the first or second pause, 'Am I right in getting the impression that you feel somehow, to some extent, you haven't had quite your share of sexual pleasure, sexual activity?' And he got the cards out and I think there was a little play acting in all this, and then counted on his fingers, and said, 'Well, you'll be interested to know that you're above average, not much above, but above.' Which amazed me."[5]

Wescott's knowledge of the Institute's work led Kinsey to ask for help with their mountains of reading material. "Then and there," said Wescott, "he asked me to help him with erotic reading matter. He asked me to come out at Christmas time, to look at their library and suggest what they might get rid of, what things to acquire, and to advise the young librarians what things to keep." Over the next five years, Wescott visited the Institute when he could, usually in midsummer and at the end of year. More often, Kinsey was in New York. Early on, Wescott came to respect his friend's devotion to science. Before taking on sexual research, Kinsey had worked in the field of zoology. "He was the greatest specialist in the individual variations in the gall wasp," explained Wescott. "And out there still, in my day, he had little things that looked like Egyptian coffins, little highly varnished hardwood boxes with lids, and inside them all the gall wasps imaginable would be on little pins along in rows according to size and color. All these were variations in the individual that didn't affect the species. And the only statistics known to zoology that had as great a range of variation as that was the human sexual statistic—that they knew. The variations were one to four hundred, I think they found, particularly as to ejaculation rate, and spread over periods of time."[6]

One difference in Kinsey's new line of study was the need for absolute confidence. That was a hard lesson for a novelist to learn. Wescott remembered, "They found one person who had only one orgasm in his whole lifetime, and that was sitting on a piano stool with a friend. It was the music that seemed to make it happen, and he had a spontaneous ejaculation. He was very young and after that he had none. And they couldn't find anything wrong with him physically. He just didn't erect and he didn't spend. And then they found somebody else, the opposite extreme, a man who had twenty-five ejaculations a week for thirty years. . . . He had the highest ratio that they found over that period of time. Kinsey said he couldn't tell me who it was. The confidence of the research was very severe, even with me. It was a terribly long time before he would even trust me with certain things. But in this case he said all he could tell me about this man was that he was a scholarly, very successful lawyer. What I wanted to know was if all these ejaculations were with one partner, or whether they were homosexual or heterosexual or both. He just didn't like answering those questions at all, just on general principle."[7]

From this point on, Wescott did not separate his interest in Kinsey from other parts of his life. He began New Year's 1950 with Carl Malouf and Tommy Sullivan in a round of parties, including one at George Platt Lynes's apartment. Then he joined Monroe Wheeler at Stone-blossom where Katherine Anne Porter was visiting. All these friends and many more were soon Kinsey subjects. Wescott still devoted himself to the Institute of Arts and Letters, taking on a term as one of its vice presidents, the first of three three-year terms during his membership. But he felt nothing was more important than Kinsey's work. What's more, Kinsey's compassionate, nonjudgmental view of sexuality was good for Wescott psychologically. He experienced health problems over the next year, and his positive response may have been due to his state of mind—much improved from periods of depression in the late forties.

In late February 1950, Wescott noticed on his upper gum a small yellow-white lump. Like so many men of his day, he was a heavy smoker.

After three decades of smoking, he awakened to the damage he'd done to his health, perhaps contributing to the bouts of pneumonia in 1935 and 1942. He admitted, "I smoked packs of cigarettes every day. I'd wake up in the night and smoke in the dark, and again the first thing in the morning. My doctor took a look and said, 'I don't think it's cancerous; it's not white enough, but you never know.' I asked if I'd have to stop smoking and he said, 'Well, if you can. Did you see that old gentleman who came in before you? He's a retired admiral from the navy. He stopped, but he stopped too late.'" The next morning, March 1, when Wescott returned to have the lump removed, he determined to give up smoking, except for one last one. "I asked for a cigarette before the operation while they were getting the knives out. They brought out a whole dish full of knives and boiling water, and he said, 'Look at the superstition of the medical profession. I've got enough sterilized weaponry here to make mincemeat of you from head to foot, with which I will proceed to remove from your mouth a thing smaller than a lima bean.'"[8]

Although there was no malignancy, Wescott kept his promise to stop smoking. "It took me six months before the urge left," he said, "but I had a dividend before that. I had the worst respiratory tract you can imagine. I used to snort and sneeze and blow, and cough and spit, and in winter I couldn't take a full breath. I'd have to take a little sip, you know, otherwise I'd choke and cough. In fifteen days that was over. My glands would ache, I'd have to rub them. My mouth would itch. And the amazing thing was I learned about breaking habits. In the past I wouldn't get into a bathtub unless I had cigarettes within reach. And so every time I got in the bathtub in the country I would shiver all over and flush and itch. And finally it got to the point where the bubble burst and it was over. But when I came to the apartment in New York, I had to go through it all over again. So, little by little I broke it."[9]

During his recovery, Wescott was treated to a rare birthday party by several of his talented friends, including Joseph Campbell, who arrived with cognac, George Lynes with red tulips, and Pauline Potter with a photo book of Picasso ceramics.

Other health problems arose. That summer, while Wescott was helping Wheeler write a museum publication and magazine article on the painter Chaim Soutine, he felt what seemed to be writer's cramp. Over months it worsened, until half his body was in pain. Finally, his doctors found a damaged disc in his neck and gave him a neck brace to correct it. The condition and treatment recurred several times later in life. More serious was the problem he discovered in the early months of 1951. "I knew I wasn't drinking any more than I had all my life," he said, "which was a good bit. I'd drink two very dry martinis before lunch and two very dry martinis before dinner, then wine if there was any, and just before going to bed I would take a little straight whisky, Irish whisky. But that's quite a lot, for a regular number of years. And I hated being drunk and never was. Suddenly, that year, I would get up from my chair and fall down on my knees, my legs would just give way. It didn't happen very often, but I knew that something was going wrong." He remembered a warm day in early April when he was working in the drawing room at Stone-blossom: "There was a table and a chair in the middle of the room, facing my Tanguy painting, with the fireplace in back of me. Beautiful room. I was writing something about Hemingway, waiting for the lunch call from Anna, and suddenly the room began to spin. Pheeww! I thought, you damn fool, drinking dry martinis on an empty stomach. I got up to walk around the house, and I saw a woodchuck behaving in a funny way in the meadow where the bulls were. I went outside to see and got up on the top post of the fence—and fell off and hit the ground with such a thud! And the whole sky went round, the field went round—I might as well have been on the Bowery! I went to the doctor the next day and he gave me estrogen for two weeks. He told me I could drink again, but recommended I didn't. I never did, except for an occasional wine or one beer."[10] Or one small strong martini made by Wheeler. And so, within a year Wescott gave up two longtime bad habits and thereby improved his physical and—it must be noted—his psychological health.

Meanwhile, he was learning much more about Kinsey's work. For example, there were studies on erotic content in the performing arts as well as in painting, sculpture, and literature. The Institute interviewed actors from three different theater groups performing Tennessee Williams's *A Streetcar Named Desire,* comparing actors in specific roles. Some were Wescott's friends. He knew that "Kinsey was very close to Uta Hagen, and very, very close to Cornelia Otis Skinner. . . . He took the histories of one hundred and fifty or more actors, and they were all different types, amateurs as well as the stars. He wanted Tennessee, and Tennessee refused. Kinsey asked me if I would intercede, and I did in a very gentle way. I urged Tennessee to do it, and said it was a most amusing experience, but I knew he would just be shirty with me if I tried to talk him into it. He was a great resister of sales talks. I think they got his history in the end. Maybe Wardell Pomeroy got it."[11] Williams finally did visit the Institute and correspond with Kinsey.

On one of his plane trips to Indiana, Wescott jotted down a few unimportant lines that reflect the novelist's eye as well as the elegance of his pen: "Half an hour has had to be wasted circling over Pittsburgh before we could get down to its foul dim atmosphere. Nevertheless a pretty atmosphere, reminiscent of Whistler, prettier than Whistler because of the bright light from on high. As we circle we keep passing two radio masts painted red and white, like masts of a festive ship sinking."[12]

At Bloomington, he read and sorted the erotic writing and pornography, and Kinsey asked about his thoughts. Wescott replied that he was

interested in it for various reasons, mostly verbal, and colloquial, and so forth. And he said, "Well, none of us have been able to read them, they're so boring." He said the second largest collection of classical material—second only to the Vatican—was there. And then as much of the contemporary as he could get. And quite a lot of amateur pornography—one bunch of which was very interesting, because in Paris there was an old millionaire who hired Henry Miller, Anaïs Nin, I forget who else, to write fancy pornographic novels, as hardcore as they could make them. He bought the manuscripts, and the writers kept copies. And Kinsey got all that. I looked forward to that with great pleasure, but found it bored me terribly. It was all just like ordinary Henry Miller watered down, and more carelessly, and cynically, and a little bit unrealistically. And as for Anaïs, it's the same all the time, you know, it's this marvelous, vaporous—you don't know whether it's the heart, or the mind, or the vagina that's doing the talking, and you're all mixed up and so is she.

I read all that. And they had cupboards three times as big for the sadomasochistic material—which at the time existed in the ratio of possibly six to one, or maybe ten to one. And they were very interested because they found there was evidence of the S/M material leading to imitation. They found more and more as they looked into it that genital pornography leads to masturbation; it doesn't lead to imitation, it doesn't change people's behavior very much. And finally they just asked me if I would read the whole thing. I'm a speed-reader so I just settled down at once while I was out there. Of course, I would zoom through, and I would skip if they were absolutely boring, and make notes. And then I delivered a quite formal speech. I took for my subject the possibility of defining pornography in the pejorative, as distinct from erotic writing, maintaining that there wasn't any difference in the degree of candor. The difference was somewhere else, and I tried to situate it. I thought I could point out in any given book a page or two that was erotic writing that approached the literary art. And some material just didn't make the grade at all, even though it might excite one. But you couldn't remember it, you couldn't even reread it. And I lectured like that. It was all rather boring. But it established my credibility.[13]

What took longer to establish was his ability to keep a secret. In the first year, Kinsey's assistants joked about Wescott's talkative nature. "They trained themselves to keep the confidence of the research," he said. "And they had a funny way of talking, so that they wouldn't be overheard in restaurants. A 'one' was a component of homosexuality out of 'six,' you know. And they tried to teach me. They got so shocked by me every time I opened my mouth. Everyone would listen to me. And I said, 'Now look, I never talk about the research in the restaurant. I only talk about myself.' Kinsey said, 'But you know, it makes a scandal for us just to be *seen* with anyone as candid as you are!' Little by little I learned."[14]

During visits to the Institute for Sex Research, Wescott worked in the library by day, then visited with Alfred and Clara Kinsey. He described Alfred as

an absolute fanatic. He was only interested in four things in life. His research. His family—he was passionate about his children and much in love with his wife, who was a wonderful woman. Then he allowed himself an afternoon of gardening, any Saturday he was home—which amounted to about one Saturday a month, or possibly two. He had a marvelous garden, all of which he'd done himself. This huge old body with this heavy chest and heavy belly, muscular old legs. He looked much older than I, and wasn't. And in the evening after dinner—Mrs. Kinsey was a great cook—was Alfred's other passion: serious music and his collection of phonograph records. After dinner we'd have a little concert, with Mrs. Kinsey, and sometimes he had some other people for dinner, other members of his family, his beautiful son, or somebody from the research. Or sometimes we'd be alone.

Then at nine thirty or ten o'clock he and I would go down to the offices, and Alfred would open the packages of material that had come in and were addressed to him, and sort out the sex journals. Sometimes Mrs. Kinsey went with us because she was the only person he trusted absolutely. He said the one thing about her that he admired most was that she was tolerant of everything except other people's intolerance. She was absolutely silent, absolutely close-mouthed, and so he assigned her the job of typing out the sex journals. They had a whole lot of sex journals coming in. They would ask peculiar people to write it all down. Clara was the most innocent woman you can imagine. She'd been one of his students and she was a scientist, a botanist, who took courses with him in zoology, and fell in love with him. She was about ten or twelve years younger than he, at least. And she was nature mad, she gave swimming lessons to the girl scouts, and she organized all the nature tours for the whole state at that time, and everybody bought her wild berries. Kinsey to amuse himself made a collection of edible and poisonous plants of the northwest United States, a part of his hobby of gardening. And she had recipes and used to cook all this. It was an atmosphere so loving and so, not only tolerant but innocent.[15]

Kinsey took histories of Wescott's friends and lovers, and was especially interested in an air force veteran named Miksche. Wescott said, "Carl Malouf, who always went to Ocean Beach, Fire Island, picked up this enormous northwestern, a Czechoslovakian man named Michael Miksche who was about six foot three. He was extremely dangerous, but a deep person. He fell in love with me."[16] A bomber pilot during the war who now made a living as a commercial artist, the muscular, crewcut, bisexual Miksche was a fascinating subject. Malouf himself remembered first meeting him in Sis Norris's, a gay-friendly bar at Ocean Beach: "A woman came up to me and said, 'You see that guy over there? He can fuck all night.' And he did, he fucked like a mink. He was an athlete, a sexual athlete."[17] Miksche was also an exhibitionist and became one of Kinsey's most important volunteers.

As Wescott learned more about the study of sexual behavior, he tried to understand it more objectively. "Sexual kindness is a rare thing," he wrote, "especially in men. Women on the whole are kinder because it is easier for them to simulate their excitements, even their climaxes. Most men are afraid of seeming impotent, especially of seeming impotent to themselves."[18]

Without a doubt, his most memorable visit to the Institute for Sex Research took place from July 7 to July 19, 1951. It coincided with a writers' conference at the School of Letters on the Indiana University campus where Wescott gave lectures with Allen Tate and Tate's wife, Caroline Gordon. Afterward he worked with Kinsey and associate Paul Gebhard, who gave him an office in Wylie Hall. One project involved grouping modern writers by categories of achievement and later penciling in their sexual identities, where possible. First, Wescott showed the researchers only the writers by type, with no sexual notations. "They showed the English professors and they said they didn't think a more impartial list could be made up by anybody," Wescott said. "I added the sexual categories afterward, by hand." His pencil notations of *ht, ho,* and *bi* for heterosexual, homosexual, and bisexual showed high percentages in the latter two categories.[19]

At night, Wescott began to see some of the films. As he recalled them later,

> Never before had I seen really hardcore films. In those days, Kinsey didn't collect any commercial "smoker" films—he was very contemptuous of them—especially the male and female ones, because you see the females can fake it, and they do. . . . But they kept samples of everything. They wouldn't show them to me. The only ones he would show to me were the amateur films that people had taken of themselves or of their lovers, and some of them were very beautiful.
>
> And all the animal films were so extraordinary. He got [Albert Shadle from the State University of New York at Buffalo] to photograph porcupines for him, and he wanted to show them to me. And this was the most beautiful film. While porcupines are in heat they copulate every twenty minutes, and in the meantime they go on nibbling their food. Then finally they start to nudge each other. Then they begin to pet each other and she rears up, they both stand up, and he throws his arms around her, and they kiss! They put their faces together, one arm on another, and they pat each other and then he feels her responses and puts his paw on the back of her neck and by main force presses her down on the ground under him. He comes down on her and in that precise moment she opens up all her quills and meanwhile his little cock is standing up—and me with my castration complex, I crossed my arms over my lap! He fornicates, it takes a number of strokes, quite fast, and while that's going on his back humps up to his neck and forward. And as he pulls out of her, up from this bed of thorns, he goes down on himself. It's a washing thing, and that's the end of it. Then he relaxes. And it happens every time, it's all built in. And Kinsey said behind me, in this excited voice, "Did you see that?" And finally he said, "Do you mind if I play it again?" And then he would sit and watch it over.[20]

By this time, there was great trust between the two friends. Kinsey at first knew little about openly gay people but came to understand the complex relationship of Wheeler and Wescott, even with all their secondary lovers. Wescott laughed, remembering:

> Of course, at first he saw that Monroe and I were what we are, the oldest living married gay couple, and then he understood about the others. He suddenly said one day, "I thought you were the least promiscuous people I've met, and now I find that you're promiscuous, only in a somewhat different way. One, two, three, four, five," he counted on his fingers! He was so funny. And of course he worked so hard all the time that his misunderstandings were haste. You see, by this time the *Male* volume was finished. But what people don't realize is that the most important writing of all, and the most important writing about the homosexual, is in the *Female* volume. And he'd asked me to come out there and help him write it. That was the last four chapters of the *Female* volume, which are: "Arousal in the Male," "Arousal in the Female," "Orgasm in the Male," and "Orgasm in the Female." And then comparison not only in charts but in things that happened in the whole body. That's an extraordinary piece of writing and in a spiritual way a kind of pornography, because fourteen things happen in the male body during orgasm. They are all specified and a great many of them also occur when you're drunk, the same things, and they traced all of that.[21]

Wescott knew that the Institute was creating films of volunteers having sex or masturbating. In fact, he had suggested a number of his younger friends, including Michael Miksche, who had been filmed having sex with the writer Sam Steward the previous year. Now Wescott was asked to volunteer. Kinsey said,

> "We want to know how people masturbate." And I said, "Well, as you probably understand by this time, my whole orientation toward sex is closely bound up with the fact that I hate my own body." I couldn't stand my horrid little penis, and then I lost one of my testicles at the time of the writing of my first book, and so on. And I've got a malformed chest, and I've never wanted to be looked at or paid attention to. I've never wanted anybody to do anything for me or to me for my pleasure. I learned to extend the range of my sexual activity to please other people. And generally speaking, I think of myself as having borrowed other people's sexual organs and physiques, and forgotten all about my own, in as far as I was happy.
>
> So I said, "I'm not the type." He said, "If it's difficult for you, you can use anything you want out of the collection." And I took not the hardcore pornography but the great picture books out of the past, the most marvelous books, old German books of the erotic Greek vases, and all that sort of thing.
>
> I said, "You may be surprised what I feel about it. I want to enjoy myself somehow or do something odd, something no one else has done." Finally I said, "Have you ever had anyone use a dildo?" "No!" said he. And they had two of the most beautiful dildos I had ever seen. Some artist in Greenwich Village had made for Kinsey two dildos of latex that were just the most comfortable degree of hardness and flexibility; soft on the surface and firm, with rather abstract curly hair, and a

seat of very naturalistic testicles. I went to my room feeling very uncomfortable. "Well," he said, "you can call it off in the morning if you funk it." He said, "We're interested in people who refuse, that's one part of the statistic, and we're interested in people who fail. This whole idea that you have to show off or do something wonderful is the furthest thing in the world. We want to know what you're like when you're failing, if you fail. I have to beat you over the head to get you to take a scientific point of view about anything!"

This was fairly early on, and I laughed. And I went to bed heavy hearted, dreading the whole thing. I went the next day and it was really amazing. Bill Dellenback, the official photographer, was up there, setting up while I ate my breakfast. Then I went up to this large room, with a pad on the floor, and no curtains around, but a curtain of lights falling down from the ceiling so that you could hear Kinsey and the photographer but you couldn't see them. If you didn't look straight out you were perfectly comfortable because there was no light in your eyes; it was just a curtain of light, very beautiful. And there in the middle of this large space was little old Wescott with his playthings. I must say it took forever to get an erection, and I wasn't very comfortable with it, but I managed.

For some reason I suffered more from these things than I expected to. I had to grin and bear it. The only condition I made was that I never had to look at the films. I said, "I hate my own body enough, I don't want to see this." He giggled and said, "Well, you ought to get over that. That's not scientific. As I've told you, we're interested in everything. You're a very remarkable man. If you were actually unique, you'd be still more interesting," said he, and he talked to me like that. The next day he came over and said, "You know, we want a second sitting out there. The boys think you faked part of it. They don't mean you did it on purpose, but you did something they'd never seen before. You jack-knifed." At the moment of orgasm, most men thrust out and pull away in the upper body. He said they wanted to see it again. So the next time I did it again, and he said, "Well, you know it isn't as crucial as we thought. Because to our astonishment, the boys found it in the animal pictures. Rabbits do it. Guinea pigs do it. Porcupines do it. And some people do it." But it's apparently very rare.[22]

One night before leaving Bloomington, Wescott was watching some of the amateur sex films with Kinsey. One film of two young men made a great impression on him. "It was of a blond German boy and a Cuban boy who was almost black," he said. "That was as beautiful as anything I'd ever seen. For me, the male human body is the most beautiful thing in nature, if it's at all well put together. And the rhythms and changes in the face and in the body as well as in the genitalia are the most thrilling things." They continued screening newly acquired films when Kinsey played a trick on him, slipping in the film of Wescott masturbating. "Suddenly, there, what's that? Looks like—'twas I! He'd put the film in there. He laughed so. And I gave a cry of horror. And he said, 'I just decided once and away to educate you a little bit. Whether you liked it or not, I was going to give you the experience. You're almost a scientist now,' said he, 'might as well have the experience of an objective view of yourself—and learn to love the way you look, learn to take an interest, anyway. Learn to share in my interest.' He was very solemn about this. And then came very interesting experiences."[23] The meaning of that last sentence remained a secret for many years.

When Kinsey came to New York, one thing that interested him was the social circle of Wescott's friend Carl Malouf. A number of Malouf's friends were fellow veterans of World War II, such as illustrator Tommy Sullivan and his giant bisexual find, Michael Miksche. Wheeler's important younger lover of the fifties was an artist and poet named Ralph Pomeroy. Although Pomeroy was outside Malouf's circle, he had a powerful impression of Miksche, who snubbed him. "I was mad for him," he said. "He was one of the most stunning sexual people I've ever met."[24] Miksche was a star among the volunteers filmed at the Institute, as were a couple named Jack Fontaine and Raymond Ungar.

Bill Miller, the handsome model, sometimes joined the group. George Lynes also got to know Kinsey, and over the next several years gave the Institute scores of photos, some for payment, some as gifts. These were mostly male nudes but also included celebrity portraits. Another interesting connection for Kinsey was the French filmmaker François Reischenbach. A frequent visitor to New York, he had known Wescott since the 1920s in Paris, as did his brother Philippe, an art dealer. François would later win an Academy Award for his documentary work and contribute two gay-themed films to Kinsey's archive.

Malouf remembered gay male gatherings of that era: "We lived in an age of innocence. A homosexual evening was so secret and hush-hush. Once, I remember, a bunch of us went to someone's apartment to see slides of some boys in bathing suits diving off a pier, photos someone had taken. For that we were all tiptoeing and shushing each other up! [W. H.] Auden, sitting on the floor, looked up when Glenway came in with Tommy Sullivan and me, and he said, 'Well, look who's here. The vice president of the National Institute of Arts and Letters.' That night after we left Glenway said, 'The nerve of Auden doing that!' Because there were others there—I think Lincoln Kirstein was there. Every time I ran into Auden he was just as rude, about other things too."[25]

Some of Malouf's parties on East Fortieth Street were mixed gay and straight and he called them "square balls" because they were tame. Some of his all-male parties were just as respectable. Malouf remembered, "We'd have a party and dinner and nothing happened. I'd say, 'Glenway, what was that all about?' And he'd say, 'Plant them now, dig them up later.' And he did! But he was a gentleman, a real gentleman."[26]

Some of the parties turned completely sexual, and when Kinsey visited New York in January of 1952, he was invited to observe one. Malouf recalled that when Kinsey arrived early in the evening he made one of his square, Midwest-innocent mistakes. On the wall was a faded photo of a real ballerina in a tutu. Kinsey turned to stocky, masculine, war veteran Malouf and said, "Is that you in drag?" The fact that Kinsey was serious made it worse. "Well!" said Malouf. "Nobody talked to me like that! Drag was something people did as a joke. We were off on the wrong foot. But Glenway immediately jumped in and smoothed it out." After dinner the party turned into an orgy, instigated by Wescott. At one point, Malouf noticed Kinsey standing in the hallway. "Kinsey was looking in one room and then another," he said, "and—just playfully—I tried to give him a little kiss. He practically went through the ceiling; that was not part of the game. Later on I told Glenway and said I was embarrassed. 'Tush, tush,' said Glenway, 'Alfred should just consider it an occupational hazard.'"[27]

As Wescott remembered it, the party had seemed in danger of remaining completely proper, perhaps because the young men were uncomfortable in Dr. Kinsey's presence. But, sitting next to Michael Miksche, Wescott decided to act: "I was playing it by ear, when I suddenly realized that I could do it; they were all acquaintances but I didn't know them too well. So I just slipped out of my chair and went down on my Michael. Whereupon, away they all went! Then I got back on my voyeuristic seat. Alfred was sitting in a corner. He made absolute dead silence! He could disappear in the room, you know, you'd forget all about him. Everybody said that. He never made a move, he didn't breathe, and the eyes were just—he was so fond, so nonnegative, so positive, and he made you feel so important and central, and suddenly there you were: you'd forgotten he was there. It was a magical effect. And suddenly he'd get up and move, and you'd think, 'My God, he's been there a long time!'"[28]

Kinsey also visited New York homosexual bars and Times Square haunts where Wescott would never be seen. "I didn't know about that; he didn't go with me, but I'm sure he went with my friends," said Wescott. "But, you see, he never told you anything, just on principle, and you never asked him anything. But he wasn't very much interested in it. He would probably go to one of each kind, and just have a look. What he wanted to do was talk. And to get to know people."[29]

Kinsey saw a party that was different from Malouf's at the Greenwich Village apartment of Ralph Pomeroy, Wheeler's companion. Pomeroy remembered that "Glenway suggested it. There may have been two hundred people, a huge success. Nothing happened. It was just beautiful young guys who gave off positive vibes. But Kinsey loved it. He wanted to see the social behavior of gays. It wasn't just about sex."[30] Indeed, Kinsey saw beyond the statistics, observing healthy relationships and love affairs. Among them was a surprising new relationship in Wescott's life.

On January 25, 1952, Michael Miksche arrived at one of Malouf's parties with a new friend. John Connolly, a twenty-four-year-old with round blue eyes, was tall, handsome, athletic, well mannered, and bright. Right away, Wescott knew he wasn't just another of the young men who drifted in and out of Malouf's crowd.

"My first impression on meeting Glenway," said Connolly, "was just an emotional feeling rather than intellectual. A kindred spirit. The first thing we both did, before saying anything, was laugh!"[31] All who knew him agreed that Connolly was highly sexed, and that was part of the attraction for Wescott. But there was much more. Connolly chatted happily in the kitchen as Wescott made dinner. Later, a jealous Miksche left early. In his journal, where he used the code name "Ronald Neil" for Connolly, Wescott described the rest of that first evening: "R. and I knelt at the foot of C. M. and W. R.'s bed, watching conjointly, turning to gaze into each other's eyes, afire, with more love than lust. . . . I love him for a particular reason: In some ways he is more like me when I was young than anyone I have ever met! Also, last night, he seemed to me the most beautiful because he was the happiest, as it happened."[32]

At first, Wescott saw Connolly only in Miksche's company, as Connolly remembers: "Glenway saw Michael and myself a good deal, and it changed my way of thinking about New York." But soon enough, they were seeing each other alone, and Wescott learned all about him. Connolly had served as a marine at Parris Island and at a navy annex in Washington, D.C. Afterward he returned to Florida to study at the University of Miami. During his three years in New York, he worked for the Alcoholics Anonymous newsletter, *The Grapevine,* then got into design work. He also did backstage work in the entertainment field, with songwriter Hugh Martin ("Meet Me in Saint Louis," "Have Yourself a Merry Little Christmas"). Together they once worked backstage for Judy Garland. And it was Martin who introduced him to Mike Miksche.

On February 23, Wescott confessed to Wheeler and Ralph Pomeroy his sudden attachment to John Connolly. Over the next two days, he wrote Kinsey a long and candid letter, detailing the goings-on of nearly a dozen friends. He gave Alfred a window not just on sexual behavior but on gay male sexuality and psychology: individual backgrounds, love attachments, jealousies, personal traits—far more than Kinsey could learn just in observing. Connolly himself was reticent and avoided interviews with Kinsey until later, but Wescott wrote about him at length. John was a nondrinker, had a good character, and held a good job in commercial design. Wescott welcomed these wholesome qualities and told Alfred he was weary of the crowd of less stable young friends: "In the course of my love-life I have witnessed so many shipwrecks—more or less loved and loving persons capsizing their own lives, clinging to the gunwales of my life until it frightens me, until their fingers weaken or until I terribly rap them across the knuckles."[33] Although he would now drift away from Malouf's parties,

Wescott was always grateful to Carl and the others for the friendship, eroticism, and balance they brought to his middle years.

During the Kinsey years, Wescott experimented with writing erotic stories, but not for publication, although they were vivid and quite good. In a lecture for Josephine Crane's "Monday Class," he praised Hemingway's decadent novel of an aging American in Venice falling in love with a girl less than half his age. The critics panned *Across the River and into the Trees,* but, Wescott noted in his journal, he, Thornton Wilder, and Christopher Isherwood were fascinated.

Only once in the early fifties did Wescott have a complete break from the Institute for Sex Research. It was during the spring and early summer of 1952 for a trip to Europe. When an invitation to an expense-paid trip to Paris for an arts conference arrived in the mail, he threw it in the trash. Wheeler retrieved it, and he, Barbara, Lloyd, and Pauline Potter pressured him to accept. The two-week International Congress of Cultural Freedom would include writers and artists he knew, including the composer Virgil Thomson and Lincoln Kirstein with his American Ballet Theater. Wescott didn't care so much about all that, but he had not been abroad since 1938. Once he agreed to go, he planned ways to extend the trip.

Instead of flying, Wescott booked passage on the ocean liner *Westerdam,* which departed on April 26 and arrived in Amsterdam on May 5. As planned, he met up with old friend Pauline Potter at a hotel. They loved each other's company and for days took boat rides on the canals and saw all the museums in Amsterdam, Rotterdam, and the Hague. The time together gave Pauline a chance to bring Wescott up to date on her exciting life. One of the leading fashion designers in the world, she lived part time in Paris and had been dating Baron Philippe de Rothschild for several years. Owner of the Château Mouton Rothschild wine properties, the baron was also a sportsman, film producer, patron of the arts, author, and poet. When they had first met at a Paris luncheon, he introduced himself and Pauline touched his heart by replying, "Oh, the poet."[34] During the war Philippe had been imprisoned by occupied France's Vichy government, and his wife, Lili, had died in a concentration camp. Now that the relationship was serious, Pauline wanted Wescott to meet Philippe when he got to Paris.

Wescott arrived in Paris by plane on May 10, 1952, after an absence of fourteen years. To avoid a hotel filled with writers and to stretch his expense money, he visited with François Reischenbach. He attended the ballet with Jacques Guérin, who took him to dinner with his controversial writer friend Jean Genet. Wescott was diplomatic. Despite the duties of the arts conference, he found time for meetings with old friend Janet Flanner, the novelist Julien Green, and many others. On May 23, he met Philippe de Rothschild and Pauline at her apartment. There was a showing of Kenneth Anger's surrealistic film, *Fireworks,* and Wescott met with Anger, who knew Kinsey and supported his work. As always, Wescott loved writing about all this to Wheeler, but now he also wrote John Connolly every day.

At the conference, Wescott was glad to see that Katherine Anne Porter was recovering from her latest failed relationship with a much younger man, this time the writer William Goyen. He remembered her statement about her early days with Goyen, whom she had heard was bisexual. "'I thought he would be rather flimsy in bed,' she'd said, 'but he was a stallion!'"[35] Porter was still writing to Goyen, and she told him she'd had lunch with "four of the most opinionated people in the world," Janet Flanner, Glenway Wescott, Virgil Thomson, and Cyril Connolly, but they had all managed to keep their manners and get along.[36]

Before leaving Paris, Wescott called on Jean Cocteau at his rooms in the Palais Royal Hotel. At sixty-two, Cocteau seemed well and was glad to see his friend from the old Villefranche days. His reputation had suffered during the war years, but he was still respected and working. Jean Marais remained a close friend but it was Eduoard Dermit who was his primary companion. Suddenly, Wescott said, their reunion was interrupted by W. H. Auden: "I went to see Jean in his rooms and it was amazing because Auden came in at the same time. And there we sat, we two expatriates, with Cocteau. Auden didn't speak very good French and Cocteau didn't know what to say to him and scarcely knew who he was, and wanted to gossip with me. Still, we sat up talking. And that was the last time I saw him."[37] Although Wheeler would see Cocteau over the next decade, Wescott did not.

Having written the long introduction to *The Short Novels of Colette,* Wescott asked about Colette, who was Cocteau's friend and neighbor at the Palais Royal. She was seventy-nine and homebound with painful arthritis, Cocteau said, but he offered to telephone her. Wescott discouraged him, not wanting to impose. A few days later, the writer Anita Loos likewise encouraged him to visit Colette, suggesting that he arrive unannounced. Wescott remembered that when his friend Patrick O'Higgins visited her a few years earlier, he used a bouquet of roses to get in the door. A florist near the Palais Royal knew exactly the type of red rose Colette loved, and Wescott arrived at her apartment. At first, Colette's friend-companion-husband Maurice Goudeket said she was too ill for company, but after remembering Wescott from their 1938 book tour to America, and after a half hour's conversation in the sitting room, he suddenly said, "She has changed her mind about seeing you."

In the bedroom, Maurice addressed his wife as "dear friend" and Wescott as "Monsieur Ouess-cote." Obviously in pain, but beautiful and tranquil, Colette had Wescott sit at the foot of her bed. When he accidentally leaned on her feet, she winced, but then smiled and said her lifetime habit of wearing sandals had left her with strong feet. When they talked books, she was impressed that Wescott knew almost all her work. She said it seemed Americans were greater readers than the French. But Goudeket quietly intoned, "Monsieur Ouess-cote is perhaps exceptional." When Colette said of her writing, "I am the person in the world the least apt to moralize or philosophize," Wescott surprised her by arguing hard in the opposite direction. He later wrote, "Whether she liked it or not, I declared, she was a thinker, she did philosophize." At the end of the visit, Colette asked him to come back to Paris soon and promised she would be better then, and they would go to her favorite restaurant down the street. Wescott recalled: "I departed with a lump in my throat, with a very natural dread of mortality. But then I reminded myself of the printed form of immortality, a sure thing in Colette's case."[38]

As planned, Wescott stayed abroad an extra month. On June 1 he flew to Rome and stayed two weeks, seeing Tchelitchew and Charles Henri Ford. Pavlik, whose health was failing, and Charles had moved there several years earlier. Ford remembered those days: "Pavlik and I lived in a villa outside the city, first one, then another; it was much less expensive. Rome was a magnet for a while. For Gore Vidal, Tennessee Williams, and so many others." Wescott had a specific reason for the meeting. Because it was impossible to ship homoerotic art safely, he smuggled back ninety-nine small erotic drawings by Tchelitchew which were given to the Kinsey Institute. That same year, François Reischenbach smuggled Jean Genet's homoerotic film *Chant d'Amour* into America under his clothes, and safely into the hands of Kinsey.[39]

Wescott visited seventy-eight-year-old Willie Maugham and Alan Searle at the Villa Mauresque on Cap Ferrat and wrote to Wheeler about swimming in Maugham's pool: "I think it is good to see one's friends naked, even at eighty. Willie is not at all disgraceful; you might say funny-looking, but certainly not pathetic. Fine brown skin scarcely wrinkled; a few moles, not the blue-black kind that may presage cancer. Beautiful legs, with not a bit of hair on them. Under a very modest pot-belly, his sex is not at all withered, just loosened, and the veins perhaps darkened."[40] In Villefranche, he lunched with the actor and playwright Peter Ustinov and the historian C. V. Wedgwood. He saw the Matisse chapel in Venice and made stops in Genoa and Lisbon. Finally he left France on June 24 on the ocean liner *Argentina*.

Soon after Wescott returned to America, Kinsey asked for help in preparing the volume *Sexual Behavior in the Human Female* for release. Wescott replied, "You don't really need me as a stylist. Do not let perfectionism in writing develop out of the necessary scruple of scientific method." He was outlining a novel inspired by his European trip, he told

Kinsey, and it would involve "not just a revelation of my homosexuality but manifestations." After all, he said, even Wheeler now said that times were changing.[41]

Some of his short visits to the Institute for Sex Research may not have been recorded, and it appears Wescott visited briefly at this time, then stopped in Chicago to meet an important friend of the Institute. He recalled,

> Kinsey knew the most extraordinary man called Sam Steward, who was an English teacher at a Catholic college in Chicago. He taught literature and he went abroad every summer and got to be great friends with Alice Toklas and Gertrude. . . . He translated Jean Genet, *Querelle* and something else, and he wrote a novel himself about Francis Rose. I spotted him through a package of erotic letters in the cupboard at the Institute library. Extraordinary, vivid writing. An exchange of letters, between an obviously illiterate person and this rather gifted person, with a gift of describing sensations, the cock in the mouth, the outside of the rectum, all this sort of thing, in an obviously self-pleasing, masturbatory and arousing way, addressed to the other. This went on for a month or two, and both sides of this correspondence were there. I said, "Well, that's the only talented person I've found here, really talented." And then Kinsey said, "Well, as it so happens, he knows all about you and he'd be delighted if you went to visit him." By this time Sam Steward had given up his job at the university because he couldn't stand it any more, and opened a tattooing parlor on South State Street, and earned a good living at it. And this of course fascinated them more and more because here he had all these peculiar sailors and such, coming in and out of his life. So I went to see him.[42]

Sam Steward, forty-three, used the name Phil Sparrow for his tattoo art and the name Phil Andros for his pornography. He had met George Platt Lynes the previous year in New York, but happened to miss Wescott. When they finally met in Chicago, he had stopped teaching at Loyola and De Paul universities for his new line of work. Wescott recalled,

> He was a smallish, lean, wiry, Irish-looking man. I met him downtown in a restaurant, and then I went to his tattooing parlor and sat with him for two hours while he tattooed these boys, one of whom got sick and had to have a cold compress on his head. They'd picked out what they wanted and sat there sweating, and he of course was in bliss, manipulating this flesh. It is slightly painful, and some of it has to go very slow. I've always wanted to have a tattoo of a star put on my hand because it's a thing sailors do: the Mount of Mars, where anger is, and I'm prone to anger. Sailors have a star put on that little muscle there. And I would have liked that but I didn't trust him, he was such a sadomasochistic character.
>
> He took me to his apartment, and when he opened the door I was never so astounded in my life. It was a small ground-floor apartment, with one small room and one immensely large room, and a tiny kitchen and bathroom. The walls above the bookshelves and the ceiling were covered with scenes of intercourse. There were penises this big and people that big fornicating all over the walls, painted by

bad amateur artists of his acquaintance. Hair-raising from the point of view of a cop coming in, you know, who would then want to know what all these boxes and file cabinets were. And scrapbooks. All over the walls were pornographic photographs. And furthermore he had a photographic journal of his sex life, which he showed me. It was the most astonishing thing I'd ever known anybody to have. He had a camera that he could operate from the bed without anyone knowing it, and he had pictures of himself making love to every type of person you could imagine, and especially young boys. He had their names and their addresses and he told me who they were, and one of the boys was the son of an important city official in Chicago. I said, "I can't remember such a courageous man as you. It doesn't shock me a bit, and it gives me great pleasure to look at it all. But it alarms me. Aren't you running a frightful risk?" He answered, "Of course, I wouldn't dare do it, except that my dream all my life has been to be in prison, and to be fucked morning, noon, and night by everyone, and beaten." I said, "If I hadn't seen this I wouldn't believe it, because what you say is so extreme, and you're so rational and intelligent and gentle and cultivated, and not the least bit cruel yourself, I should think. You wouldn't want to hurt anybody, and you're so vigorous, I can't imagine you letting someone hurt you." I felt really frightened. And all through dinner he had been talking Jean Genet talk, about how thrilling it would be to be in prison, and I came away with that impression. He was the most extreme masochist that Kinsey ever found.[43]

Wescott learned something else about Sam Steward that he later reported to Paul Gebhard: "He gave me an amusing, resentful little account of his having had sex with [Thornton] Wilder passingly in Paris some years ago; no one else has ever told me any such thing."[44]

Even before meeting Steward, Wescott knew that he had been teamed up sexually, on film at the Institute, with his own friend Michael Miksche. A tragic character, Miksche was Steward's sexual opposite. Wescott explained,

Michael, who was very much in love with me, was the most fascinating person of all for Kinsey. He was a giant Paul Bunyan type, very strong, with a magnificent physique. He had gone to war at about twenty, and within a year he was in command of four or five jet bombers, and he went on two flights a night over Berlin and bombed it all to pieces. At that age he hadn't had homosexual inclinations, and didn't have much experience with women. One of the men in his flight crew was in love with him and confessed it. And Michael just said, "This is all nonsense. I'm not going to report you. We'll be friends, but we're not going to talk about it anymore." He had this tyrannous, psychological sadism.

One of the greatest tragedies having to do with sex is that S/M has been understood as only the physical experience, which is the smallest part of it. Because it's really Coercive/Submissive. They've now got lots of names, "bondage" and "domination," and I don't know what all. But it's built-in: it can be father and son; older brother and younger brother; black and white; brainy and brawny; soldier and civilian; older and younger—all these things.

Well, Michael was very multifarious in love and very bossy, because he wanted to dominate everybody, by his very nature. He took this boy and told him to calm down, that it was an idealistic thing, and they were having a love affair without sex. Two or three nights after this, the young man opened the door of the plane and threw himself out over the Rhine. And Michael almost went mad. I think he came back from the war with a sense of guilt and a sense of frustration, because by that time he wanted to go to bed with that boy.[45]

After the war Miksche drifted from California to New York. He was twenty-six when Carl Malouf met him on Fire Island. By that time a boyfriend had taught Miksche how to be a commercial artist. Wescott remembered, "He was a very successful amateur artist and made twenty thousand dollars a year, way back then, doing windows for Bloomingdale's and trashy advertising of all sorts."[46]

Without a doubt, Miksche was the most interesting of the men Wescott recommended for Kinsey's sexual films: "I sent out about eighteen combinations—both paired-off people or one person of mine that he would match with someone else. He did a lot of films with Miksche, one or two I looked at but most of which I didn't want to see! Michael was a terrific performer, not a sadist by nature, but he was such a showoff." Deliberately, Kinsey had matched the aggressive Miksche with the masochistic Sam Steward for two days of filming. Wescott said, "They were the rarest pair, you see, because masochists especially are very shy as a rule, and here we had an exhibitionist masochist."[47]

In his memoir, *Chapters from an Autobiography,* Sam Steward remembered his two-day sex session: "Mike was quite a ham actor; every time he heard Bill Dellenback's camera start to turn, he renewed his vigor and youth like the great bay tree; and at the end of the second afternoon I was exhausted, marked and marred, all muscles weakened. . . . Later that evening Kinsey left Mike and me in separate parts of the library to do some reading; and suddenly Mike appeared, wild-fire-eyed and excited—having stimulated himself with some typewritten S/M stories—and had his way with me on the cold cement floor of the library stacks."[48]

Miksche was also a pornography artist who worked under the name Scott Masters, and Wescott recalled a film of his drawing with an electric beam, naked outdoors at night: "He made an exhibition piece for Kinsey to show a professor who wanted to know what a homosexual aesthetic sense was. Stark naked with an electric pencil, he drew pornographic pictures, fornication, dancing and so on, in the air, and they were photographed in the movie. I must say it's one of the most extraordinary things you can see on earth." Kinsey was impressed, but he warned Wescott that Miksche could be dangerous. In a long letter, Wescott conceded, "A good many of the young masochists express fear of him. They fancy he will murder someone someday."[49] While Miksche was not a danger to Wescott, whom he loved, Kinsey's instinct would prove correct.

Sexual Behavior in the Human Female was released in August 1953. The first print run would total 150,000 copies, Kinsey told Wescott, followed by another 150,000 in September. "Nearly three years of intense work on the manuscript," he said, "with only an occasional breath of more interesting atmosphere in gathering new data, has left me a bit groggy. Certainly we have appreciated the many evidences of your continued good wishes and specific good work for us."[50] He also mentioned encouraging news about his recurring heart problems.

Wescott replied, "Of course I was thrilled by the great news item . . . and proud to be written to so promptly—and deeply relieved in my affection, and for science's sake and literature's sake, to hear that you can catch up on your health, that your heart hasn't really been harmed." In his ten-page letter, he mentioned that Wheeler would be visiting his parents in the Chicago area at the end of the month and was likely to visit the Institute in Bloomington. Wescott thought he might come to Bloomington at the same time, but admitted some awkwardness about Wheeler. "There is an odd reticence between us about everything erotic. . . . We never hesitate to tell each other secrets or scandals—but not for fun. He thinks of my sex life with sufficient sympathy but no empathy at all." Wescott recalled the days of their triangular relationship with George Platt Lynes and how it upset him when he accidentally saw the two of them making love. "I am not sure that his desire for me has entirely burned itself out; perhaps it never will," he mused—though he would acknowledge to friends that they'd not had sex after the Paris years.[51] These remarks were one of the few hints in all of Wescott's letters to Kinsey of possible sexual intimacy between himself and Kinsey, and between Wheeler and Kinsey. Yet most of Wescott's letters to Kinsey, nearly two hundred pages, vanished from the Institute files in later years—very likely the work of associates who feared scandal would help critics undermine the work.[52] However, Wescott kept photocopies.

One of Wescott's ongoing discussions with Kinsey and others was sexual honesty in writing. He told a friend: "As to Forster's ceasing to write fiction, I am inclined to think he did himself an inner injury by not publishing the homosexual novel, *Maurice*."[53] Yet Wescott's idealistic homosexual-love story, "A Year of Love," was never developed beyond excerpts from letters and other material relating to Mark Pagano, who inspired it, as well as John Connolly and Bernard Perlin. And his fifteen-year-old story "A Visit to Priapus," completely and beautifully written, remained unpublished. In contrast, the younger Sam Steward/Phil Andros seemed determined to write everything. On a postcard in 1953, Steward wrote prophetically from San Francisco, "Dear Glenway: A real exciting place to be, with something to do every minute of the day and night. It's my first trip to San Francisco and I'm making every moment count. Such tales to be told!"[54]

In September, Wescott sent Kinsey profiles of John Connolly and Ralph Pomeroy, his and Wheeler's younger lovers respectively, along with a heartfelt response to the *Female* volume, and his own role in it. He wrote, "I spent yesterday and today reading your book. It is superb, not disappointing to me in any respect, holding my interest and touching my deepest sympathy in every detail. It reminds me of a phrase of Marianne Moore's: 'That which is able to change the heart proves itself.' It is beautiful in form and composition, with great orderliness, and unity as well as clarity of language. It is a masterpiece. But you will not be displeased to hear, my mind runs on ahead—even to the little contributions I fancy making myself, as to the homosexual in one phase and another. Sometimes it flashes through my mind that I would like to have nothing else to do."[55]

That fall, one of Wescott's young friends, designer Chuck Howard, visited Bloomington and reported back that Kinsey was ill. Wescott wrote to Kinsey in November to express his concern. He also mentioned his disappointment over what he called a "weak" article that E. M. Forster had written about the "recent scandals in England." Clearly he was referring to homosexual scandals. Among his papers is another article entitled "The Unspeakable Crime," which appeared in *Time* magazine on November 1, 1953. The piece recalled the 1895 court case of Oscar Wilde and mentioned three current cases, particularly that of Lord Edward Baron Montagu. A Tory Party member, Montagu was involved in a scandal linking upper class gentlemen with working class boys, and, like Oscar Wilde, he made the mistake of going to court. The other scandals involved two celebrities who pled guilty to "importuning males in public": Labour Party member W. F. Field and the actor John Gielgud. Wescott was horrified by the homophobic witch hunts and hoped Kinsey would get to his proposed book on reforming sexual freedom laws: "I long to have you get through the volume on the laws and the prisons with strength enough left over to produce a further study of the homosexual."[56]

Many years later, Wescott reflected: "Kinsey told me shortly thereafter that there were a great many more [gay] people in prison in England than there were here. And the extraordinary and rather distressing thing about that was that in England only the lower class people went to jail—until Lord Montagu, whom I knew, committed a hideous indiscretion. He and two or three other rather grand young men got a lot of the boys from the village and had a sort of orgy party, and one of the boys stole a very expensive camera from the host. The host yelled bloody murder and insisted on prosecuting, and the boy was the son of the head of the police department in that part of England. Ha! And he wouldn't back down. Two or three of them had to serve short prison sentences. He was in prison for a year. And all of that led to the liberalization."[57]

Aside from their correspondence and meetings, Wescott sometimes accompanied Kinsey on his public appearances. "I went to a public speech he made in Princeton . . . where he talked about the research in general and picked up some histories to take. A man got up at the end and said, 'Doc, would you like to take the history of a castrated man? I'm speaking of myself. I've learned not to be too sensitive about it.' And of course Kinsey almost fainted away with the mixed emotions of compassion and curiosity, and he took his history. The man had corrupted a little girl, or girls, he'd had a sex offense of that kind, and the judge gave him a choice of going to prison for a long sentence or being spayed! And he chose that. Interestingly enough, Kinsey told me that it didn't make him impotent; it weakened him and embarrassed him. For several years a castration doesn't make much difference, as one knows in animals, horses and so on. But the horror of that! And Kinsey went all the way down to Oklahoma, to a man who had been in a terrible accident but still had love affairs. He was interested in people like that."[58]

Wescott's friend Carl Malouf remembered one of Kinsey's visits to the Wescott farm in New Jersey. By the fifties, Lloyd was a noted cattle breeder, and he kept prize bulls and sold their semen for large fees. Malouf had seen how this part of the business worked: "There was a kind of ramp, like those you use to work under an automobile. The bull clambered up on that while the cow was below. Almost immediately the bull ejaculated into the air. A very brave worker stood there with a contraption that caught the semen in midair. Well, once they tried it with a prize bull and it didn't work; he wasn't interested in the cow. One of the farmhands spoke up and said, 'I've seen this bull very interested in a young bull in the herd. Why don't we take out the cow and put the young bull down there?' So they did, and the prize bull shot all over the place! Glenway loved telling that story and Kinsey wouldn't believe it. Finally, he went out to the farm and saw it with his own eyes."[59]

Stone-blossom provided another service for Kinsey's study. In 1954 Wescott's friend François Reischenbach filmed part of *Last Spring* there. In this short, chaste, homosexual love film, two handsome farmworkers are separated when one leaves to live in New York. At night the one left behind dreams of the city's homosexual haunts, such as Times Square and a bar room. The film ends happily when the two reunite in the countryside. John Connolly and Dick Kushner, a model and artist, play the two young men. Reischenbach gave Kinsey a copy of the film for the Institute archive.

The positive work of the Kinsey years was tainted by the public backlash to the *Female* volume. Criticism of the *Male* volume five years earlier had come largely from academics. Now, in the Joe McCarthy era, it was impossible to fight the relentless flood of inaccurate and sensational magazine articles and hack books. Despite media rumors of its failure, the *Female* volume sold successfully, but the public relations defeat was nearly fatal. Kinsey associate Wardell Pomeroy wrote, "The book appeared to have stirred up every kind of exploiter, every moralist, every psychotic in the country." Right-wing Republicans initiated a House investigation in which unsubstantiated charges were filed and no defense witnesses were allowed. The intimidated Rockefeller Foundation under Dean Rusk withdrew all funding for the Institute, after more than a decade of support. At the same time, the Foundation gave more than ten times as much, over half a million dollars, to the Union Theological Seminary, presided over by Kinsey enemy Harry Fosdick, "to aid in the development of vital religious leadership." Pomeroy reflected, "I believe that the loss of foundation support, coupled with the severe strain of trying to find more money, added to his already impossible schedule, hastened Kinsey's death."[60]

In early July 1954, Wescott and Wheeler visited Wheeler's parents ("the healthiest and most lovable of octogenarians," Glenway called them), and Wescott went on to Bloomington. There he made a private notation: "K's heart attack," referring to one of Kinsey's cardiac emergencies.[61] Wescott remained at the Institute until July 14, working with Paul Gebhard on a socioeconomic study of homosexuals. Despite the bad press, the Institute still had support from Indiana University and others, along with book royalties.

No one could convince Kinsey to slow down, and he took a research trip to Peru in August. He wrote Wescott from abroad: "The trip is as interesting and profitable as I had anticipated. We already have one thousand negatives of ancient Indian art which have erotic content." Bad health prevented a visit to Stone-blossom on his return. Concerned, Wescott wrote his friend a story with a pointed message. In her youth, he said, Katherine Anne Porter had tuberculosis and her doctors forbade her to see people, even to receive letters. "Then they feared that books tired her, and limited her reading time. Not good enough!—the restlessness of her eyes around the room made her feverish, so finally, for rest-periods, they covered her face with a green baize cloth, as one does a canary, to silence it. One of the admirable things I know about her—the will to live, in the form of passivity."[62]

Like Paul Gebhard, Sam Steward, and others, Wescott noticed Kinsey's memory lapses and bouts of temper over the next year. During the last three months of 1955, Kinsey escaped his problems with a celebrated European trip that renewed the joy in his work. He spoke at universities, visited prisons and other institutions, and recorded his observations.

Returning to America meant getting back to the problem of fundraising, which Kinsey hated, and facing his own mortality. Wescott remembered, "Actually, my role in his life was more important as time went on, because he was absolutely heartbroken with the knowledge that he was going to die. And the Rockefeller Foundation had bounced him out. . . .

They just left him high and dry. He knew he was going to die and leave the boys with no money, and went desperately around trying to get funding. And the nearest he came was Huntington Hartford."[63] In May of 1956, Kinsey met with Hartford, an A&P supermarket heir, but the two men couldn't connect, and Kinsey came away with no support. Wescott couldn't forget that gloomy night:

After a lot of correspondence, Kinsey had a meeting with Hartford. He came to me afterward and almost died in Monroe's apartment! He had the worst heart attack I'd ever seen anyone have, turned green and panted, lying on the bed, and I thought he was going to die right then and there. We were pushing the nitroglycerin pills down his throat, and eventually he was coming to life again. I was so angry and he was so angry. But by that time it was like that and we knew he was going to die and he was very unhappy.

During all that period I was the only person he confided to, because he didn't want to tell the boys about it, he didn't want to tell them how he felt. And he wanted to be a moralist, he *was* a moralist, but within the context of the research. I remember once he said to me, "I suppose you may be disappointed in me in that I may seem sentimental and moralistic and all that." He said, "If you knew how my young men beat me up every time I let my mind wander into speculations of right or wrong or better or worse or good influence or the future or what ought to be or how morality would develop, and so on." At the end, he talked to me a good deal along that whole line, and we were very, very close. And I think at the end he was fonder of me, but of course he wasn't so lovable at that point. He was sad and severe.[64]

Others also witnessed the deline in Kinsey's health. On one of his last trips to California, he visited Sam Steward's apartment and fell behind as they climbed the three flights of stairs. Steward recalled his friend standing on the landing below. "Oh Sam," he said, "what have you done to me?"[65] In New York, Paul Cadmus witnessed an attack almost as bad as the one at Wheeler's apartment.

In Kinsey's last year, Wescott and Wheeler suggested that he stop appealing to politically controlled foundations and turn to wealthy liberal philanthropists. Wescott gave one example:

The most emancipated man I've ever known in my life was Leonard [X] of the great family in Cleveland. For some reason or other, Monroe never managed to bring Kinsey and him together. He was a big stout man who came to New York often for fun and games, and he was an adorable big lug of a provincial queen, not very effeminate, but stout, baldish, and always had young men. Finally he had strokes that affected his arms and legs so that he had to be wheeled around, and he came to New York constantly, collaborating with Monroe on Museum of Modern Art shows. And he would come with this beautiful boy pushing him in the wheelchair. Monroe would say, "How brave you are, it's incredible, how do you get in and out of a plane, why don't you make us come and see you?" Leonard said, "It's no credit to me. It's that angel behind there pushing me. He has to heave me to the pot and heave me into bed, and I couldn't live without him." And when he died he left twenty million dollars to the Cleveland Museum and just a kennel of expensive dogs to that boy. And the family and friends were so embarrassed that they got together and made up capital funds, enough for him to live on. This was probably because for some reason or other, Leonard, in the "hour of death," with his lawyer bullying him, he couldn't—and people hate to make their wills anyway. Who *knows* what that meant? It shocked us, a shiver went through us. And that's the sort of person Kinsey could have had if he would have done things differently.

I said to him, "Reform is the thing that most needs doing; that's what the best people care for in this research. Science isn't all that interesting to people who aren't trained to be scientists. And everybody hates injustice, everybody hates false imprisonment, everybody has a relative, a son, or cousin or somebody who is queer. If you will undertake to ease that hideous business which has been going on since the Old Testament, you will get support you can't get now!" And he said, "I can't do it without sacrificing my scientific status and my principles."

Monroe also said that the Institute should have been brought here to New York, because Alfred had to run it out there, with a predominantly Catholic legislature. Again and again the Knights of Columbus would try to get the legislature to put the Institute out of existence.[66]

Clara Kinsey told friends that Alfred never recovered from his trip to New York in May 1956. On June 1 he suffered several light heart attacks and was hospitalized. His doctor explained that he might live several more years if he limited his workday to a few hours. But Kinsey would cut back to only eight hours of work, and spent the rest of the time in the garden and with Clara. Finally, he returned to the Bloomington hospital and died on the morning of August 25. Wescott and Wheeler attended the funeral. The praise and kind words for Kinsey in the mainstream press came from many who were silent when he was under attack. Among his true friends were gay artists and activists of the era. The Los Angeles gay rights periodical *One* entitled its August–September 1956 issue "A Tribute to Dr. Kinsey" and carried his portrait on the cover.

Thereafter, Wescott occasionally visited and worked at the Institute. On a personal level, he missed the great friend who had helped him resolve some of the unhappiness and conflicts within himself. Remarkably, both Wescott and Wheeler kept a lifelong secret—even from those closest to them. Four decades after Kinsey's death, two biographers revealed that he had some sexual experiences with men, including Wescott, and possibly Wheeler. The revelation came as a great surprise to John Connolly, Ralph Pomeroy, Bernard Perlin, and others.

Biographer James H. Jones—who as a young man interviewed Wescott at the Institute on June 27, 1972—reported that Kinsey had some unusual sexual habits, and some sexual experiences with men. The conservative Jones sensationalized this aspect of Kinsey's private life, referring to him as "homosexual," and questioned the conclusions and statistical merit of his work. A number of reviewers found the Jones book not only homophobic but strangely antisexual. Martin Duberman wrote, "Jones's crude psychologizing (which is really moralizing) is far too formulaic to inspire confidence. Indeed, several of Kinsey's surviving colleagues guffaw at Jones's reductive view of the complicated man Kinsey was."[67]

British author Jonathan Gathorne-Hardy replied with his own biography. By coincidence a nephew of the midcentury writer Robert Gathorne-Hardy who knew Wescott, he concluded that Kinsey had a few sexual liaisons with Wescott, mostly likely during July 1951 in Bloomington. He also believes Wheeler's few visits to Bloomington may have included sex. In nongay naïveté, Gathorne-Hardy misuses the word "lovers," but he takes a balanced view and presents a welcome defense of Kinsey and the Institute during (yet another) conservative American era.[68]

It is likely that Wescott considered the personal facts unimportant but a threat to Kinsey's name. Idealistically, he saw Kinsey's work as humanitarian and loved his friend's joy as a scientist in the study of human sexuality. He said, "I remember one day, among all the guinea pigs I introduced him to, there was a silly creature called Ed who was attached to Bill Miller. And he was very, very handsome, a muscle man, and dumb, and he said to Kinsey, 'Doctor Kinsey, don't you ever get blasé?' And Kinsey laughed, but not aloud. Kinsey had a sort of lugubrious face, a solemn face, with terribly piercing eyes, but they would also sparkle. If he wanted to laugh, he wouldn't move his mouth at all, his eyes would jump around. And the rest of the time they would bore right through you. He didn't laugh at the question. 'Well, I don't think anything is very likely to shock me or surprise me,' he said, 'but you know, I'll tell you something that's very important. No two sexual histories are alike!' And he had a beaming smile, just rejoicing!"[69]

9

Inside the Circle

Farewell to George

PARK AVENUE is one of midtown Manhattan's most spectacular urban sights. The wide boulevard extends for miles, with enclosed flower beds and trees dividing the steady traffic flow on uptown and downtown streets. Monroe Wheeler's apartment at Park Avenue and East Fifty-fifth Street was ideal for his celebrity-filled gatherings and a moderate walk from his office at the Museum of Modern Art.

When Ralph Pomeroy interviewed at the museum in 1951, Wheeler didn't have an opening but he helped him with contacts and invited him to a party. Pomeroy, twenty-five, had had a difficult time in the military, studied at the Art Institute of Chicago, and spent some time in Europe. He remembered his first visit to the apartment of Wheeler and Wescott. The walls were an unusual shade of gray turning to lavender; Wheeler said his friend Tchelitchew had mixed the colors seven times to get it right. On that first visit, Pomeroy met and left with another guest, a sexy young playwright, but Wheeler pursued him. A budding poet, Pomeroy got an editing job with *House and Garden* and later with *Travel and Entertainment,* and Wheeler set him up with a Bank Street apartment. He became Wheeler's companion, on and off, for a decade, but he also greatly enjoyed Wescott. Pomeroy remembered, "At first Glenway disapproved of this pushy little *arriviste.* But we became good friends. My reading on Glenway was that he was generous. And with him you could talk honestly about sex. Monroe disapproved." At 410 Park Avenue, he got to meet some of their famous friends, including the Sitwells, Lincoln Kirstein, Brooke Astor, and Philip Johnson. "Lincoln Kirstein was homosexual but would never say it. Never, never." One strange moment occurred when Wheeler celebrated the publication of one of Pomeroy's poems in *Harper's Bazaar.* He was left alone for a moment with the great Marianne Moore, who said, "You know, Ralph, I've never been published in a national magazine."[1]

Wescott's new lover, John Connolly, also visited the apartment often. Connolly said, "I remember a large living room, small dining room, large bedroom, tiny kitchen, and long foyer. There I met Porter, Rebecca West, Bill and Emily Maxwell, Dorothy Parker, and many more."[2] Despite his wild private life, Connolly was accepted by Wheeler because of his sense of discretion and his love for Wescott.

Wescott's friends from the Carl Malouf circle were less welcome at the apartment. Malouf, who considered Monroe "a stuffed shirt," said, "I resented all this business of Glenway at 410 asking Monroe for money so he could take us out to dinner. When I read Monroe's art articles, I saw the fine hand of Glenway Wescott. He should have been paid for editing!"[3] While some resented Wheeler's formality, his accomplishments could not be disputed. In April of 1951, French President Vincent Auriol presented him the Legion of Honor at a ceremony in Paris to honor his work in bringing exhibits to France and especially in arranging exhibits of French artists in America. At the time, he was planning a Matisse exhibit for the Museum of Modern Art.

Wheeler loved to share his travels and success with Wescott through letters. When preparing for the Matisse exhibit, he wrote from Nice: "Yesterday I began to work on the Matisse loans in Paris. . . . I phoned Matisse as soon as my plane landed and he asked me to come see him tomorrow afternoon. Then I called Willie, who asked me to come to dinner, and Alan called for me in the car." After dinner at Maugham's restored Villa Mauresque, he said, he ran into the brother of Jacques Guérin, Wescott's French lover of the twenties: "I took a stroll along the Promenade des Anglais and found Jean Guérin sitting alone, drunk as an owl. . . . Would you enjoy seeing all these ghosts from our past? How goes the Colette preface? I love you. You are the one who has lasted best. —Monie."[4] Days later, he wrote again to say he had had dinner with Jacques Guérin himself and Jacques's new friend, Jean Genet.

Later, Wheeler wrote from Venice, "My dearest, no eyes but yours can perceive all the wondrous human and human-willed beauty of this place, and without you I feel as though only half of me is here." Finally, he wrote in triumph from Paris, "I have a lot of work with Matisse, who is now in Paris, and with Mr. Elanger regarding French government financing of the show." When he returned to New York, Monroe received a note from museum board member Nelson Rockefeller: "I just read with great interest about the Matisse Exhibition and the financing of the show. I can't imagine how you worked it out. We'll have to give you our own Legion d'Honneur."[5]

Wheeler reported that Willie Maugham, richer than ever, was treating faithful Alan Searle badly. As Wescott saw it, Maugham was building up wealth in fear of illness and death. In a journal note, he saw the contradiction in Maugham's study of religions at the same time he sought material things. He wrote, "The success-seeking life does *not* lead to philosophy, because it goes counter to the grain and pattern of existence, which is tragic."[6]

While Wheeler was the perfect host, his gatherings could go awry. Once, Katherine Anne Porter began a witty tirade against Truman Capote after he left the party. Wescott replied sharply, not because he was really a friend of Capote but he realized how many other gay writers she berated: André Gide, Maugham, Forster, Isherwood. He came to believe that her bouts of homophobia were "an expression of her deadly lonesomeness."[7] The next day, Marianne Moore thanked Wheeler for the evening with a wry note: "What boundless giving, forethought, patience last evening. Not to mention the flowers and the taxi. I must disrupt your practice regarding taxis even if it amounts to coming by tricycle. . . . I thought Truman Capote was very pleasingly unpleased."[8]

Through the fifties, the Sitwells were highly entertaining guests at 410 Park Avenue. Edith Sitwell began one of her American tours with a costumed reading as Lady Macbeth at a Museum of Modern Art members' evening. She needed a partner to read as Macbeth, and Wheeler offered to get Basil Rathbone or José Ferrer, who had been married to actress Uta Hagen. But Sitwell felt more comfortable with Wescott.[9] Rehearsed and dressed for the role, he did well on the strength of his exceptional speaking voice. James Mason Brown of the *Saturday Review of Literature* thought far less of Dame Edith at sixty-three as Lady Macbeth. Wescott felt she was more convincing in George Platt Lynes's photo of her in her outfit and crown, hands outstretched with her fingers pointing forward. Lynes had a similar success with his famous photos of Marianne Moore in oversized hats.

Osbert Sitwell was seeing New York doctors for his Parkinson's disease, and Marianne Moore commented to Wheeler: "I said not a word to Edith till she had partly gone. And might not have spoken to Osbert, I suppose, if you had not led me to him—I am sad to see that he has to fight to maintain an illusion of contentment."[10] Moore's compassion and humility were part of her greatness. She felt too shy to talk to the Sitwells, even at age sixty-seven, in a year in which she'd been awarded the Pulitzer Prize, the National Book Award, and the Bollingen Prize for her *Collected Poems.*

The novelist Frederic Prokosch was probably remembering the same evening with his comical essay "The Shrimp." When the guests of honor arrived, Edith, larger than he expected, moved across the room with authority and made for the sofa. Osbert moved in halting uncertain rushes, once toward an open window, then toward a bookcase. Wheeler gently took him by the arm and led him toward Marianne Moore, who was sitting alone in a corner. Osbert suddenly lurched sideways toward Katherine Anne Porter and, thinking she was Marianne, began praising her poetry. Wheeler said smoothly, "This is Miss Porter, not Miss Moore. Miss Moore is a poetess, but Miss Porter is a raconteuse." Prokosch had the courage to sit beside Edith and start a conversation about poetry. Edmund Wilson stood above them holding a drink and joined in the conversation. When a boy passed with a tray of shrimp, Wilson took one. Prokosch remembered, "I watched with frozen horror as the shrimp slid from its toothpick and gracefully landed on Miss Sitwell's coiffure." But Edith seemed unaware of it and everyone else pretended not to notice. So the shrimp remained in her hair like an amulet while she discussed Alexander Pope and Percy Shelley. And Prokosch was so enchanted by "Edith's witchery" that he forgot the shrimp too.[11]

Wheeler's social life, work, and travel made him seem indestructible, but he often had health problems. Once, an attack of shingles persisted for months and threatened his eyesight. Marianne Moore worried: "I am pained, Monroe, to hear from Marion Kauffer of your hardships—this intolerable suffering, if Marion understood correctly—shingles in your left eye. Serum administered immediately should counteract it, we were told." Through it all, Wheeler hardly broke his routine. Ralph Pomeroy remembered, "Nothing, not even pain, would stop Monroe. Even then, he'd put on an eye patch and keep going." Nearly five months later, Marianne wrote: "I am rejoiced, Monroe, that your eye is restored. . . . I cannot intimate the depression I felt that your sight was threatened—even temporarily limited."[12] In fact, his eyesight was partly impaired.

There was a public perception of Wescott and Wheeler as a highly cultivated and formidable couple. Their friends understood the more complex dynamics. But again and again, it is their private letters that capture the bond between them. A letter from Wheeler when he and Raymond Mortimer were traveling through Germany is characteristic: "Most dear: We had a very bumpy flight through electrical storms from Amsterdam here, via Nuremberg, and the plane was late. We arrived just in time to get to the opera at the Prince Regent Theater. . . . We went to the Hamderkunst where I was overwhelmed by the Rubens and Poussins—also magnificent Flemish paintings. . . . Munich is still a shambles and the ruins everywhere are hideous and very depressing and it hasn't stopped raining since we arrived. Raymond is a godsend—reacting brilliantly to every sight and telling me long tales of his friends in England. Raymond returns to England tomorrow and I fly to Venice on Saturday. Thrilled by your three letters which were waiting for me. I love you.—Monie."[13]

Aside from Wheeler's domain, Wescott's New York life now centered on John Connolly. He kept keys for Connolly's apartment, first one on West Fifty-seventh Street, then one of many years on West Sixtieth Street. There was enough substance and mutual loyalty to sustain the relationship, despite predictable problems. Wescott was disappointed when one of Connolly's young boyfriends encroached on his time. And in the midfifties, he felt let down when Connolly accepted François Reischenbach's offer to summer in Europe and work in the film business. In a low moment, he expressed his complaints to Connolly, but also his understanding that it was a mistake to rely too heavily on a younger lover: "I could not expect you to resist François' temptation to go abroad," he admitted, putting that issue aside. Then going on to the others, he said, "What altered our sex-life was not a failure of love or anyone's fault—it was a change in you; perhaps in me also. . . . I am in despair about my writing because I haven't had time to write, or freedom of mind, or assurance as to the future. I have wanted you to help me manage myself in my difficult transitional circumstances—but I understand your not knowing how to; not being able to." Two days later, Wescott added a journal-like note to his copy of the letter: "Lloyd always speaks of self-pity as the worst of all vices of the mind. I believe in both pity and self-pity. But not self indulgence."[14]

Possessed of a happy nature and devoted to Wescott, Connolly could smooth over the problems. Wescott saw him off on his trip, and Connolly recalled, "François was creating a documentary, a travelogue. I went from Paris to Luxembourg to Brussels to Amsterdam to Copenhagen to France to Spain!"[15] He also took on related chores, such as driving the temperamental writer Violette Leduc through Italy. The experience led him back to Wescott and later to a career in the film business.

As always, Stone-blossom balanced Wescott and Wheeler's world. There they celebrated the golden anniversary of Bruce and Josephine Wescott.[16] Ralph Pomeroy found that what he loved at Wheeler's apartment, he also found at Stone-blossom, but more so. "This was an eighteenth-century household," he said, "filled with art, music, literature, sculpture, wonderful talk." He was amazed by Barbara and Lloyd's house, the Mill, especially the artwork, antiques, and the picture window through which cows would look over a stone wall into the living room. Of Lloyd and Barbara, Pomeroy said, "I've always been upset by accusations that Glenway and Monroe orchestrated that marriage. Ridiculous! Barbara was a free spirit. And Lloyd was hot! He was D. H. Lawrence—white silk shirt and overalls."[17]

Connolly recalled, "The first time I came to Stone-blossom I didn't know what to expect. Glenway had a magnificent old house, hard by the road, white clapboard, long and wide." Contributing humor, folk wisdom, and loyalty to the household was housekeeper/cook Anna Brakke. A tiny treasure, Anna lived on one side of the house with a handyman brother and ancient mother. Connolly learned of Anna's personal story: "As a girl she'd married an extremely beautiful Czechoslovakian boy, but only weeks later he died in a factory accident, for which she got no compensation. She kept his picture but never again considered marriage." Anna enjoyed the democracy at Wescott's small corner of the farm. Once, in a kitchen fight with Wescott, who preferred healthful cooking, Anna argued, "Just what you like, and what goes good, that's it. After all, Mr. Wescott, when we disappear, we're not going to come back and eat, are we?"[18]

Connolly also remembered the Wescott parents. "Bruce was bemused by the sophistication of his brood. Josephine was quite small and very sweet. But what character they instilled in their children!" Of Lloyd and Barbara, Connolly said, "They were very handsome together, but Barbara depended on Glenway more and more for sociability." Bernard Perlin also remembered Barbara's dependence on Wescott: "Barbara was a lovely person, quiet, shy, rarely self-assertive. Then she'd say something to knock your socks off! But Glenway was her substitute husband, he was her entertainment, he was her life. He earned whatever he got." Wescott escorted Barbara to local museums and New York concerts. A number of times they visited the Philadelphia Museum and trustee Henry McIlhenny, who was himself a great collector of nineteenth century French and English masters. As to the power structure at the farm, Connolly said, "Lloyd could put his foot down. But when Barbara put her foot down, that was it. She was a matriarch."[19]

Lloyd Wescott was more than a gentleman farmer. He was a director of the local Hunterdon County Medical Center and a board member of a women's prison in Clinton, and he held a high level position with the New Jersey Department of Agriculture. On March 22, 1952, Wescott and John Connolly were dining at the main house when Lloyd fell seriously ill. An ambulance took him to the hospital where he had late-night surgery for a perforated duodenal ulcer. A strong man at forty-five, Lloyd recovered, but he would have related illnesses over the years. Barbara suffered a less serious ulcer later that year, after missing Glenway during his European trip.

A major family crisis occurred the following year with the unexpected death of Bruce Wescott. Glenway wrote to Alfred Kinsey about his father: "It was one of those rapid abdominal cancers that make one think of being burned at the stake."[20] After drastic surgery on November 12, Bruce Wescott died on November 18 at the Hunterdon County Medical Center in Flemington, a facility that Lloyd helped found. Since Lloyd was having a relapse of his stomach ulcer, and Josephine was ill herself, Glenway took charge, staying at the hospital as much as possible, sleeping there the last three days. At 2:15 A.M., a nurse left the room for coffee and Glenway was alone with Bruce in the final moment. Long forgotten was the trouble between them during Glenway's unhappy childhood. "The love and good understanding between me and the hopeless dying man was extraordinary," he told Kinsey.[21] His four sisters arrived for a private family service.

During these difficult weeks, Monroe Wheeler was in Latin American and Glenway was forced to make a decision alone. Josephine Wescott was ill after two minor strokes, and her house in nearby Clinton was lonely and sad. Certainly Barbara was too high strung to take in her mother-in-law. Finally, Lloyd sat down to talk finances with Glenway, and suddenly asked if he and Wheeler would be willing to take in their mother. Unable to consult Wheeler, Glenway immediately said yes. Agreeing meant accepting a more sober, mature lifestyle at Stone-blossom. Having earned little income in recent years, he told a friend: "As Lloyd and I are inclined to see things, this is the sort of responsibility he paid me for."[22] His new bedroom was a small side room, and weekend guests would be rare for some time. Losing his study seemed a symbolic comment on his productivity.

Yet Wescott took on the care of his mother gladly. Over the next several years he turned down invitations to Europe from both François Reischenbach and Pauline Potter. Pauline was now settled in France as Baroness Pauline de Rothschild, having married Philippe. Wescott's concern was justified. Returning from his annual Cape Cod trip to the Cranes' summer home, he was surprised to see how much his mother had declined. Loyal housekeeper Anna agreed that Josephine depended on him to give her life meaning. Wescott cheered Josephine with talks and outings and read to her. A joyful photo of this period shows Wescott and his mother at Stone-blossom, laughing together on the steps of the front porch.

At the edge of Wescott and Wheeler's world was George Platt Lynes. He had returned from California with only his furniture, cameras, and a boyfriend/model named Randy Jack. At first he stayed with his brother, Russell, then got a cold water flat and finally a grand place on Sixtieth Street. "God, he had style," said Bernard Perlin, "even without money. He was borrowing. He was working, but not much, and he sold photos to Dr. Kinsey and *Der Kreis* magazine."[23] Kinsey was able to buy some of the nudes and portraits for the Institute, and Lynes gave him others. *Der Kreis* (The Circle) was a monthly European gay journal of the forties and fifties, edited by Karl Meier. Printed in German, French, and English, it attracted work from writers such as James Barr and Sam Steward, and artists and photographers such as Paul Cadmus and Lynes. Lynes published male nudes under the pseudonyms Roberto Rolf and Robert Orville.

Although Lynes's glory days were behind him, he was still widely respected for his sense of style and, of course, for his celebrity portraits, ballet photos, and male nude photography with its dramatic use of light and shadow. Steward remembered, "George's name had a magic all its own in New York." Lynes showed him his apartment, filled with the work of major artists he knew, let him help himself to fifty of his own photos, and took him to the kind of place Wescott would never go. "On one evening of that New York visit," Steward recalled, "George and I went to a hustler's bar on Forty-second Street near Times Square and sat in a dim booth to meet Bill Inge, the enormously popular playwright of *Picnic* and *Come Back, Little Sheba*."[24] They remained friends, and Lynes encouraged Steward to write his "Phil Andros" pornography stories and novels.

One of Lynes's best friends, Paul Cadmus, remembered Lynes fondly and with humor. "People often thought that Lincoln Kirstein and George were great friends when they went to prep school together," Cadmus said, "but George said, 'No, I hated him. He had all the football players!' He was jealous of Lincoln's success there. But they got to be quite good friends. I remember a statement George made that describes him perfectly. He said, 'There's *nothing* unpretentious about me!' And it was absolutely true. But he was a very good host. Everybody loved to be photographed by him and took off their clothes as quickly as they could, as soon as he wanted."[25]

Cadmus knew Lynes's situation was bad after he returned from Hollywood: "He got terribly in debt. George had no sense about extravagance. He had no money, but he loved buying things, he loved jewelry, and giving presents." Bernard Perlin joked, "George was very generous, whether or not he had money."[26] When he returned from a sabbatical in Rome, Perlin stayed with George briefly and, like others, gave him as much money as he could. He preferred to remember the heady days of the forties when Lynes let him use part of his large studio, a space Lynes previously shared with Marsden Hartley, and later with Richard Avedon.

Steward believed that Lynes knew his health was failing as early as the spring of 1954. If so, Lynes had no proof, no diagnosis beyond colds and bronchitis. But he may have suspected the worst. He had sent photos to Kinsey's Institute before, but in April 1954 he turned over negatives for hundreds of photos. His health declined throughout the year. Wescott noticed that Lynes was conspicuously absent from a party of close friends at designer Chuck Howard's apartment in January 1955. He sent him a kind note and mentioned giving an essay about Lynes's photography to Sy Kahn of Beloit College, who was writing about him.[27] Later that month, Christopher Isherwood and Don Bachardy were in town and took Lynes out to a restaurant. But by late winter and spring, he was suffering from headaches, chest pain, and a cough. Finally in mid-May, he agreed to undergo more than a week of tests at New York Hospital and was diagnosed with a lung tumor. Exploratory surgery revealed that both lungs were affected and nothing could be done. The doctors spoke to Lynes in euphemisms but told his brother the whole truth, and Russell Lynes immediately told Wheeler and Wescott.

From a Yaddo writers' retreat, Pomeroy wrote to Wheeler about his writing project there and was surprised by the moving letter Wheeler sent in reply:

"Death Has Closed Eyes" is a good title for your story. And to my grief this evening it is, before many months, to close those of my dear former love George Platt Lynes. His brother phoned me. . . . The operation took place today, and I obtained a report from Russell this evening. It is a cancer so advanced . . . the only way to prolong his life was not to touch it, but to alleviate it as much as possible with radium treatments. The doctors cannot say how long it will be, but they must know by now ways to prevent too much suffering, and he has a large and devoted family and circle of friends to divert him. For twenty years, from the age of twenty to forty, he had a life anyone might envy; then folly took control as he was incapable of reason, and of maintaining the golden present and near. But his capacities were fully realized, and who can do more? Many people will enjoy seeing his photographs for a long time to come, and he has given pleasure to many, which is a marvelous thing.[28]

Wescott wrote Isherwood on May 24 with the news and said Russell Lynes, the successful *Harper's* editor, was already clearing out his brother's apartment, on which Lynes owed months of rent. Isherwood replied from Santa Monica: "My dear Glenway, Thank you so much for writing. I can't tell you how much your news of George saddens me. I had heard he was sick but imagined that at worst it was T.B., which is rarely a menace nowadays. And now this awful shock. Don is very upset too. George was so sweet to him. . . . Let this tragedy at least cause us to stay closer together in the future, even if it's only short notes."[29]

Wheeler was leaving on a six-city European trip with Raymond Mortimer. Before he left, Lynes, barely out of the hospital, photographed him on June 16—his final portrait of Wheeler, in his last studio. Lynes was feeling a little better but growing restless living with his brother and sister-in-law. In Venice Wheeler learned from Wescott that new antibiotics were helping Lynes and that François and Philippe Reischenbach had offered Lynes a trip to Paris in the fall.[30] In late July, Wescott helped Lynes clear out his studio. In the charged atmosphere, he found they were having their best talks in many years. Katherine Anne Porter, who was also moving from her city home to Connecticut, bravely joined in their high spirits and humor, though she was well aware of the bad news.

In late August, Lynes wrote to Wheeler, who was at the Cranes' Cape Cod home, from his family's summer home in North Egremont, Massachusetts: "I'm sick of the parade of symptoms, etc. So, let's just say I'm feeling quite a lot better and let it go at that." In a blunt phone conversation, Lynes told Sam Steward: "I am taking 20-odd kinds of pills, and there are terrible pains in my chest, as if an elephant were sitting on me." Bernard Perlin was with Lynes and remembers putting salve on the burns from his cobalt treatment and that Lynes was taking cortisone. Perlin also remembered that "George suddenly developed an obsession for an Australian tennis star and dragged us to the tennis matches!"[31]

Before leaving for Europe, for what Lynes called his "sentimental journey," he destroyed much of his fashion photography, including negatives, and asked Wescott to deliver some final nude photos to Kinsey's Institute. Wescott told James Charlton in California that it was fitting he had heard the bad news from Bernadine Szold, because it was she who sent Lynes to them in the twenties. In a note to his teenage niece, Wescott wrote: "Item from Paris: poor George Lynes has had his hair dyed."[32]

Kinsey and Lynes crossed paths in Paris that year, but it was not a happy reunion. Kinsey told Sam Steward: "We had arranged to have dinner at a very expensive restaurant, but George looked ill and his mood was black. Suddenly in the midst of everything he made a nasty scene, grew furious with the waiter and indeed all of us, pushed away from the table leaving his steak untouched, and left the restaurant in great anger. I never saw him again." John Connolly also reported seeing George in Paris: "The last time I saw him was in a cafe and he introduced me to Gloria Swanson."[33]

In the face of their impending tragedy, Wescott wrote one of his characteristic aphorisms in his journal. Decades later it would be quoted in reference to AIDS: "The answer to death is *not* love, in which the suicidal spirit enters too frequently; it is sex: the all-forgetting sensation, the paroxysm of present tense, and relief from will power."[34]

Lynes came back to New York with a short Canadian friend named Glen McCourt. Perlin said, "McCourt was not George's cup of tea, so it wasn't about sex, but Glen was a godsend at the end, because George was extremely difficult. He was spending money on narcotics, and selling things, including a small Picasso that Barbara had given him." Lynes was hospitalized in November. On a few nights he was able to leave the hospital to attend the ballet with friends, but he was declining quickly. Connolly said, "He was smoking in his hospital room at the end. He just didn't care." Wescott saw him with ice packs, heating pads, and pain-killers. By the first week of December, he was sleeping most of the time. Wescott and Wheeler remained in the city. Wheeler left his office at the museum every afternoon to visit. Josephine Wescott was visiting family in the Midwest but sent a telegram that Wescott kept and marked, "For George." It read, "Dear, Cannot express pity and anxiety. Convey profound sympathy."[35]

When Wescott visited the hospital on Tuesday, December 6, Lynes was sleeping and looked handsomer than he had all year. But that impression and the nurse's kindness made Wescott realize the time was close. Although agnostic, he went to the hospital chapel and prayed, he noted in his journal, for release, and in the hope that they might all understand Lynes's story correctly. That night, Wheeler took Wescott and Pomeroy to see a play. When they returned, Russell Lynes called and said it was over. Wheeler put the down phone and said, "Now I have a lot to think about."[36]

Wheeler and Russell Lynes arranged the funeral at Saint George's Church on Stuyvesant Square for Thursday, December 8. Lynes was buried in Woodlawn Cemetery, the resting place of his father and grandfather. Later that day, Marianne Moore sent this note: "I have been thinking about you, Monroe, affording strength and courage to us all, needing it yourself; taking your afternoon time to go see George and struggling to make up for it; refusing to let me bear any part of the heavy expenditure of today, or of your flowers. But Mildred and Russell certainly will do as I asked and let my offering diminish the expense of yours, in securing the special flowers. The finality of these partings—with life seeming to offer years of usefulness ahead, but for the inexplicable."[37]

Holidays were observed quietly that December. On Christmas Eve, Wescott's recorded reading of Walter De la Mare's poetry was broadcast on WEVD radio.

Lynes's circle of friends helped protect his place in photography. He had chosen his executor well in Bernard Perlin, who placed negatives and photos with archives, with advice from Lincoln Kirstein. Perlin also warned *Der Kreis* magazine and others about unpermitted use of photos. Although Kirstein had been estranged from Lynes, he now praised his ballet photos anew. He told Wescott that reviewing more than twenty years of Lynes photos of his and Balanchine's ballets had contributed to his knowledge of art. Lynes mastered the use of light, he said, and didn't use retouching as a substitute for focus. Lynes created style, he realized, and the impression strengthens with time.[38]

Kirstein then met with Wheeler and Perlin about future Lynes exhibits at the Museum of Modern Art and City Center. When Wescott suggested a book of ballet photos, Kirstein responded that the idea was thrilling and he would try to make it happen soon. In fact, a beautiful book was in print within a year. When Katherine Anne Porter thanked Wescott for her advance copy, she admitted that she hadn't cried for Lynes yet, because "his fate was so hard, and the homeless wretchedness of his last months was too tragic to cry about."[39]

Wescott remembered Lynes fondly in a note to his niece, Debo: "We are all profoundly moved—he had the gift of keeping friends, no matter what grievances developed. Also, in a way which I may try to explain someday, he was our scapegoat. Of course we are grateful for the fact that his suffering did not go on and on. He slept almost all the last week."[40] To friends, he explained that Lynes was their scapegoat because his extravagances made everyone else's behavior seem moderate.

Years later, Paul Cadmus said of Lynes's work, "Well, I think he's better than Maplethorpe. And I think Maplethorpe was influenced by him."

Of his life he said fondly, "His friends forgave him all his faults. He had such charm."[41]

Ralph Pomeroy recalled, "My memory of George Platt Lynes is of a big party at his apartment on the East Side. All the walls in the bedroom were covered with raspberry silk. There was photography and art that had special meaning to his friends. I was dazzled. To me it was a time that will never happen again."[42]

10

Beyond Fiction

The Valley Submerged

ACCORDING to Bernard Perlin, "Glenway dedicated himself to society more than to writing. He liked being a personage, a storyteller, a conversationalist. It was as though he was never contented with just publishing. He had a very strong ego, a very strong sense of who he ought to have been, of who he had been."[1]

Caroline Newton from the early Chicago days was thrilled to renew her friendship with Wescott in the fifties. Hearing his captivating voice again, she said, reminded her of many stimulating and happy hours she owed him. Wescott replied, "Thank you, but I hope I shall be able to write more, talk less." But the part of himself he called "Wescott the Talker" clearly outpaced "Wescott the Writer." No one could deny he was one of the great conversationalists of his time. Even his letters hinted that hours of fascinating talk could follow. His reply to Newton mentioned recent atom bomb testing: "What a strange era we live in, worse than anyone has any idea." And he said he found proof of Lord Byron's long-rumored love for a French boy named Giraud—in a bookseller's catalog, which offered a draft of a will by Byron that left most of his fortune to Giraud.[2]

Increasingly, he was sought after as a public speaker. When Bard College awarded an honorary doctorate to Wallace Stevens, Wescott was asked to lecture. The event reminded him of his own boyhood: "Mr. Stevens was the first poet I loved. I memorized 'Sunday Morning' and 'The Comedians,' and cut his poems out of the magazines before his books came out." Stevens had praised Wescott's first book of poems in 1920. Now, on the same platform at Bard College, Wescott gave a talk about

Virginia Woolf's *Mrs. Dalloway.* Concerned that the students didn't understand, he feared he had done it badly. Then it was Wallace Stevens's turn. Wescott remembered, "Stevens was the stuffiest man you'd ever know. He was the vice president of an insurance company in Hartford. And he'd walk to work and make up a few lines of whatever poem he was writing . . . then sit down and play insurance man all day. Most people loathed him, and I must say he wasn't a barrel of laughs. But he got up in front of the students at Bard College and said, 'I want to tell you something, boys and girls, about Mr. Wescott's lecture. I want to call your attention to the fact that every word of it was the direct result of a life—and it's getting to be rather a long life—dedicated to literature.'"[3]

Wescott's life in literature was often entertaining. When he nominated Carson McCullers to the National Institute of Arts and Letters, Katherine Anne Porter and William Faulkner resisted. "But I got her in," he said, "Carson kissed me with her mouth wide open, I'll never forget it, ha!" And he remembered, "She'd once fallen in love with Katherine Anne Porter at Yaddo, that's all come out now. Katherine Anne just couldn't stand this crazy, limping, drunk, pale, chinless-wonder rival writer coming and saying, 'I'll die if you don't talk to me.' And one night Carson got carried away and slept all the summer night long at the door of Porter's room. When Katherine Anne opened the door in the morning and found Carson there snoring away her hangover and stinking up the place, she kicked her—just gave her a good kick! Porter admitted it, she said she couldn't help it. And Carson fled and never came back again."[4] Years later, Wescott helped McCullers make revisions to *The Square Root of Wonderful* when advance reviews were unkind, and the play did have at least a short Broadway run.

Events at the Academy often produced colorful stories. John Connolly remembered that Wescott took him to a dinner there in the late fifties and introduced him to a new member, playwright Arthur Miller, and his wife, Marilyn Monroe. "When it ended," Connolly confessed, "I took Marilyn's glass, which had her lipstick on it." Bernard Perlin was also there and recalled Marianne Moore's saying, "I'm the other 'MM' at this party."[5]

An interesting dimension of Wescott's powerful public presence was that he and Monroe Wheeler never hesitated to appear together as a couple, even at the most formal affairs. In a piece on architect Philip Johnson, Brendan Gill noted: "Until well into the sixties, it was convenient for hostesses to pretend that homosexuals were unattached bachelors; they were certainly not to be invited in pairs. In Johnson's circle, the novelist Glenway Wescott and Monroe Wheeler, a member of the staff of the Museum of Modern Art, were an exception to the rule. Wescott and Wheeler were inseparable and, wearing wedding rings, were accepted as a married couple in the forties and fifties by even the most indurate of homophobes."[6]

Though Wescott and Wheeler were among the most accepted and privileged gay couples in America, Wescott remained sensitive to the cases of antigay discrimination and police harassment. He recorded in his journal: "News Item: Thirty-two men have been arrested in a Turkish bath. The *Herald Tribune* listed their occupations: social worker, tailor, schoolteacher, nightclub entertainer, Transit Authority patrolman, undertaker, broker, interpreter, doctor, and traffic consultant. Michael Miksche called this to my attention, somewhat rejoicing in the fact that the arts and literature were not represented."[7] Headlined "32 Men Seized in Vice Raid at East Side Bath," the article reported that Herbert Weinberg, fifty-five, owner of the Saint Marks Baths at 6 Saint Marks Place, was arrested along with thirty-one patrons. The fact that most of the men refused to plead guilty foreshadowed a changing decade ahead.

Although Wescott had removed himself from Carl Malouf's circle after meeting John Connolly, Michael Miksche remained a disturbing presence. The bomber pilot turned illustrator, the sadomasochist whose instability had worried Alfred Kinsey, decided to marry a woman. Wescott could not escape his tragic story. "Michael fell in love with a boy called Gino who was a ravishing little Italian who had been in jail, and who was oversexed in the way of absolute abandon. This boy had no culture at all, moral culture, except in Italian opera, you know, the killing. Michael had been unfaithful to him, and Gino had caught him. One day Michael came in and found Gino with an empty bottle of gin on the floor and feeding Michael's select artwork into the fireplace. Michael trembled from head to foot and decided to kill him, but turned back out and slammed the door." Miksche got a friend to warn Gino to leave immediately, then met with Wescott. "He said, 'I never expect to experience with anyone the bliss I experienced with Gino. But I never will see him again because if I do I'll kill him, and you know I'm quite capable of it.' And I did know that. He said, 'I've decided the only thing for me is to go back to women, get married, make a living, frequent heterosexual society, and avoid all the bars and the rest of it.' He said, 'Do you think it will work?' I said I thought it would work physically, I didn't know about the rest of it. Well, Kinsey, when I told him this, was so angry. He said, 'Don't you know that man is a killer? How can you recommend such a foolish thing, he can't possibly live happily with a woman.' I said I didn't say he would live happily, but that it would be a success sexually, and it was. But what I hadn't known was that he'd get so bored."[8]

Even after Miksche's marriage, he would still try to see Wescott. "Michael would call. His wife was a very admirable strong female, a successful advertising person, but she was two-dimensional; she only wanted this great character. They had a hideous little baby. He would ask me to dine with them and then he would get on the bed with her and fondle her and I would sit on the bottom of the bed and talk or read to them, and he would hope to go to bed with both of us. And I just wasn't playing that game, I knew she was in anguish. I cleared out. Then he never called me at all, except when he was drunk in the middle of the night or when he was sobbing with sorrow."[9] Miksche would return, Wescott knew, as would the memory of Kinsey's warning.

In contrast, the people Wescott wanted to see most, he saw less. In 1957, John Connolly accepted the position of assistant to William Inge and spent six months a year in California. Connolly kept his apartment on Fifty-seventh Street, and Inge his on Sutton Place. Otherwise they lived in opposite wings of Inge's house in Hollywood. Already experienced in the business, Connolly now became accustomed to rush deadlines and travel. He said, "Bill Inge liked to write at night and I'd have to rush the follow-up work the next day. He also wanted me to deal with the lighting at all the theaters where his plays were going on."[10] Although Wescott regretted Connolly's absences, he appreciated the job's importance to his career. Ralph Pomeroy remembered Wescott's opinion of Inge: "Some people thought Inge was second rate, despite all his success, but Glenway said, 'He has a certain talent. And it tracks.'"[11]

Another of Wescott's closest friends was also absent. Since Pauline Potter had married Baron Philippe and moved to Château Mouton Rothschild, their contact was limited to letters. Wescott complained, "I miss you grievously, passionately." Yet his life was filled with the demands of a busy schedule. Caring for his mother, he avoided lengthy trips, but often lectured. While visiting Paul Gebhard at the Institute for Sex Research, he took part in the writers' conference across the Indiana University campus. He described one day to Bernard Perlin: "A conference with a colleague and a pupil at seven a.m., all the morning preparing a new lecture, and perusing and annotating five manuscripts, then lunch with my boss, and my lecture out under a tree, attended by a squirrel also, then the big evening lecture of the rival prima donna here, Mizener, the Fitzgerald biographer, followed by a debate conducted by me, deliberately provoking, to stir up discussion—to bed at twelve, wild with weariness, requiring a pill."[12] Arthur Mizener interviewed Wescott for his book, as did another F. Scott Fitzgerald biographer, Andrew Turnbull. Over the decades, dozens of biographers would interview him about his literary contemporaries.

Wescott's lecture topics of the fifties included Virginia Woolf, Ernest Hemingway, André Malraux, Somerset Maugham, Ford Madox Ford, Colette, Thornton Wilder, Gertrude Stein, E. E. Cummings, Isak Dinesen, and Thomas Mann. His lecture venues were Josephine Crane's "Monday Class," City College, the Poetry Center at the Ninety-second Street YMHA, and universities around the country. At the fiftieth anniversary of the MacDowell Colony in 1957, he spoke about Marianne Moore and presented her with an award. As he sat with Miss Moore and her brother, Warner, on a platform under a green and yellow tent, he realized it was thirty-six years since he had been there.

He also took on numerous appearances and duties for the Academy and other writers' organizations. Marianne Moore once warned him, "You don't speak of your own work. You participate so charitably in many a person's enterprise, I wonder that you can gain headway at all."[13]

While not producing a major work in the fifties, Wescott was becoming a master of the big literary essay and article, in his intimate, educating style. His introduction to *The Maugham Reader* examined the author's work but also praised Maugham's dedication: "Regularly every morning he goes to his desk and labors at his writing. For months at a time he will not skip a day." In "A Transatlantic Glance" in the *Griffin,* he reflected on reasons that some writers translate well to other languages, such as timeliness and subject matter.[14]

Wescott wrote a lengthy introduction to *The Short Novels of Colette,* and no writer in America was better qualified. As a birthday present Monroe Wheeler had given him the French language edition of the complete works of Colette and had it bound in Holland: fifteen volumes, seven thousand pages, two million words. Wescott read and reread every word. When his introduction of nearly twenty thousand words was on deadline, he took half a Benzedrine as needed.[15] In one paragraph he summed up the plight of the serious artist, whether great like Colette or merely good: "It is an essential feature of the artist's temperament: pride of greatness—and heartbreaking ideal of greatness for those who know that they personally are second-rate, which keeps them from declining to third-rate or fourth-rate—taking all that has been done already as a matter of course, a matter of no further interest; climbing up on the previous proud accomplishment, not to glory in it, just to see what may lie beyond, perhaps accomplishable, if one lives long enough. From which must derive from aging artists a certain chronic bitterness, and for second-raters, a sickness at heart. For we never do live long enough."[16]

The piece also appeared in *Vogue,* and later Wescott recollected his Paris visit to Colette for *Town and Country.* Among his ongoing published work in *Proceedings of the American Academy and Institute of Arts and Letters* were discussions of Edith Sitwell, works of art, Robert Frost, and other poets.[17]

At the suggestion of the poet Louise Bogan, *New Yorker* editor William Maxwell urged Wescott to write for the magazine.[18] But they never agreed on a role. Wescott wanted a column, not an office position like Bogan's. Somehow the opportunity was missed, on all sides.

Wescott was always capable of writing something completely unexpected and unusual. Such a work was a new edition of *Twelve Fables of*

Aesop. Under Monroe Wheeler, the Museum of Modern Art publications department was creating not only beautiful exhibit catalogs, art books, and reproductions but also some deluxe specialty books. Years earlier Wheeler had created for Harrison of Paris *Aesop's Fables* with illustrations by Alexander Calder. Now he wanted a selection of fables, illustrated by Uruguayan artist Antonio Frasconi, with a modern rewriting of the tales. When Marianne Moore turned down the offer, Wheeler turned to Wescott.

Frasconi's linoleum plate illustrations were humorous, and Wescott's retitled and retold tales bore his special touch. The moral of "The Hare with Ability and the Tortoise with Staying Power" is "Persistent ambition without talent breaks no record. Talent without character wins no race." In "The Stag in His Own Opinion," a great stag is proud of its powerful antlers but embarrassed by its thin feet and weak ankles. When a hunting dog gives chase, the stag's legs carry it away quickly but its antlers get caught in underbrush as the dog closes in. Wescott's dry rendering of Aesop's moral: "Self-opinion often is a snare and a delusion. One's pride and joy may be deadly, and one's inferiorities functional in some circumstances." The deluxe original edition of *Twelve Fables of Aesop* was printed in a black slipcase with a red cover and gold lettering on the spine. The less expensive edition that followed was sold and reprinted for twenty years.[19]

At the same time, Marianne Moore published a ten-year project, her verse translation of La Fontaine's 231 fables. With her usual outlandish modesty, she told Wescott that his twelve fables were "more dashing" than hers: "You amaze me. I envy you; I could not possibly have got individuality and charm into the book as you have, or proceeded with your firm light touch." Later, she added, "Tales with a bite, Glenway; amazing the novelty, the naturalness; the sure diction—a department in which you have always starred. . . . And the morals! 'Talent without character wins no race.'" Wescott scholar William Rueckert saw *Twelve Fables of Aesop* as truth-telling narrative in a straightforward style, with an execution that was "faultless." Once again, Rueckert noted, Wescott showed the ability to perfect a form, then move on.[20]

Wescott's most important works reappeared in the fifties. *The Pilgrim Hawk* appeared in a new German edition and in the anthology *Six Great Modern Short Novels* (the other five were *The Dead* by James Joyce, *Billy Budd* by Herman Melville, *Noon Wine* by Katherine Anne Porter, *The Overcoat* by Nikolai Gogol, and *The Bear* by William Faulkner). The mass market paperback of *Short Novels* has been reprinted many times. Harper and Brothers published a Modern Classics edition of *The Grandmothers* in 1955. An old story Wescott considered one of his best, "The Sailor," was reprinted in a paperback anthology along with stories by

Denton Welch, Shirley Jackson, William Faulkner, Jean-Paul Sartre, and others.[21]

Writing projects that went unfinished included the idealistic novel "A Year of Love"; his poetic first glimpse of England, "The Yellow Fog" (see chapter 2); and "The Leider Singer," a long story based on Elena Gerhardt. His idea for a collection of essays and memoir, "A Dust Basket," would eventually lead to a book of essays, under a different name. The greatest loss was the book that should have been Wescott's fifth novel, "Children of This World."

Carl Malouf said, "Glenway was always talking about his journals. I thought, 'Journals? I want another novel.'" Wheeler especially wanted that last novel. He confided to Katherine Anne Porter: "Glenway is in good health. Needled by a young professor who wants to write a Ph.D. thesis on him, he started looking for certain early pieces and has got himself in an insuperable task of sorting and ordering millions of papers and letters. At this point he would rather do anything than write another story, but something will come of it I feel sure. His mother is an awful burden, and he is a saint." The young professor Wheeler referred to, Sy M. Kahn, wrote a major dissertation on Wescott and published an excellent bibliography of his work.[22]

Unfortunately, Wescott confused the need to write a new novel with his financial dependence on Lloyd and Barbara. He once confessed to Lloyd "my overwhelming disappointment and guiltiness" and said, "The real reason for my unproductivity has been just my weakness, foolishness, self-indulgence, pursuit of pleasure, laziness. All my life I have had to force myself to write; sitting at my desk somewhat longer than anyone else has to, in grim determination and concentration, waiting and waiting to feel my talent. . . . No inadequacy of talent as such; in any case no diminishment, no change. I have only grown impatient and cowardly about it."[23] Yet Wescott's self-criticism is excessive; he wrote every day and he wrote a great deal.

Remembering his two experiences with best sellers, Wescott told old friend Raymond Mortimer: "Twice in my lifetime, as by chance, great reverberating illusion-inducing success—and in-between it has all been rather like the watercolors of the handless, the weaving of the blind."[24] With bitter humor he added: "Don't quote any of this to William Maugham—my 'career' as a writer always inclines him to a sort of mercy killing." As for Wheeler, Wescott called him "my great unpardoning undiscouraged consort."[25] But what Wheeler really wanted, Wescott knew, was another novel, and not for the money, although there was nothing wrong with that, but for Wescott's happiness and, most important, for the sake of creating another wonderful book. Behind Wheeler's stinging comments was love, and love of literature. They understood each other too well. In a handwritten journal note, Wescott commented, "Monroe: Oh, he has the courage to hurt me!—and sometimes with uncertainty, or perhaps double meaning, whether it is disciplinary, for me, for my benefit, or whether self-expressive upon impulse, to relieve some grief of his own."[26]

Wescott had to make up his mind about "Children of This World," the book he called "the Chicago novel," originally titled "Cain and Abel." He had dated an early draft during Maugham's years in America "Yemassee, January 1946." Many years later, he attached a cover note, explaining that he gave up on the book because it was "too populous and too inventive for my capacity."[27]

The autobiographical first chapter begins, "My grandmother cautioned me against Chicago." Alwyn Tower has won a scholarship to the university, and his Wisconsin family worries over him as he packs to leave the farm: "I was sixteen years old, unworldly and ignorant though not innocent. I had experienced blissful sex, a year and a half of love, and then renunciation of love; and had learned things about myself that made me very uneasy, if not desperate, imaginative and alertly selfconscious. Even the one I had loved knew only my behavior, never my entire feeling."

Before leaving, Alwyn says, "That night I slept not very well at all, in the bedroom in which, come to think of it, I was born, and in which, as it happened, I had lost my virginity." Once the novel moves to Chicago, Wescott's notes show a plan for the story structure: "The four planes or dimensions: My Life; Others' Stories; Others' Lives; Collective Life." An outline for the early chapters reveals vivid autobiographical subjects: "University and Poetry Club; Furnished Room on North Dearborn Street; Dream of My Father; Burning of Lloyd's Hands; Analyst! False Homosexuality: Mrs. Moody etc.; Villefranche; Edward Sheldon."

Some scenes are well drafted, such as Alwyn's escape from a robbery attempt on Peach Street, which actually happened to Wescott at twenty when returning from Wheeler's home to his downtown boarding house at night. There is also a sympathetic talk with a prostitute, and the short-lived job at Hart, Shaffner and Marx. The Poetry Club material is especially good. Of Imagist poetry, his fictional self says, "The point was to write as vividly as possible while keeping a maximum of reticence." As for the young poets, "We fancied ourselves inventing our aesthetic as we went along—deducing most of it in fact from the work of the elders we most admired who had the most singularity, the least popularity. . . . Above all we wrote for one another, to impress one another, not in competition or to be judged by some outsider."

Chapter 2 includes material on Clement Auer, the boy who tried unsuccessfully to seduce Wescott, once by remaining nude while Wescott visited his rooms and once by menacing him with a pistol. Chapter 3 includes his last visit to the tragic girl who loved him in her last months, Maurine

Smith. Broaching subjects of sex and sexuality honestly makes "Children of This World" intriguing, as in chapter 5: "The evil elements in sex are seduction, temptation, craving, frustration, humiliation, immoderation and insatiability—no matter how ideal your relationship, how elysian your happiness, you'd better face it, it's there, woven in, criss-cross in the very fabric. Furthermore, it is in life itself."

The major problem with the book is that Alwyn Tower is the narrator but not the main character. That person is Jock, a character Wescott's handwritten notes say is drawn from Paul Humphrey, the big, handsome, masculine fellow from the real Poetry Club. While not a great talent, Humphrey was an ideal heterosexual hero for Wescott, in fact and fiction. Starting with Alwyn Tower and then turning him into a secondary character is a mistake he had made before. Here, more than four hundred pages ran aground.

It is likely that Wescott's instinct to limit his Alwyn Tower character was a reluctance to develop the early sexual references in the novel. A homosexual narrator was still unwelcome in mainstream publishing, as Gore Vidal had learned with *The City and the Pillar.* And Wescott's divided feelings came from internal as well as external pressure. A fifties journal note confessed, "My feeling of being prevented from writing about homosexuality (by Monroe + Lloyd + Barbara) equals in an important degree my own inhibition, more or less cowardly, fear, dread of punishment, uncertainty of the moral ethics and the psychology."[28]

More significantly, Glenway's financial dependence on Barbara and Lloyd made him feel undue pressure about producing another major novel, and reluctance to give up the effort. On one occasion, when Lloyd forgot to deposit a check for his brother, Glenway felt embarrassed about mentioning it, and confessed all his mixed feelings about the situation. Barbara responded with a tough-love but loving message: "As to your further problems, if Lloyd or I shrink from them (or seem to) it is rather from a feeling that whatever helpfulness we might offer—whatever mere brotherly love or money—it must inevitably fall short of the scope and complexity of your needs and problems (your life, or lives, and not just the surface!)—and not in the least from any disapprobation or disillusionment about you! (If I ever 'disapproved' of you, dear, I never knew it.) . . . Where your troubles are financial, Lloyd and I can help, and shall want to go on helping as much and as long as possible. Especially in relation to Mother this seems picayune compared to the sacrifices you've made and are making for her. . . . With so much love and admiration always, Barbara."[29]

Several years later, after another discussion of the uncomfortable subject, Barbara responded in the best way possible: "Tho I am delighted and flattered when you do talk about work on hand, or up ahead, I do not expect you to do it any more than I expect to hear about your sex life or your dreams! . . . As to my 'right' to reproach you—dear Glenway, inspiration and creation can't be owed, nor bought, nor sold—nor held by anyone but yourself. As between you and me the books have been balanced long ago, and on your side the credit stretches up into the future! Sometimes I realize that the indebtedness is all on my side, and ask myself to what extent the 'security' I have provided for you has not in fact hindered and burdened you."[30]

Sometime shortly after those reassuring words, Wescott made a clear decision when he told Wheeler and everyone else that he was abandoning "Children of This World." He had a great deal more to say and his instincts told him to move beyond fiction and concentrate on the nonfiction areas of literary and personal essays, where he now felt more comfortable. That also meant accepting a practical reality. He could no longer hope for the brass ring of a financial windfall, such as he had known with *Apartment in Athens*. Nonfiction articles and even books could not promise that. His writing and lectures would earn limited income, but he would still be dependent on Lloyd and Barbara. Humorously, he referred to himself as "a bird in a golden cage."

The problem of finances was worse when he had an extra expense. For example, in February of 1957 he had a bad fall at a country railroad station, gashing his head and chipping a tooth. When his birthday came around that spring, Barbara gave him an authentic Etruscan bronze. Beautiful as it was, he admitted to Raymond Mortimer that he wished he could sell it to pay his doctor, dentist, and lawyer.[31]

Aside from the demands of his family and work for the Academy-Institute, Wescott's life remained crowded with people and events. In fact, from his middle years to old age, the details of his and Wheeler's world are best summarized or reflected. When Pavlik Tchelitchew died in Rome, Bernadine Szold told Wescott her favorite memory of the artist: "I found a notation I'd made of what he once said about Monroe: 'His heart is like a red ruby.'" When a fire closed the Museum of Modern Art for much of 1958, Wheeler assured Osbert Sitwell that damage to Tchelitchew's controversial "Hide and Seek" and another painting could be repaired and the closing was an opportunity for refurbishing. When Wescott let Alice B. Toklas know of his lecture on Gertrude Stein, Toklas replied with two enthusiastic pages, edge to edge in her tiny script. "It was fabulous to hear from you," she wrote, "I think of you often. Your final call at the rue de Fleurus with Mina Loy is still vivid." But she expressed sorrow about George Platt Lynes: "He was the sweetest of the young men of whom I was fond."[32]

Even on holiday, Wescott and Wheeler kept up a busy pace. On June 20, 1958, they joined Janet Flanner and her American lover Natalia Danesi Murray for three days at Natalia's house at Cherry Grove, Fire Island. On

June 23 they rushed back so Wescott could attend Eleanor Roosevelt's appearance at Clinton Farms, the women's prison Lloyd supported, while Flanner accepted an award for journalism from Senator John F. Kennedy at Smith College. That night they reunited at Flanner's party for journalist Mary McCarthy.

Wescott had enjoyed Fire Island with friends since the twenties and still visited Paul Cadmus at Saltaire, but they were intrigued by the emerging gay community of Cherry Grove. Cadmus remembered, "We walked to Cherry Grove when the sand was hard, eleven miles each way. It was a wonderful walk. We'd go just to check the gay life there. . . . I remember there was a sign in front of one of the houses, 'The *Lesbins* must leave our young boys alone.' I never heard gays called 'Lesbins' before—they got it wrong in every way!" Wescott recorded a glimpse of Cherry Grove in his journal: "Just beyond these bungalows, just over the dunes, there lies heavenly landscape, sandscape, with delights of the flesh and the weather more selfish than anything in the world. Friday night when we arrived they took me down to the beach, the harvest moon had just risen. It seemed to have come up terribly excited, like a bull into an arena."[33]

Good friends and familiar retreats—including Cape Cod with the Cranes—were welcome during a year of illnesses. In 1958, Josephine Wescott suffered a stroke and made a partial recovery. Wheeler was hospitalized with another attack of shingles, which affected his right leg, but he recovered quickly. Barbara, now fifty-four, suffered a coronary thrombosis and was hospitalized for six weeks at Hunterdon County Medical Center, which Wescott praised as "Lloyd's perfect little hospital and great specialists."[34] Barbara organized annual fundraising art auctions for the Karen Horney Psychoanalytic Clinic and Institute in Manhattan, and Glenway and his young friends saved the day, gathering and framing three hundred pictures. Lloyd himself needed surgery for an intestinal lesion, related to his operation years earlier.

That year Wheeler learned that the grand old building at 410 Park Avenue would be demolished and replaced by a ghastly office tower. He found a small apartment at 215 East Seventy-ninth Street in a tall pale-blond brick building called the Thornely. It barely served their purposes for only two years. Far more unsettling news was delivered to Lloyd personally by New Jersey Governor Robert Meyner. After years of drought, the state decreed that the Raritan River would be diverted. The entire valley, including Mulhocaway farm, with Stone-blossom, would be submerged and turned into a reservoir. Farmers and homeowners would be compensated.

While Wheeler was on a long museum trip to Japan and France, Lloyd found a farm that was for sale by bandleader Paul Whiteman. Glenway wrote to his mother, who was making her last visit to Wisconsin, "Lloyd has come to an agreement with Mr. Whiteman. The lawyers are drawing up the papers." He expressed regret to Bernadine Szold: "Now the last seasons of our beloved valley. . . . For me it will take all that time to prepare to move—twenty years of these attics and archives. . . . Monroe's as well, very massive now that he has moved from 410 Park Avenue into a small flat." But after seeing the new farm, he praised Lloyd to William Maxwell: "My brother has bought another farm between Rosemont and Stockton in Delaware township, and is letting me have the handsomest old stone house on it. So, beyond the ordeal of moving, my way of life will not be greatly changed. My good fortune puts me to shame." Glenway gave the name Haymeadows to the stone house and grounds being refurbished for himself and Wheeler. John Connolly drove Glenway to the property and remembered, "When I first saw it, there was a farm worker named Leroy living there with a house full of kids."[35]

Life at the Wescott farm was never dull. In keeping with his public role, Lloyd sometimes gave jobs to former inmates of the nearby women's prison. Even before moving to the new farm, he hired the most famous of these, Ethel "Bunny" Sohl, forty-one, who had served twenty-one years. According to the *New York Daily News,* Ethel, "a tough, reefer-smoking, gun-toting tomboy, was sent away for life in 1938 for the $2.10 holdup and murder of a bus driver in Belleville, New Jersey. The ex-gungirl's new life is a job as a herdsman on the Hunterdon County, New Jersey farm of wealthy Lloyd Wescott, president of the State Board of Control for all New Jersey penal institutions, who has known Ethel for the last fifteen years." The article also described the Wescott farm as having 275 Guernsey cattle, including show stock. A vintage 1938 photo showed two attractive young women, "Tomboy Ethel" and a girlfriend-accomplice, in handcuffs and smiling after their arrest.[36] Ethel, a reliable worker and loyal friend, stayed with the Wescotts for more than twenty years. Glenway sometimes referred to her as "our transvestite murderess."

During one of Wheeler's long trips, Wescott kept him up to date with news of the present and future farms. Letter excerpts reveal much about their life and love: "Dearest of all: Have you noticed? Neither of us has wanted to say goodbye. . . . Baba took me to Haymeadows this afternoon, and I put in another dozen irises. The horsey-faced Irish boy dropped a plank on the hot-tempered stout carpenter's leg and asked to be transferred to another job. . . . Poor Anna! The raccoons came back last night and ravaged her sweet corn, swinging the stalks down for fun, dirtying a great many ears with their nibbles, scarcely hungry. . . . I ought to have tackled the Dinesen piece when up this morning . . . but there has been some household or family flurry every fifteen minutes. . . . Anna is gathering crab apples for jelly, cursing the squirrels, who drop the finest fruit from the highest bough, all scored by their teeth. . . . Mr. Whiteman called on

Lloyd yesterday, in a red suit, affable . . . he wants to buy back a piece of the land and build a new home there."[37]

As Wheeler traveled from country to country, Wescott's letters awaited him at the next hotel. The best thing to come of the change of farms was a long lyrical essay, "The Best of All Possible Worlds," a title he briefly considered for a book of reminiscences. Using the loss of Stone-blossom as metaphor, the essay has a sweeping theme about modern times in art and society, including technology and the nuclear bomb: "Past versus future . . . science versus religion . . . science perhaps also versus democracy." Among the worry and prophecy are luminous moments of hope or magic. One passage recalls a morning on the farm during the worst days of drought: windless heat, dying grass, damaged trees, and a brook gone silent and dry. Suddenly an image rises above despair: "Then our male catbird of the last couple of years, whom we recognize and love because he has two or three notes more than the regulation song of his family, came dartingly around the garage and perched there. . . . He sang, and I stood there watching him sing, so ecstatic that when he got to his high notes, he threw his head all the way back and pointed his bill straight up to the stricken blue sky. Upon which I shed tears; and it occurred to me that whereas my sadness had been building up about the drought and the inundation of the valley, and homelessness up ahead, what had actually triggered that little moisture in my own eyes and on my cheeks was the love of the bird, the delight in the freakish extra bit of song, rather like Pascal, tears of joy." Originally read at the Academy-Institute, the essay appeared in the *Proceedings* and was later revised and published as "The Valley Submerged."[38]

In concentrating on nonfiction, Wescott hit on a pattern of writing essays to be read as lectures and later published. His slow, exacting way of writing was unchanged. He told Caroline Newton, "How laborious I am, upon every line of my slight production! But that, I suppose, is what I have to offer, my specialty: little wood-carvings against the grain." To Carl Malouf he described his writing as "carving peach pits."[39]

Wescott's lectures took him beyond New York to Baltimore, Virginia, Houston, and elsewhere. Caroline Newton arranged several readings and a lecture on Thomas Mann at Haverford College in Pennsylvania where she taught. He also made more radio appearances, including a British Broadcasting Company interview on the post–World War I expatriates in Paris.[40]

In late January 1959, Wescott reported to Pauline de Rothschild, "Last week I was elected President of the National Institute." The *Herald Tribune* and the *New York Times* announced his election on February 3 with articles and photos. Almost immediately, he was drawn deeper into literary politics. Knowingly, Marianne Moore wished him luck with "this captious Zoo's miscellany of contending personalities." One early victory was winning a membership for Janet Flanner. Wescott recalled a humorous moment when W. H. Auden scolded him for wearing a casual jacket: "Auden said, 'Don't you realize, you haven't the slightest sense of decorum. You've got to wear a dinner jacket. You've got to *get* one!' And when I looked down, Wysten was standing there in bedroom slippers!" He told William Maxwell of another feisty member, a well-known artist: "Georg Grosz, who is German to the point of craziness, drank too much before and during lunch—and I had to take him in both hands and hold him to the microphone." More often, his work was routine, planning awards and grants, or drafting a statement against censorship. When Marianne Moore pressured him with her choices for memberships and prizes, she realized her friend's difficult position and teased, "Dear Glenway, martyred, heroic Glenway."[41]

What Wescott could not change was his increasingly conservative image. Even mainstream young writers, such as Bill Maxwell's protégé Harold Brodkey, saw him as old school. He never understood the concept of the antihero, which put him off such writers as Genet and William Burroughs. But in general, he was open minded about most forms of literature and younger writers.

Wescott didn't mind showing his enthusiasm for certain writers such as Baroness Blixen, better known by her pen name of Isak Dinesen and as the author of *Out of Africa.* In 1959 Dinesen was the Academy-Institute's guest of honor for its annual award ceremonies. Traditionally limousines took members and guests to its inconveniently located building at West 155th Street and Broadway. Wescott enjoyed his first meeting with the frail seventy-three-year-old as they rode along the West Side Highway with E. E. Cummings and Marchette Chute. After the ceremonies, he continued to escort her to readings and events. He brought together Christopher Isherwood and Katherine Anne Porter at Ruth Ford's party for Dinesen at her apartment in the Dakota building. Ruth, sister of Charles Henri Ford, was now married to the actor Zachary Scott. Isherwood enjoyed Dinesen's taste for champagne and sang, "We've been mixin' with Baroness Blixen."[42]

Dinesen told a story of having undergone spinal operations years earlier and being unable to sit up, type, or write. Determined to finish one last book before she died, every day she lay on the floor and dictated, asking her secretary to go for another hour, another page. Finally, the book was finished, she recovered, and went on to write much more. Wescott quoted her: "'That taught me a lesson,' she told us. 'When you have a very great and difficult task, perhaps something almost impossible, if you will do only a little at a time, every day a little, *without faith, without hope,*' and she underlined those words with her spooky deep voice, 'suddenly the work will finish itself.'" The anecdote became part of a Wescott essay that included his own aphorism: "Despairing of what we want to do often helps us to do what can be done."[43]

Originally written as an introduction to her readings, Wescott's piece mentions that Dinesen's African servants called her reading of poetry "talk like rain" and believed the stories she told aloud were a new Koran and asked her what god had inspired her to write. The essay also describes Dinesen's American tour. She was in delicate health, and her favorite meal was oysters, grapes, and champagne. Time after time, he witnessed her storytelling from memory, which enchanted audiences. It was scholar Jacques Barzun who made Wescott promise to submit his introductory talk as an essay to Russell Lynes at *Harper's Magazine*.

In April of 1959, Wescott met a writer and editor who could give him the kind of creative support he had never known before. Robert Phelps, thirty-six, had published a novel, *Heroes and Orators,* and was a masterful literary editor. Like Wescott, Phelps had attended the University of Chicago. He helped found Grove Press and ran it for three years before selling it. At present he was editing for George Braziller, Inc. Louise Bogan, who had introduced them, enthused: "Tell me what you thought of young Phelps. He has certainly read everything."[44]

Phelps was delighted by Wescott's personality and humor and intrigued by the shelves and boxes of manuscripts and binders he found at Stone-blossom. Soon he suggested a large volume of Wescott essays, reviews, fiction, and poetry to be called "A Windfall." Though he was living in Woodstock, New York, with his wife, painter Rosemarie Beck, and child, Roger, Phelps began a close friendship with Wescott.

Whenever possible, Wescott visited his future home at Haymeadows. He told Bill Maxwell, "I spent five hours the other day with a Huckleberry Finn and a Tom Sawyer, measuring the rooms, doors, windows, closets, fireplaces, etc." Still caring for his mother, he again turned down Pauline de Rothschild's offer of a trip to France. Missing him, Pauline remembered her last visit to New York: "Without noticing it perhaps, I haven't been thinking of you, then suddenly you are in the room. I am at Stone-blossom. You are in your velvet chair. . . . Monroe would mix a martini. . . . How important our conversations were to me, how extraordinary they must have been to still seem an essential in my life, as if they took place yesterday or today. . . . I still remember the last ride to the corner of 79th Street with the same ache. . . . You would again be very far away and for too long a time. . . . Except for moments like these, I lead the most enchanted and enchanting of lives. . . . And by my side this wonderful man, Philippe, entirely well now, and strong as two yoked bulls."[45]

But Wescott was right to stay by his mother's side. In September, he told Caroline Newton, "Mother is in the hospital since Wednesday, for intravenous feeding, etc. . . . The doctors say that she may die at any moment, from extreme weakness, but I am afraid that she is more willful, more spiritual, than they know." He was right. Josephine Wescott lingered for months at the hospital. When she could no longer speak and was in an oxygen tent, she one day pantomimed to him her discomforts and frustration, a terrible moment. He told Maxwell, "I couldn't keep her out of the hospital, and they saved her life three times. . . . Tomorrow I remove her from the hospital to a luxurious nursing home." As for the farms, he said, "We are still at Stone-blossom—and will stay a few months. The state is having legal problems with some of our poor neighbors, therefore not pressing us. Haymeadows is not ready. My brother and sister-in-law will start moving next week. Half the books are there already. But the cows will have to stay here until spring—the new modernistic barn is not ready."[46] Along with the livestock, he stayed behind, lingering as long as possible in a place that held fond memories.

"The Valley Submerged," one of Wescott's most heartfelt and important essays, describes this moment in time. It is partly about the lessons of giving up the farm at Mulhocaway for the Spruce Run Reservoir: "Displacement and resettlement may teach one not to despair too quickly, even of great changes." But it is also about the tragedies of the animal kingdom and mankind, and the great poet Yeats's philosophy of all that. At the same time, "The Valley Submerged" remains a farewell to the beautiful farm and valley, and memories of lives and loves left behind. In it, Wescott describes how the dawn broke over the landscape and distant houses: "At daybreak, that is, in the quarter before daybreak, from some point below the horizon in the east or the southeast, the preliminary sunbeams would arch up across the valley, behind my back, over my head, illuminating those houses of my neighbors first of all. Suddenly I would see them at the foot of my bed amid the darkness: the sunrise singling them out before it had actually risen anywhere else, pouring itself into them, and transfiguring them into magic-lantern architecture, palaces of porcelain, as in a fairy tale; or as it is described in the last few pages of the Bible, New Jerusalem, battlements of glass and pearl measured in golden reed."[47]

The great partnership, Wescott and Wheeler at Stone-blossom, 1959.

"Luncheon at Haymeadows" painting in three time perspectives, by Harold Bruder. With permission of the artist.

Katherine Anne Porter with Wheeler and Wescott, Summer 1960.

The younger partner: Anatole Pohorilenko, faithful companion to Monroe Wheeler, 1977. With permission from John Stevenson.

Wescott with attentive barn cat at Haymeadows.

Dinner conversation with Wescott.

At home on the farm, Wescott in denim overall.

Wescott prepares to award the MacDowell Medal to Marianne Moore at the artists' colony, August 20, 1967.

Tennessee Williams enjoys a 1975 reunion with Wheeler and Wescott. Photo © Gerard Malanga. With permission from Gerard Malanga.

Barbara Harrison Wescott, art lover and patron, family matriarch, with Magritte painting at New Jersey State Museum.

Love springs eternal: John Stevenson and Wescott, dated January 8, 1979 and signed by the photographer, Jill Krementz.

Tigers at Haymeadows! Wescott said, "You know, they can get over the fence. They just don't know it."

Wescott siblings: Lloyd, Beulah, Glenway, Katherine, and Elizabeth, 1978.

Monroe Wheeler at 81, 1980. With permission from John Stevenson.

The magician's wand: Wescott with a branch of blossoms at Haymeadows, 1980. With permission from John Stevenson.

11

The Great Divide and Images of Truth

JOSEPHINE WESCOTT died before dawn on January 4, 1960. "Mother, beautiful as she lay dead—pale gray and pale yellow," Wescott recorded. He looked at his sister Elizabeth sitting at the foot of the bed and saw in her face his mother's expression. Louise Bogan wrote kindly, "It was sad to hear of your mother's death. Both my mother and father died in the winter: it is a stern season, but it gives our mortality a kind of blessing."[1]

Glenway handled most of the phone calls, telegrams, and letters. After a private service and cremation, Josephine's urn was placed in Glenway's care, along with that of Bruce Wescott. Over the years the parents were misplaced more than once, and it would be three decades before the whole clan found a resting-place on the farm.

Wescott instinctively turned to work, especially lectures, and he was more popular than ever as a speaker. William Rueckert described his effect on an audience:

A handsome man who speaks with a slight British accent, Wescott was apparently born to talk: he is articulate, open, vital, informed, and enthusiastic. As in most of his published work, his own presence in a public talk is overwhelming; that is, one is always conscious of Wescott personally, not so much because he intrudes himself in an offensive way into the subject, deflecting the interest to himself, but because he experiences everything personally and presents it that way, using his own experience of the work or just his own experiences as part of his method of conveying the subject. His manner, then, is not really informal but personal. Like his dress and deportment, his manner is actually quite formal, even elegantly so; but the formality is softened by his warmth and enthusiasm. There is no boredom, no elaborate critical or methodological machinery; and no sense that one is hearing (or reading) a formal lecture. There is just the man who is discoursing on his own experience of a work, a subject, an author, a period of time, a place, and whose object is to convey, through himself, a sense of love for a particular work or author and the truth as he understands it.[2]

Wescott's decision to move away from fiction seemed reinforced by Truman Capote when they met at a party in Manhattan. Capote had just returned from Garden City, Kansas, where he was researching and writing his nonfiction classic, *In Cold Blood.* Wescott asked him how he found life in the small town. "At first it was hard," Capote said. "But now I'm practically the mayor."[3]

When Wescott's Isak Dinesen piece appeared in *Harper's Magazine,* Katherine Anne Porter wrote, "What strikes me, every time I read one of your appreciations of writers you care for, is how truly generous and selfless you are in your praise."[4] Porter said she hoped the essay would go in Wescott's next book. She referred to *Images of Truth,* the book of criticism and remembrances he was completing. Although *Images of Truth* was the book they wanted first, Harper and Brothers gave Robert Phelps a contract for "A Windfall," the big volume of Wescott selections. Editor-in-chief Cass Canfield sent Wescott a note saying he had the manuscript of "A Windfall" in front of him and would be glad to publish it. But Phelps didn't know what he was getting into. The plans included art, literary and personal essays, poems, stories, reviews, his Fitzgerald piece, the retold fables of Aesop, and more. Somehow things went wrong. Wescott wanted the newer essays moved to *Images of Truth,* which made sense, but there were many other disagreements as well. Here, it must be said, Wescott was at fault, and Monroe Wheeler grew angry with his costly indecision.

The time to move to Haymeadows drew near. One night the family saw it by flashlight after a dinner in Rosemont. In April, Glenway moved during the same week that Lloyd moved the cattle. The beautiful two-story stone house reserved for Wescott and Wheeler had a living room, hallway, dining room, a library with desk, and a big kitchen that looked out at a rolling lawn and a small red barn. Behind the kitchen was a pantry and storage room with shelves for Wescott's many three-ring binders and boxes. Upstairs were three comfortable bedrooms and an attic. There was a basement wine cellar, and they soon added a flagstone terrace.

Across cornfields and cow meadows, and beyond a large stainless steel barn, Barbara and Lloyd were settled in the big house at the front of the farm. In honor of *The Pilgrim Hawk,* a neighbor called his small farm Peregrine Hill. Their new home was soon filled with activity. Katherine Anne Porter celebrated her seventieth birthday with them on May 15.

Bernadine Szold visited. Barbara organized another art sale fundraiser. Daughter Debo, at only eighteen, married Dr. Leon Prockop of Maryland.

In New York, Wheeler found a new apartment, number 8M of 235 East Fifty-first Street on the northwest corner of Second Avenue. Its size was adequate, Wheeler could walk to work, and it became his and Wescott's permanent city home.

As president of the National Institute of Arts and Letters, Wescott comfortably filled the role of literary arbiter and spokesman. He noted the work of contemporaries, such as Ernest Hemingway's installment of *The Dangerous Summer* in *Life* magazine. Just as with *Across the River and into the Trees,* Wescott appreciated his old rival's work better than most. He saw that this wasn't just about bullfighting, that Hemingway, in failing health, was giving an affectionate farewell to Spain. The mature Hemingway made him think of the French Romantic writer François René de Chateaubriand: "More than anyone else he is like Chateaubriand (Chateaubriand in the *Mémoires d'outre-tombe*): the music, the affectations, the fewness of themes, and the really powerful sentimentality."[5] After Hemingway's suicide the following year, the *New York Times* published a letter by Wescott that urged the preservation of the author's neglected manuscripts. Mary Hemingway saw the letter on a day when she was supervising a bonfire at the Hemingway's house in Cuba. But she wasn't burning manuscripts, only stacks of Ernest's magazines and newspapers.

More personally, Wescott wrote to John Knowles about *A Separate Peace:* "I love your book. . . . I picked it up in a sorrowful fit—my mother has died, after an illness that stays in my mind, and I am having to move from a house in which I have lived for twenty-three years—and it thrilled me. It is praiseworthy in language and pace and perspective; and it is genuinely intelligent."[6]

On his sixtieth birthday, Wescott's duties at the Institute led to a profound experience. The honored guest that day was Robert Frost, and the elderly poet was lobbying the administration of President John F. Kennedy to create a sort of secretary of the arts position. But when Wescott introduced him, Frost surprised him by saying, "First, let me tell you something about Glenway; he is now one of my oldest friends. I've watched him ever since Mrs. Moody, the wife of the poet Moody, sent him to see me when he was twenty."[7]

Wescott was struck by that memory. It was the summer of 1921 when he and Wheeler traveled to the MacDowell Colony in Peterborough, New Hampshire, to see the intimidating Mr. Frost. Forty years later he was reminded again of that exciting time of his youth, when the promise of his life as an artist opened before him. As he described it, "For a moment on the April evening great Frost disappeared from my mind, and with him all of the company of the Institute and the great library–dining room where we were, about fifty of us. I stood as though all soul, alone upon one of the great divides of my life. . . . I felt it at the roots of my hair, at the juncture of my lips on either side, and in the tips of my fingers, hot and cold: thanksgiving for one thing, having had more than I deserved always, and the tragic desire to live forever."[8]

Meanwhile, as president of the Institute, Wescott was disturbed by the Kennedy administration's plans for its emerging National Cultural Center. The new center seemed to claim the same purpose as the Institute of Arts and Letters, yet it was clearly focusing only on the performing arts. Its first appointed members included entertainment and sports people. Wescott told an Institute council meeting that some of the proposed federal spending should be used to support writers and artists: "The greatest American cultural problem is the poor remuneration of the lifework of so many creative men and women, even famous ones, including members of the Institute."[9] Just a small part of the money being proposed in Washington could help establish $4,000 annual pensions for the Institute's 250 artists and writers and its small number of honorary foreign members, he said, and it could also create three new international prizes larger than the Nobel Prize. But his modest proposal was never seriously considered in Washington.

Many years later, Institute member Norman Mailer looked back at Wescott's frustration at this time: "Glenway Wescott was a tall, spare, distinguished, and handsome man with fine white hair and a youthful face; it is painful to think of how intensely he desired an American nation imbued with literary arts. Few presidents of the Institute could have given as much of themselves as he did, yet with it all he was a profoundly divided man, radical to the core, yet always overaccommodating to the traditions of the Institute."[10]

After Frost's appearance, Wescott joined the poet in Washington on May 1–3, 1961, for what he hoped would be productive meetings with the administration. But it was essentially a ceremonial event with cabinet members, senators, and Supreme Court justices and a luncheon with Secretary of the Interior Stewart Udall. Wescott wrote to the president and received a reply that was mostly courtesy, saying in part, "Dear Mr. Wescott . . . I am hopeful that this collaboration between government and the arts will continue and prosper. Mrs. Kennedy and I would be particularly interested in any suggestions you may have in the future about the possible contributions the national government might make to the arts in America. . . . Sincerely, John Kennedy."[11] It became clear that no real changes were forthcoming, but the government did heed one specific suggestion by Wescott and former Institute president Douglas Moore: the National Cultural Center was renamed the National Center for the Performing Arts.

The early months of 1962 held exciting news for Wescott, Wheeler, and Barbara Wescott. Katherine Anne Porter turned in the galleys of the novel she had been writing for decades, *Ship of Fools,* and dedicated it to Barbara. Porter nervously asked her editor, Seymour Lawrence, if the large book made sense as a whole. "Yes," he answered, "it is like a great wave."[12] Over the years, the Wescott clan had stood by Porter through her disastrous love affairs and problems of finances, work, and health. Now their friend would earn over a million dollars for the book and movie rights and treat herself to a house in Washington, D.C., a $20,000 emerald ring, and a long European vacation. And suddenly her work sold easily—even a letter to Barbara sold to a travel magazine for $1,000.

Wescott's article "Katherine Anne Porter: The Making of a Novel" appeared in the *Book-of-the-Month-Club News* in March, in *Atlantic Monthly* in April in a longer version, and in translation for the *Japan-America Forum.* The piece contains personal anecdotes, explains Porter's background as a short story writer, and reveals that *Ship of Fools* was inspired by an ocean voyage of 1931 and outlined in a letter to Caroline Gordon Tate. When Porter despaired of her class-conscious story of tragic characters at sea, Wescott confessed, he almost advised her to give it up and salvage stories and essays from the manuscript. But his closest friend—Wheeler—stopped him. Months later, he wrote, when Porter read aloud several new chapters, "I suddenly caught sight of what was in her mind, the great novel structure; the whole so very much more than the sum of the parts."[13]

As a publicity gimmick, *Ship of Fools* was released on April Fool's Day. Porter spent part of the month at Haymeadows, and on April 29 Wescott joined her in Washington for a White House dinner in her honor. On Sunday, May 13, they appeared together on the NBC television program *An Open Mind* with Eric Goldman. Goldman later said that the show was one of the most popular in his series. Late in the program, Wescott praised his friend's big, complex novel, and remarked, "My novels aren't novels; they're stories pieced together or novellas expanded. And in the novella expanded, you have three or four people and a deep problem, and you go inward introspectively." Porter replied, "I love that, too. I think that's a marvelous way to write. There are so many ways to write, and the artist does what he can. He works according to his own heart and his own mind."[14]

Next, Wescott turned to his own page proofs for *Images of Truth.* But he had a problem with Caroline Newton, who had arranged his Thomas Mann lecture at Haverford College. Newton, who had translated the German writer Jacob Wasserman and corresponded with Thomas Mann, was possessive of Mann's legacy and planned to make a deluxe chapbook of

Wescott's lecture.[15] In a letter, Wescott politely referred to it as "your essay." But his final essay was vastly expanded from the lecture. When *Images of Truth* was in galleys, Newton left phone messages that Wheeler misplaced. "He disapproves of the telephone—except for secretaries and such," Wescott explained, and said he wondered if she would like his Thomas Mann chapter.[16] He soon found out.

Caroline Newton, Wescott's friend since the early twenties, sent a letter through her lawyer to Harper and Row, claiming the Thomas Mann chapter as her property. Wescott responded: "Naturally, all this has angered me and hurt my feelings. No one has ever sicced a lawyer on me, if I remember correctly, and if it comes to a matter of legality we will not be able to communicate with each other personally." He pointed out that her lawyer offered no details. "Therefore I am hastening to make one last personal statement, hoping to stem the folly. . . . Of course I know that you wanted me to let you publish the text of my remarks at Haverford, but there was no publishable text; and I have no remembrance or record of my having agreed to produce any such text for you. In any case, you must understand that the Mann chapter is a very different and subsequent work, which would not be covered by your claim or understanding."[17] Newton dropped the matter immediately.

Images of Truth, a unique collection of remembrances and criticism, went forward. All the essays have Wescott's storytelling quality: intelligent, fond, deceptively meandering but always making his heartfelt points.

The introductory chapter, "Fiction Writing in a Time of Troubles," reflects on literature and its purpose: "What we call creative spirit really does not create anything," he says. "It evokes and recollects and relates. It is a mere inclination of our good nature and our good will, stooping and bending close to evil in order to understand it. It is a flashing of our small individual light, as best we know how, into the general darkness." The chapter mentions themes that run from ancient literature to the modern novels his essays discuss, and also explains different kinds of narrative. And it gives his philosophy of moral fiction: "In order to last a novel must be functional. To be sure, it must entertain, and it must convince, and it must thrill somehow; but it must also help."[18]

The second chapter, "Katherine Anne Porter Personally," puts together his new and old Porter pieces at the height of her fame. In contrast, "Somerset Maugham and Posterity" is in part a defense of the author's high place in English literature, insisting that Maugham's eight or so best works ensure his immortality. Reworking his previous criticism, Wescott reviews novels and stories objectively and Maugham's career with due respect.

Chapter 4 is his large, masterful "Introduction to Colette," revised and expanded, and chapter 5 is his fond, personal "Call on Colette and Goudeket," recalling his visit to the Palais Royal in summer 1952, two years before her death. His essay on narrative, "Isak Dinesen, the Storyteller," makes an interesting and different chapter 6.

The book concludes with two large chapters of previously unpublished work that grew from lectures. At thirty-five thousand words, "Thomas Mann: Will Power and Fiction" is the work Caroline Newton thought she could claim somehow. Wescott prefers *The Magic Mountain* and shorter pieces to Mann's other novels. He considers the homosexual theme of the novella *Death in Venice* not true to life, but finds the story atmospheric, and believes the Aschenbach character to be modeled after the major gay poet Stefan George. Wescott analysis always includes his poetic voice: "*Buddenbrooks* is sheer and soaring as though thrust up by some young earthquake, cloud-capped and breezy. *The Magic Mountain* is a vast Andean plateau with environing abysses. *Joseph and His Brothers* is loftier than the foregoing, but distantly, as it is a historical novel, wall-like along the horizon. . . . *Dr. Faustus* stands up highest of all, blackly wrapped in historic storm, flashing with superstition, avalanching down in its concluding chapters according to the old legendary plot." Wescott concludes that "Mann's breakthrough . . . his specialty and innovation, was the philosophical novel." More than three decades later, biographer Anthony Heilbut remarked in *Thomas Mann: Eros and Literature,* "Glenway Wescott, a gay novelist, proved to be one of Mann's best critics, perhaps because his approach strayed from the academic."[19]

The concluding chapter, "Talks with Thornton Wilder," best achieves the book's goal, balancing the personal and the critical. It examines Wilder's major works, framed by their talks over the years. Wilder, too, had not produced a novel in some time, and Wescott suggests Wilder is drawn to writing for the theater, rather than "the novelist's lonely, uncertain, haunted desk." He praises the sense of discovery in Wilder's fiction: "At times he made me think of a boy climbing a tree."[20] And he reminds the reader of how the ambitious, quality writer can lose confidence in a dark moment, like Wilder at the New York premiere of *Our Town.* He points out that Wilder's historical novels are about the present day, and he praises *Ides of March* as a great work of moral fiction. The theme of *Images of Truth* is the higher truth at the heart of fiction, and the book's dedication reads "To Monroe Wheeler, lifelong."

While Wescott awaited publication, *Time* magazine photographed him at Cape Cod on vacation with the Cranes. Advance copies of the book brought congratulations from Christopher Isherwood, Diana Vreeland, Anaïs Nin, Uta Hagen, and others. Finally, Harper and Row launched *Images of Truth* with a party at the Saint Regis Hotel and a newspaper ad that read, "Coleridge on Poetry, Wescott on Fiction."

A well-known writer with a sound-alike name, Orville Prescott, reviewed *Images of Truth* in the *New York Times* and concluded, "Mr.

Wescott has the intellectual equipment to be a major critic, plus a prose style simpler and more graceful than that of any critic now writing." *Time* magazine's positive review included a perceptive comment: "Like the pre-*Ship of Fools* Katherine Anne Porter, Glenway Wescott is a somewhat melancholy yet tantalizing figure. His novels—including *The Grandmothers* and *The Pilgrim Hawk*—earned him a special reputation as a prose craftsman and subtle prober of the wheels and springs of emotion that turn the clock of character." Although Wescott readers want a new novel, *Time* went on, "*Images of Truth* is not their long-awaited work of fiction, but it is an eloquent, at times fascinating, celebration of the art of fiction writing."[21]

During the last three months of 1962, Wescott took on an exhausting schedule of book signings, readings, and television and radio appearances that included the far West and much of California. At Stanford University, he saw the Winterses, his old friends from the Chicago Poetry Club days. On a note planning their get-together, Yvor Winters grumped in his big brother tone, "You are excited beyond the occasion."[22] Janet Lewis Winters was now known for such novels as *The Wife of Martin Guerre,* on which the movies *The Return of Martin Guerre* and *Sommersby* were based.

At Berkeley, Wescott told students that he had proofread *The Apple of the Eye* in 1924 while bedridden with mumps and "covered with ice packs to my knees." Asked about the current literary scene, he said, "This is a cheapskate era with relation to literature and the arts in the United States." He called for a revival of the true literary magazines that "print the young writers side by side with the masters . . . for educational and inspirational experience."[23]

There followed a hectic eighteen-day stretch of appearances throughout the Midwest, then a return to the East Coast for a series of readings. A note from Marianne Moore awaited: "Dear Glenway, A cosmos, a composite for me of how to write—*me,* impervious to sophistication! . . . your Katherine Anne is really the person; Thornton: so is he ('like a boy climbing a tree'). . . . You are fearless. It is a great satisfaction to me to see you in your glory, shed on you by shedding it on others."[24] On December 31, Wescott appeared on a PBS television program about William Faulkner, then returned to Haymeadows for New Year's in a great, blanketing, silencing snowstorm.

Months after the success of his book and tour, Wescott was unpleasantly surprised by another reemergence of Michael Miksche, who phoned during a dinner with Barbara and Lloyd, Monroe Wheeler, and Ralph Pomeroy. Wescott learned that "very shortly after our last talk, he'd thrown himself in the Hudson River, and got fished out and put in a nut house." That day, after seven months in Bellevue Hospital, he had been released. "I talked to him for about twenty minutes. He told me how, when he'd walked into his room at Bellevue, the first thing he'd seen was a *Time* magazine and he opened it and saw my face, in their review of *Images of Truth*. He said, 'Oh, I hated you so. I paced up and down that room and wanted to kill you. You're the source of all my troubles. And suddenly my mood changed, and I remembered I love you so, and I never will love anyone else, never have loved anyone else.' He was weeping."[25] Wescott got Miksche off the phone and remembered the words of Dr. Kinsey: "Don't you know that man is a killer?" He had confessed to Paul Gebhard at the Kinsey Institute, "I must admit that I am a little afraid of him."[26]

It was nearly a year later when Wescott saw the troubled man one last time. After seeing a ballet with a friend, he stepped out of a taxi at Third Avenue and Fifty-third Street to get a newspaper. Standing at the newsstand, he heard a voice behind him say, "You won't find what you're looking for." It was Miksche, standing large, calm, and tragic in the night. "I said, 'I can't talk to you now. Earl Butler is there in a taxi waiting for me. I'll call you in the morning.' He said, 'No, you won't. Because you don't have my phone number.' I said, 'Oh, you're not living with your wife. Well, then you'll have to call me.' And two weeks later he was dead."[27] Michael Miksche, the World War II bomber pilot, underground artist, and sexual athlete, took his life with pills on a Manhattan rooftop. Wescott could not miss the irony of such an end for an exhibitionist. "Imagine that: him going alone," he said.[28]

In contrast to the fate of Miksche was the charmed life of John Connolly. Wescott's important friend loved working in Hollywood and New York with William Inge. At one point, he considered working for Tennessee Williams, and he and Bill Miller visited Williams in Key West. But he remained loyal to Inge. Carl Malouf, who was seeing little of Wescott by then, remembered getting a glimpse of Connolly's life in California in 1962. "I was painting murals all over the West," Malouf said. "John Connolly drove Inge's car to San Diego to pick me up and drove me to Hollywood, to Inge's house. . . . That afternoon a lot of boys came to the swimming pool. This was entertainment for me, which I thought was very sweet. And they were very pretty boys, the kind I imagine that today would be in movies—you know the kind of movies I'm talking about. And one of them appeared at the edge of the pool with an Oscar, and dived in, Oscar first! That was the very day that Marilyn Monroe died. I heard the news while I was still in the pool."[29] She had died of an overdose in nearby Brentwood. The more reticent Connolly didn't remember details of the day, but he recalled that he and Inge had dinner that night with the director George Cukor, who said he was about to hire Monroe back to the film from which she had been fired.

During one of his stays in New York, Connolly took Wescott to Inge's

Sutton Place apartment for dinner with film star Sal Mineo. On another occasion, in Hollywood, Connolly remembered, "Monroe came out to see some people about paintings they were going to give the museum. I took him on the set of MGM's movie *Mutiny on the Bounty* and introduced him to Marlon Brando. I had to go off for a moment and left him and Marlon talking as they sat between decks of the film set of the ship. Monroe loved it."[30]

Connolly's work with Inge ended in 1963, and Wescott told a friend, "My John looked beautiful with a joyous Florida tan and a sad expression. His parting of the ways with Inge finally took place yesterday, after six years; the great man having finally found someone else who wants to live in California, and who furthermore could be had for a much smaller salary."[31] That night Connolly and Wescott hosted composer Ned Rorem's birthday party, and Truman Capote joined them. As for Connolly's work, he went on to a successful career in lighting direction for television.

Whatever their other relationships, Wescott and Wheeler's partnership was the foundation. At Cape Cod, Wescott would rewrite Wheeler's introduction to the "Last Works of Matisse" catalog. As a surprise, Wheeler would give Wescott a handsome suit. In a moment of low spirits, Wescott's words to Wheeler reveal more than the routine of his days: "Dearest, Yesterday was a bad futile day—my fatigue is a little cumulative now and doubtless will be to the end. I write this as one might a prayer. Think of me with all your heart. Dinner with Rebecca West was not enjoyable—it seemed to me there was a wild desperation under her would-be wittiness. . . . Last night I cooked hamburgers and tomatoes and mustard, for John and Earl, but gave up going to the movies, sent them packing, went to bed. I finished the introductory essay with some exaltation. . . . Your loving Gl."[32]

Together, Wescott and Wheeler entered the time of life when longtime friends are lost. Proudly they visited the Art Institute in Chicago for a George Platt Lynes exhibition. In Isak Dinesen's last months, Wescott spoke honestly: "Dear Tanya: I wish you a happy New Year—but at your age and at mine, newness is not likely and perhaps not desirable; and to be specifically concerned about happiness may not be auspicious." Amusing to them both was the feisty example of Marianne Moore during her stay at Brooklyn Hospital: "I don't want flowers. . . . I shall soon resemble a pig in clover. . . . I feel like the dragon when St. George finished it off. I hope *you,* Monroe, are becoming hardy. . . . Have taken every step possible to be clinical and stark but have been embowered in flowers which I had to take care of like a gardener."[33]

A death that tugged at the memory of their youth was that of Jean Cocteau on October 11, 1963. Cocteau's last film, *Le Testament d'Orphée*—in which Yul Brynner appeared—had hauntingly portrayed the event. Wescott remembered of Cocteau: "His was a life marked by exhibitionism, intense love affairs, reconversion to Catholicism, and addiction to opium over a long period of time. . . . He used to tell me that he felt he was a victim of all these boys who used him as if he were a kind of altar. He was one of the greatest celebrities in the world, although he didn't have top rank in any of the arts that he practiced. I think his poetry was too mannered, too tight. He learned to draw and he drew and drew and drew, almost as much as Picasso, and Picasso admired him very much and taught him a lot. His best prose is like Colette and she was his last great friend. If it weren't for drugs, he could have been, for one thing, the next Sarah Bernhardt of France. His own plays that he put on were the most beautiful and most fascinating things you could imagine. I wish the American Theater would use the theatrical effects Cocteau put into his plays. I think it makes a difference." Remembering Villefranche, he said, "I'm afraid that people who learn of Cocteau's sorrows, drug problems, religious problems and love affairs will think it all tragic. But it wasn't like that, because we laughed all the time."[34]

Edith Sitwell thanked Wheeler for an exhibit of Tchelitchew, just eight months before her own death: "I am so happy that Pavlik's show is being a great success. But isn't it like the world that it should happen now, when he who longed for recognition so much is dead! You were one of the wisest and kindest of his friends. How much you helped him." When Sitwell herself passed away, a day after selecting photos for her last memoir, Wescott wrote: "Lucky Edith! Lucky she was in many ways, in spite of her magnificent father's cruelty and her beautiful mother's disdain." To her brother Osbert he admitted, "Of course, Edith's death was like a vast tree falling in the forest, annihilating underbrush, hiding young trees—and frightening me, as to the general death-sentence and as to the health and staying power of other friends, and of my own."[35]

Alan Searle wrote to say that his life was sad because Willie Maugham was beginning to fail, and he couldn't imagine life without him; they had known each other for more than thirty years. When Wheeler himself visited the Villa Mauresque, he sent Wescott this report:

> Night before last I dined again with Willie at the Mauresque. In contrast to the preceding night, when I arrived he was slumped low in a big chair in the far corner of the living room under the Zoffany stage scenes of Macklin, and he seemed in a less good mood. We had cocktails on the terrace. While talking I mentioned Josephine Crane, and he had no recollection of her whatever. (Alan told me later that one of his old friends, Lady Bateman, came to lunch the other day; halfway through the meal, Willie leaned across to Alan and said, "Who is that woman?") Willie told me another story about a recent visit to Churchill. He had thought in advance of a story that would amuse him, and told it, as loud as he could. When he finished, Churchill asked, "What's that you said?" I told him about Katherine

Anne's new book; he remembered her, said she had written one of the best stories he ever read, but couldn't recall the name of it. I did my best to entertain him, and after dinner I thought of some story and asked if he had heard it. "No." "Shall I tell it to you," I asked. And he replied softly, "No." And shortly after he made his excuses and went to bed.[36]

Maugham lingered for several years. When Wescott sent greetings for his ninety-first birthday, Searle replied that his sweet thought gave Willie his first bit of pleasure in some time. He said Maugham now lived in a twilight world of horror and rarely touched reality. Sometimes he didn't recognize Searle.[37] Maugham's death on December 15, 1965, made headlines around the world. Months earlier *Life* magazine had asked Wescott to write a memorial piece. What he did not publish was a considerable amount of journal material on Maugham, including an entry entitled "Cremation in Marseilles," which reads in part:

> Alan sat on a hard straight bench in a sort of waiting room that was rather like a private chapel in a stupor of grief and weariness. At last the director of the proceeding came in to tell him that it was all over, and he had in his hand a tray covered by a napkin. He removed the napkin and displayed several longish objects, white or gray-white. "Whatever is that?" Alan exclaimed, not in real ignorance, but in stupefaction and wild grief. It was bone, pieces of bone that had not sufficiently deteriorated in the fire, a forearm or two, a shinbone. "They are too big for the urn I've brought," Alan protested. The crematorium employee knew that; he had to have permission to break them in pieces. He suddenly produced a small hammer out of his pocket and wielded it with some dexterity: *tock, tock, tock*. Alan Searle fled out into the street and vomited, which weakness surprised and saddened him almost as much as the gruesome relic had done.[38]

As for Maugham's interment at King's College in England, Wescott added, "It interested me and touched me, I told Alan Searle, to learn that the extremely aged man had wanted his ashes to go back to the place, Canterbury, where he had as a small boy been unforgettably mistreated and unhappy, where he had been perhaps the most miserable schoolboy who ever lived."[39]

Other losses in the sixties included Nancy Cunard, the poet and founder of Hours Press, and Elizabeth Shepley Sergeant, the biographer of Willa Cather. Wescott had first met her in Santa Fe. He eulogized her movingly before a crowd of one hundred at the Cosmopolitan Club, saying, "She suffered from the worst sort of pride, which is humility about one's talent."[40]

At Haymeadows, Glenway was still "a bird in a golden cage," and not just a financial cage because he cared about the emotional needs of Lloyd and Barbara. His brother and sister-in-law gave up the intimacy of their youth long ago, but they generally lived together peaceably. John Connolly said simply, "Barbara just refused Lloyd her bed. She was very polite about his lovers." Ralph Pomeroy remembered, "Lloyd was absolutely open about his mistresses. Sunday morning he went to see the longtime one. Everybody would say, 'Lloyd has gone to get the newspapers.'"[41] One time, Barbara accompanied Lloyd when he served as a judge at an international Guernsey show in Capetown, South Africa, and then on a long European vacation. But normally she traveled with friends or relatives. Glenway was essential as a mediator and a joyful presence. Barbara and Lloyd loved nothing more than for Glenway to read to them.

The Wescotts did pull together in a crisis. In the fall of 1965, shortly after Lloyd helped open a new wing at the Hunterdon County Medical Center, he was diagnosed with a malignancy on his lung. After successful surgery, Glenway and Barbara took him home to the farm. In early 1967, Lloyd and Glenway's sister Marjorie MacLeid in San Francisco was terminally ill with cancer. Glenway had what he called a long, heartbreaking phone call with her. Lloyd made two trips to see her, but he implored his brother to resist going. As Glenway understood it, "She scarcely seems to recognize anyone; all that is left of her life is a bad dream."[42]

Reflecting on the family loss, Barbara and Lloyd commissioned several paintings by the artist Harold Bruder. One oil on canvas, "Luncheon at Haymeadows," shows Glenway, Lloyd, Barbara, and Monroe at a table on the lawn. Glenway in jacket and tie is the one figure laughing, chin down. "I never laughed that way," he often joked, "but since the painting I catch myself laughing like that all the time!"[43] The painting captured the feel of their personalities, the stance of their bodies, and the casual elegance of their world.

In real life, Barbara was more than a patron to individual writers and artists. She and Lloyd gave much to the community, including seventy-two acres of land for a public park, the Wescott Nature Reserve. She continued her art fundraisers and testimonial dinners for the Karen Horney clinic, once renting out the Terrace Room of the Plaza Hotel. The *Newark Sunday News* mentioned her gift of a Gauguin painting to the Newark Museum, and a 400 B.C. marble bust of Venus to the National Gallery in memory of her father.[44] Her other donations to museums included works by Monet, Soutine, Utrillo, Bonnard, Renoir, Tchelitchew, Morandi, and many others.

On the other hand, Barbara didn't pretend to have Lloyd's democratic, common touch. Lloyd was a public figure, and New Jersey Governor Robert Meyner once gave a surprise birthday party in a state park, introducing him as "The First Citizen of New Jersey." During the time of antiwar and civil rights demonstrations, Glenway joked with dark humor about Barbara, who needed to shop before taking a long vacation with her sister Verna: "I felt duty-bound to go along with her. What if she had a flat tire? What if she encountered angry Negro boys in Trenton?" More seriously, he jotted in his private daybook, he now saw her as "fond, lonesome, possessive."[45]

Away from family obligations in the country, Wescott was increasingly popular as a public spokesman for the arts. In addition to Eric Goldman's *Open Mind* show, he made television appearances on a program about copyright law, on a CBS show called "Paris in the Twenties" with Janet Flanner, and in a PBS interview with Anita Loos. In radio interviews he discussed Edith Sitwell with Arlene Francis and *The World of the Paperback* with the host of a syndicated program by that name.[46]

Appearing with Karl Shapiro at a conference on the arts at Wingspread in Racine, Wisconsin, Wescott again called for public support for serious writers, with stipends or paid positions. But when he looked around the room, Wescott realized that the attendees were mostly salaried professors, not struggling writers. Months later, in the *Authors Guild Bulletin,* he recalled how his words fell on deaf ears at the Wingspread conference. The professors seemed shocked, he wrote, that he should speak about mercenary matters. But what about nonacademic writers, he asked: "When a famous or once famous old author ends his life in penury . . . it sends a message to all and sundry that writing is a second class way of life."[47]

During his Midwest trip, Wescott met with Earl Kuelthau for the last time. Married and now age sixty-three, Earl had been Wescott's first love—"Carl" in the story "Adolescence." Another stop on the lecture circuit was historic Union College in upstate New York. He complained to Lloyd, "Schenectady is a grim uncomfortable town and Union College almost embarrassingly unwelcoming—very odd." He misread his hosts, if not the town. In addition to paying Wescott for three lectures, Union devoted a complete issue of its journal, *Symposium,* to his lectures, photographs of his visit, and an interview by Frank Gado. The glossy white cover had a strikingly handsome illustration of him. Wescott said of his current writing status: "I'm not a novelist. . . . I know now what I can do," referring to essays and memoir. When Gado asked a smart question about his fiction—"Did you feel you were going for a cleanness of line and simplicity of words?"—Wescott gave an immediate and perceptive answer: "More for narrative prose as an expressive instrument rather than as a display of art or as a way of showing off, or as a way of changing anything." Three years later, Union College presented Wescott with an honorary doctor of letters degree. (Rutgers University too had awarded him an honorary degree, in 1963.) At the MacDowell Colony, Wescott presented Marianne Moore with the Edward MacDowell Medal, then spoke about Moore, Frost, and other poets he had met there in his youth.[48]

Throughout the sixties, Wescott found himself enjoying a third period of celebrity, now as an urbane New York literary figure. It was the result of the Institute presidency, *Images of Truth,* more public appearances, and more frequent articles in popular magazines and newspapers. Once, he was surprised by an ovation from a large Authors Guild crowd at the Biltmore Hotel. In July 1963 *Esquire* magazine's special issue, "The American Literary Scene," included a two-page color spread with Gertrude Stein's comment, "You are all a lost generation," and a group photo in which Wescott, casual and laughing in a youthful turtleneck shirt, appears with Marcel Duchamp, Kay Boyle, Malcolm Cowley, Caresse Crosby, Carl Van Vechten, Dawn Powell, Man Ray, William Slater Brown, Matthew Josephson, and Virgil Thomson.

Wescott now reviewed frequently for the Sunday *Book Week* in the *Herald Tribune,* having started with the first printing in the United States of Ford Madox Ford's *The Fifth Queen* and Colette's memoir, *The Blue Lantern.* Another piece, "The Choreographer" in *Show* magazine, was an appreciation of George Balanchine's decades in ballet with director Lincoln Kirstein. He remarked: "Kirstein is a phenomenal man, with the artistic temperament to an almost extreme degree and a multipotential of talents, only no vocation, other than as an animator, a benefactor, a cultural publicist."[49]

One of his most important *Book Week* reviews pointed out the unique skills of John Cheever in *The Wapshot Scandal:* "You might call Cheever an existentialist, in an American way. He reveals his people by what happens to them, and by what they happen to be doing at a given moment, and what they remember having done, rather than by exact analysis on his part or important articulateness of their own." He reviewed Diana Forbes-Robertson's biography of her aunt, actress Maxine Elliot, and Eleanor Clark's *The Oysters of Locmariaquer.* He noted that Clark's book was less about the rare oyster from the northwest coast of France than about the town, region, and people. It was exactly the kind of small or special theme—with deeper meaning—that interested Wescott himself more and more. Other *Book Week* reviews included Cyril Connolly's collection, *Previous Convictions,* and *The Journal of Jules Renard.* One of the more personal was "A Face to Laugh, a Face to Cry," about Edith Sitwell's autobiography, *Taken Care Of.* Even in her memoir, he wrote, "My departed friend's poetry echoes and re-echoes in its prose with so much emotion."[50]

When Janet Flanner published her pieces from the *New Yorker* as *Paris Journal,* Wescott wrote, "Her great quality is her immediacy and candor of impression—a greatness that journalism is inherently capable of (and history is not, as a rule)." Wescott's was "the most loving and considered of all the reviews," said Flanner's biographer, Brenda Wineapple. For the *New York Times,* he reviewed Garson Kanin's light memoir of Somerset Maugham.[51]

Wescott's own perspective on Maugham reached much of America in

Life magazine. His "Passing of the Old Party" included amusing recollections. Once, he revealed, two elegant middle-aged ladies interrupted Maugham's writing in a Cape Cod hotel. He tolerated it because the ladies were full of praise, but after they left he realized they had stolen his two fountain pens as souvenirs! Another time, at a Hollywood dinner party, comedienne Fanny Brice and friends tried to pantomime the title of one of Maugham's novels. When Willie, exasperated, couldn't guess it, they realized they were thinking of someone else's novel. Wescott recounted Maugham's life and work and said the passing of the Old Party—a grand elder—marks the end of an era. Personal as always, he added, "My books did not impress him much, and, in his friendly way, he would have liked me to be more successful, financially independent of my family, freer to travel around the world. He was a born teacher and tried to teach me."[52]

One can imagine Monroe Wheeler restraining a smile at Wescott's bold "financially independent of my family" statement in *Life* magazine. Comically, when it appeared, Wescott was forced to move in with Barbara and Lloyd because a massive blizzard covered the farm in deep snowdrifts. Each day he struggled to the Haymeadows side of the farm, to get books, shirts, and paper and to refill his bird feeder.

Apart from reviews, Wescott's "The Valley Submerged" finally appeared, in the summer 1965 issue of *Southern Review.* He wrote an art essay for an exhibit of Bernard Perlin's paintings and noted, "He is a master draftsman, especially in silverpoint: unforgettable likenesses of Katherine Anne Porter, Maugham, Mrs. Russell Lynes, Martha Gellhorn."[53]

While Wescott had turned to nonfiction, his fiction remained in print. *The Grandmothers* was released in 1962 as an Atheneum paperback, and his long out-of-print story collection, *Good-bye, Wisconsin,* was published by Signet Classics/New American Library in 1964. The cover shows people waiting at a small train station and carries a quote from Horace Gregory: "Glenway Wescott at his best . . . An American classic." That year, the "Good-bye, Wisconsin" essay also reappeared in a textbook published by Lippincott, *The Personal Voice.*[54]

Although *The Pilgrim Hawk* consistently appeared in new printings of *Six Great Short Modern Novels,* Harper and Row brought out a handsome hardbound edition in 1966. Wescott's biography note stated, "Though a Middle Westerner by birth, an expatriate in Germany and France for about thirteen years of his young manhood, a country dweller by family connection and preference, he considers himself a typical New Yorker." A jacket blurb by Christopher Isherwood praised the book as "truly a work of art, of the kind so rarely achieved or attempted nowadays." The novelist John Hawkes commented to Cass Canfield, "For me, the artistic perfection of *The Pilgrim Hawk* is brilliant and terrifying and wholly admirable." Old friend Osbert Sitwell, now an invalid at his home in Florence, wrote, "So much time had elapsed since I last read it that I came upon it quite new and immensely enjoyed it." The short story writer Jean Stafford wrote about the book and its characters in *Vogue:* "The tragedy of the pair is that beneath their antagonisms and their contempt for each other (the counterpoint of Mrs. Cullen's complicated bird is her husband's alcoholism) there is the habit of authentic love on which they are hamstrung—they cannot change and they will not flee."[55]

Months later, Wescott was interviewed over lunch by Cocteau biographer Francis Steegmuller. Afterward, he remembered, he met up with William Maxwell, who had a surprise. "Bill said, 'I'll give you a copy of the *New Yorker,* one day in advance. Open it up, you'll see why.'" Inside was "Love Birds of Prey," Howard Moss's major appreciation of *The Pilgrim Hawk* and of Alwyn Tower as storyteller: "We believe in him as a character, but we become suspicious of his point of view. He reveals more than he knows and what he reveals is himself, without seeming to be quite aware of it. We are dealing with two things at once: the story Tower tells and Tower's story. The effect is something like watching a movie whose main character turns out to be the cameraman."[56]

As Wescott left Maxwell to walk uptown, he felt a profound sense of redemption. "At any rate, I walked down the street with tears streaming down my face. Because that was success for me, to have a big, full length, high brow essay by the poetry editor of the *New Yorker.* At least it would bring me to the attention of what ought to have been my audience, if I had an audience at all."[57]

New editions of his books, new admirers and praise would always remind Wescott of his early fame and the expectations that it caused. In 1966, his agent, Helen Straus of the William Morris Agency, had a near miss in placing *Apartment in Athens* with a British film producer. It was the kind of tease he had heard before, from Hollywood when the book was new. Years later, he commented, "A play and/or movie could be made of this someday, I am often told—I no longer believe any such thing. It made a broad-based reputation for me, but cost me some of my prestige as an unsuccessful highbrow writer."[58]

Writing aside, Wescott's life was so busy that it can only be highlighted. He was in good health and longevity ran in his family. He was also wiser, and was generous when John Connolly met a serious lover in 1967, British merchant marine Ivan Ashby. He knew John would remain in his life, as would others, such as Bernard Perlin, Earl Butler, John Yeon, and Will Chandlee III, an ex-Marine from Philadelphia. He told Paul Gebhard at the Institute for Sex Research, "Promiscuity and constancy are the two great traits of homosexual men; which is the more extraordinary. I took Will to spend last weekend with Bernard Perlin in Ridgefield."[59]

Kinsey's work and the goal of sexual freedom remained sacred to him.

After one visit with Mrs. Kinsey and other Institute workers, he complained to Raymond Mortimer about Midwest antigay witch-hunts: "Just before I got to Bloomington, a distinguished and beloved professor—not, needless to say of the Institute for Sex Research; an ordinary professor of English literature—was arrested for his letter writing, with odious headlines in the local newspaper, which drove him to despair. He tried to commit suicide but only crippled himself. There have been a good many such casualties, hateful; and almost no one seems to think of this in terms of civil liberties, invasion of privacy, seizure of personal records, etc." He told Gebhard, "I keep wondering and (in a sense) praying about the welfare of the Institute for Sex Research, and your labors and projects."[60] Over the years he would write and visit the succession of directors in Bloomington.

Wescott did notice signs of change in the sixties. He saw the newest gay resort on Fire Island, the residential Pines, east of Cherry Grove. At the increasingly festive Grove, he visited Janet Flanner and Natalia Murray at their house on the bay. He saw Tennessee Williams at a bar called the Sea Shack, and stopped at the Beach Hotel's discotheque, then called the Bat Cave. In the city, he first met Andy Warhol at Ruth Ford's apartment in the Dakota building. It was Ruth's brother, surrealist Charles Henri Ford, who introduced Warhol to one his young film stars, Gerard Malanga. "That's when Pop was popping," said Ford.[61]

The journals of gay men, including his own, were on Wescott's mind. He told Raymond Mortimer, "I am composing a letter to Lincoln Kirstein in order to persuade him *not* to destroy his journal of the thirties. He is under the influence of Auden, that Ostrich, who has been plodding the theory of the irrelevence of biographical knowledge, of the desirability of not publishing documentary literary material and, to be on the safe side, of destroying it." Bernard Perlin agreed with Wescott and wrote, "After [Hubert Selby's] *Last Exit to Brooklyn,* everything goes." In turn, Wescott encouraged Ned Rorem to publish his tell-all journals: "Who was it (was it Milton?) who said truth always comes into the world as a love child, with some scandal for the mother."[62] In 1966, the *Paris Diary* of Ned Rorem appeared, with an introduction by Robert Phelps.

On the establishment side of the fence, after his term as president of the Institute of Arts and Letters, Wescott did all he could for the arts in committee work. On one special awards project, he met a difficult deadline and got $375,000 in grants for fifty writers and artists. When the *New York Times* announced "A Revision of Copyright Laws Approved by House Committee," Wescott commented on his years of work for copyright reform by noting on his clipping of the story, "Half a loaf." When A. E. Hotchner was being prevented from publishing his memoir of Hemingway by Ernest's widow, Mary, who preferred the scholar Carlos Baker, Wescott wrote Hotchner: "I find myself scandalized and fascinated by the account of Mrs. Hemingway's legal action against you in the morning's *Times.*" As Wescott saw it, the fight involved "matters of privacy, author executorship, the power of widows to destroy literary material, the competitiveness of great publishing houses, and famed university professor versus regular writer. And in all these counts, I think it is safe to say, I am on your side." Hotchner decided to fight the lawsuit and eventually won. Many years later, Hotchner recalled: "Wescott's letter of support could not have come at a more propitious time. *Papa Hemingway* was my first serious book and I was totally unprepared for the legal firestorm that Mary created. Although quite irrational (she contended that conversation was protected by copyright) the court proceedings she induced were very threatening. To receive an unsolicited letter of support from a writer of Wescott's stature was precisely what I needed at that moment. It strengthened my resolve not to make the changes in the manuscript that Mary was demanding. In the end, Mary's legal attack was turned aside by the court of appeals. I always felt deeply indebted to Wescott, whom I had never met, for his strongly worded message of encouragement."[63]

Felicia Geffen of the Academy-Institute remembered Wescott's working visits to her country home in Pawling, New York: "He would take long walks in the woods and come back with his arms full of exquisite wild flowers, which he would then arrange in vases. He would sit down in the kitchen and spread his papers all over the table while I was preparing a meal and he would write and also talk, and talk, about all manner of things. Always astute, always amusing, of people and places, and of himself."[64]

Talk and humor were the greater part of Wescott's charm. At Wheeler's formal parties, Wescott contributed wit and fun. One evening, he complained to art historian Sir Kenneth Clark about Aldous Huxley's address to the Academy-Institute, and they had an exchange of very British humor. He recalled: "At Monroe's dinner party for the Clarks and Mrs. David Rockefeller and Marianne Moore, I told Sir Kenneth that Huxley's Blashfield address had disappointed us; all about the future, in his way. 'Such a mistake!' Sir Kenneth said. 'It is a rule of life: never talk of the future. Never drink vin rosé; never discuss the future.' I recalled Emerald Cunard's saying that summer in New York was quite bearable if one observed two rules: 'Never dine before nine o'clock, and never listen to a note of Beethoven.'"[65]

A high moment at the East Fifty-first Street apartment was the night of Truman Capote's Black and White Ball at the Plaza Hotel. Capote had asked Wescott and Wheeler to host one of the preliminary dinners. Janet Flanner planned to fly in from Paris, but as the date approached Capote kept forgetting to invite her lover, Natalia Danesi Murray, who ran Rizzoli Books in Manhattan. Flanner was upset, and Wescott wrote an angry letter to Capote, but the letter was not sent. Wescott wrote on the unmailed page, "Monroe, almost in tears, forbade me to send it." Wheeler had a horror of vulgar fights and scenes, and suggested a brief telegram. Capote phoned right away and apologized. On the night of the Black and White Ball, Monday, November 28, 1966, Wescott cooked minced lamb for Wheeler, Monica Sterling, Anita Loos, Virgil Thomson, Janet, and Natalia. Later they joined the other masked guests at the Grand Ballroom of the Plaza, everyone from Rose Kennedy to Frank Sinatra. Natalia recalled, "The best part, in fact, of Truman's ball was the reunion of old friends at the dinner given by Glenway Wescott and Monroe Wheeler. . . . Once in the Plaza ballroom, with the five hundred guests, the occasion became a *grande mêlée* of the beautiful, the famous and the infamous, ogling one another, dancing and greeting one another under spotlights. Truman had reached the height of social success with that ball."[66]

Away from the social world where they were an institution, Wescott and Wheeler were still developing their unique relationship, now five decades old. Wheeler's life was more glamorous—he traveled around the world, and charmed and escorted socialites, including Brooke Astor. Wescott wrote Fred Wheeler, now in his nineties, "Monroe spent the weekend with Adlai Stevenson and others at Mrs. Astor's in Rhinebeck, then off to Paris."[67]

Wheeler put off retirement for three years, until 1968, then told a local newspaper, "I really wanted a motorcycle for my eighteenth birthday, but instead my father gave me an expensive printing press." But, even at sixty-nine, he had an incredible memory and art contacts throughout Europe, Japan, the Philippines, and Latin America. He gave art lectures, remained a member of the MoMA board as an honorary trustee, worked on committees, and took on assignments and travel well into old age.[68]

In New York, the new Lincoln Center became an important part of their world. Lincoln Kirstein's New York City Ballet moved from City Center to the New York State Theater, and Wescott and Wheeler followed it, as a treasured part of their lives.

At the farm, Wescott was amazed when Wheeler with poor eyesight drove his big Buick through a thick fog all the way from Trenton at a snail's pace. Another time, in a severe snowstorm, he drove houseguest Raymond Mortimer to the Barnes Collection exhibit. Wescott called it, "Monroe Wheeler's sacred willfulness."

Wescott's kitchen table notes put poignant moments into words. On one occasion he wrote, "Dear lifelong-beloved Monroe: I am sorry for what I said." On a memo pad sheet imprinted in red with the words Don't Forget he wrote, "I love you more than I can tell."[69]

At long last, they began to accept Pauline's open invitation to Christmas and New Year (her birthday) at Mouton Rothschild. After nostalgic days in Paris, they would take a train to the Bordeaux region, to the centuries-old Rothschild vineyards at Mouton, near Pauillac. Pauline had refurbished the original stone house and large stables into Petit Mouton and Grand Mouton. The red-tiled buildings were filled with antique furniture, statues, and modern art. There were luxurious guest rooms and a large library. Even the labels of Philippe's wine bottles were designed by artists, from Matisse and Picasso to Tchelitchew and Warhol. When hosting friends such as Wescott, Wheeler, Janet Flanner, Raymond Mortimer, and Stephen Spender, Pauline selected each day's china, silverware, tablecloths, and napkins from photo and swatch books with more than 175 patterns. She and Philippe also created the Museum of Wine in Art, filling it with artifacts, glassware, tapestries, and paintings. Thousands of tourists visited.

To Wescott, the baroness was still his old friend Pauline and they loved each other's company as much as ever. In January 1967, he helped her with the galleys of *The Irrational Journey,* her diary of Moscow, Leningrad, and Russian art, poets, museums, and architecture. At Wescott's suggestion, the manuscript was edited by Robert Phelps's talented friend Peter Deane, who was also credited with two of Wescott's book jacket portraits. "Dearest Baba," Wescott wrote, "The art of living at Mouton is of using up every hour gregariously, in conversation, eating and drinking, taking walks. I worked an hour or two every morning with Pauline . . . and had three serious sessions with Janet as well."[70] Returning from Mouton, Glenway enjoyed welcome weeks in Paris, Amsterdam, and London.

By the late sixties, Wescott was still in generally good health, but he admitted to Earl Butler how the years were affecting him: "The aging process is not a slope; it is a sequence of plateaus and precipices, like a vast, obscure and jarring staircase. One goes along it seemingly unchangingly, especially in the latter part of life, when there isn't much change in oneself; then suddenly one steps into a space, comes down with a thump on another level, with unfamiliar problems and prospects, and with a horrible fatigue."[71]

In June of 1968, Wescott misstepped less metaphorically, on a loose piece of concrete at a neighbor's turkey farm, breaking a bone in his left foot, which required a cast for six weeks. Aside from this accident, life in the country was becoming more appealing than the demands of the city. About this time, Barbara established a trust fund of stocks for him, giving him some sense of security at last. The household missed retired housekeeper Anna Brakke, who wrote in her sweet, wise way from Vero Beach, Florida: "It's very lonely where we are living. If it wouldn't be for the birds, it would be a sad life." Haymeadows still had a great cast of characters, including transvestite ex-convict Ethel Sohl. He joked fondly: "I am up at four a.m. to clean house because Monroe's friend Mrs. Astor is about to visit us. As a rule it gets done by our man Ethel, but she couldn't find time."[72] Ethel lived with her lover in a small rented house near Haymeadows. In Wescott's sacred archive of papers, he tucked away a Christmas gift label that read, "To Glenway and Monroe, from Ethel and Lillian."

Wescott's love of nature included all animals. He never owned a pet but fed the birds and roaming farm cats, and especially loved the antics of squirrels, even picking favorites and noting sadly the final absence of one. He wrote to Trenton State College professor Hugh Ford, "One of my beautiful, teenage red squirrels, possessed of the devil, came up to see what I was doing in *its* attic—a problem!" Another time, he freed a red squirrel from a rat cage-trap, risking a bite, "because its almost suicidal hysterics made me unhappy." Once, after some misunderstanding, his sister Beulah sent him a card with an illustration of Saint Francis preaching to the birds. On it she wrote, "Just to say I'm lonely for you and love you." Wescott saved it, and inscribed: "I kept this unopened for nine days, knowing what it was; nevertheless wept when I read it."[73]

Obligations of literary history seemed to pursue Wescott. Hugh Ford was writing *Published in Paris,* about the deluxe presses of the expatriate years, and devoted a chapter to Harrison of Paris. Robert Phelps continued to press Wescott for a project. Phelps had success with *Earthly Paradise,* his autobiographical selections of Colette. And he co-edited with Peter Deane a lavish book of photographs and text called *The Literary Life, 1900 to 1950.* He amused Wescott with city gossip, such as that of a young writer they both admired, Susan Sontag, who he said was teaching at Columbia University by day and prowling nightclubs in a leather jacket at night. But, friendship aside, what Phelps wanted was a Wescott book. His proposed volume of selections, "A Windfall," became a lost opportunity. Sometimes Wescott added a few pages to his old fiction manuscript, "The Stallions," but never tied it together. And for years he wanted to produce a book of letters between himself and Porter, including some of her correspondence with Wheeler, Barbara, and both Lynes brothers. It was to be called "Letters to a Circle of Friends," but it was never finalized. Another book that should have happened was "The Old Party," a second volume of literary essays that would have contained his later Maugham pieces and other essays crafted from lectures. He had more than enough material. Yet he complained to John Connolly of "my failure to function as a writer, even when I have ten thousand dollars dangling in front of me—'The Old Party' is more than a year and a half overdue."[74]

What emerges as a pattern in Wescott's late years is an inability to follow through on excellent book proposals. He could write a specific piece beautifully, and intellectually he could—and did—command any room. But after his midsixties, the evidence seems to show, he lost the skills of organization needed for a book-length work. In truth, any strong editor could have solved this easily. But he never in his life had a forceful editor. He was too successful too early. He had too formal a relationship with Cass Canfield. Young Harper editors didn't presume to offer suggestions to Glenway Wescott. Nor could Phelps sway him. To many, he was an intimidating figure.

Frustrated, he complained to Janet Flanner of depression, "the worst since 1949. In many ways my life is so fortunate that as a rule I hide the bad beneath the good." He told Bernadine Szold, "My life seems unmanageable at this point and I am trying to figure out how it can be simplified, short of pretending to be a Christian and entering a Trappist monastery." And he hinted at the specific problem to the poet Babette Deutsch: "I have been absorbed in a bit of melancholia, for the third time in my life—no danger. . . . For months my study has just accumulated every kind of paper, more scribbled than written, and when I lost sight of something in the disorder I often forgot it."[75]

Katherine Anne Porter once told Wescott that Russell Lynes had taken stacks of her manuscript, laid them out on the floor, and chosen some to take away to create a magazine article. She joked, "Honey, you should have an editor like that, ha ha!"[76] She was so right.

Porter, who was awarded the Pulitzer Prize and National Book Award for her *Collected Stories,* became ill in her late seventies. Wescott began visiting her in Washington, D.C., and on one trip reported to Ivan Ashby, "She naturally is fearful of pneumonia, with which she has been at death's door a good many times in her life; the first is portrayed in *Pale Horse, Pale Rider.*" Later, he added, "I have just walked down to the drug store, about a mile, to buy a thermometer. Feverish K.A.P., out of patience with her life, and no wonder, bit the one she had in two!"[77]

In late December 1968, Wescott and Wheeler met in Spain at the Ritz Madrid and traveled to Paris, where Pauline sent a telegram: "Hurry please. You are so late getting here. Mouton is waiting for you." Wescott added in fountain pen: "A tug at the reins."[78] At Mouton Rothschild, Baron Philippe and Pauline were seldom seen in the first half of the day, and daily lunch and dinner menus boasted great meals and vintage wines. Amid the holiday, Pauline confided to Wescott that her heart was weakening; she was experiencing insomnia and night fevers. Wescott stayed on with Pauline until January 10, before rejoining Wheeler in London. Ivan Ashby, who was awaiting immigration clearance so he could live with Connolly in America, remembered, "Monroe stayed at a hotel convenient for him, and Glenway stayed with me. On my drive to work, I'd drop him at the Waterloo tube station and off he'd go!"[79]

During the week of his next birthday, Wescott saw a Bernard Perlin exhibit in Connecticut and remarked about a beautiful building at Yale that would be important to his future: "New Haven has another first-rate building: [Gordon] Bunshaft's vast strange jewel box, the Beinecke Library of Rare Books and Manuscripts."[80]

In May 1969, at a time when he was thinking about archives and his own legacy, Wescott was surprised to receive a letter from a popular poet and the author of the novel *Deliverance*. James Dickey had read Wescott's essays and sent a letter from his South Carolina home, through Harper and Row: "Last week I picked up your *Images of Truth* in an airport newsstand. . . . I liked what you said about Katherine Anne Porter and the others. . . . I am quite sure that Somerset Maugham will never again have such an eloquent defense. . . . There has never been anyone more absolutely *right* about Thomas Mann than you are. And that is a very great deal. I remember meeting you at the National Book Awards the year I won for poetry. . . . Know that I think of your work with admiration and honor, in criticism, in fiction, and in other things you do, like some of the personal reminiscences in 'Good-bye, Wisconsin.'"[81]

Dickey's friendly letter came during a bad month. Old friend Osbert Sitwell had died on May 4 in Florence. And Wheeler was embarking on the most dangerous and controversial journey of his career.

Wheeler was close to many artists and museum officials in Latin America. MoMA trustee Nelson Rockefeller also loved the region and had a house and businesses in Venezuela. Unfortunately, President Richard Nixon, after four months in office, pressured Governor Rockefeller to make a goodwill tour, tied to the museums but representing the White House. After decades of CIA operations and rightwing dictators, the United States' Latin American relations were never worse. Nixon had a hand in that history. Rockefeller, with his own political ambitions, called on his old friend Wheeler, who had made four Latin American trips the previous year, to join the mission.

The mission was ill fated from the start. Both Peru and Venezuela refused them entry. The CIA prepared spiral-bound briefing books, labeled *Rockefeller Presidential Mission,* covering each country's politics, history, economy, and revolutionary activity. A Secret Service flyer listed rules and warnings for the dozens of Americans.[82]

There were rock-throwing street demonstrations in Bolivia, Ecuador, and Colombia. On June 3, 1969, the *New York Times* reported, "The White House announced today that it supported Governor Rockefeller in his determination to continue his tours of Latin America on behalf of President Nixon despite the violence that has plagued the mission." That week, the syndicated column of Drew Pearson and Jack Anderson said Rockefeller was a hero in Latin America but Nixon had disastrous history of anti–Latin American decisions.

Wheeler, at seventy, stayed with the mission to the bitter end, over three months and forty-two thousand miles. Back in New York, he was asked to submit a report to Rockefeller. Wescott helped Wheeler with most of his writing projects, and that seemed true of his "Revised Report RE Cultural Affairs." The five-page report noted the extreme division of classes in the countries and recommended a cultural exchange, but only if American help came through Latin institutions and universities. In Wescott-sounding prose, it praised Latin Americans' desire for the higher arts: "For in true concern for the things of the spirit, in their warmth of heart and liveliness of mind, and in their aspirations, they are second to no other population on earth."[83] How far in Washington the document traveled is unknown, but, at a serious time in polarized America, a longtime gay couple was speaking as one about a major issue of foreign affairs to the highest branch of government.

Only weeks earlier, the modern gay rights movement crossed a threshold with the Stonewall riots, days of protest around Sheridan Square after police harassment of a Village bar called the Stonewall. Even Wescott's and Wheeler's younger friends felt a gap between themselves and the new generation of gays. Ralph Pomeroy remembered, "I'd been to that bar a week before. As I walked in, there were four Italian thugs. They didn't pretend to hide it. It felt uncomfortable to me in that scene, loud music and dancing—and the Mafia. I left and went elsewhere. When it happened, I had mixed feelings. Proud, yes, but worried what might be the repercussions. But then I thought of that younger crowd at Stonewall: Well, we didn't have the guts to do it, and you did. And I realized it was an important moment in history."[84]

For Wescott, the decade was ending with private emotions as well. Marianne Moore was slowly recuperating from a stroke. On September 17, he received a hand-delivered page of scribble from Moore, mostly in red ink. "I received a note dictated to and addressed by her nurse," he wrote on the sheet. But the illegible script seems in more than one handwriting. What is discernible in the red ink are the phrases "makes me feel" and "ten feet underground." On top of the page Wescott wrote, "Wonderful terrible image."[85] Fortunately, Moore made progress and lived several more years.

In late September and early October, Barbara felt moved to visit the places of her youth and persuaded Wescott to join her. Lloyd did not enjoy traveling, and Wheeler was in Rome with Raymond Mortimer. Wescott and Barbara saw friends in London, Vienna, the Netherlands, and Paris. When they returned to Kennedy Airport, Wescott rushed off the plane to make sure Barbara didn't pay tax on a duty-free tapestry. Only in Manhattan did he realize he'd left behind his raincoat with all his keys to Wheeler's, John Connolly's, and Haymeadows. He complained to Bill Maxwell: "Disorder is a disease and haste is a symptom."[86]

Among his work that year was an introduction to a new printing of

Maugham's *Summing Up* and preparations for the December appearance of the Argentinean writer and poet Jorge Luis Borges at the Institute of Arts and Letters.

On December 18, Wescott joined Wheeler for a week in London, including a full day together at the National Gallery, then Paris, and finally to the Rothschilds at Mouton on January 1 to bring in the new decade. On this visit, they kept some black-and-white photos of themselves strolling outdoors with short, dapper Baron Philippe and tall Stephen Spender with his walking staff—Wheeler looking elegant and Wescott in his favorite British overcoat. All seemed relaxed and peaceful, their different stories known, their accomplishments almost complete.

12

"Quail and Strawberries"

He is the wall of this place whose hair
has the look of splash from a puddle.

Here, where a catbird gives problems to prose,
stone wall becomes room, becomes home, becomes whole
him.

"When I die, I want to lie in that wall."
(The one by the road where grapes crawl and walnuts huddle.)

He is the wall of this place, whose chest
is crooked and whose stance converses.

How many kinds of weather make a novel?
How many singers can sing exactly when wanted?

How many reds can penetrate the blue?
How explain the swing of sex, the bugle, the flair

of horses running through Hunterdon County,
the mythical waters of Broadway on which ships pass?

He is the wall of this place, whose eyes
are sky-held-in-check. Whose words are disordered order.

How many words to a house? How many houses turn hovels?
He is the wall of this place, whose crewcut splashes,

who captures the tilt of heaven for his chapters,
whose novels lean and, in slow water, double.

—Ralph Pomeroy, "The Novelist at Home in New Jersey,"
dedicated to Glenway Wescott

AFTER bringing in 1970 at Mouton Rothschild, Wescott visited the museums in Paris and London with Wheeler. He wrote to Barbara, "Pauline's health has worsened; and now, not too late (I hope) her old doctor and two specialists have ordered her to the Leahy Clinic in Boston for, they presume, surgery. She sets out Friday next, the sixteenth."[1]

At the end of the month and in early February, Wescott made several trips to Boston. While Pauline was in the hospital, Philippe took rooms at the Ritz-Carlton. Renowned cardiologist Bernard Lown was surprised to learn that Pauline, who traveled with trunks filled with books, refused to see doctors in the morning. He liked her but was disappointed when she refused the heart valve surgery he recommended.[2] After alternative surgery in New Zealand failed, she eventually had Lown's operation and was given an experimental drug, Tolamol. In his autobiography, Baron Philippe de Rothschild wrote, "From that time on she was an invalid. . . . She gained a little strength from time to time, but she was never again the Pauline I had known. She began to dress simply, in clinging trousers and loose shirts, a bright scarf at her neck in the evenings."[3] Photos of the time show that Pauline made the casual look very attractive. Wescott cheered her with letters and praised her travel writing in his lecture "Women at Letters." Over the next six years, he traveled to Boston for Pauline's hospital visits, and they would take walks, go to restaurants, and reminisce.

He also devoted time to Katherine Anne Porter, whose health remained poor. Commenting on one of his most complex relationships, he quipped to John Connolly, "I am going to Washington to visit Porter, chief personifier of my psychic blocks and general futilities."[4]

A hard loss was that of Marianne Moore, at eighty-four. She had been a fixture in Wescott and Wheeler's world for half a century. In her last years she had returned to Greenwich Village, but her funeral was at the Lafayette Avenue Presbyterian Church near her Brooklyn home of decades. On the printed program he saved, Wescott wrote, "Program of the memorial service for Marianne in Brooklyn, planned in every detail by herself. Her body in commonplace coffin lying all soul alone around the corner from her apartment, disappointingly visited by Monroe and Robert [Phelps] and me at 4:30 p.m. on Monday." Under one of the famous pictures of Moore in her tri-corner hat, he added, "The Smile of a Ghost."[5]

When another great, E. M. Forster, passed away at ninety-one, Wescott and Christopher Isherwood were anxious to publish their friend's gay-themed novel of 1913–14. After several months, Isherwood wrote, "Dearest Glenway: It seems that my claim to have the disposition of the American rights to publish *Maurice* is now legally recognized in England and very soon I'm to have the papers which say so. Then I shall be able to go ahead and hand over the rights to the Institute. . . . I must have a copy of the definitive *Maurice* before I can offer the book to publishers, or rather, before you can, or the agent you recommend. . . . Much love to you both as always, Christopher. P.S. Have just finished my book at last—*Kathleen and Frank*. What a relief."[6]

When *Maurice* was finally released in the fall of 1971, Wescott published "A Dinner, a Talk, a Walk with Forster" in the *New York Times*, recalling the novelist's 1949 address to the Academy-Institute, as well as the dinner party at Wheeler's that included Dr. Alfred Kinsey and Joseph Campbell. The article describes Forster's visit to Stone-blossom and his touching relationship with his married policeman friend, Bob Buckingham. It also reveals that it was Wheeler who delivered a copy of the manuscript from Forster in London to Isherwood in 1952. Forster made revisions later. When the novel was finally in print Wescott wrote, "One of my reasons for living—that is, for caring about my health and avoiding self-destructiveness and facing up to the pain and shames of old age—seems to be to live long enough to read books like *Maurice* and other withheld manuscripts that one knows about; the whole of Virginia Woolf's diary, for example."[7] Weeks later, he read part of *Maurice* to a large crowd at the historic Poetry Center of the Ninety-second Street YMHA and YWHA.

While Wescott helped bring Forster's important gay novel into print, he had doubts about the cart-in-front-of-horse priorities of some in the gay rights movement. Wheeler was in Puerto Rico with Bill Miller—who had inherited a San Juan condominium from a physician friend—when Wescott wrote him about the Reverend Troy Perry: "What do you think of homosexual men feeling so much need of religion? And note that the Reverend Mr. Perry wants to make marriage irrevocable, until death do them part. Really, the human race can't let well enough alone, or mind first things first," he said, pointing out that there were still no laws for the most basic gay civil rights protections.[8] That point could be made thirty years later.

Early gay activist Dick Leitsch, executive director of the Mattachine Society, remembered writing to Wescott in February 1971: "I was very interested in the legend of Saint Sebastian, and I'd been in touch with Christopher Isherwood, who sent me Wescott's entry from his *Calendar of Saints for Unbelievers* and Glenway's address." The entry stated in part that "when Rome was most immoral, it became a convention for the popes and lesser ecclesiastical lords to have their boy-sweethearts painted as St. Sebastian." Some, including Dr. Kinsey, have claimed that the Vatican has an embarrassingly large number of paintings of the martyred, near-naked Saint Sebastian in storage. "At any rate," Leitsch recalled, "I wrote Wescott and asked if he could help us understand Sebastian's legend in homosexual lore."[9] Wescott kept the letter but didn't answer. He preferred to let his writing speak for him—not just the subtle gay references in his first three novels, but his "out" remarks in *Images of Truth* and in the new personal essays he wrote in the seventies.

Complex relationships were still part of Wescott and Wheeler's world, even after they had been together more than half a century. Wheeler's new young companion was Anatole Pohorilenko, a friend of Will Chandlee, who was raised in Philadelphia and worked at the Philadelphia Museum of Art. In his early twenties, he had studied art history and already traveled in the highest circles of gay society. Like all Wheeler's earlier companions, Pohorilenko was attractive, sophisticated, and loved the arts.

At first there were problems. "About two or three months into our relationship," Pohorilenko remembered, "I had a run-in with Glenway. It was about my presuming to want to know everything. Monroe and I were supposed to go to London to see the National Gallery, but I told him I didn't know if I should, that Glenway was angry with me. Monroe said, 'Don't worry. I'll take care of it.' The next day or so, Glenway phoned me and told me to have a good time in London, and to be sure Monroe took his medicine."[10] A truce had been declared. Over time, Wescott came to respect Pohorilenko's devotion to Wheeler.

While he couldn't match Wheeler's still-active sex life, Wescott remained uncommonly candid in his journals: "What has vanished from my sensual memory is the pleasure of being fucked; despite the power and importance of it in three or four relationships. . . . Can I cut myself down to the realities and to the last lap of life? But the last lap may be a totality of love once more: body-soul."[11]

Honesty was the chief quality of Wescott's journals, but putting them in publishable form was the problem. He had notebooks, loose pages, cards, and hundreds of three-ring binders. Included were many hundreds of letters, which could be mined for excerpts. There were also strange scrapbooks of clippings and photos with his commentary, such as one of seventies images called "The Eye," one of oddities called "Bizarries," and one of erotic male photos called "American Beauties." Yet it was all intriguing. A large, pasted-down newspaper portrait of President Nixon's crewcut chief of staff, H. R. Haldeman, was annotated, "The worst face in our present nightmare news."[12] Next to photos and clippings of handsome Olympic gold medal swimmer Mark Spitz he wrote: "Doctor Kinsey said that there was homosexual vulnerability on both sides of the [Senator Joseph] McCarthy struggle."[13]

Robert Phelps was not discouraged by the mountain of material stored on shelves and in banker's boxes in the large room behind Wescott's kitchen. Phelps's latest book, *Professional Secrets,* was a success. The work consisted of Phelps's selections from Cocteau's autobiographical writings, as translated by the poet Richard Howard. Phelps, who called Wescott "the most multifarious man who ever lived," was anxious to create a time line of excerpts from his archive at Haymeadows. He visited the farm and put together a sample chapter of selections from his journals of the early 1950s. In late 1971, they signed a contract for three volumes of edited journals. Wescott received a larger advance than he had known in years, though it meant a break with his longtime publisher, Harper. When he read Phelps's masterfully edited selections to small gatherings, he was excited by the positive response. He devoted time and energy to the project, and Phelps borrowed from Haymeadows what he called the "matrix" of his work. But looking through old material was not always good for Wescott. He referred Phelps to his journal excerpt about a graveyard in East London. It was a true story about workmen digging up a centuries-old graveyard, with instructions to relocate bodies as necessary. Suddenly they began falling seriously ill and the work was stopped. Doctors diagnosed what the men were catching—Bubonic plague! "Searching through these papers," Wescott said, "I feel myself weakened by illnesses of the past."[14]

As the journals became his main focus, he finally gave up on a project that had frustrated him for years, the Katherine Anne Porter correspondence, "Letters to a Circle of Friends, 1933–62." After much arranging, studying, and considering, he realized what was wrong. Katherine Anne's letters were simple and direct, sticking to one or two topics, and could be published as is. His letters were brilliant in places but often covered too many topics. And it wouldn't do to publish his letter excerpts alongside her complete letters. Devoted friend Ralph Pomeroy remembered that moment in time: "Glenway just realized Porter's letters were better than his. And that was tough to admit."[15] The manuscript went to Porter's collection at the University of Maryland.

Now, however, Wescott was free to start something new. At seventy, he no longer wanted or needed to write book reviews. Buoyed by the work of Phelps, he was inspired to his last period of important writing. Coburn Britton, a poet who lived next door to Paul Cadmus on Saint Luke's Place, had started a deluxe journal called *Prose* and was willing to pay fifteen hundred dollars for anything by Wescott. At first, Wescott tried to resurrect his old fiction manuscript, "The Stallions." In his journal he noted, "Sadly inspired by my difficult manic-depressive laboring away at my 'Stallions' for Coburn Britton's quarterly *Prose;* in which connections I have read a good deal of my sketches, letters and jottings on the eve of 1938–39—I wrote *The Pilgrim Hawk* in three or four months in 1940. It amazes me how closely the good and bad in my work is interspersed."[16] He told Wheeler that at Parker's Ferry Willie Maugham once suggested that Wescott revive the old eighteenth-century novel in letter form, in a new way: mailing it to some real correspondent in daily installments. He reflected, "Wouldn't it be strange if he were right about me after all?"[17]

Finally, Wescott began writing a series of new personal essays that were filled with his characteristic charm. In the first, "The Odor of Rosemary," in *Prose* number 2, he remarks that he wants to be more like Marianne Moore and Jorge Luis Borges, who would write "whatever pleases them, whatever comes into their lives or their heads." Indeed, his new essays are like that, meandering delightfully from one topic to another, yet always returning to the theme. "The Odor of Rosemary" touches on the lore of the herb rosemary, in history, in vignettes about Moore's poetry and her cooking, in folk tales from his former cook Anna, with personal asides along the way. For example: "I remember my mother, a few years before her death, with very little eyesight, but with a love of sweet odors and a detestation of the opposite as keen as my own, as she took her autumn walks, pausing to hold up her head and savor the dying breath of the vegetation, then peering down to the ground at every step, picking out of the vagueness that she could see a leaf here and there, stooping and collecting leaf after leaf. And I have begun to catch myself behaving like that, though with senses still almost intact."[18]

Seemingly unrelated memories and tales offer lessons. The essay ends with a detailed recollection of his 1935 ocean voyage to Europe. Leaving honeymooners Barbara and Lloyd alone, he befriends a young Californian. His friends might assume he was attracted to the youth, he writes, but that was not the case. Instead, the tragic boy was attracted to Wescott as a writer and told him the whole story of his father's suicide. Then, embarrassed, the young man said, "My God, let's talk about something cheerful," touching Wescott's heart. As their ship passed the coast of Spain, the breeze brought the scent of wild rosemary out to sea. "It is the details that persuade us of great things," Wescott writes. "It is the uninventable that we choose to believe and to love in the end. Down from the steep mountainside fields, impossible to cultivate, buzzing with the wings of bees and sharp with their stings, down came (and down still comes) the musky and honied odor of the herb."[19] The essay ends on a note of compassion toward the youth, toward humankind, that leaves the reader moved and wondering what he has just experienced.

Old friend Anita Loos wrote to Wescott, "It is a treasure to be read and reread—a reminder that charm and grace can still exist in this sorry world of today."[20]

The next essay for *Prose* was "The Emperor Concerto," which referred to Wheeler's favorite piece of music, Beethoven's Piano Concerto no. 5, op. 73 ("Emperor"). The opening paragraphs recall his first ocean voyage to England in 1921, when he met a woman who boasted of her brother, the pianist Wilhelm Backhaus. The narrative jumps to 1933 in Paris when Backhaus is performing the "Emperor" concerto and Wheeler whispers to Wescott that he wants the piece played at his funeral. Without mentioning Jacques Guérin's name, Wescott reveals that at the time he was breaking up with his French lover, and his mind wanders between the loss of the man's satiny flesh and pleasing scent to the chill he felt at Wheeler's words. He recalls them walking home through Paris that night, "with an odd inability to keep step, which has persisted. His steps are longer than mine, though I am taller. The reader may suppose that I mean this figuratively, to symbolize our differences of thought and moral orientation; but no, it was (it is) a fact."[21] The essay touches on other memories, and questions of morality and immortality—an odd and understated piece. All his new writing referred to gay relationships in a matter-of-fact way.

"Memories and Opinions" in *Prose* number 5 recalls the twenties in London and Paris. He remembers that the colorful R. B. Cunninghame-Graham was kind to him during his first visit to London, but later was offended by the sexuality in *The Apple of the Eye,* which Wescott had dedicated to him. "Thus I began to learn," he notes, "that the moral liberations of the future were more likely to develop in my native land than in Europe, despite the philosophy and the sophistication across the sea."[22]

The essay remarks that the American expatriates admired Ford Madox Ford and his novels, such as *The Good Soldier,* and adds, "I vowed then that to the day of my death I would keep advising young people, indeed anyone who might give attention to my reminiscences and enthusiasms, to try reading Ford, or to try again."[23]

Of Gertrude Stein, "monumental, strong and calm," he suggests: "She must have realized that Hemingway's way—a powerful perfectionism, carefully fitting every one-syllable word into place as though it were a bit of mosaic or a note of music—and even my way, my inhibited sweetness, my diffidence when I have pen in hand, were a reproach to her, a rivalry with her, in principle if not in fact or intent." And of James Joyce he recalls a Left Bank party when the writer was talking about Catholic saints with a man he discovered to be an ex-priest. "'Oh,' said Joyce, 'it is worth my immortal soul to sit here discussing theology with an unfrocked priest!'"[24]

The section "Hemingway's Contempt for Me" recalls Hemingway's attacks on Wescott's talent and his sexuality. In response, he criticizes Hemingway's deliberately lowbrow vocabulary, "laying on his democracy with a trowel, making a business of the common touch." And he rejects his colloquialism, "the basic baby talk of the universal animal which never grows up." Hemingway's inability to understand cause and effect hurt his novels, he adds. But in his short stories, "he often achieved perfection. They are nuggets of pure experience set apart from all the matrix of the world, distinct from the gravel of ordinary existence and from the bedrock of our conventional, inherited, and collected understanding of life."[25]

Wescott dedicated "Memories and Opinions" to Bernadine Szold, to whom he long ago had dedicated the poetry collection *Natives of Rock.* When he mailed her a copy, he told her that he had meant to put together a book of personal essays and fiction under the title of the lead essay, "The Odor of Rosemary," but instead he put it aside, in order to help Phelps with the journals. This was a mistake, because the potential new book of prose selections was too promising to put aside.

One other new piece, "The Breath of Bulls," appeared in the Doubleday anthology *Works in Progress No.6,* which described it as part of the would-be volume "The Odor of Rosemary." A memory of Stone-blossom, the essay opens at dawn with Wescott in bed with a thermos of coffee to inspire early writing, but instead he is reading about Greek mythology. He reads that the god Zeus, when taking the form of a bull, had a breath like the delicate odor of crocus. Knowing there is nothing delicate about the breath of real bulls, Wescott goes outdoors on the wet lawn in only his bathrobe, picks a crocus, and checks its minimal scent. Caught!—by his housekeeper, Anna, who scolds him for being outdoors in his "altogether! Under that old thin, worn-out bathrobe." He knows she hates the old bathrobe, and that was her real complaint. Rather than explain about the crocus, he makes up a story about losing his favorite fountain pen—but Anna just gives him a one-sided smile. Wescott concedes, "I could look forward to repeated solicitous inquiries about my favorite fountain pen, for days perhaps, or even weeks; and I resolved to begin trying to decide what sort of bathrobe might suit me, and what it should cost. I was as respectful of her mystifications as she was of mine."[26]

The humorous self-portrait had another side: the supernatural knocks and clunks in the Stone-blossom house, attributed to late nineteenth-century murders there. He recalled the previous owner of his house, a widow whose husband had been killed by a bull. The widow died soon after he met her, "one of several ghosts who haunted that happy though intensely emotional house and presumably haunt it to this day, when it is a ghost itself, down under the small shiny waves of the water reservoir."[27]

Enchanted, Pauline de Rothschild sent him a crocus from Mouton. The surviving member of the writing Sitwells, Sacheverell, praised Wescott's new work to Wheeler: "I found them quite fascinating—and how beautifully and clearly he writes. He has a wonderful gift for recovering the past; and I am hoping he is writing and publishing about the early years in Paris."[28]

The Wescott legacy seemed to be a popular topic. He even appeared in fiction as himself in *Poetic Justice* by Amanda Cross [Carolyn Heilbrun]. When a new critical work appeared, he told Malcolm Cowley: "There arrived today *Glenway Wescott: The Paradox of Voice* by Ira D. Johnson. The Rueckert book, which I haven't seen, must have been better, and that isn't much to say."[29] The earlier critical appraisal, by William Rueckert, considers all his work up to that point and is more favorable. Ira Johnson's book examines only the fiction and has mixed opinions, though it says *The Grandmothers* fulfilled Wescott's early promise and *The Pilgrim Hawk* is the culmination of his career. There is validity in Johnson's central point, about the "paradox" of voice: despite the success of his Alwyn Tower character, Wescott had a philosophical instinct to move away from it. And the more he moved away from autobiographical fiction, the more abandoned manuscripts he compiled. Of course, Wescott was beyond that kind of analysis. His legacy was in the books on the shelves and, he believed, in his journals.

Publisher Cass Canfield informed him of a new library edition of *Images of Truth.* He also offered his own perspective on Wescott the writer in his memoir *Up and Down and Around:* "From the earliest days I have known and admired Glenway Wescott; among his books *The Grandmothers* is his best novel. Although he was not the first writer of quality to evoke the American past, he brought unusual freshness to a kind of personal narrative that has grown in popularity over the years. Glenway's brilliance in conversation matches the quality of his literary style. Once president of the National Institute of Arts and Letters, he's an important figure in American letters; his writing style is a model of distinction. I hope that, someday, he will permit the publication of his vast correspondence, for he's one of the great letter writers."[30]

At about the same time, a new edition of *Contemporary Novelists* defended Wescott against all the publicity announcements of the latest "major" novels and novelists: "When the inflated press-releases are consigned to their place as part of the history of advertising rather than as part of literary judgment, however, Glenway Wescott will take his place as one of the finest literary artists in this period's prose," it stated. As for his out-of-print novels, "one hopes that in the not too distant future, Wescott's prose fiction will again be in print so that it can take its place as one of the truly distinguished achievements in twentieth century literature in English."[31]

Wescott, like Katherine Anne Porter, paid little attention to scholarly criticism. He was looking ahead, and he named his planned first volume of journals "Halfway." Curious, the novelist Isaac Singer wrote as one craftsman to another, "Dear Master, I am very much interested in your work because only those who can be silent when they feel like it, can talk well when the time comes. I also had years when I wrote almost nothing. Lately I work a lot."[32]

Flattering comments and book expectations were fine, but Wescott's priorities were best expressed in this note to Wheeler in Paris: "A weary day, a lonely day, but not unhappy. In the midst of the past week's discontents and wild sorrows, I seem to have reached a number of little practical decisions. Nothing worries me except your health—and I do not refer to surgeries, etc., but to wear and tear of moving. . . . Will you receive this? No matter. You know what it is intended to convey: Love. Yours ever, Glenway."[33]

Amazingly, Wheeler's travels and Wescott's routine of country and city had changed little over the decades. Joseph Campbell wrote to say he was happy to retire from teaching because it meant more time for other things. But to Wescott and Wheeler, it was keeping up their grand lifestyle that made their golden years special. In a postcard from San Francisco, Wheeler told Wescott of meeting friends, and added, "Quail and strawberries for dinner."[34]

Among their friends, Janet Flanner was in New York more often, and at the apartment of Natalia Danesi Murray they met Kurt Vonnegut Jr. At Cherry Grove, Natalia's house was just west of the firehouse, at the first right turn on the bay. A Fire Island lover since the twenties, Wescott gave his late impressions to composer David Diamond: "This past weekend I spent at Cherry Grove chez Mrs. Danesi Murray with my old, old friend Janet Flanner (Genet). . . . The people I was knee-deep in, or with, were all rather elderly friendly acquaintances of years and years standing; the young I saw were all a little loony and a little too drunk. I still love the place and the principle of it."[35]

Through the early seventies, they spent Christmas and New Year's Day at Mouton Rothschild, and Wescott's reading of his new essays was a highlight. Pauline remained in delicate health. Fashion magazines still wrote of "le style Pauline" but she was now reclusive. Her apartment in Paris and castle in Denmark were not enough of an escape from being Baroness de Rothschild. She announced that she was taking a London residence in the Albany, Piccadilly. Modern and sympathetic, Philippe accepted this decision. The fact that he was a notorious womanizer went unspoken. For Wescott, the holiday trips included visits to Paris, Belgium, Spain, and London with Wheeler. Their American friend Will Chandlee now worked for and was close to the filmmaker Tony Richardson, who had been married to the actress Vanessa Redgrave. Ivan Ashby remembered that Richardson hosted a party for Wescott and Wheeler, and Cecil Beaton invited them to his lavish home, Reddish House.[36]

On reflection, Wescott had enjoyed too little travel all through his middle years. Now, in his later years, he shared at least a bit of Wheeler's lifestyle of great European hotels, restaurants, museums, and friendly households. Yet he was unchanged in his liberal beliefs and passions. When President Richard Nixon was reelected by a landslide, Wescott consoled a losing Democratic candidate for Congress, Helen Meyner, and asked her to stay in politics: "I cannot say that the triumph of Nixonism has broken my heart, having foreseen it for several years. I am a kind of pessimist, and that protects one a little. The 'triumph' is harder on Lloyd; until a couple of months ago he thought that our party might pull itself together and drive out the wrong doers."[37] Helen, wife of ex-Governor Robert Meyner, was later elected to Congress. The Wescotts were friends of the state Democratic Party, but they did have one Republican friend in eccentric, pipe-smoking Congresswoman Millicent Fenwick.

By 1973, Wescott was still in fairly good health, though he underwent three days of hospital tests for circulatory problems. But Wheeler's arthritis required stronger and stronger pain-killers. Wescott's datebook once noted his lover's "desperation of pain." When home, Wheeler took a hot bath in the morning and Wescott would bring up his coffee and juice, and read to him, as he had since their earliest days. Whether it was a newspaper or book, Wescott's reading to Wheeler was familiar to everyone who knew them.

The passing of time was the theme all around them. Janet Lewis sent word that she had seen Kathleen Foster recently.[38] Kathleen was Wescott's fiancée from the Poetry Club days half a century earlier! In midyear, Wescott saw Janet Flanner off to Paris, with some concern. Poor health had kept her in New York with Natalia Murray for eight months. Natalia and Flanner's longtime companions in France, Solita Solano and Noel Murphy, all tolerated Janet's attempts to keep their relationships separate. Biographer Brenda Wineapple commented, "However, Janet's lovers were now linked by their concern over her unsteady health."[39] Another old friend, William Inge, in poor health and depressed, took his own life in June.

Even some younger friends were becoming historic figures. Bill Miller never seemed to get over being the handsomest man of the forties, and by midlife was becoming reclusive. Another beauty from the past, red-haired Patrick O'Higgins, reemerged. A gadfly in the late forties and fifties, O'Higgins had made a career as a portrait photographer and a publicist for Helena Rubinstein—and authored a fine memoir of the cosmetics queen called *Madame.*

Wescott himself was still young enough at heart to care about romance and sex. Young couples visiting Haymeadows were sometimes offered a heavy rug for their lovemaking in front of the fireplace (the very buffalo rug from his early childhood). On a loose journal page, Wescott noted, "Back to one of the formulas of my middle life: The only sexual encounters that I feel ashamed of are those that I haven't enjoyed."[40] A big change in his private life was his willingness to go to an X-rated movie theater. Ever since Stonewall, there had been more legal gay businesses and less risk. Convenient to his city routine was a theater in the West Fifties: "*The Super* has been running at a small squalid theater called The David. . . . I went once more and found more to admire in it than before, and some wild beauty even in passages of crazy lust."[41] He preferred films by the directors Toby Ross or William Higgins, filled with plot and young beauties. His favorite was *The Experiment,* a romantic story of young love. He sometimes recommended a film to Wheeler, if the theater seemed respectable enough. Bernard Perlin remembered that Wescott could also get emotional about well-written gay erotica.

At the same time, the public Wescott remained a writer's writer, especially for those in need of a literary quote. Columnist Pete Hamill quoted from *Good-bye, Wisconsin* when writing a loving piece about New York

City: "New York is halfway between the South of France and Wisconsin, always halfway between any two such places; that is its importance." Several quotations from Wescott's early writings appeared in the text of Michael Lesy's highly praised book of photographs, *Wisconsin Death Trip*. Ayer Press released editions of *Images of Truth* and *Good-bye, Wisconsin*.[42]

Overall, life seemed to be winding down pleasantly and predictably for Wescott. He and Wheeler drew up wills that gave important roles to Anatole Pohorilenko, John Connolly, and Peter Deane. It seemed reasonable that there might be good years ahead, but no more surprises. Yet a surprise was coming.

After spending the holidays at Mouton Rothschild, Wescott was at Haymeadows on January 7, 1974, when Earl Butler arrived for the weekend. Butler had told Wescott he would be bringing along a friend, a man in his twenties named John Stevenson. Born to a military family in Texas, Stevenson had traveled and acquired unusual sophistication in his youth. He was tall, handsome, fair, possessed great charm, was successful in advertising, and was already a gifted photographer. The moment Stevenson and Wescott met, they delighted in each other.

A romantic, Stevenson had never heard anyone speak so enchantingly, and he sensed magic about Wescott. It was a comfortable winter's night at Haymeadows, and after dinner they stepped onto the moonlit lawn. Stevenson remembered, "Glenway walked ahead and suddenly vanished, like a wizard! I was stunned. Then I saw a movement and realized he'd only been hidden for a moment by a tree. But in that moment I was prepared to believe anything."[43] The mutual feeling of that first meeting lingered. At first they spoke often by telephone. Wescott felt absolutely sure of this new relationship, but he kept quiet about it for months. After all, he had a bond of over twenty years with John Connolly, even though Connolly lived with Ivan Ashby, now a Merchant Marine captain. And there was respect for Earl Butler's feelings, because Butler was devoted to Wescott and fond of Stevenson.

In April, Wescott was on a plane to Miami with Connolly when he wrote to Wheeler about the effect of "new, more love" in his life. "What I think it amounts to is a new confidence in myself, as to peacefulness between you and me, prerequisite to the kind of work I have undertaken; a matter of detachment and regular hours, silent solitary hours, a page or two or three at a time."[44] The trip was one of several spring and summer vacations with Connolly. After his years with William Inge, Connolly had fashioned a successful career in television, including fourteen years as lighting director for *Ryan's Hope,* as well as work for *One Life to Live,* sports programs, and the *Peter Jennings News Hour.* Though seldom free, he took Wescott occasionally to the Florida Keys, where his mother, who loved Wescott, joined them.

Now the spring and summer of 1974 brought joyful days and evenings with John Stevenson. Sometimes they met when Stevenson was with Earl Butler, sometimes not. Stevenson's office was near the East Fifty-first Street apartment and he often took Wescott to lunch at the city's best Chinese restaurant. Wescott took Stevenson to the New York City Ballet and visited his charming studio apartment on Minetta Street in Greenwich Village, in a courtyard building where Aaron Burr once lived. As improbable as it seemed, at this late date, Wescott knew that he was completely in love with this much younger man, and was loved in return. At an age when he needed little, he found Stevenson's intelligence and romanticism irresistible.

Wheeler curated a Miro exhibit in Paris that year. When he returned, Wescott invited Stevenson to one of the Fifty-first Street cocktail parties. Stevenson's conversation, looks, and manners won Wheeler's approval. In late August, Stevenson was at Haymeadows and Wescott read his most enchanting essay, "The Valley Submerged," and inscribed a copy to him, "with the good beginning of my love." On other visits, he was invited to dinner with Lloyd and Barbara, and saw the Wescott clan as they were in the seventies. "Sitting at Barbara's table, I often observed the dynamics of their menage," he said. "Lloyd was sort of the manager. Barbara was the center of gravity. She clearly deferred to Glenway, and was warmer to him than to anyone. Monroe was there as Glenway's consort; his relationship to Barbara seemed polite and official, and to Lloyd, distant and cool."[45]

As Stevenson learned, Wescott still lived a busy life. That year, he visited Katherine Anne Porter in Washington, D.C., met Pauline de Rothschild on her trips to Boston and New York, and visited the Kinsey Institute in midsummer. At the Academy-Institute of Arts and Letters, he showed objectivity in his support for Gore Vidal, who was not a friend. Wescott wrote Tennessee Williams, "Will you join me in seconding dear Isherwood's nomination of brave, brilliant Vidal for membership in our Institute? I delighted in being hugged by you at Don Bachardy's exhibition. Furthermore, you said, 'Why Glenway, you're going to live forever!' Which did me good to hear, as I have begun to have heart disease. No matter. We are immortal; you certainly, I possibly. I need two or three years for my masterpiece."[46] He was referring to his journals. When Vidal was offered membership, he declined, upset that he wasn't invited sooner. Decades earlier, Vidal and Wescott had argued about Truman Capote. Vidal had pointed out that Capote hadn't written many books, and Wescott replied that quality is more important than quantity of books.

Stevenson also witnessed the start of Wescott's recording sessions.

Robert Phelps had convinced Wescott to read a little and talk about his early years on tape. At first, the recordings were made during unplanned gatherings of Phelps, Stevenson, Earl Butler, Wescott, and his sister Beulah. Later they became more organized and productive. After one of these late evenings, Beulah sent Wescott a note from the Harper and Row office—"I called this morning but found that you had already left for the country. What energy!"—to tell him that she was retiring from her longtime job there.[47]

I met Wescott that October of 1974. After college, I had briefly been a suburban newspaper reporter, then a junior copywriter at the publisher where John Stevenson worked. Early that year I witnessed his reaction to meeting Wescott. A long-haired kid in a conservative office, I was feeling the effects of a wild weekend—yet it was John who was beside himself with excitement as he described the mystic experience of Glenway at Haymeadows. A voracious Hemingway reader, I knew of the expatriates, including Wescott, but hadn't read him yet. I heard more of Stevenson's meetings with Wescott. Then in the fall I was invited to meet him.

One day after work, Stevenson and I walked up to Wescott, who was wearing his long British overcoat as he waited at a little park on Minetta Street at Sixth Avenue. His smile and eyes were exceptional. A slightly crooked stance made him appear frail at first, but I quickly saw he was quite sturdy and walked briskly. Just over six feet, he was strikingly handsome, with a resonant, articulate voice—the very image of a distinguished author. More important, one came away impressed by the joy of life he expressed—it seemed to extend to a large space around him. I came to know him well and was present at many of the events that followed.

There was no celebration at Mouton Rothschild at the end of that year. Pauline was in Boston for treatment and tests, and Wescott spent several days with her, quietly sharing her birthday and New Year's Day.

January 1975 marked a milestone for both Wescott brothers. Lloyd announced his resignation as trustee of the Hunterdon County Medical Center, two years after he had stepped down as chairman. The medium-sized, model hospital, at 2100 Wescott Drive in Flemington, New Jersey, honored him with a brass plaque in its lobby. At the same time, Glenway turned over to the New York Public Library a considerable amount of material for its Berg Collection of English and American Literature. The sale, arranged by curator Lola Szladits, included manuscripts and partial drafts of the published and unpublished novels, along with poetry, some correspondence, galley proofs, rare editions, and miscellaneous early items. Wescott enhanced the Berg material with explanatory notes and cross-references. Included was his earliest diary, a composition notebook from the days of West Bend High School. Not included was a massive amount of three-ring binders and banker's boxes containing manuscripts, thousands of letters, and various journal material. Wescott recommended the Berg to ex-lover Jacques Guérin, who was now one of the most important bibliophiles in the world. During this period of literary housekeeping, he received a page proof of his biographic entry in the forthcoming thirty-eighth edition of *Who's Who in America*. To his surprise, it included a 1933 novel, *The Deadly Friend*. He crossed it off his list of publications, just as he had long ago.

Early in 1975, Wescott told Ralph Pomeroy of his relationship with John Stevenson—"the first old friend to whom I have unnecessarily confided my new involvement of friendship and desire."[48] He loved having a young friend with the charm and taste of Stevenson, who that spring had bought from Sotheby's a first edition of Walt Whitman's *Leaves of Grass* and a handwritten letter by Henry Wadsworth Longfellow. When Stevenson moved from his small studio to 51 Bond Street, a large East Village loft with a wood beam cathedral ceiling and a skylight, Wescott was delighted. He gave a number of readings there.

Wescott wrote to Wheeler in Antigua to say he was hosting a party at "*chez toi*" for Maugham widower Alan Searle and a friend, and that he was inviting "my two Johns."[49] That meant even Connolly was beginning to see Stevenson's place in Wescott's life. Other guests included Robert Phelps, Will Chandlee, and Tony Richardson. Richardson and Wescott, sitting in facing armchairs, seemed to be sparring lightly for control of the room. When Wescott mentioned his new interest in working sessions on cassette, the famous director interrupted, "I only use recordings now. I hate to write." And Wescott replied, "Funny, it's the one thing I love."

That spring, Wescott made trips to Boston for Pauline, and to Chicago's Art Institute with Barbara. He was so busy, he confessed to John Stevenson, that he had neglected to write Wheeler, who was spoiled by decades of letters waiting at foreign hotels: "My beloved old traveler has had nothing from me except one apologetic cablegram—he has written me three times."[50]

Happiness was Wescott's real distraction. He scribbled in his datebook: "'I have learned more from being happy than from any of my misfortunes or sorrows,' said I to John Stevenson. 'Write that down,' he demanded, just as John R. C. is apt to do."[51] Through Stevenson, Wescott met other young friends. One evening he arrived by himself in casual jacket and tie at a youthful rock-and-roll party on Bleecker Street. He didn't mind the loud music, drinking, and marijuana. It surely reminded him of Village parties in the twenties. At one point a star-struck boy sitting beside him said, "I want to become famous." Wescott smiled and asked, "Why?" The youth didn't have an answer. Later, in a side room, Wescott was lying full length on the carpet, his head in his hand like a boy, talking to the youngest guests there, teenagers who sat close to him on all sides.

Behind the happy diversions, there was some concern about the journals. Robert Phelps had continued editing, right up to the 1955 material, but release of the first volume was delayed. People at the publishing house wanted changes but there was no clear communication among the highly civilized publisher, the star editor, and the temperamental author. Still, the work was promising. Wheeler made perceptive remarks about Wescott's life at that moment in time: "John Stevenson is a good friend for Glenway at present because he is romantic about literature, inspiring Glenway's intense, even painful self-criticism, which he then mediates with enthusiasms. The journal is unlike anything he had done before—rough, uneven, opinionated and often surprising. A good deal of the time he minds Robert's editing but he probably wouldn't want to publish it at all if Robert had not handled it so cleverly."[52]

Wheeler's fulfillment was in his flair for life, no matter the passing of the years. In January 1976, he sent Wescott greetings from Panajachel, Guatemala: "The arrival of the Warburgs and the Heintzes turned our quiet house party into a jamboree. Today we motored through beautiful mountains to the prettiest lake in the world, on whose shores we are lunching. . . . Will you be in New York to dine with me on the 31st?"[53]

Yet the reality was that the years were passing. Their friend Janet Flanner became too frail to live abroad and came home to stay with Natalia Murray. Shortly after Janet left France, her other longtime companion, Solita Solano, passed away at eighty-seven.

In February, Wescott sent Pauline a routine letter but she was already on her way back to Boston. By telegram her doctor had told her to stop taking her heart medication, Tolamol, and to come immediately. When she arrived she called Wescott and he quickly joined her. Philippe could not come for several days. The doctors had learned that Tolamol, which she had been taking for years, could cause cancer, and their examination of Pauline revealed that it had. Treatments started immediately, and a new heart medicine was prescribed. Wescott stayed by her side. Eight years younger than he, at sixty-seven Pauline was still youthful, sweet, and brave. For the first time in decades they were alone for days without any formal ceremony or their partners or famous friends. They talked and talked, as only best friends can. In Wescott's *Apartment in Athens,* his character Major Kalter said of his dying wife: "We were like a god and a goddess, there in the grim hospital, with her frightful bandages, in our grief and loss. Wonderful days!" Surely, it was something like that. After Baron Philippe arrived from France, Wescott stayed on a little longer, then returned to New York. He wrote to Raymond Mortimer, "I had a magical four days in Boston with Pauline before Philippe arrived. His two or three lengthy calls on the phone were pessimistic and pathetic. . . . I am afraid that her health is not holding up as we hoped."[54]

In his autobiography, Philippe recalled, "Boston, the hospital, the hotel, were now a part of a deadly daily routine." Pauline took treatments through the end of February and then Philippe flew her to Santa Barbara, California, hoping to lift her spirits. They stayed at the Biltmore and quickly drew a crowd of admirers. "My poor Pauline," he wrote, "so many wanted to know her, to lionize her."[55]

On March 7, 1976, Pauline sat on the beach much of the afternoon, watching the Pacific. Philippe was swimming and came back to the hotel to find that she had collapsed in the foyer and died. In their room, he found that she never opened the new heart medicine that had been prescribed. He telephoned friends and sent telegrams around the world. That evening, he received this telegram reply: "Thank you for two decades of care and devotion to our darling. Your heartbroken Glenway and Monroe."[56]

A lengthy obituary in the *New York Times* the next day mentioned only a previous hospital stay, not the most recent, stating only that she had been recovering from influenza. It described her beginnings in Baltimore, her fame as a clothing designer, her celebrity as a Rothschild, her various homes, and the wine museum at Mouton Rothschild that now drew twenty-five thousand tourists every summer. It included Diana Vreeland's description of Pauline: "She can dominate a room from a footstool." Philippe arranged for a service in Santa Barbara, then transported her home to Mouton Rothschild for burial.

In his own last years, Ernest Hemingway had repeated a phrase that greatly annoyed his wife, Mary: "People are dying who never died before." He meant, of course, people of quality, true peers. Wescott had lost many peers, but Pauline's was a rare friendship few others understood. Philippe made a stopover in New York on his return to France, but Wescott was too upset to see him. He sent an apology, referring warmly to Pauline's ghost, and saying that she might not have lived as long without Philippe: "As an even older friend of Pauline's than you yourself, thank you for making a great blissful life for her, well into the third decade. . . . Certainly yours was one of the most creative marriages I have ever known."[57]

For months, Wescott put off routine activities. Then he began to meet again with Robert Phelps, and he attended Lloyd's fund-raising party for New Jersey Governor Brendan T. Byrne in June. He was surprised when a publisher asked to reprint his humorous book of 1932, *A Calendar of Saints for Unbelievers.* Peter Neill of Leete's Island Books in New Haven used an unbound copy of the Harrison of Paris edition to produce a paperbound facsimile of the original, as well as one hundred hardbound copies numbered and signed. The beautifully typeset tales of famous and dubious saints were reproduced, including Pavel Tchelitchew's drawings of the signs of the Zodiac. Phelps wrote a brief appreciation of *Calendar of Saints* for the August 1976 issue of *Mademoiselle*. He said in part, "Even if it were not a book so brimming with the extremities of human nature, I would love it for its form: several hundred squibs, orts, marginal notes, glimpses, memos, *historiettes,* profiles, after-dinner anecdotes, and all arranged around our calendar year."[58]

At seventy-five, Wescott kept up his various interests. Harper and Row still invited him to its annual party, a retreat at upstate Mohonk Mountain House. In the city, Charles Henri Ford lured him to a screening of his homoerotic *Johnny Minotaur,* which immediately acquired cult status. At the Academy-Institute of Arts and Letters he kept up committee work, and artist Georgia O'Keeffe praised him for getting the long-distance members to vote.

Wescott had a proud moment at the Academy-Institute when he opposed a commercial deal with Franklin Library, a division of the Franklin Mint, which specialized in newly created collectibles of all kinds. In return for financial considerations, the Franklin Library wanted to produce a series of Academy-Institute Gold Medal–winning books. Wescott argued that their Gold Medal was awarded for an author's life work, not a single book, and that the publisher would surely pick only the work of famous authors. He opposed the selling of their reputation and criticized the Franklin Library: "Their presentation and packaging is vulgar; their advertising language in brochures and on huge pages in newspapers is boastful and misleading, but perhaps not more than it has to be to minister to the cult of culture in the minds of the uncultivated."[59]

After a divided vote of the membership, the Institute withdrew from the book series proposal. Another notable moment for literature was the last appearance of Katherine Anne Porter, eighty-five, at the Ninety-second Street Poetry Center, accompanied at each arm by Wescott and Wheeler. Photos at the Center record the event.

Still a political romantic, Wescott awoke on Election Day 1976 to an auspicious sign: "A great pheasant on my doorstep." He listened to election results until late at night. In the morning, the first words he heard on the radio were, "Jimmy Carter, who has won the election . . ." He wrote down, "Joy, joy, political joy."[60]

Despite all the subject matter in his life, Wescott now became more reluctant about publishing his journals. Revelations in Truman Capote's *Answered Prayers* had upset society people, some of them Wheeler's friends. One of Capote's *Esquire* installments, "Unspoiled Monsters," had mentioned Wescott by name, as one of the celebrated friends of the editor George Davis ("Boaty" in the novel). Far less kind were the portrayals of Tennessee Williams and Katherine Anne Porter, by pseudonym, and Cecil

Beaton and especially Ned Rorem, by name. When Wescott tentatively agreed to an interview about Kinsey for a gay magazine, he admitted, "What makes me timid about these unveilings of oneself in magazines is simply that I talk more naked than other people. Paul Cadmus and Isherwood can say whatever they like, and it isn't ever indecent." At the same time, he admired Isherwood for his candid interviews in the gay press: "Christopher told me, 'I've just decided, as long as the police keep arresting my young friends, I must speak up.'"[61]

Although he didn't want an interview published any time soon, he did speak candidly and enthusiastically about the whole Kinsey experience, leaving out only his most private experience with Alfred. He even joked about magazines in Times Square that showed larger penises than Kinsey's scientists ever found. "There is *Over Nine Inches,*" he said, "and the one I bought, *The Hundred Biggest.* The beautiful man was on the cover, and he really was astounding, and the rest were the most dreary looking human beings I ever saw—woebegone faces and sunken chests and some enormous-looking useless thing hanging down sideways. Ha! It cured me of being a size queen forever."[62]

The day after talking about Kinsey, Wescott shared an important moment for sexual liberty. Accompanied by John Stevenson and Wheeler, he joined Christopher Isherwood at the Algonquin Hotel for the book launch of Isherwood's autobiographical *Christopher and His Kind.*

Despite such positive moments, 1976 had begun with the loss of Pauline and ended with equally grave news. In late summer, Barbara and Lloyd announced that Barbara's doctor had found cancer and planned for surgery in New York. She was hospitalized on August 31 and Glenway gave her a note through Lloyd, asking her to be patient with the "pains and clumsinesses" of the hospital. He added, "We'll all be holding our breaths while you're away—not in fear; you are still too beautiful, too clear-voiced, too determined, too non-selfish. But our lives, which ought to immortalize you, ache in their foundation."[63]

After exploratory surgery the next day, Lloyd called Glenway from the hospital. It was inoperable. Barbara came home that week with a schedule of radiation treatments. The routine of their lives fell back into place, but a cloud hung over it. Glenway found Debo "beautified by emotion." Debo's daughter, Joanna, asked him, "Grandmother said she's going to 'beat it' and get better. Will she?" He answered the twelve-year-old tactfully: "Well, yes, maybe she will. But, you know, dear, none of us can beat it forever, can we?"[64]

As the tragic year wound down, Wescott admitted a surprising fear to Bernadine Szold: "Tolling in my head for days amounting to a week has been the thought that I may never revisit France again. My old dearest of all will not tolerate this; isn't likely, indeed, to believe it."[65] Wheeler, courageous despite his own health problems, promised Wescott that they would travel together to France in the next year.

Barbara showed improvement for a time and the whole family surprised her with a party on New Year's Eve. Two weeks later, the Friends of the New Jersey State Museum held a dinner in her honor. On January 22, Glenway had dinner alone with Barbara and Lloyd, and just as in old times he read to them afterward, choosing Turgenev's stories "The Quail" and "Nightingales."

Worry about Barbara may have affected Wescott's health. He had circulatory problems and complained of short-term memory loss, but no serious trouble. Then on March 13 he wrote to Wheeler about his difficulty writing for the previous two weeks. The letter was in an unsteady hand, a poor attempt at his usual beautiful script. A page of journal that he wrote that day, describing the time he had spoken harshly to his father as a child, was barely legible.[66] Sometimes his rough drafts were scribbled, but this was much worse.

Alone in the house, that very night, he had a scare, and afterward wrote five pages in fine, clear handwriting describing it to Lloyd. He had fallen asleep in his little bedroom, formerly a pantry behind the kitchen, reading the newspaper and listening to the heavy rain, "Whereupon, I had what I took to be a stroke—breathless, immobilized, struggling to get on my feet, blinded, standing up at last, just able to stumble into my study, into the kitchen, into the dining room, meaning to telephone you, unable to remember your number, still unable to see, shifting dark shadow and blazing light; and I took up the telephone to ask the operator to call you—and then I woke up, in bed, that is, on my bed and holding the *Times*. No sign of its having been anything but a bad dream; unlike any dream I have ever had; worse. Pulse normal, eyesight clear, a little nausea, a little fear."[67]

Wescott put on the radio, not wanting to telephone and worry Lloyd. The phone rang and it was John Stevenson, who promised to call again in the morning to be sure all was well. Wescott concluded the letter to leave for Lloyd, "if the dream should prove to be a prelude to the worst of realities. I must provide you with a key. I must remake my will. I am not afraid. . . . Thank you for all that you and Barbara have meant to me—your perfect love and care. I should ask to remind Monroe that I have loved him exceedingly since 1919 until this day, this night, and he has been able to give me inspiration to write, and may do so once more."[68]

He left the folded pages in the kitchen with a note to Ethel, the farmhand: "If you find me ill, give this to my brother. If not, let me have it." Then he read himself to sleep. Waking as usual at dawn, he tucked the letter away in one of his boxes of loose papers.

Of course, the dream simply reflected the bad year. Philippe de Rothschild wrote: "I have now been for two weeks living in Pauline's Paris house.

Blissful. Though I have not yet put a definite end to six months of a nightmarish time. . . . Here in her house, she is still there, and for me it is now comforting. She also is in Mouton. . . . I am leaving tomorrow for three weeks in London. So, wherever I am, you both are also there with me. Love & love & love, Philippe." He added a postscript: "I have heard some disturbing news of Barbara. I hope it is wrong. Fond messages to her."[69]

Barbara Harrison Wescott's months of reprieve wound down in early April. She was taken to Hunterdon County Medical Center and died in her sleep at 3:30 A.M. on April 7, 1977. It was like a shifting of the ground, for Barbara had been one of them since the Paris years, for five decades—her different relationships with Lloyd, Glenway, Monroe, and George Lynes stronger than those with her distant and widespread relatives.

On May 1, the New Jersey State Museum held a groundbreaking ceremony for a sculpture garden in Barbara's memory, centered by mosaic murals of Ben Shahn. On May 2 the *Trenton Times* reported, "400 Celebrate Memory of Barbara H. Wescott." Photos there and in the *Flemington Democrat* of May 5 showed Lloyd and his granddaughter, Joanna Prockop, as the girl turned a spade of soil at the groundbreaking. Another showed Wescott at the lectern. Museum director Leah Schlossberg remembered Barbara's decades of support, calling her "missionary, emissary, patron, benefactor, hostess and reporter-writer." Governor Brendan Byrne said Barbara had achieved "the kind of immortality we all strive for." Former Governor Robert Meyner was present, and his wife, Congresswoman Helen Meyner, recalled Barbara's twenty years of friendship. Representatives were present from three organizations Barbara had long supported, Friends Fine Arts Committee, Hunterdon County Medical Center, and the Karen Horney Clinic. Speaking last, Wescott described her as she was in the days that inspired *The Pilgrim Hawk,* in her youth in France: "She had a great big Mercedes. . . . Once she took me to an open track to show me how it went. She was a tremendous sportswoman. She went shooting, salmon fishing, and horse riding, and she always had a fast car."[70]

Wescott's strength in bad times was a comfort to others. Months earlier, he had eulogized his friend Anaïs Nin at New York University. But much of Wescott's strength was drawn from Wheeler. Shortly after Barbara's memorial, Wheeler had museum business in Mexico and France. Wescott wrote to him in Paris. "Upon your departure," he admitted, "I have found myself weak, empty, useless—but the light of your love keeps shining on me. Credo: your ambition for me, my belief in order and rest." But the subject of order was a touchy one at Haymeadows. In telling Wheeler they had to get serious about organizing their wills and possessions, he mentioned his brother's horror of Glenway's mountain of material: "Oh, Lloyd was funny the other day. . . . He said, 'If you and Monroe predecease me and I have to cope with all this, I'll go mad!'"[71]

Yet Wescott felt more protective than ever of his huge archive of papers, because he knew it held their story. Early that year he had done a reading of their early letters and Brooke Astor insisted that Wheeler and Wescott have their lifelong correspondence edited and published.[72] Having once traveled to Japan and Taiwan with Wheeler, she had seen his delight in Wescott's letters and his pleasure in writing home about his adventures. For his part, Wheeler never despaired of the proposed books of journals or letters, but he liked to have something symbolic in hand. In Europe, he had two copies of *The Grandmothers* lavishly leather-bound and embossed with their initials.

Another comfort that Wescott found in old age was the beauty of country life, he told John Stevenson, in a letter decorated with pieces of blue-green shell from a fallen robin's egg.[73] As a project between them, he lent John his copies of the ninety-nine erotic Tchelitchew drawings he had given to the Institute for Sex Research in the fifties, so that John could make negatives with his view camera. Wescott also took him to the Dakota building to meet Ruth Ford, whose apartment was filled with paintings by Tchelitchew, the late lover of her brother, Charles. He told Ruth of John, "I love him, differently from past attachments."[74] At Haymeadows, Stevenson photographed handsome platinum print portraits of Wescott. In New York, they saw an exhibit of George Platt Lynes nudes and mythology photos at the Sonnebend Gallery.

Lifting Wescott's spirits even more was a trip to Europe, just as Wheeler had promised. He flew to Paris on November 10 and they met at the Hotel de Calais. Walking through the Louvre one day Wheeler pointed to a spot where they once stood with Will Chandlee. That prompted Wescott to send Chandlee his impressions of the nostalgic trip: "For twenty-four hours I fancied it might suit me to live and work here—until the French, my French, got into the act. Lunch and all afternoon with Jacques Guérin, scarcely getting a word in edge-wise: his quarrels, his exploits of buying and selling, his treasures. He is too stingy even to answer questions. After that, three grand meals with Philippe de Rothschild in thirty-six hours. . . . I wonder if I have the courage to see François [Reischenbach]—is our friendship restorable? Has either of us the time for it?"[75]

Next they went to Amsterdam, then London, staying at the Ritz in Piccadilly and visiting with Kenneth Clark, Stephen Spender, and other friends.

As 1977 ended, Wescott and Wheeler appeared together at a party of Stevenson's youthful friends in the city. In the country, they joined Lloyd's charity fundraiser in Barbara's memory, and Wescott read his "Valley Submerged." In beautiful script, he made a revised version that was photocopied for all the guests.

Happily, the last two years of the seventies were a testament to

Wescott's love of life and the people in his life. "What joy your telephone call gave me," he wrote to Stevenson. "It must slightly resemble the experience of the souls of believers in Purgatory, if and when they pass from one level of that perilous location to the next, upward, heaven-ward, or perhaps I should say, Nirvana-ward."[76]

In the middle of New York's worst snowstorm in a decade Wescott met Stevenson and a friend in Chinatown for dinner and then, in his buttoned-up overcoat, walked through snowdrifts to a nearby arcade to see a famous dancing chicken. Another evening, a boy prostitute at the notorious corner of Fifty-third Street and Third Avenue met his eye, then followed him for blocks. Wescott ducked into the safety of his apartment building and later told friends coyly, "I don't know *what* that young man thought I could do for him!" Another time, he was introduced to the painfully young and beautiful French Canadian artist Denis Gaudreault. He spoke to the talented but narcissistic artist in fluent French, and afterward commented to the youth's friend, "French boys are the most expensive thing in the world, if I remember correctly."

Stevenson and friends took Wescott to see Quentin Crisp's one-man performance at a theater on MacDougal Street early in 1979. The British wit was the new celebrity in New York after his memoir *The Naked Civil Servant* inspired a popular BBC production starring John Hurt. After Crisp's funny monologue, he answered questions from the audience. When that began to lag, Wescott rose and spoke, and got a predictable reaction. He praised Crisp's courage as a survivor and his recent success. But the intoxicating sound of Wescott's voice, his elegant but warm manner, turned the entire audience toward him. The burst of applause was clearly not just for the man on stage. And it's possible Crisp felt a bit upstaged.

Ten days later, Wescott and Wheeler held one of their East Fifty-first Street parties, and John Stevenson invited Crisp, who arrived in his black outfit and black fedora after that evening's performance. Among the other guests were Christopher Isherwood, Don Bachardy, book dealer Bob Wilson, and an assistant to Liz Smith—a society columnist who had greeted Wescott at the previous week's performance and would report on this party the next day. Crisp seemed on guard in this company. He sipped wine and enjoyed grapes and Black Forest cake. Only when he spoke with the youngest guest did his eyes open wide and he seemed for a moment unreserved and youthful himself.

Isherwood joked with Crisp about their recent experiences with television talk show hosts. "Oh, I found Tom Snyder very easy," said Crisp for all to hear. "All I had to do was say, 'Oh, yes, I've suffered!'" Everyone laughed. Isherwood said, "I can't believe we never met before! How is it that we never met in London?" Crisp smiled slightly, hesitated, then said with a little edge, "We lived in different neighborhoods." Then Wescott asked, "When can we have you here again?" Quentin paused, then caused another burst of laughter with his most theatrical voice: "Oh, eee-ternally."

Shortly after that party, Wescott wrote one of his journal notes on a blue index card at his kitchen table in the country: "Quentin Crisp: Not all things to all men, but all things to one man, to wit, himself."[77]

Wescott seemed to develop a mischievous rebelliousness in his late years. He was as bohemian as Wheeler was fastidious. On one occasion friends were helping Wescott sort journals and papers at the East Fifty-first Street apartment, which was in shocking disarray that day. The living room carpet and every surface were covered with books, open binders, folders, and loose papers. Wescott said, "It's all right. Monroe won't be home from Europe until tomorrow." But only an hour later, a key turned in the apartment door. Wheeler put down his suitcase, announced he had taken an early plane, and immediately began picking up the books and papers. Wescott did the same as a frozen silence fell over the room. Despite the tension, their fights were often humorous to others.

On another occasion, Wescott and Wheeler were at a private dinner in the Princeton University community. Brooke Astor and other notables were present. Some undergraduate men were seated at a separate table. One of them remembered, "Glenway Wescott came over and I can't describe how he talked to us, he was so entertaining and full of life. Then he looked at place markers on the other table and told the butler, 'I don't know where our places are assigned, but I want to sit with these boys.' And he did! I don't think the other guests liked it at all."[78]

Wescott took his public appearances seriously. In April 1978 he spoke at Rutgers University about his creative friends at a conference on women of the twenties. An account in the *New York Times* included a photo of Wescott with Kay Boyle, Janet Flanner, and the photographer Berenice Abbott. He was still active at PEN and the Academy-Institute. He recalled for friends a time that the esteemed Ralph Ellison spoke too long at an Academy-Institute gathering and criticized a fellow member too harshly. Pretending to pass Ellison a note, Wescott said, he leaned over the podium and whispered, "Shut up, Ralph!"

Like other members, he had to acknowledge changes at the Academy-Institute. He was amused when a friend reported discussing Wescott with new member Allen Ginsberg and Peter Orlovsky at a raucous Punk Rock show at legendary Mabuhay Gardens in San Francisco. Ginsberg wrote a poem about that night called "Punk Rock, You're My Big Crybaby." Though allied with the older members, Wescott liked Ginsberg. "I once had a gathering of poets at Monroe's apartment," he recalled, "and Allen arrived wearing sandals. I said, 'Allen, shall I wash your feet?' He didn't understand the reference, but LeRoi Jones, who was a preacher's son, burst into laughter."[79]

Wescott's happy spirit contrasted with his strange reluctance to publish. He sometimes talked about his journals, the "Windfall" anthology, or even "A Visit to Priapus," but, perhaps subconsciously, he seemed resigned that these works would be posthumous. He told Berg curator Lola Szladits that his publisher "scolded" him for giving Maugham biographer Ted Morgan generous interviews. Yet Wescott had not granted his publisher's request to see his binders of Maugham material, which editors could have turned into a book. When Truman Capote asked a Wescott friend about Wescott, he was told he was fine but still reluctant to release his journals. Capote smiled and rolled his eyes. Naturally, Robert Phelps was frustrated that the journals he had edited seemed indefinitely stalled. He would have accepted some changes by the publisher, if only Wescott would come to a decision. "It's all about locks," he complained to friends. Over time, it seemed that Wescott in his late years worked harder at not being published than most writers do at publishing.

It was revealing when Wescott told several friends two true stories that he had never managed to write, as if passing them along. One was about a single mother who lived in fear of her beautiful but evil twin sons, who were arsonists. Another was about a young pianist whose male lover was killed by his enraged father, who was then acquitted of the crime.

Indeed, storytelling, the essential love of literature, still defined who Wescott was. His readings at the apartment kept the promise of his journals fresh and alive. Among the regulars were Jane Gunther, widow of author John Gunther, and Connie Bessie, an editor at *Newsweek*. Bessie, whose husband, Michael, had reprinted *The Grandmothers* in the sixties, was a woman of great warmth who sometimes brought knitting to the readings. The special evenings seemed a tribute to a rich, bygone era.

On November 7, 1978, when Wescott was out, Wheeler left a note, signed with a little drawing of a heart: "Dearest, Robert Phelps called. Janet died last night—heart, of course. I phoned Natalia—no answer. Another of our oldest and dearest gone. Robert said she had spent a happy day. Bless her heart."[80]

In fact, after a pleasant day, Janet Flanner was stricken late at night. And at the hospital, Natalia was kept waiting in the lobby all night because she was not a "family" member. Such losses were a part of longevity that Wescott was forced to accept. But in a late journal note he revealed that he still lived with Janet, Pauline, Barbara, Osbert Sitwell, Frances Robbins, and others: "Remembrance sometimes is like seeing and hearing ghosts, friendly ghosts. A number of my dead friends were gurus, which went unnoticed because of the energy, stir, and originality of their everyday life style, and their sweet humility toward me. Now, dead, they have nothing to do for me except speak, re-speak."[81]

Bernadine Szold sent her own timeless memories. She reminded Wescott that she took the last photo of Isadora Duncan, as Duncan sat beside handsome Wheeler and put on his beret, and she remembered that she had written Paris columns for the *New Yorker* before Janet Flanner did. Thinking of her own mortality, she sent Wheeler old correspondence and photos. Included were pictures of herself—an attractive, round-faced woman wearing a turban—with Wheeler and Barbara during their 1932 trip to China.[82]

Of course, Wheeler and Wescott were practically living legends by now. It didn't matter that Wheeler took Percodan every day for his arthritis, or that Wescott sometimes wore a neck brace. Together they appeared at the Riverside Church funeral of Wheeler's longtime friend Nelson Rockefeller. They took part in Lloyd's fundraiser for Democrats Bill Bradley and Helen Meyner, and in Governor Byrne's party for art patrons. At the Museum of Modern Art's exhibit of twenties and thirties portraits in fall 1978, there were drawings of both Wescott and Wheeler by Tchelitchew, Cadmus, and Cocteau.

Their lives remained active–and colorful. In the seventies people were often shocked to learn that Haymeadows now had a fenced compound with large tigers! Deborah Wescott's second husband, Thane Clark, had originally brought aggressive dogs to the farm, and Lloyd insisted they go. Then he took in tiger cubs, which once were used in an automobile commercial. Quickly the cubs grew. One playfully pounced on Wescott, knocking him against a parked car. Another bit a neighbor. Finally, four tigers were placed behind a fifteen-foot fence on an acre of land, close to Wescott's house. The arrangement went on for years, just another dimension of their extraordinary world. Wescott said he once dreamt the newspaper headline "Author Eaten by Tigers."

Since death by tiger or natural causes was a possibility, Wescott settled some financial decisions. To John Connolly he would leave much of the trust fund of stocks inherited from Barbara. He sold his Tanguy painting "Peril Solaires" at a large profit and would sell more. He also owned Coubert's "The Beach at Saint Aubin" and "The Wave" (or "Stormy Sea"); Tchelitchew's "The Lion Boy," "The Hanged Man," and six drawings; Hyman Bloom's "Amputated Leg"; and Bernard Perlin's "Bombed Yokohama" and six silverpoint drawings.

But possessions and finances were a minor concern. When Wheeler underwent some serious hospital tests, Wescott confided to John Stevenson, "Last night, thinking of Monroe as perhaps at death's door, I dined alone with Dorothy, then tried to stay awake, afraid of my fright." Only months later, Wheeler was in Alpes-Maritimes in France with Baron de Rothschild, worrying about Wescott's journals. He wrote, "I think of you and your predicaments every moment, but know that you will vanquish them. . . . I miss you desperately. I love you. Monie."[83]

Often alone at Haymeadows, confronting his papers, decisions, and reflections, Wescott wrote: "It takes half a lifetime to learn to grow old, without indignity, without advisors in my case."[84]

One day, he found his galley proof for "The Cat Reformed by Matrimony," a rewritten fable not included in his *Twelve Fables of Aesop,* and gave it to Wheeler with this inscription and a drawing of a heart on the envelope: "Given to my Monroe . . . when our old hue and cry about trivialities and incompatibilities seems to be waning; little tasks of sorting and storing and also, in fact, giving and selling, our strange small possessions take too much out of us; we haven't the strength to quarrel."[85]

13

Golden Leaves and the Birthday Book

ALONE in the Berg Collection reading room at one of its noble four-chaired tables, 10:30 a.m.," Wescott wrote on a stray page while reviewing his material at the New York Public Library. Archives and journals were his concern now. When he wanted thousands of pages of material photocopied and stored in the city, he was persistent and skillful in getting the job done.

Although his role at the Academy-Institute was diminished by this time, he still attended meetings. As always, he gave interviews to scholars, such as biographers Gilbert Harrison on Thornton Wilder, Ned O'Gorman on Allen Tate, and Martin Duberman on Paul Robeson. And he still gave readings. After one gathering, actress Ruth Ford told him, "I love being with you and hearing you talk like nobody on this earth can do—I wish you had a tape recorder around your neck so no one of your words could be lost."[1] He was lured to San Francisco to give a lecture about Alfred Kinsey's work to students at the Institute for the Advanced Study of Human Sexuality, where former Kinsey colleague Wardell Pomeroy was academic dean.

On July 8, 1980, John Stevenson set up an unlikely meeting. The author of *City of Night,* John Rechy, was in town from Los Angeles for a production of one of his plays. Stevenson had known him since they were both schoolboys in Texas and invited him to East Fifty-first Street. Wescott was on the sofa in jacket and tie, and Rechy, a muscular weight lifter in a pullover shirt, sat in an armchair. Rechy always wanted to be known for his other books, not just the famous sixties novel about a hustler's life, but he was pleased when Wescott praised the book's importance to sexual liberation. In turn, Rechy was equally polite to the man he plainly saw as a distinguished figure from a bygone, glamorous era.

A week later, Wescott met with Jack Woody of Twelvetrees Press and helped identify and date many of the photos for *George Platt Lynes Photographs 1937–1950*. The book included nudes, celebrity portraits, and mythological subjects with an introduction by Wescott. Just a year earlier the Nicholas Wilder Gallery in Los Angeles had presented a Lynes exhibit, and now the Institute of Contemporary Art in Boston was showing his "Photographic Visions." Wescott and Wheeler knew that Lynes's reputation in photography was secure.

While he wanted to stay active, Wescott's journal showed that the pace sometimes exhausted him: "I woke up at two a.m. and found myself too tired to go back to sleep. Leftover nightmare flowed up around me. Fatigue of yesterday led to the fatiguing day ahead. Poor old fool!" Other times there was weariness of spirit: "My mind in the early morning is lined with mirrors of memory, unavoidably tormented with every sort of realization of myself, past and present and seemingly future."[2]

There were losses that year. Patrick O'Higgins, the red-haired charmer who had written a memoir of Helena Rubinstein, died prematurely of heart trouble. Wescott attended the funeral at Saint Patrick's Cathedral. When Katherine Anne Porter died at ninety, he and Wheeler attended her memorial service in New York. In London, they lost Cecil Beaton and Wheeler's close friend, Raymond Mortimer.

Balancing the dark moments was the evidence of his fortunate life. Wescott was honored at the governor's reception for New Jersey artists on September 14. Governor Byrne presented him with an award from the New Jersey State Council on the Arts for his lifelong contribution to American letters. The *Newark Star-Ledger* story included a photo of him receiving the award at Princeton University. Monroe Wheeler and John Stevenson accompanied him to the ceremony and an evening party at the Schlossbergs'. In December, he joined Wheeler on a holiday trip to London.

After this point, Wescott's stamina became unpredictable. At Earl Butler's apartment, *Boss* magazine publisher Reginald Guy was planning an issue on Tchelitchew. From his heavy suitcase Wescott brought out photos of Pavlik and photocopies of his erotic drawings. He remembered amusing quotes: "Pavlik told me, 'I like a boy to have the face of a girl and the cock of a horse.'" He said Pavlik's great admirer, Edith Sitwell, once said that her high school biology teacher had explained homosexuality as a part of nature. Surrounded by her artist friend's homoerotic paintings, Sitwell had proclaimed, "My teacher prepared me for all this." Sitwell was a "giantess" at six feet, he said, handsome in her way, but she considered herself ugly because her mother had told her so.[3] After his storytelling, Wescott seemed suddenly distant from the high-spirited party, with a look of troubled weariness.

Yet just five days later on Saint Patrick's Day he was in his best form, cohosting Wheeler's party in memory of Isadora Duncan. He had recently been interviewed about the dancer by Jeremiah Newton of Andy Warhol's crowd. Now Wescott reminisced and a young poet, Daniel Diamond, read his amusing poems about Isadora. Along with the regular guests on this cheerful night was an Italian countess who had just visited Gore Vidal in California. Wescott was also in good form when he and Wheeler joined Stephen and Natasha Spender at the Rittenhouse Square mansion of the Philadelphia Museum's Henry McIlhenny.

On his eightieth birthday at Lloyd's house, he was impatient with the party and the amateur photography, though he was surrounded by Wheeler, Anatole Pohorilenko, John Stevenson, Will Chandlee, and Wescott relatives. On another occasion that spring, he asked a group of friends to meet at John Stevenson's loft. He reportedly wanted to take everyone to a small gallery that was slow in returning some Lynes photos. Robert Phelps joked, "Here we are again, Glenway Wescott's Marching Band." But the gallery problem had been solved, and a grinning Wescott arrived with his famous deviled eggs and other delicacies, interested only in a pleasant evening of friends, warmth, and humor. Despite normal ups and downs, he was in reasonably good health in the early eighties.

There was an unexpected scare at Haymeadows in the spring of 1982. One night when Wheeler was in the city, Wescott was awakened by a crash of lightning that seemed very close to the house. Taking a flashlight, he went out into the storm in bathrobe and slippers. He flashed the light straight ahead toward the cornfields, then closer, on either side of the lawn. A large old tree had fallen near the tiger compound. Stepping closer, Wescott realized part of the fence was down and he was standing in the dark with nothing between him and the tigers. He retreated to the house, and temporary repairs were made. Lloyd's son-in-law, Thane Clark, actually had six tigers and leopards now. But his marriage to Deborah was failing and he agreed to have the animals taken away to a big cat reserve in Florida that summer.

The Fourth of July weekend of 1981 was eventful. Lloyd's cook, Dorothy Smith, who really played a larger role on both ends of the farm, amused Glenway and his guests with stories about her house cats. "The cat don't live with you," she said, "you live with the cat." Near Lloyd's large aluminum barn were shackled massive bulls and a field of grazing cows. At the big house across the farm, tall, gregarious Lloyd told funny stories of his recent vacation to China. Wheeler was reserved, but Glenway seemed surprised and delighted by Lloyd's humor. Whatever the complications of their family history, it was clear that he loved his brother. At one point, conversation stopped when a large flock of geese flew low over the house, just above the rooftop, the sound of their cries and wings creating a wonderful effect. Nature-loving Lloyd was known to tolerate noisy raccoons in the walls of his house. After dinner that night, Lloyd enjoyed a show of small fireworks near the backyard deck, laughing like a young boy at the flashes, explosions, and whistles.

That morning a group of professional cat handlers arrived with trucks and equipment. The four tigers and two leopards were tranquilized, caged, and loaded onto two trucks. Wescott watched this unpleasant business from a distance. He wanted the cats in a more sensible setting and away from him, but he was always saddened by any mistreatment of animals. He also saw tragic imagery in it, especially on the Fourth of July, the day his teenage affair with Earl ended, the day he and Wheeler had one of their worst fights, among other ill-fated occurrences. Later that week, Wescott learned that during the trip to Florida one of the tigers died from the combination of barbiturates and summer heat. Its brother then became enraged and had to be shot. Reportedly, such a risk is common in transporting big cats.

The years when the tigers were fenced in at Haymeadows made an obvious metaphor for Wescott. He could have solved his publisher's problems and got his journals on track. But by now he seemed locked into the comfortable thought of a posthumous book. Robert Phelps, however, was tired of waiting. "It's a shame," he told friends, "because no one loves to be lionized more than Glenway." After publishing *Letters from Colette,* which he selected and translated, Phelps tried to break the deadlock of the journals. He gave some of his Wescott interview material to George Plimpton at *Paris Review.* When nothing happened immediately, he offered a section of the edited journals to Ben Sonnenberg, who was starting up a deluxe literary journal, *Grand Street.* Not only did Sonnenberg want it, he scheduled it to be the lead piece in the premier issue. Wescott received proofs for the fifteen-page excerpt of his 1938 trip to Paris, and predictably he fussed over them for too long. But Phelps got it in print, alongside work by Alice Munro, Ted Hughes, James Salter, and others. Wescott had mixed feelings, but he appeared at Sonnenberg's launch party.

"Paris 1938" is entertaining, complex, and sad. Entertaining because of Wescott's descriptions and humor, and complex because of numerous names and Phelps's copious footnotes. And sad because, while his Paris holiday was filled with French friends, Wescott's lonely side is revealed in those pages. With familiar candor he mentions a sexual fling: "Having had my way, with my familiar willingness to be ignored, I sprang out of bed, but he followed me and threw his arms around me from behind, and at the touch of his hand I swooned and fell on the floor, really swooned, in a softly whirling darkness with little stars like forget-me-nots, which was lovely."[4]

It was an impressive first glimpse of the journals, but Wescott remained unusually sensitive about it, calling it "better and worse than I expected."[5] What the *Grand Street* piece showed was that Wescott's sensitivity was about literary quality as much as worry about scandal for Wheeler or people in the book. Those who knew him longest understood this about him, and one was Janet Lewis Winters. Wescott saw Janet for the last time on October 30 when they met at Saint Catherine's College in Springfield, Kentucky, for a forum in memory of their Poetry Club friend Elizabeth Madox Roberts.

Of course, the person who understood best was Monroe Wheeler. His sympathy counted most, but it wasn't always forthcoming. Whatever people thought of Wheeler, he was still, in his eighties, a great man and he expected no less from Wescott. After Wheeler solved some crisis about a Museum of Modern Art catalog, trustee David Rockefeller, like his brother Nelson before him, sent a compliment: "I sometimes wonder what problems we would still be bogged down with if you had not been there to nudge things forward." When Indian Prime Minister Indira Gandhi visited the museum, Wheeler, who had made numerous art pilgrimages to India, was among the trustees who greeted her.[6]

At times, Wheeler could be quite flinty with Wescott. The poet Daniel Diamond remembered being at Haymeadows to help Wescott take a van full of papers to the city. "First, Glenway told one of his stories," Diamond said, "and Monroe, sitting with an art book, said, 'You've told that story before, and it hasn't gotten any better.'" After an exchange of words, Wescott rushed out the front door and actually ran off down a country road—just as he had when they were very young men in West Cummington, Massachusetts, and on other angry occasions. Wheeler, unblinking, turned a page of his book and said, "This performance goes on every two hours. Miss this installment, don't worry, you can catch the next."[7]

Wescott reached yet another audience, thanks to the Canadian poet Ian Young, editor of the popular poetry anthology *The Male Muse*. Bearded and dressed in black leather, Young made it through the gates of a Wescott party when Wheeler was away. An activist, anarchist, historian, publisher, and S/M spokesperson, he was also the guest editor of Dennis Cooper's journal, *Little Caesar*. A previous issue had been an instant collector's item, with a New Wave artists theme and rock star Iggy Pop naked on the cover. Now Young was doing an issue called "Overlooked and Underrated" about underappreciated writers. He wanted an essay on Wescott and insisted on a particular picture for his cover, a 1930 Lynes portrait that he saw at the apartment. Wescott was willing to send the photo, but Wheeler, when he heard all this, resisted. He thought the picture would wind up in some sort of gay, leather, motorcycle magazine. A month or more passed before Wescott prevailed.

Among the contributors to "Overlooked and Underrated" were Edmund White on James Schuyler, James Purdy on Denton Welch, and Oswell Blakeston on Mary Butts. It seemed that Wescott was the most successful, least sympathetic figure. Always curious about the mysteries of literature, Wescott admired Young's introduction, which examined the reasons writers are underappreciated, such as accidents of life, critics, subject matter, locale, politics, prejudice, shyness, audience, and timing. Young wrote: "Why then are our favorite writers under-rated? Just because they are *our* favorites and the gods are cruel? It makes for interesting conversation, but in the end must remain something of a mystery—just as why so many of our contemporaries are over-rated. Who? you say, a bit belligerently. Well, Updike, Cheever, Barth, Rechy, Irving, Gardner, just to begin with the few whose first name is John."[8] When Wheeler finally saw the journal, he was surprised and pleased, and Wescott was vindicated for his trust in the young and the bohemian.

One night, while Wheeler was at the ballet, Nancy Rica Schiff was at East Fifty-first Street to add Wescott's photograph to her collection of famous octogenarians. As the hour grew late, Wheeler arrived home. Schiff insisted on photographing them together, in armchairs placed in front of their bookcase, and looking handsome in their white shirts and ties. Published several times, it was a tribute to their century-spanning relationship.

Wescott offered some wide-ranging thoughts on his career and life in an interview at Haymeadows in August 1982. He agreed to talk about *The Pilgrim Hawk,* the one book he usually avoided discussing. His fame in the twenties was followed by frustration in the thirties, and it was *The Pilgrim Hawk* that resurrected him—not as a financial success, but as a short novel widely recognized as one of the finest in the language. Yet his reputation still seemed tied to his early Midwest fiction and the World War II bestseller.

At the heavy lawn table and chairs outside his kitchen on the summer evening, Wescott said, "I really don't think I know anything about it. I know when I wrote it and what else was going on at the time." But over the next few hours he remembered the afternoon at Barbara's house in Rambouillet that inspired the story, and the trained hawk of Barbara's guests. He said that the story wasn't fiction at all because it was based on true incidents. But he laughed when reminded that he had three copies of Samuel Butler's *The Way of All Flesh* in his library, the 1903 classic that made autobiographical fiction a standard of modern literature.

Wescott discussed the form of his short novel. "Mrs. D. H. Lawrence sent word to me that I should have acknowledged that the book was like Lawrence. I wrote her and said, 'I see what you mean.' Because after

Lawrence we all wrote those novellas, 'The Mountain Lion,' 'The Woodchuck,' 'The Runaway Horse,' and everything under the sun. It was the form that suddenly struck all our literature. It knocked the real novel right out. The big novel is only written now by the hacks."

Aside from Lawrence's novellas and Maugham's technique, Wescott, who earlier said he didn't think he could remember anything about *The Pilgrim Hawk,* thought of deeper influences. "It's like an eighteenth-century French novel. It's like *Manon Lescaut.* It's like *Les Liaisons dangereuses.* And it's like *Adolphe.* But most of all, it's like Mozart, it's based on an opera."

When told that his female characters are generally sympathetic, he thought of Alexandra Henry and Mrs. Cullen in the novel, and said, "The women talked the same language, they understood each other, you know. And I [Alwyn Tower] could only talk to the drunkard. I am perhaps the only man who has refrained from pretending he understood women. I think men have been abusing women in their novels more than they have in reality. I just didn't do it."

The subject changed to Thomas Wolfe, and Wescott recalled when Wolfe became a Harper author in late 1937. "Thomas Wolfe quarreled with Max Perkins at Scribner's and came over to Harper and sat on the back of my neck! He got all the attention and all the advertising. I was just teacher's pet." When it was suggested to Wescott that, with his style—subtle, descriptive, and intellectual—he wasn't meant to be a popular writer, he said softly, "Well, I wanted to be." Then, with a smile, "I've always said that if I could have *read* Thomas Wolfe I would have *been* Thomas Wolfe! Because actually his rough drafts are like mine. He scribbles and rewrites and piles things up, until gradually he gets out of the picture. Or he becomes a character; he ceases to be the author writing about himself."

Twilight fell over the farm and there was just the sound of crickets and of wind sweeping through the cornfields. Wescott's mood shifted. He said, "The professors who come out here just want to talk about *The Apple of the Eye* and *The Grandmothers.*" Those novels had immediate success. The first edition of *The Pilgrim Hawk* sold little, even though the critics praised it and it wound up in important anthologies. When he first wrote that manuscript, even before he had anyone else's opinion of it, did he feel vindicated for the unsuccessful years of the thirties? "Oh, yes," he said. "I felt it was the most original thing I ever wrote and the most original book I ever read! Absolutely. I've always been adoring of it. And my disaster is that I can't write another. Every time I've written a book I thought I could do another like it—until I tried."

Even so, when a writer does succeed, with just the right form and technique, isn't even once enough? "Well," Wescott said, "I can't at the moment educate you by telling you how many of the great novels were single books. And the writers who wrote them could never write anything else. It's part of—you see, writers don't sell their work; we don't have the commercial advantage painters have. Painters are shopkeepers, you know, and they can sell and they get the money and they paint another. We can't do it; nobody can bully the public into reading a book. And the critics don't matter a bit."

A three-legged cat appeared behind a bush and Wescott called, "Hello, cat," and got up to bring it some food. When he came back to his chair the summer night had settled, the candle on the table was the only light. Something made him think of the first summer he knew Wheeler. "When Monroe came to see my mother, I knew he was going to take me over and save me." Then he spoke of his triangular relationship with Monroe and George Platt Lynes. "When we left Paris, and he realized I was going to accept George, Monroe loved me more than he'd ever loved me before. He felt sorry for me."

Wescott smiled sadly, no longer thinking of 1920 or 1934, but of 1982: "He doesn't feel sorry for me anymore, alas. He's sorry for himself, and he's sorry for himself because he's got to die. And he's sorry for himself because I'm so beastly to him. I'm so thin-skinned and I hate so to be a servant, and he's really made a servant of me, as if I were a half-witted person he's adopted. And I think this is all his drug, actually."

He drifted into the tragedy of George Lynes, who became reckless in his affairs and obsessed with George Tichenor, who died in the war, then with his brother Jonathan, who left him. He believed Lynes's bad choices ruined his health. "Evil subject matter," he called it. "George was so beautiful, right up until the time he collapsed, when that boy destroyed him—that man destroyed him! There was a time he came out here and wanted to come back, couldn't he come back he asked. And I said no. He said, 'Well, what if I just stay?' I said, 'Then I'll go.' And, ahh . . ." For a long moment, there was just stillness and the sound of crickets, then Wescott breathed, "Poor George."

An outdoor telephone bell that was attached to a pole rang timidly. "Now that is probably John Stevenson," Wescott said, standing up. He paused. "I don't think I've ever answered these questions before without backing away from them. I've remembered and said things I haven't said before." Then he walked to the house and disappeared behind the kitchen's creaky screen door.[9]

Clearly, Wescott was sharp in his thinking but the publishing blocks stayed in place. He tentatively agreed to a restructuring of his journals—to fewer volumes—but nothing happened there. He even told his publisher that he wanted to resurrect "The Stallions" novella, but admitted, "It was realistic years ago, but now suddenly it warms my heart and expresses my innate fears."[10] When Wheeler needed help writing an introduction for a publication describing three generations of Rockefellers, Wescott was not up to it. Worse, Wheeler's habits, writing on both sides of a page, mixing important and unimportant jottings, drove Wescott to distraction: "There is scarcely a piece of paper or notebook or other blank surface that my poor darling will not adorn or deface with some reminder or factual detail or promise to himself or to me."[11] He ignored invitations to contribute something, anything, to *Southern Review,* Charles Henri Ford's revival issue number 10 of *Blues, Boss* magazine, and Ralph Pomeroy's own poetry magazine.

Glenway often admitted the conflict between Wescott the talker—who could hold a room or large hall spellbound—and Wescott the writer, who was always struggling to catch up. As a friendly gesture, Jacques Barzun sent Wescott a copy of *American Scholar* that contained his article on William James with this sentence underlined: "For there is nothing more inimical to writing than talking." Appropriately, Wescott found a lecture among his papers that could be published with little editing and published it as "A Succession of Poets" in *Partisan Review.* It recalls poets he had known, especially Marianne Moore and Robert Frost. It spans the decades, remembering not just the poets' works but their strange personalities and quirks. He quotes Frost on his visit to Greece: "The Acropolis, the Parthenon, meant more to me than any place on earth. But I just stayed sitting in the hotel; I never went up there. I knew that I could make it out better in my mind's eye than I could have seen it climbing around squinting in the sun. It was the same in Jerusalem. I carried the holy places all in my head.'" Of Miss Moore, he remembers their first meeting in her Greenwich Village apartment, includes samples of her poetry, with his keen perceptions. For example, he says, her conversation reminded him of the flight of a sparrow hawk: "I have one, residing in the spinnery behind my barn in New Jersey. As it departs helter-skelter, as my eyes bid it farewell, I wonder whether, in its native emptiness, high up, out of earshot, it gives a little laugh, as our dear conversational poetess sometimes did."[12]

Finally, he describes the spirituality of Moore, beyond her humor and sophistication: "She had much of that gaiety that Yeats extolled in his theory of tragedy, an exalted, almost exuberant submissiveness to what is, what must be—and I refer, and she thus responded, not only to the major fatalities but to meannesses, wastes, leaks, vulgarities of our everyday life. They were a jest to her as well as a weariness unto death."[13] Like most of his essays, "A Succession of Poets" is subjective, literature loving, and compassionate. It was the last authentic new piece published in his lifetime.

That last publication, in the fall of 1983, marked a transition in Wescott's remaining years. In October, he and Wheeler had dinner with country friends in nearby Stockton, and Wescott read a selection from *The*

Grandmothers. It was likely the last time he gave a public reading. He also admitted to several friends, "The other day I was reading to Monroe, as always, and in the middle of it I thought I stumbled. I stopped and asked, 'Did I misspeak?' 'Yes,' said Monroe." He captured Monroe's neutral but gentle tone.

On December 2, Wescott attended an Academy-Institute luncheon. He seemed fine but two days later, a minor calamity struck. That evening his old friend Joseph Campbell was being honored at the Princeton Club, and Wescott had promised to give a five-minute introduction. John Stevenson, who was there, remembered painfully, "We all let Glenway walk right into that, because we weren't sure. Some days he was fine, some days he was not. But I had a foreboding."[14] Wescott was introduced and received applause from many who knew him as a great public speaker. He stepped up to the microphone, started to speak, and stopped. He started again, stumbled in his words, and stopped. A silence fell over the room. Wescott couldn't seem to begin. Campbell, seventy-nine himself, left his wife Jean's side and walked to the microphone. Stevenson recalled, "He put an arm around Glenway and said, 'Glenway and I have been friends for many years. When I first wrote *A Hero with a Thousand Faces,* he was one of my strongest supporters.'" Campbell said Wescott had told him that his was the kind of book that did good, rather than the kind that made money, but he predicted that in time it would be appreciated. He spoke of Wescott's friendship and then went on to his prepared talk. The bad moment passed, but it was telling.

Wheeler had his own physical problems. A doctor warned that his right eye was threatened by macular degeneration. He had a bad fall and spent several days in Lenox Hill Hospital. Yet he still wanted a car for local driving in New Jersey and replaced his failing Cadillac with a large Chrysler. John Stevenson half joked, "It's a perfect metaphor for their world now, both of them bombing down the road in a big car, with Monroe barely able to see over the steering wheel."[15]

Wescott made far fewer trips to the city in 1984. He declined interviews and left off correspondence. He did attend Wheeler's party for Philippe de Rothschild on March 14. During the week of his birthday, he met Robert Phelps for lunch in Greenwich Village. Phelps remembered, "It was a beautiful day and after lunch we strolled and bought ourselves ridiculously large ice cream cones. When I put him in a taxi, he was holding his ice cream and beaming with amusement."[16] Generally, Wescott's stamina faded late in the day. Meeting for dinner one night in September, he seemed frail, almost spiritlike. He spoke softly, but with clear, cogent remarks. He said, for example, that the AIDS crisis reminded him of the widespread terror of the Spanish flu.

Wescott was very much himself in the morning hours. At the request of a teacher in New Jersey, he spoke to students at Del Val High School in Hunterdon County about the expatriate writers of the 1920s. On October 18 the *Flemington Democrat* reported that he told the young writers, "Don't try to imitate anyone else. Be yourself. Develop your own writing skills." A boy told the reporter, "He was kind of like a literary museum, all in himself." A girl said, "It was sort of like being there with Ernest Hemingway and F. Scott Fitzgerald."

The problem was that he became tired and disoriented by evening. Perhaps in frustration or fear, Wescott printed the words "dementia" and "Alzheimer's" in the back of his now little-used datebook. Yet he never had any such diagnosis. His real trouble seemed to be that his circulatory problem was growing worse. On December 7, 1984, he appeared at the Academy-Institute for a ceremony and dinner. As always, limousines took members home. The poet Howard Moss shared a ride, and when it stopped at East Fifty-first Street, he was surprised when Wescott stumbled badly from the car.[17]

Finally it was clear that trips to New York made no sense for Wescott. He had spent the previous New Year's Day with his sister Beulah in Saint Louis, but now he stayed close to home. The workers at Haymeadows who loved him, Dorothy, Jerome, and Ethel, watched him more protectively. The warm environment and rest helped. Sounding much better, he telephoned friends and suggested visits to Haymeadows. Wheeler gave him reports on who he saw in the city and what ballet. He wrote his schedule in Wescott's datebook. When traveling, he didn't expect Wescott's letters now, but sent his reports as always. A message from Munich read: "Dined last night with Stephen Spender and his son. The museums are a joy—the weather all snow and blizzards."[18]

The dynamics were changing at Haymeadows. Anatole regularly drove up from Philadelphia. John Connolly was arranging to buy the house and surrounding acres from Lloyd, and he and Ivan Ashby made frequent weekend stays. Lloyd had built a smaller house and was planning to sell off other parts of the farm. John Stevenson was often in California on business, but he would telephone Glenway often and occasionally come out to visit. Without Barbara, there was more of a chill between Lloyd and Monroe, but Lloyd sent polite notes, sometimes about routine household matters, once stating that he was "out-of-pocket $7000" on expenses for Glenway over the previous year.[19] Aware of the different factions, sympathies, and perspectives, Glenway often joked about the open warfare that would follow his death. But while he remained healthy, peace prevailed.

When a literary journal published Wescott's memories of Cocteau, Wheeler was unusually pleased and excited.[20] The reason was clear. The piece quoted Wescott the talker at his absolute best, and Wheeler's lifelong pride in Wescott surged. In turn, Wescott as always was joyful in pleasing

Wheeler. And for both of them, the article contained anecdotes of their youth in Villefranche and Paris.

There was no more talk of journals but Wescott continued to fuss with his papers, to no good purpose. Finally there was a family decision to move the many boxes of papers to the upper floor of the garage, formerly a barn loft. Wescott was content with the decision, but occasionally wanted to get to the material.

Wescott and Wheeler remained wonderfully rarefied and witty. Sometimes they fell into an old-time sparring contest. Once, while discussing Haitian art, Wheeler said, "I knew the man who introduced it to America." Wescott cracked: "Wouldn't you know?" Wheeler, taking the arrow, didn't bat an eye. Yet the old affections remained. Mornings were always a painful, hours-long process of revival for arthritis-ridden Wheeler. As always, Wescott brought up his juice, coffee, and newspaper, but now slowly, one step at a time. When Wescott heard that another of his interviews would be published, he immediately said, "Dedicate it to Monroe."

At Wheeler's suggestion, Wescott gave a friend his collection of old pornography novels, nearly twenty small paperbacks, several covered in brown paper. Though he spoke more haltingly, he was thoughtful and clear, even remembering details of conversations from years earlier. He was as spiritual as ever, in his nature-loving way. Sometimes, when a friend was leaving the farm, Wescott liked to stand alongside the car and put beautiful colored leaves in the friend's hand, with a knowing smile. In "The Odor of Rosemary" essay he said he inherited his mother's habit of gathering colorful and fragrant foliage. And in *The Apple of the Eye,* the older boy said good-bye by pressing a clover leaf into the hand of the younger one.

On Thursday, February 20, 1986, Wescott was taken to Hunterdon County Medical Center with discomfort that proved to be a mild heart attack. Wheeler himself was ill, but friends and family visited the hospital and found Wescott fairly well, though a bit confused. He said to John Stevenson, "I disgrace myself with boredom and loneliness and vexation." But when they sat at the large picture window looking out at the countryside, he came around. He praised Wheeler's good humor of late. He said, "I want to come to the city soon, and I want to have a party." Stevenson suggested a party for his birthday. Doctors released him after only four days.

Before Wescott's birthday, Arbor House published a new edition of *The Grandmothers,* as part of its Contemporary Americana series of modern classics. Created from the original pages of the first edition, the thick paperback was much more pleasing than smaller reprints of the past. The previous Atheneum edition had a cover design of a quilt pattern with a small illustration of a rocking chair. The Arbor House artist, Scott Jackson, created a colorful cover illustration in downward perspective of a young Alwyn Tower in a busy street scene. It could have been Holden Caulfield on the cover of *Catcher in the Rye.* Or it could have been Wescott as a teenage college student in Chicago. In the new introduction, John W. Aldridge writes: "What impresses one today—as it did so many of the critics in 1927—is the remarkable clarity with which the young author was able to conceive and describe in extremely realistic detail the daily lives of people who are obviously modeled on his Wescott ancestors, but most of whom he knew only from fragmentary stories told within the family and passed down from generation to generation. . . . Wescott's tone throughout the novel is gentle and compassionate. His respectful sympathy for the brave and troubled lives of his characters is everywhere in evidence."[21]

Though Wescott had not seen the book yet, it appeared in stores at the time of his birthday, and he was pleased by telephone calls of congratulations. His eighty-fifth birthday was on a Friday and a local newspaper reported that he celebrated with family and friends at a restaurant in New Hope.[22] Wheeler had to leave for Spain for two weeks, but Connolly and Ashby were at Haymeadows for the weekend. When Stevenson and a friend drove out on Saturday, Wescott was waiting in jacket and tie—the lavender tie he wore for special occasions. Stevenson had brought a bottle of champagne, a birthday cake, and an oil painting of Wescott by artist Susan Haeni, who had worked from photos and included a hawk in the background. He also brought a boxful of the new edition of *The Grandmothers,* and Wescott admired the cover illustration. When a caller offered birthday greetings and more congratulations on the book Wescott protested, "I had nothing to do with it. It came through the trees, looking for me."

When asked to inscribe two books, he was upset that he could manage only a shaky scrawl. Stevenson quickly cheered him and suggested a drive to New Hope and lunch in Lambertville. Wescott loved a certain heavily wooded country lane in New Hope called Laurel Road and said, "I dreamed of it last night, but I didn't think that would be enough to bring it on."

It was a cloudy day and spring was late that year, so Laurel Road and its adjacent embankment and stream were barren and wintry. But they stopped at public flower gardens and walked among colorful beds of bright tulips, roses, and irises (Wescott's favorite). There they ran into John Connolly and Ashby, and Wescott laughed as his two Johns fussed over him. Later, at a small restaurant in Lambertville, he surprised his friends with perceptive personal comments. Wescott always had the ability to see through people, but he also had a midwestern politeness that usually left personal remarks unsaid and questions unasked.

What mattered was that Wescott seemed content. He was proud of what he had accomplished, even with some regrets. And in words and manner he seemed confident that his legacy, in journals and new editions like *The Grandmothers*, would take care of itself.

The following month, his doctors suggested he would be better off with a pacemaker, and he and Monroe agreed. In midsummer, Monroe told one of their friends by telephone that he was leaving for Europe and was worried about leaving Wescott. "He's physically all right," he said, "but more slow moving and more forgetful than ever."[23] When he took the phone, Wescott sounded fairly good, though still restless about remaining in the country.

Three months later, in the first week of October 1986, Wescott suffered a stroke. At the hospital, he couldn't walk and his speech was affected. Yet, when he mistook the voice of a patient for Wheeler's, he said, "What did you say, dear?" in his usual, perfectly distinct voice. Except for that moment, he was unable to speak clearly. Distressed at first, he was cheered by Wheeler, friends, and family. Doctors found him stable and, after two weeks of testing, were willing to grant his wish to go home.

At Haymeadows, a bed for him was placed in the library downstairs, alongside windows that looked out to the lawn and the cornfields beyond. A nurse visited every other day, and Dorothy took on a major role as caretaker. Some stroke victims make a major recovery after several months. Wescott's improvement was only fair. He could communicate better and move around a bit.

Anatole remembered, "Once Glenway had his stroke, the equilibrium of everything changed." Lloyd, Monroe, John Connolly, and Ivan all cared about Glenway equally, but from very different perspectives. Monroe was also dealing with worsening arthritis and recent cataract surgery. At Haymeadows he would spend part of the time with Glenway and part of the time alone. Anatole said, "Monroe never liked to talk about his illnesses. He'd hibernate instead. He didn't dwell on the problems. He liked a good martini."[24] Wheeler's stoic, restrained behavior was nothing new. He alone had shared most of the century with Wescott, and no one could know all he was feeling.

During one of Wheeler's stays in the city, John Stevenson took him to dinner at the Oak Room of the Plaza Hotel. "As we entered," Stevenson recalled, "a man with a heavy accent got up from his table, called, 'Hello, Monroe,' and started a conversation. It was Henry Kissinger!"[25] (Kissinger and Monroe had met through Nelson Rockefeller.) More than emotional support, Stevenson also provided crucial decision making. Wescott had planned for him to be his temporary executor, and he became the ambassador among the different parties at Haymeadows.

On January 30, 1987, Stevenson drove out to the farm. Dorothy had prepared Wescott, who was eating alone at the dining room table, dressed in jacket and tie. Hearing Stevenson enter, Wescott put down his fork and slowly turned and saw him, his eyes filling with tears. Stevenson sat down beside him and they embraced and had a peaceful visit alone.

Afterward, Stevenson drove directly to Lloyd's lawyer's office in Trenton, as planned. Both he and Lloyd were surprised when the lawyer suggested they make a memorial of a room in the Haymeadows house for Glenway. Stevenson said, "I told them it was far more important to let things out, and surprised them with the news that libraries were asking about Glenway's papers."[26] Decisions were made. Lloyd had discussed a nursing home for Glenway, and Stevenson ended that talk. John Connolly now owned the house and had agreed that Glenway should stay. Lloyd would be reimbursed by Glenway's estate for medical expenses. They also arranged for a load of Glenway's papers to be returned from storage in the city.

Another key supporter in Wescott's behalf was Hugh Ford, an English professor at Trenton State College. Ford's *Published in Paris* had glowingly recalled Harrison of Paris books. His new book on the expatriates, *Four Lives,* had a foreword by Wescott that was really a patchwork of paragraphs from his "Memories and Opinions" essay joined with other memories in what is apparently Wheeler's prose. Now Ford had a grant to write a biography of Wescott. In mid-February, Stevenson and Robert Phelps made a plan. In late March, they and Hugh Ford and one or two others would stay several days at Haymeadows. There was plenty of real work to be done, but more than anything the group looked forward to being together with Wescott again, as in happier days.

On the night of Sunday, February 22, 1987, however, Glenway was in bed when another stroke took him. Monroe was in the house, and when Lloyd was called from across the farm the two men spoke quietly and consoled each other. Then Lloyd telephoned his sisters, Beulah in Saint Louis, Elizabeth in Philadelphia, and Katherine in Beverly Hills. He knew his brother's wishes and arranged for cremation. Monroe asked Hugh Ford to contact the newspapers.

The next day, the media gave major attention to the unexpected death of Andy Warhol, who had passed away early Sunday after routine surgery. A deadly oversight between the hospital staff and a private nurse had caused a scandal. On Tuesday, February 24, the *New York Times* obituary carried a three-column heading, "Glenway Wescott, 85, Novelist and Essayist," and a handsome photo of Wescott by Peter Deane. The piece recalled "one of the last of the major American expatriate writers who lived in France in the 1920s and 1930s," quoted Hugh Ford as likening Wescott in America to E. M. Forster in England, and stated, "Everything he wrote was done in high style—almost Flaubert-like in certain ways." After describing his novels and essays, it mentioned, "*The Babe's Bed,* an allegory that revealed his uneasy, oscillating attitude toward his home and toward an America that he said 'is not a rich country, not in real values, not yet.'"[27]

Other obituaries appeared around the country that week and in the *International Herald Tribune* on March 2. But the most interesting was a quirky and poignant four hundred words in the *Times* of London on February 27. After Wescott's early success, it said, he was criticized for his silence in the thirties. "But in 1940 he confounded his critics with what is usually granted the status of a masterpiece: *The Pilgrim Hawk,* a haunting, poetic, compressed story of love and art, freedom and captivity." It noted that *The Grandmothers* had often been compared to Proust, and recalled Edmund Wilson's praise for *Apartment in Athens.* Despite Wescott's abandoning fiction in the second half of his career, it said, "he will be remembered for the near-perfection of his subtle love story, *The Pilgrim Hawk,* and for his dedication to the literary art. He felt that his talents were outstripped by his ideals, but the view that his is one of the truly notable achievements in English fiction is not too rare a one." Though the *Times* of London referred to Wescott as "the elegant and rather tragic writer," it concluded, "He did enough to be remembered so long as fiction is read."[28]

On the personal side, Wescott likely cherished a more private assurance. At the end of a long and happy day with John Stevenson at Haymeadows, they walked by purple mandrake plants—a narcotic plant used by magicians, Wescott said—and then came to the beehives that could be traced back to the Civil War. "These are my grandfather's bees," he said, as they stopped to rest. Then he smiled and said with some emotion, "I want to live forever." Stevenson hugged Wescott, looked in his eyes, and answered, "You will!"[29]

Epilogue

Other Voices and Continual Lessons

"When I die it's going to be like a Balzac novel."

—G.W.

WESCOTT humorously predicted a Balzac novel of plot and intrigue if he died and left friends and family to fight out disputes over property and possessions. He was right, but his own journals, papers, and legacy were also at stake.

Until Wescott's last four months, Wheeler never expected to outlive him. Now, on the day after Wescott died, Wheeler returned alone to his city apartment, not knowing he would never again see Haymeadows. He called friends and designed invitations to the memorial service at the Academy-Institute of Arts and Letters.

The next morning, Wheeler experienced what he thought was a heart attack. Losing his balance, he fell hard against the large sink in the bathroom, breaking two ribs. He managed to telephone the doorman and was taken by ambulance to Cornell Medical Center. Anatole Pohorilenko was teaching an art class in Philadelphia when he was contacted, and when he arrived that evening Wheeler was still on a gurney in the emergency room. It wasn't until one o'clock in the morning that he had a room, and in all those hours he hadn't been given Percodan for his arthritis pain.

Living between the apartment and the hospital, Pohorilenko followed Wheeler's directions for the paper stock, typography, design, and mailing of Wescott's memorial invitations. Many friends who were numbed by Wescott's passing felt warmed when they received the handsome invitations—but didn't know that Wheeler himself was hospitalized.

While still keeping the secret of his illness, Wheeler managed to be transferred to Hunterdon County Medical Center in New Jersey. "At exorbitant cost," Pohorilenko said, "we got an ambulance to make the transfer." Only at Hunterdon did doctors discover that Wheeler had actually suffered a stroke. "If Monroe died we would have sued," said Pohorilenko. "It would have been 'Andy Warhol' all over again."[1]

At the hospital, Pohorilenko one day found a handsome young man visiting Wheeler. All his life, Wheeler had had protégés in the arts who were devoted to him. Now he admitted to two more: Joshua, who worked in a gallery, and Ted, straight, on staff with a national photography magazine. Amused, Pohorilenko later said, "There was one thing Monroe couldn't do, and that was lie."[2]

On Wednesday, March 11, 1987, the Academy-Institute of Arts and Letters sent white limousines for the invited guests. Nearly one hundred members and friends gathered in the second-floor library–meeting room where chairs were arranged. Many learned for the first time that Wheeler was hospitalized. In the adjoining room, ornate leather chairs bore brass plates with the names of voting members of the Academy, the higher body of the organization then. Wescott's name appeared on chair number thirty-two.

When the memorial program began director Margaret Mills revealed that Wheeler had discussed the plans three months earlier and had said that Wescott was pleased to know his friends would eventually gather there to remember him.

Former director Felicia Geffen recalled the friend she had known since the forties: "Handsome, always charming, compassionate, dedicated to whatever he was doing, keenly interested in everyone and everything that came into his ken. To me, his style and use of language were a joy." Over the decades, she said, they had planned their organization's special events. "Before each dinner or luncheon meeting he would come to my office and we would spend hours planning the tables—one of the great pleasures, always knowing who to sit next to whom." She remembered his visits to her country home and his love of nature. "He was an iris fancier, and he would send me dozens of iris of all colors, many of which are still growing in my garden. . . . When I was in the hospital for an operation, it was he who greeted me at the door with a bouquet of flowers when I arrived home."

Jane Gunther eloquently described Wescott's tape-recorded readings and talks: "It was an enchantment," she said. "Sometimes one thought of his led to another in tumultuous disarray. But there was always a point, and the point was usually a profound one. It was moving, riveting, and very good fun. . . . Here was a man of convoluted sophistication, witty and wicked, utterly civilized, and yet totally honest, simple and never afraid to be candid." Even though he had bouts of melancholy, she said, Wescott's charm was in his "sunny" disposition. "His smile could tell you that. It was an aware smile, which revealed that he looked at the world objectively.

He smiled, not with contempt and irony, but with curiosity and secret delight. To be a person in this world is an adventure, which I believe Glenway understood better than most of us. It amused him, and so it made him gentle. He was not fighting, but watching."

The editor and author Russell Lynes, George's younger brother, remembered when he was a teenager and Wescott gave him a copy of *The Grandmothers,* which was then in its seventeenth printing after only three months. "He was the first famous man I ever knew," he said. "I should have been awed, but Glenway would not permit that. He was respectful, not tolerant, of the young—true of him always."

The novelist William Maxwell, then seventy-nine and a past president of the Institute, began by saying, "What a wonderful life. A life dedicated with a saintlike monomania to the art of writing and the world of letters—so crammed with friendships with gifted people, so rich in the pleasures of the eye and the mind." Maxwell said his correspondence showed how much valuable time Wescott devoted to the Academy-Institute. If he had a fault, he said with a smile, it was the childlike candor he brought to any literary cause; he couldn't imagine that anyone would disagree with him. He added, "No harm came of it. He would not for anything have given up being affectionate. In loving people, he had to take care of them and take on their problems.

"He believed that young writers should become acquainted with the masters of the older generation and he went to considerable trouble to bring this about. Through him I met Cummings and Richard Hughes and Mina Curtis and Georgia O'Keeffe." Even in everyday life, he said, Wescott was a born storyteller, his conversation always filled with stories fully articulated.

Finally, Maxwell expressed what only a writer of his stature could, touching on the enigma and the triumph of Wescott: "From the very beginning the literary world expected and demanded of Glenway things he didn't have in mind, or perhaps even had it in him to give. This gave him a feeling that his career had gone astray, though it actually had not. One of the happy memories of my life is of sitting in the public library in Hamilton, Bermuda, and reading *The Pilgrim Hawk,* which had been serialized in *Harper's Magazine.* I was in my early thirties, the tropical rain was coming down outside open, unshuttered windows in a solid noisy way, making a curtain that enclosed the room and the other readers and the work of fiction that had seized upon me. Every once in a while a sentence would give me pleasure so intense that I would have to stop reading until I could accommodate it."[3]

Composer and pianist Ned Rorem accompanied vocalist Debra Vanderlint. Because Wescott loved Bach, he said, he played a Bach piece, as well as one of his own early compositions. The touching, lilting notes of Rorem's piece seemed to linger as the formalities ended.

Two days after the memorial, Wheeler had a visitor from a university library. Several major libraries were now vying for Wescott's papers. On pain-killers and with limited vision, Wheeler did not sign the document the visitor had brought but asked him to leave it. Arriving the next day, Pohorilenko saw that it was a one-paragraph contract that would have turned all of the Wescott and Wheeler archives over to the library, with terms to be decided later. "When I told Monroe what the paper was for," he said, "he turned toward the wall and wept."[4] Determined to recover and take charge of these decisions, Wheeler transferred to the Merwick rehabilitation facility at Princeton for months of therapy.

Interestingly, Wescott's will left everything to Wheeler—unless Wheeler were to die before the eleventh day after Wescott's death. In that case, his net assets would have been divided among John Connolly, John Stevenson, and nephew Bruce Hotchkiss. Estate lawyers warn clients that longtime mates often die within a short time of each other, and a will like Wescott's prevents long delays and double taxation. And Wheeler nearly had died two days after Wescott. Wescott also had told friends that Wheeler, addicted to pain-killers for his arthritis, kept a hidden stash, in case he ever decided to use them. It appears both men's deaths were natural, but Wescott's will seemed to allow for several possibilities.

Wheeler was released from Merwick in July, but he no longer had a home at Haymeadows and without professional help he couldn't live at East Fifty-first Street. As a temporary solution Pohorilenko took him to his family home in Philadelphia. But first he went alone to get some of Wheeler's personal possessions from Haymeadows. John Connolly and Ivan Ashby were away, and Lloyd was forced into the awkward position of gatekeeper. He admitted to Pohorilenko that there were strained feelings all around. He knew Monroe had loved Glenway and Barbara. But, he said, he sometimes felt Monroe treated Lloyd as if he were the foreman of the farm. Yet Lloyd wrote to John Stevenson that he now felt badly for Monroe. And as for all the disputes over artwork, paintings, books, and furniture, he declared, "The easy solution would have been to burn the house down."[5]

In Philadelphia, Pohorilenko recreated Wheeler's Haymeadows bedroom, from the brass bed to the paintings and how they were arranged. But it was difficult. Wheeler was in a wheelchair, and his right side was paralyzed. His vision was blurred and spanned only about four feet. Nevertheless, he was mentally sharp and spoke well. By the fall, he was back in his New York apartment, with the help of a visiting attendant.

On October 19, 1987, the stock market plunged 508 points, more than

20 percent of its whole. The fact that Wheeler lost $100,000 in a matter of hours explained his state of mind thereafter when arguments about paintings and furniture flared up. In particular, at Haymeadows were two side chairs and a needlepoint day bed designed by Jared French and executed by George Platt Lynes. Wescott had verbally promised them and a French table to John Connolly. Wheeler claimed the pieces. In extremely palsied handwriting, he wrote to Connolly, beginning with a quote from E. B. White: "The only sense that is common in the long run is the sense of change—and we all instinctively avoid it." He admitted that Pohorilenko suggested he give up his claim to the furniture. However, "Upon much reflection about my present and future situation, namely the immense expense for my continued existence as a stroke victim and the uncertainties of the market, I have decided instead to let you purchase them." He named a price and said the furniture would otherwise be removed for auction, then closed, "Please forgive my wretched calligraphy. Cordially, Monroe."[6]

The letter went through Haymeadows like a mortar shot. Lloyd politely but firmly supported Connolly's position, and lawyers got involved. Wheeler dropped his claim in return for Connolly's dropping several additional claims.[7]

Meanwhile, Wescott's assets were appraised at over $200,000, including his unsold literary archive. The estate owed more than a third of that, including $40,000 to Lloyd for expenses he took on during his brother's last three years. All that legal business would go away eventually, guided by temporary executor John Stevenson and lawyers on all sides.

Seven libraries were interested in the Wescott archive. To the surprise of many, it wasn't nearby Princeton but Yale's Beinecke Library that won out. Its Collection of American Literature housed a number of Wescott's contemporaries and the library wanted Wheeler's archive as well. Pohorilenko and Will Chandlee supervised the removal of more than 120 bankers' boxes of material from Haymeadows. "We drove off the farm at the same time," Pohorilenko remembered, "and for a while we saw the truck with Glenway's archive up ahead on the country road. What a feeling it was to see that big truck turn off, heading north, and disappear."[8]

In February 1988, Wheeler celebrated his eighty-ninth birthday during a one-month stay in Philadelphia. At his New York apartment, there were problems, as when book dealers took advantage of his incapacity. One day Pohorilenko arrived from Philadelphia to find that a well-known book dealer that had contracted to buy five or six rare volumes was about to remove two cases of books. He stopped that, but there were some losses. "People were tricking, and downright stealing," he said. "Once a small painting was actually taken from the wall!"[9] Finally, an ideal staff secured the household. Longtime friend Jane Gunther recommended a woman who had cared for one of her parents. Pohorilenko found a young man,

Bill Shepard, who took control and was a great companion to Wheeler. A third aide filled the gaps.

In May, Wheeler attended a ceremony at the Museum of Modern Art where a reading room was named in his honor in the Prints and Illustrated Books Galleries. Thereafter he received only a small number of old friends at his apartment, including Will Chandlee, Ralph Pomeroy, Robert Phelps, and a few others. Despite his condition, he made a last trip to England with the MoMA international council in late July. He told several people, "I want to see London again, to see a certain painting, and to visit a certain friend." He traveled in his wheelchair, accompanied by his assistant Bill Shepard.

Like Wescott, Wheeler died on a Sunday night, on August 14, 1988, in his apartment. The *New York Times* obituary recalled his early acquaintance with Picasso, Renoir, Chagall, and other artists, and his efforts in bringing their work to America. It cited his supervision of more than 350 books on the visual arts, and of his curating dozens of major shows. MoMA director Richard Oldenburg said, "He reached out and created a whole new public for the Modern. The museum became known for the quality of its books. He was passionately devoted to quality of illustration and design, and he developed the first-rate publishing by museums that we know today."[10]

On the morning of November 3, about two hundred people attended the museum's memorial for Wheeler in its Titus Theater. The event seemed much more formal than Wescott's, the most informal speaker being David Rockefeller. It was a reminder of how much self-educated Wheeler had achieved in the conservative world of large museums, a field that esteems degrees and academia. His colleagues recalled how he had helped build the reputation of MoMA in Europe during its early years. Whatever their differences, Lloyd had shared the same lifelong story with Monroe, and he was at the memorial. Towering over most people, he greeted Monroe's and Glenway's friends, and he showed no sign of having had cancer surgery only months earlier.

At last, Wescott's journals were addressed. John Stevenson and the publisher had changed the contract to only one volume, *Continual Lessons,* with final editing by Robert Phelps. Adding more years to the book was an improvement over the proposed first volume, "Halfway." By including excerpts up to 1955, *Continual Lessons* reflected the book's title: Wescott seemed to grow wiser, more at peace with himself, in middle age.

The journals seemed on course—but they were not. Phelps's health declined and time passed as he was unable to complete the project. He was only sixty-five but he had been taking medication for Parkinson's disease for a long time. He was a gentle, literature-loving man, and the irony was striking. For so many years he had waited while the journals were stalled.

Now, as fate would have it, he and the journals were stalled together. In the winter of 1989, he grew very ill. It was typical of his quiet dignity that Phelps himself walked to his publishers with the manuscript and suggested an editor to finish it. When he passed away on August 2, the *New York Times* remembered him as the man who helped introduce the works of Colette and Cocteau to America.[11]

In *Continual Lessons* Wescott quotes Edgar Allan Poe as saying any man could be immortal if he would simply write a memoir called *My Heart Laid Bare,* and live up to the title. Poe added, "But to write it—*there* is the rub. No man *could* write it even if he dared."[12] Yet, Wescott's journal did live up to that challenge. It would have been easy enough for him to concentrate on his successes and famous friends. Instead, he was self-critical and included even embarrassing truths. Often he was too hard on himself, but that also revealed a truth about the person he was.

A number of Wescott friends were helpful as the book moved closer to publication. The most poignant was Carl Malouf, who had fallen out of touch with Wescott in the sixties. The host of Wescott's weekend parties in the Kinsey years, Malouf had made a career of creating murals all over the country, among them a mural at the Sheraton hotel in downtown Washington. Retired and in delicate health, he said of Wescott, "He was a marvelous man, the most interesting, compelling, and fascinating person that I'll ever know. I never thought Glenway would die. I thought he'd go on and on and I'd die." Above Malouf as he spoke was a relic from the days when his apartment was Wescott's escape from Stone-blossom obligations and the formality of Wheeler's 410 Park Avenue apartment. It was a large, glittering, amber-colored chandelier with baubles and balls. Malouf remembered, "Glenway thought this chandelier was perfect for our parties because, he said, it was the color of whiskey."[13]

By the fall of 1990, Lloyd's health was failing but he was pleased to see an advance copy of the book jacket for *Continual Lessons.* He said of his brother, "I miss him very much." Lloyd passed away on Christmas Eve 1990.

Seventy years after the Poetry Club days, two of Wescott's oldest friends lived to read *Continual Lessons.* One was Kathleen Foster, who had been Wescott's fiancée until he committed to Wheeler. The other was the novelist Janet Lewis, who in her nineties wrote a remembrance of her Poetry Club friends. She said of Wescott's journals: "For myself, I cannot read it without often hearing his voice, and encountering acquaintances we had shared. . . . It gives most certainly his great enthusiasm for life—for music, art, letters, people and things—garden snakes, frogs and iris. This is what I remember most from knowing him. He could cast a glamour over almost anything from his great delight in it."[14]

Continual Lessons was well received in the mainstream press. In the

Washington Post, Hortense Callisher's review carried the same name Edgar Allan Poe suggested for a totally honest journal: "A Heart Laid Bare." In her enthusiastic comments, she noted the hold of Wescott's family on Wescott: "Lions are kept on the farm. So is he." The title of a review in the *Chicago Tribune* also commented on the journal's honesty: "Glenway Wescott's Amazing Candor." In the gay press, a few literary writers praised the book as literature, but most saw its importance as gay history. As novelist Stan Leventhal put it, "Our history is slowly returned to us."[15]

There were few examples of the homophobic reviews Wescott feared. And yet, since *Continual Lessons,* several heterosexual critics have painted Wescott as effeminate or a dilettante—both assumptions completely false, and a kind of homophobia.

Wescott continues to appear in other writers' fiction, such as Alfred Corn's novella *Part of His Story.* Edmund White's three-page parody in *The Farewell Symphony* is more gentle and amusing than the novel's other author parodies. Less kind is a Richard Hall short story, or William Burroughs in his last journals.[16] Some could never forgive Wescott his Academy-Institute establishment image.

As always, Wescott's work speaks for him. *The Pilgrim Hawk* lives on in reprints of the *Six Great Modern Short Novels* Dell paperback and in new English, German, French, and Italian editions that have appeared in recent years. Once again a major appreciation of *The Pilgrim Hawk* appeared in the *New Yorker,* this time by Susan Sontag. *The Grandmothers* was republished in 1996.[17] Further editions of these books and *Apartment in Athens* are forthcoming. A private printing of "A Visit to Priapus" was praised by playwright Robert Patrick as "classic gay fine-writing," and by Ned Rorem as a "posthumous masterpiece."[18]

It was Anatole Pohorilenko and Will Chandlee who took Wescott's and Wheeler's ashes to the small farmers' graveyard, hidden behind a rock wall and trees at Haymeadows. As part of their private ceremony, they read poems from *Natives of Rock.* Today the hidden graveyard at Haymeadows has a large marble marker, listing the remains of Bruce and Josephine Wescott, Lloyd and Barbara, Beulah, Elizabeth, Glenway, and Monroe.

After his friend Wescott died, and shortly before his own death, Joseph Campbell was finishing the last of his PBS film series *Masks of Eternity,* with Bill Moyers. Campbell said, "I've lost a lot of friends, my parents and all, and a realization that has come to me very, very keenly is that I haven't lost them. That moment when I was with them has an everlasting quality about it that is now still with me. What it gave me is still with me. And there's a kind of intimation of immortality in that."[19]

Notes
Index

Notes

In citing collections in the notes, shortened forms have been used as follows:

Beinecke	Beinecke Rare Book and Manuscript Library, Yale Collection of American Literature, Yale University
Berg	Henry W. and Albert A. Berg Collection of English and American Literature, New York Public Library
GW	Glenway Wescott
MW	Monroe Wheeler

The Glenway Wescott Papers at the Beinecke library are arranged in thirteen series. Research for *Glenway Wescott Personally* drew particularly from the series entitled "Correspondence, Journals and Notebooks, Writings, and Personal Papers." Wescott's "journals" are not journals in the sense of daily records of thoughts and occurrences. Generally they consist of three-ring binders filled with all types of notes, drafts, and copies. The overall arrangement is chronological. The notebooks are more closely related to Wescott's creative writings.

The Glenway Wescott Papers in the Berg Collection are generally arranged by book and manuscript title, and include author's editions, galleys, working drafts, and related materials. The collection also includes Wescott poetry, correspondence, and the author's 1970s annotations for the Berg.

CHAPTER 1. WISCONSIN FARM BOY TO MIDWEST PRODIGY

1. GW, interview by Robert Phelps, January 16, 1976.
2. Ibid.
3. GW, journal/diary, December 1917–May 1920, Berg.

4. GW, "Memories and Opinions," *Prose,* no. 5 (fall 1972): 177–202.
5. GW, journal note, n.d., Beinecke.
6. GW, interview, January 16, 1976.
7. Ibid.
8. GW, "The Odor of Rosemary," manuscript binder, 1970, Beinecke.
9. GW, interview, January 16, 1976.
10. Ibid.
11. Ibid.
12. Ibid.
13. Ibid.
14. Ibid.
15. Ibid.
16. Yvor Winters, *Yvor Winters: Uncollected Essays and Reviews,* ed. Francis Murphy (Chicago: Swallow Press, 1973), 311.
17. GW, interview by Robert Phelps, January 30, 1976.
18. Ibid.
19. GW, journal/diary, December 1917–May 1920, Berg.
20. GW, interview by author, December 8, 1976.
21. GW, interview by Robert Phelps, March 13, 1976.
22. GW, interview, January 16, 1976.
23. Ibid.
24. GW, interview, January 30, 1976.
25. Ibid.
26. Ibid.
27. Janet Lewis, "The Poems of Maurine Smith," *Chicago Review* 37 (winter 1990): 52–63.
28. Ibid., 62.
29. Robert Cooke, "Solving a World War II Riddle," *Newsday,* March 21, 1997, 8; Malcolm Gladwell, "The Dead Zone," *New Yorker,* September 29, 1997, 52–65.
30. GW, interview, January 16, 1976.
31. Ibid.
32. Ibid.
33. Ibid.
34. Ibid.
35. Ibid.
36. Ibid.
37. GW, journal/diary, December 1917–May 1920, Berg.
38. GW, interview, January 16, 1976.
39. Ibid.
40. Ibid.
41. GW, "Poems," fall 1919, Berg.
42. GW, interview, January 30, 1976.
43. Ibid.
44. Ibid.
45. Ibid.
46. Ibid.

47. Ibid.
48. Ibid.
49. Ibid.
50. Ibid.
51. Ibid.
52. Ibid.
53. Ibid.
54. Ibid.
55. Ibid.
56. Quoted in Glenway Wescott, *Continual Lessons: The Journals of Glenway Wescott, 1937–1955,* ed. Robert Phelps with Jerry Rosco (New York: Farrar Straus Giroux, 1990), x–xi.
57. GW, interview, January 30, 1976.
58. Ibid.
59. Ibid.
60. Ibid.
61. Ibid.
62. GW, journals, [1970s], Beinecke.
63. GW, interview, January 30, 1976.
64. Ibid.

CHAPTER 2. THE NEXT STEP

1. GW, interview by Robert Phelps, January 30, 1976.
2. Ibid.
3. Ibid.
4. GW, "A Succession of Poets," *Partisan Review* 50 (1983): 395, 393–94.
5. Ibid., 398.
6. MW, diary note, possibly letter fragment, September 20, 1921, Beinecke.
7. GW, interview by author, December 8, 1976.
8. GW, "The Emperor Concerto," *Prose,* no. 3 (fall 1971): 163–80.
9. Wescott often said that he intended to write a piece called "The Yellow Fog," about the first time he arrived in England, but apparently he never did. He did, however, write about it briefly in this letter to Ivan Ashby, September 12, 1976, Beinecke.
10. GW, "The Emperor Concerto."
11. Ibid.
12. Ford Madox Ford, *It Was the Nightingale* (Philadelphia and London: J. B. Lippincott, 1933).
13. GW, interview, December 8, 1976.
14. GW, interview by author, September 15, 1978.
15. Harriet Moody to Josephine Wescott, January 5, 1922, GW correspondence, Beinecke.
16. GW, interview, December 8, 1976.
17. GW, interview, January 30, 1976.
18. *New Republic,* July 2, 1922. Wescott's unsigned reviews appeared in the *Chicago Tribune* and the *Chicago Evening Post* from October to December 1922,

including two in the Literary Review section of the *Post* on December 9, 1922. Signed reviews appeared in the *Chicago Tribune,* October 12, 1922.

19. Moore to MW, February 23, 1923, Marianne Moore Papers, Berg.

20. GW, "Mr. Auerbach in Paris," *Harper's Magazine,* April 1942, 469–73.

21. GW, interview by Robert Phelps, March 13, 1976; GW, "The First Book of Mary Butts," *Dial* 75 (September 1923): 282–84.

22. GW, "Sacre de Printemps," unpublished story, Beinecke.

23. Paul Mariani, *William Carlos Williams* (New York: Norton, 1981), 205–6.

24. GW, foreword to *Four Lives in Paris,* by Hugh Ford (Berkeley, Calif.: North Point Press, 1987), xviii.

25. Moore to MW, October 1, 1923, Marianne Moore Papers, Berg.

26. GW, interview, March 13, 1976. The affair of Betty Salemme and Robeson is reported in Martin Duberman's *Paul Robeson* (New York: Knopf, 1988), 68–70.

27. GW, interview, March 13, 1976.

28. GW, review of *Riceyman Steps,* by Arnold Bennett, *Dial* 76 (March 1924): 287.

29. GW, interview, January 30, 1976.

30. Frank Gado, ed., *Conversations on Writing and Writers* (Schenectady, N. Y.: Union College Press, 1973), 4–5.

31. GW, journals, n.d., Beinecke.

32. In an interview by the author on July 5, 1981, Wescott acknowledged that the character Dan Strane in *The Apple of the Eye* is the same autobiographical character known as Alwyn Tower in much of his later fiction.

33. GW, *The Apple of the Eye* (New York: Dial Press, 1924), 54, 79, 95, 144.

34. Kenneth Burke, "Delight and Tears," *Dial* 77 (December 1924): 513–15; "An Epic Novel of the Middle West," *Boston Evening Transcript,* November 29, 1924; Burton Rascoe, "Books," *Vanity Fair,* December 1924; Herschel Brickill, "Books on Our Table," *New York Evening Post,* February 13, 1925; Cleveland Rogers, "*The Apple of the Eye* Grips and Hurts, but It Also Convinces," *Brooklyn Eagle,* December 6, 1924.

35. Ford to MW, January 1, 1925, GW Correspondence, Beinecke.

CHAPTER 3. THE EXPATRIATE TWENTIES

1. GW to Newton, January 29, 1925, Berg.

2. GW to Newton, February 16, 1925, February 23, 1925, April 9, 1925, Berg.

3. GW to Newton, May 13, 1925, Berg.

4. GW, interview by author, February 15, 1979.

5. Ibid.

6. Ibid.

7. GW, with decorations by Pamela Bianco, *Natives of Rock: XX Poems, 1921–1922,* (New York: Francesco Bianco, 1925), ix.

8. Marianne Moore, "Natives of Rock," *Dial* 81 (July 1926): 163; Llewellyn Jones, review, *Chicago Evening Post,* January 1, 1925; William Rueckert, *Glenway Wescott* (New York: Twayne Publishers, 1965), 27.

9. GW, interview, February 15, 1979.
10. Ibid.
11. Ibid.
12. Ibid.
13. Ibid.
14. GW, "Venus on the Shore," Berg.
15. GW, journals, n.d., Beinecke.
16. Oswell Blakeston, "The Lady Who Enchanted Cocteau," *Little Caesar* no. 12 (spring 1981): 19–22; GW, interview by Robert Phelps, March 13, 1976.
17. Sy Myron Kahn, *GlenwayWescott: A Critical and Biographical Study* (Ann Arbor, Mich.: University Microfilms, 1957), 276.
18. GW, interview by author, August 19, 1982.
19. Burton Rascoe, "New Works of Fiction," *Bookman,* September 1927, 87–90; C. P. Fadiman, "The Grandmothers," *Nation,* October 12, 1927; "A Celebrity at Twenty-seven," *New York Herald Tribune,* December 18, 1927.
20. GW, interview, August 19, 1982.
21. GW, *The Grandmothers* (New York: Harper and Brothers, 1927), 1.
22. Ibid., 377–78.
23. GW, "Flight and a Victory," manuscript, Berg.
24. GW, interview, August 19, 1982.
25. Ibid.; GW, *The Grandmothers,* 385.
26. GW quotes Hemingway in "Memories and Opinions," *Prose* no. 5 (fall 1972): 177–202.
27. GW, interview, February 15, 1979.
28. Carlos Baker, ed., *Ernest Hemingway: Selected Letters 1917–1961* (New York: Scribner, 1981), 213.
29. Ernest Hemingway, *The Sun Also Rises* (New York: Scribner, 1926), 21.
30. GW, interview, February 15, 1979.
31. Carlos Baker, *Ernest Hemingway: A Life Story* (New York: Scribner, 1968), 164.
32. Peter Griffin, *Along with Youth: Hemingway, the Early Years* (New York: Oxford, 1985), 61.
33. *The Complete Short Stories of Ernest Hemingway,* Finca Vigía Edition (New York: Scribner, 1987), 250–52, 316–19, 302–5; Ernest Hemingway, *The Garden of Eden* (New York: Scribner, 1986); Ernest Hemingway, *A Moveable Feast* (New York: Scribner, 1964), 118–19; Ernest Hemingway, *Death in the Afternoon* (New York: Scribner, 1932), 70–72, 180–82, 204–5; *Selected Letters 1917–1961,* 278.
34. Peter Griffin to author, November 24, 1986; Baker, *Ernest Hemingway: A Life Story,* 188–89.
35. See GW, "The Moral of F. Scott Fitzgerald," *New Republic,* February 17, 1941.
36. GW, interview, August 19, 1982.
37. GW, interview, February 15, 1979.
38. GW to Zena Naylor, 1926, Beinecke.
39. GW to George Platt Lynes, June 24, 1927, Beinecke.
40. GW, interview, August 19, 1982.

41. Ibid.

42. Ibid.

43. GW, "Talks with Thornton Wilder," *Images of Truth* (New York: Harper, 1962), 242–308.

44. GW, *Good-bye, Wisconsin* (New York: Harper and Brothers, 1928), 279.

45. F. Scott Fitzgerald, *Letters,* ed. Andrew Turnbull (New York: Scribner, 1963), 507.

46. GW to author, inscription, January 9, 1975.

47. *Boston Evening Transcript,* November 3, 1928; Theodore Purdy, *Saturday Review of Literature,* November 17, 1928; *New York Times,* September 16, 1928.

CHAPTER 4. PARIS AND A NEW FAMILY

1. GW, interview by author, February 15, 1979.
2. Ibid.
3. Ibid.
4. GW to Lloyd Wescott, Beinecke.
5. *The Babe's Bed* (Paris: Harrison of Paris, 1932), 11.
6. Ibid., 13.
7. Ibid., 39–40.
8. GW, interview, February 15, 1979.
9. Barbara Harrison to GW, August 12, 1929, Beinecke.
10. GW to Lloyd Wescott, October 22, 1928, Beinecke.
11. GW and MW, Correspondence, Beinecke.
12. "The Babe's Bed," *Times Literary Supplement,* February 19, 1931; John Chamberlain, "Glenway Wescott's *The Babe's Bed,*" *New York Times,* January 25, 1931.
13. GW, interview by author, August 19, 1982.
14. Hugh Ford, *Published in Paris* (New York: Macmillan, 1975), 338.
15. GW, interview, August 19, 1982.
16. Ford, interview by author, November 3, 1990.
17. Janet Flanner, *Paris Was Yesterday, 1925–1939,* ed. Irving Drutman (New York: Viking, 1972), xviii.
18. *Good-bye, Wisconsin* (London: Jonathan Cape, 1929); "The Whistling Swan," *Neue Schweizer Rundshaw* 8 (August 1929); "The Runaways," *A Twentieth Century Anthology of Modern Stories* (New York: Modern Library, 1930); "In a Thicket," *Les romanciers Americaines* (Paris: De Noel et Steele, 1931).
19. Roberts to GW, November 10, 1929, Beinecke.
20. GW, "A Personal Note about Miss Roberts," *Bookman,* March 1930.
21. GW, interview, August 19, 1982.
22. GW, "The Dream of Mrs. Cleveland," manuscript with notation by GW dated May 5, 1975, Berg.
23. Robbins to GW, August 7, 1931, Beinecke.
24. Josephine Wescott to GW, February 12, 1930, Beinecke; Bruce Wescott to GW, [February 12, 1930?], Beinecke.

25. GW, "Fear and Trembling," manuscript, Berg.
26. Glenway Wescott, *Fear and Trembling* (New York: Harper, 1932), 59, 93, 97, 367–68.
27. GW, interview, August 19, 1982.
28. Carlos Baker, ed., *Ernest Hemingway: Selected Letters 1917–1961* (New York, Scribner, 1981), 357.
29. Isabel Paterson, "A Reed Shaken by the Wind," *New York Herald Tribune Books,* May 3, 1932; John Chamberlain, "Glenway Wescott's Own Dilemma," *New York Times,* May 15, 1932; Laurence Stallings, "Good-bye Wisconsin, Hello Economics," *New York Sun,* May 4, 1932; Gilbert Seldes, "Wescott Worries in Fine Words about Us," *New York Journal,* May 4, 1932; Gerald Sykes, "Reviews," *Nation,* June 15, 1932, 684; W. E. H., "Fear and Trembling," *Boston Transcript,* May 28, 1932, 21.
30. Moore to MW, July 11, 1932, Berg.
31. GW, journals, 1951, Beinecke.
32. GW, *A Calendar of Saints for Unbelievers* (Paris: Harrison of Paris, 1932), 121, 40.
33. William H. Rueckert, *Glenway Wescott* (New York: Twayne Publishers, 1965), 78.
34. Horace Gregory, "Books," *New York Herald Tribune,* July 1, 1933, 5; H. M. Chevalier, "Reviews," *Nation,* July 19, 1933; Betty Drury, "A Calendar of Saints for Unbelievers," *New York Times,* July 23, 1933, 5; Ernest Bates, "Books," *Saturday Review of Literature,* July 29, 1933.
35. GW to Saxton, April 9, 1933, Beinecke.
36. GW to Newton, May 16, 1933, Berg.
37. Harrison to GW, March 13, 1932, Beinecke; MW to GW, April 12, 1932, Beinecke.
38. GW to Sackville-West, April 10 and May 6, 1933 (two-part letter), Berg.
39. GW, journals, April 11, 1933, Beinecke.

CHAPTER 5. LOST IN AMERICA

1. Bruce Bawer, "Glenway Wescott," *New Criterion,* May 1987, 36–45, 40.
2. GW, interview by author, August 19, 1982.
3. GW to Newton, May 17, 1934, Beinecke.
4. GW, "The Deadly Friend," manuscript, Berg.
5. GW, journals, n.d., Beinecke.
6. GW, "A Sentimental Contribution," *Hound and Horn* 7 (Spring 1934): 523–34.
7. William Rueckert, *Glenway Wescott* (New York: Twayne Publishers, 1965), 102.
8. *Letters of Katherine Anne Porter,* ed. Isabel Bayley (New York: Atlantic Monthly Press, 1990), 110–14.
9. GW to Porter, July 18, 1934, Beinecke.
10. Moore to MW, December 29, 1934, Berg.
11. Szold to GW, [1934], Beinecke; Szold to GW, July 24, 1934, Beinecke.

12. GW, interview by author, July 5, 1981.
13. Josephine Wescott to GW, date obscured, 1935, Beinecke; Josephine Wescott to GW, April 1, 1935, Beinecke.
14. GW, "The Odor of Rosemary," *Prose* no. 2 (spring 1971): 171–204.
15. GW, interview by author, February 15, 1979.
16. Ibid.
17. GW, "Poor Greuze," *Wadsworth Atheneum Bulletin* 13 (January–June 1935): 2–8.
18. GW, *Images of Truth* (New York: Harper and Row, 1962), 88.
19. GW, interview, February 15, 1979.
20. GW, *Continual Lessons,* ed. Robert Phelps with Jerry Rosco (New York: Farrar Straus Giroux, 1990), 6–8.
21. GW, "The Sight of a Dead Body," *Signatures* 1 (Autumn 1936): 135–38; and GW, "The Rescuer," *Life and Letters Today* 15 (Autumn 1936): 150–56.
22. GW, "Biography and Impression: Kristian Tonny," Julian Levy Gallery, February 23–March 15, 1937.
23. Cadmus, interview by author, November 3, 1996.
24. Ibid.; GW, *Continual Lessons,* 5; Cadmus, interview.
25. Ford, interview by author, November 3, 1990.
26. GW, interview by author, November 23, 1982.
27. GW, interview, August 19, 1982.
28. Ibid.
29. Ibid.
30. Cadmus, interview.
31. GW, " New Jersey Farm—Christmas Images," December 1937, Beinecke.
32. August Derleth and Raymond E. F. Larsson, eds., *Poetry Out of Wisconsin* (New York: Henry Harrison, 1937); GW, *Continual Lessons* and subsequent journals.
33. GW, *Images of Truth,* 302.
34. GW, interview, February 15, 1979; Moore to MW, March 10, 1938, Berg.
35. GW to MW, March 16, 1938, Beinecke.
36. GW, interview, February 15, 1979.
37. Ibid.
38. Ibid.
39. Ibid.
40. Ibid.
41. GW, "Paris, 1938," *Grand Street* 1 (autumn 1981): 105–20.
42. GW, interview, February 15, 1979.
43. Ibid.
44. GW, interview, August 19, 1982.
45. GW, "The Stallions," 1938, and additions, Beinicke.
46. Ibid.
47. Ibid.
48. GW, "An Example of Suicide," 1938, Writings, Beinicke.
49. GW, "Long Island," 1938, Beinicke; GW, *Continual Lessons,* 44–47.
50. GW, "A Visit to Priapus," 1938, Beinicke; private printing, New York: Jerry Rosco, 1995.

51. GW, "Images of Mythology" with photographs by George Platt Lynes, *U.S. Camera,* January–February 1939.
52. Cadmus, interview.
53. Rueckert, *Glenway Wescott,* 103.
54. GW, "A Commentary," Jared French exhibit, Julian Levy Gallery, January 24–February 7, 1939.
55. GW, *Continual Lessons,* 51.
56. GW, "The Summer Ending," *Poetry* 54 (September 1939): 306–7.

CHAPTER 6. THE LITTLE MASTERPIECE AND WILLIE MAUGHAM

1. GW, interview by author, August 19, 1982.
2. Ibid.
3. "The Pilgrim Hawk," notebooks and typescripts, Berg.
4. GW, *The Pilgrim Hawk: A Love Story* (New York: Harper and Brothers, 1940), 11.
5. GW, interview.
6. Ibid.
7. Ibid.
8. Ibid.
9. Ibid.
10. GW, *Pilgrim Hawk,* 1.
11. GW, interview.
12. William Rueckert, *Glenway Wescott* (New York: Twayne Publishers, 1965), 109; GW, *Pilgrim Hawk,* 23–24, 25.
13. Ira Johnson, *Glenway Wescott: The Paradox of Voice* (Port Washington, N. Y: Kennikat Press, 1971), 131.
14. GW, *Pilgrim Hawk,* 75.
15. GW, interview; GW, *Pilgrim Hawk,* 84.
16. GW, *Pilgrim Hawk,* 49–50.
17. Ibid., 106.
18. Rueckert, *Glenway Wescott,* 113.
19. "Pilgrim Hawk," typescript with inscription dated July 16, 1940, Berg.
20. GW, *Continual Lessons,* ed. Robert Phelps with Jerry Rosco (New York: Farrar Straus Giroux, 1990), 74; GW, interview; Cass Canfield to GW, August 27, 1940, Beinecke.
21. Marjorie Wescott to GW, October 26, 1940, Beinecke; Robbins to GW, September 27, 1940, Beinecke; Tate to GW, November 19, 1940, Beinecke.
22. Rose Feld, "Books," *New York Herald Tribune,* December 8, 1940, 5; Sterling North, "Wescott's Return," *Chicago News,* December 11, 1940; Mark Schorer, "Return of Glenway Wescott," *Kenyon Review* (summer 1941): 375; Katharine Woods, "The Pilgrim Hawk," *New York Times,* December 1, 1940, 7; "Fresh Start," *Time,* December 2, 1940.
23. GW, "The Dream of Audubon," *Dance* 8 (December 1940–January 1941); *The Best One-Act Plays of 1940,* ed. Margaret Mayorga (New York: Dodd, Mead, 1941).

24. Rueckert, *Glenway Wescott,* 107.

25. GW, "The Moral of F. Scott Fitzgerald," *New Republic,* February 17, 1941 (reprinted in *The Crackup,* ed. Edmund Wilson [New York: New Dimensions, 1945], 323–37, 332); John Dos Passos to GW, February 21, 1941, Beinecke.

26. GW to Newton, January 8, 1941, Berg; Forster to GW, February 16, 1941, Beinecke.

27. Porter to GW, April 18, 1941, Beinecke.

28. GW to Schorer, April 30, 1941, Beinecke.

29. GW, interview.

30. Ibid.

31. Ibid.

32. Ibid.

33. GW, *Continual Lessons,* 69; Cadmus, interview by author, November 3, 1996.

34. GW, interview.

35. Ibid.

36. Klaus Mann, *The Turning Point* (New York: L. B. Fischer, 1942), 297; "The Writer's Problem in the World Today," *Chicago Sun,* January 3, 1942. Wescott developed the piece into "Fiction Writing in a Time of Troubles" for his book of essays, *Images of Truth.*

37. Wescott made the statement about a Maugham/Haxton scandal in Italy to the author on August 19, 1981, but in 1975 he had been more vague when Maugham biographer Ted Morgan interviewed him. Morgan checked with the British Home Office and found that a 1919 criminal record of Haxton exists, but it is sealed until the year 2019—a rare application of the so-called hundred-years rule.

38. GW, interview.

39. Ibid.

40. Maugham to Sheldon, December 19, 1943, copy, "The Old Party" material, Beinecke; GW, interview.

41. GW to Newton, October 16, 1941, Berg; GW, "A Fortune in Jewels," manuscript, Berg.

42. GW to Pauline de Rothschild, February 22, 1971, Beinecke.

43. "Mr. Auerbach in Paris," *Harper's Magazine,* April 1942, 469–73.

44. "The Frenchman Six-Foot-Three," *Harper's Magazine,* July 1942, 131–40; "The Frenchman Six-Foot-Three," annotated typescript, Beinecke; "The Sailor," *American Harvest: Twenty Years of Creative Writing in the United States,* ed. Allen Tate and John Peale Bishop (New York: L. B. Fischer, 1942), 325–38.

45. Cadmus, interview.

46. Lynes to MW, February 24, 1943, Beinecke.

47. GW to Lloyd and Barbara Wescott, February 26, 1943, Beinecke; Barbara Wescott to GW, February [?], 1943, Beinecke.

48. GW to Lynes, March 3, 1943, Beinecke.

49. GW, interview.

50. Fiction and verse of Frances Lamont Robbins, GW miscellaneous, Beinecke.

51. GW, interview.

52. GW, datebooks, June 1943; Tennessee Williams, *Memoirs* (New York: Doubleday, 1975), 73.

53. GW, journals, December 12, 1943, Beinecke.

54. GW, "Erich Maria Remarque," Knoedler Galleries catalog, October 18–November 18, 1943.

55. "I Love New York," *Harper's Bazaar,* December, 1943, 53.

56. Ibid.

CHAPTER 7. THE BESTSELLER

1. GW, "A Fortune in Jewels," manuscript and annotations, Berg.

2. GW, "Apartment in Athens" drafts, including pages titled "A Change of Heart" and "Children of Wrath," Berg.

3. GW to Barbara Wescott, February 17, 1944, Beinecke.

4. GW, *Apartment in Athens* (New York: Harper and Brothers, 1945), 13.

5. Ibid., 27.

6. Ibid., 42, 49.

7. Ibid., 232, 236.

8. GW, reading of journals with commentary, October 22, 1975.

9. GW, 1975 note to Berg curator Lola Szladits.

10. GW, miscellaneous, Beinecke.

11. GW, annotation, 1975 note to Szladits.

12. Szold to GW, December 4, 1944, Berg; GW, interview by author, July 5, 1981.

13. Ferber to GW, February 22, 1945, Beinecke; Maugham to GW, March 1, 1945, Beinecke.

14. "Apartment in Athens," *Kirkus,* January 1945; Rebecca Ranking, review, *Library Journal,* February 15, 1945; Diana Trilling, "Mr. Wescott's War Work," *Nation,* March 17, 1945, 312–13; Edmund Wilson, "Greeks and Germans by Glenway Wescott," *New Yorker,* March 3, 1945, 76–78; Eudora Welty, "Told with Severity and Honesty," *New York Times,* March 4, 1945; A. C. Spectorsky, "Apartment in Athens," *Chicago Sun Book Week,* March 4, 1945.

15. Carl Malouf, interview by author, April 23, 1990.

16. GW, journal note, "Buchenwald 1945," July 31, 1971, Beinecke.

17. GW, *Continual Lessons,* ed. Robert Phelps with Jerry Rosco (New York: Farrar Straus Giroux, 1990), 128.

18. Porter to MW, September 15, 1945, Beinecke.

19. GW, journals, January 1945, Berg.

20. Ted Morgan, *Maugham* (New York: Simon & Schuster, 1980), 499–501.

21. Maugham to GW, September 3, 1946, Beinecke, and *Continual Lessons,* xvi.

22. GW, review of *Razor's Edge, Wings* 18 (May 1944): 4–9; GW, "Somerset Maugham and Posterity," *Harper's Magazine,* October 1947, 302–11.

23. Maugham to GW, August 22, 1947, Beinecke.

24. GW, interview, July 5, 1981.

25. GW, "Paintings of Paris by Camille Pissarro," Carstairs Galleries, catalog, April 1944; GW, "Stories by a Writer's Writer," *New York Times Book Review,*

September 17, 1944; GW, "Elizabeth Bowen's 'The Heat of the Day,'" *Saturday Review of Literature,* February 19, 1949; GW, "A Portrait of Country Life," *Tomorrow* 11 (July 1947): 35–37; GW, "The Moral of F. Scott Fitzgerald," in *The Crackup,* ed. Edmund Wilson (New York: New Directions, 1945), 323–37.

26. *El Halcón Errante,* trans. Ricardo Latcham, in *Antología de escritores contemporáneos de los Estados Unidos* (Santiago, Chile: Nascimento, 1944); *The Pilgrim Hawk* (London: Hamish Hamilton, 1946); *Great American Modern Short Novels,* ed. William Phillips (New York: Dial Press, 1946); *Pilgrimsfalken,* trans. Brigitta Hammar (Stockholm: Albert Bonniers Forlog, 1949); *Apartment in Athens* (Cleveland: World Publishing Company, 1946); *Apartment in Athens* (Toronto: McClelland and Stewart, 1946); *En un Departamento en Atenas, Omnilibro* Ano II, April 1946; *En un Departamento en Atenas,* trans. Maria Rosa Oliver (Buenos Aires: Editorial Lautaro, 1945); *Casa in Atene,* trans. Spina Vismara (Milan: Bompiani Press, 1947); *Appartement à Athènes,* trans. Madame Jeanneret (Paris: Delamain et Boutelleau, 1947); *Athenska Domacnost,* trans. Prelozila Hofmanova.(Prague: Vaclav Petr, 1947); *Apartment in Athens* (New York: Bantam, 1949).

27. Writers who expressed interest in doing a screenplay of *Apartment in Athens* in 1945 included playwright Paul Green and the team of Richard Friedenberg and Donald Wisely. Correspondence, Berg.

28. GW, outline, notes and partial text for six-act play, "Apartment in Athens," Berg.

29. GW, journals, February 10, 1949, Beinecke.

30. Felicia Geffen, address at American Academy of Arts and Letters, New York, March 11, 1987. In 1977 the two organizations became one, the American Academy and Institute of Arts and Letters, or the Academy-Institute.

31. GW to Thornton Wilder, April 11, 1947, Berg.

32. GW to Thornton Wilder, January 1, 1949, Berg.

33. Charles Henri Ford, interview by author, November 3, 1990.

34. Cadmus, interview by author, November 3, 1996.

35. Ames to GW, April 9, 1949, Beinecke.

36. GW to Wilder, April 28, 1949, Berg.

37. GW to Maugham, April 27, 1946, Beinecke; Porter to MW, July 26, 1945, Beinecke.

38. Barbara Wescott to GW, May 22, 1947, Beinecke.

39. Moore to MW, July 16, 1947, Berg; GW, *Continual Lessons,* 213.

40. Kirstein to Lynes, 1946–48, Beinecke.

41. Pomeroy, interview by author, September 21, 1998; Perlin, interview by author, June 29, 2000; Charles Kaiser, *The Gay Metropolis* (New York: Houghton Mifflin, 1997), 10.

42. GW, interview by Robert Phelps, March 13, 1976.

43. GW to Perlin, September 9, 1945, Beinecke.

44. GW to Wilder, April 11, 1947, Berg.

45. Malouf, interview.

46. Malouf, interview.

47. GW to MW, March 11, 1949, Beinecke.

48. GW, interview, August 19, 1982

49. Ibid.
50. Ibid.
51. Ibid.
52. Ibid.
53. Cadmus, interview.
54. GW, *Continual Lessons,* 179–80.
55. MW to Forster, September18, 1949, Beinecke.
56. GW, *Continual Lessons,* 259.

CHAPTER 8. DR. KINSEY AND THE INSTITUTE FOR SEX RESEARCH

1. GW, interview by author, December 8, 1982.
2. Ibid.
3. Ibid.
4. Ibid.
5. Ibid.
6. Ibid.
7. Ibid.
8. GW, reading of journals with commentary, October 22, 1975.
9. Ibid.
10. Ibid.
11. GW, interview, December 8, 1982.
12. GW, journals, December 28, 1950, Beinecke.
13. GW, interview, December 8, 1982.
14. Ibid.
15. Ibid.
16. GW, interview by John Stevenson, January 28, 1979. As an aid to his memory when he was organizing material, GW recorded conversations with several people besides Phelps and Rosco. John Stevenson kept several such recordings.
17. Carl Malouf, interview by author, April 23, 1990.
18. GW, journals, Beinecke.
19. GW, interview, December 8, 1982, and documents.
20. GW, interview, December 8, 1982.
21. Ibid.
22. Ibid.
23. Ibid.
24. Ralph Pomeroy, interview by author, September 21, 1998.
25. Malouf, interview.
26. Ibid.
27. Ibid.
28. GW, interview, December 8, 1982.
29. Ibid.
30. Pomeroy, interview.
31. John Connolly, interview by author, July 11, 1998.
32. GW, *Continual Lessons* (New York: Farrar Straus Giroux, 1990), 313.
33. GW to Alfred Kinsey, February 24–25, 1952, author's collection. Among

Wescott materials passed on to the author by Robert Phelps were photocopies of GW letters to Kinsey. Most of the originals disappeared from the Kinsey Institute files. See note 52 below.

34. Joan Littlefield, *Baron Philippe* (New York: Crown Publishers, 1984), 290.

35. GW, journals, Beinecke, and conversation, October 22, 1975.

36. Joan Givner, *Katherine Anne Porter: A Life* (New York: Simon & Schuster, 1982), 383.

37. GW, interview by author, February 15, 1979.

38. GW, "A Visit to Colette," *Town and Country,* January 1953; GW, *Images of Truth* (New York: Harper and Row, 1962), 148.

39. Ford, interview with author, November 3, 1990; Thomas Waugh, *Hard to Imagine: Gay Male Eroticism in Photography and Film from Their Beginnings to Stonewall* (New York: Columbia University Press, 1996), 395.

40. GW to MW, June 15, 1952, Beinecke.

41. GW to Kinsey, July 14, 1952, author's collection.

42. GW, interview, December 8, 1982.

43. Ibid.

44. GW to Paul Gebhard, January 18, 1957, Beinecke.

45. GW, interview, December8, 1982.

46. Ibid.

47. Ibid.

48. Sam Steward, *Chapters from an Autobiography* (San Francisco: Grey Fox, 1980), 102.

49. GW, interview, December 8, 1982; GW to Kinsey, March 18, 1953, author's collection.

50. Kinsey to GW, July 19, 1953, Beinecke.

51. GW to Kinsey, August 1, 1953, author's collection.

52. Jonathan Gathorne-Hardy, *Sex the Measure of All Things: A Life of Alfred C. Kinsey* (Bloomington: Indiana University Press, 2000), 356.

53. GW to Will Chandlee III, October 22, 1953, Beinecke.

54. Steward to GW, date obscured [1953], Beinecke.

55. GW to Kinsey, September 4, 1953, author's collection.

56. GW to Kinsey, November 25, 1953, author's collection.

57. GW interview, December 8, 1982.

58. Ibid.

59. Malouf, interview.

60. Wardell B. Pomeroy, *Dr. Kinsey and the Institute for Sex Research* (Harper and Row, 1972), 338, 379, 381.

61. GW, datebooks, July 5, 1954, Beinecke.

62. Kinsey to GW, August 22, 1954, Beinecke; GW to Kinsey, September 15, 1953, author's collection.

63. GW, interview, December 8, 1982.

64. Ibid.

65. Steward, *Autobiography,* 105.

66. GW, interview, December 8, 1982.

67. James H. Jones, *Alfred C. Kinsey: A Public/Private Life* (New York: Norton, 1997); Martin Duberman, *Nation,* November 3, 1997, 40–43, 40.

68. Gathorne-Hardy, *Sex the Measure of All Things,* 35–69.

69. GW, interview, December 8, 1982.

CHAPTER 9. INSIDE THE CIRCLE: FAREWELL TO GEORGE

1. Ralph Pomeroy, interview by author, September 21, 1998.

2. John Connolly, interview by author, July 11, 1998.

3. Carl Malouf, interview by author, April 23, 1990.

4. MW to GW, June 8, 1951, Beinecke.

5. MW to GW, July 6 and 12, 1951, Beinecke; Rockefeller to MW, July 26, 1951, Beinecke.

6. GW, *Continual Lessons* (New York: Farrar Straus Giroux, 1990), 294.

7. Ibid., 302.

8. Moore to MW, October 10, 1951, Berg.

9. GW's dialogue notebook with comments for "Macbeth" reading, November 1951, Berg.

10. Moore to MW, December 9, 1952, Berg.

11. Frederic Prokosch, *Voices: A Memoir* (New York: Farrar Straus Giroux, 1983), 283–90.

12. Moore to MW, March 26, 1953, Berg; Pomeroy, interview; Moore to MW, August 14, 1953, Berg.

13. MW to GW, June 28, 1955, Beinecke.

14. GW to John Connolly, April 14, 1955, Beinecke.

15. Connolly, interview.

16. Bruce and Josephine Wescott's fiftieth anniversary was on June 27, 1950.

17. Pomeroy, interview.

18. Connolly, interview; GW, *Continual Lessons,* 373.

19. Connolly, interview; Bernard Perlin, interview by author, June 29, 2000; Connolly, interview.

20. GW to Alfred Kinsey, November 25, 1953, author's collection.

21. Ibid.

22. GW to Caroline Newton, November 23, 1953, Berg.

23. Perlin, interview.

24. Samuel Steward, "George Platt Lynes," *The Advocate,* December 10, 1981, 22–24.

25. Paul Cadmus, interview by author, November 3, 1996.

26. Ibid.; Perlin, interview.

27. GW to Lynes, postcard, January 6, 1955, Beinecke.

28. MW to Pomeroy, May 20, 1955, Beinecke.

29. Isherwood to GW, June 1, 1955, Beinecke.

30. GW to MW, June 27, 1955, Beinecke.

31. Lynes to MW, August (date obscured), 1955, Beinecke; Steward, "George Platt Lynes"; Perlin, interview.

32. GW to James Charlton, September 16, 1955, Beinecke; GW to Deborah Wescott, September 20, 1955, Beinecke.

33. Kinsey quoted in Steward, "George Platt Lynes"; Connolly, interview.

34. GW, *Continual Lessons,* 374; quoted by Charles Barber, "AIDS Apartheid," *NYQ,* November 3, 1991, 42.

35. Perlin, interview; Connolly, interview; Josephine Wescott to GW, December 5, 1955, Beinecke.

36. GW, *Continual Lessons,* 398.

37. Moore to MW, December 8, 1955, Berg.

38. Perlin to E. Gauthier, GW correspondence, July 14, 1956, Beinecke; Kirstein to GW, November 16 and 17, 1956, Beinecke.

39. Kirstein to GW, November 22, 1956, Beinecke; Porter to GW, January 1, 1957, Beinecke.

40. GW, *Continual Lessons,* 399.

41. Cadmus, interview.

42. Pomeroy, interview.

CHAPTER 10. BEYOND FICTION

1. Perlin, interview by author, June 29, 2000.

2. GW to Newton, September 13, 19, and 23, 1951, Berg.

3. GW, reading of journals with commentary, Beinicke, and conversation, October 22, 1975.

4. Ibid.

5. John Connolly, interview by author, July 11, 1998; Perlin, interview.

6. Brendan Gill, "Philip the Bold," *New Yorker,* November 14, 1994, 139.

7. GW, journals, February 11, 1957, Beinecke.

8. GW, interview by John Stevenson, January 28, 1979.

9. Ibid.

10. Connolly, interview.

11. Ralph Pomeroy, interview by author, September 21, 1998.

12. GW to Rothschild, March 23, 1957, Beinecke; GW to Perlin, July 12, 1957, Beinecke.

13. Moore to GW, April 22, 1951, Berg.

14. GW, introduction to *The Maugham Reader* (New York: Doubleday, 1950), xxi; GW, "A Transatlantic Glance," *Griffin* 1 (1951).

15. GW, *Continual Lessons* (New York: Farrar Straus Giroux, 1990), 296; GW, journals, Beinecke, and conversation, October 22, 1975.

16. GW, "An Introduction to Colette," *Short Novels of Colette* (New York: Dial Press, 1951), liv.

17. GW, "Colette," *Vogue,* December 1951; "A Visit to Colette," *Town and Country,* January 1953; GW, "In Praise of Dr. Edith Sitwell," *Proceedings of the American Academy of Arts and Letters and the National Institute of Arts and Letters,* 2d ser. 1 (1951): 49–52; "The Old and the New," *Proceedings,* 2d ser. 5 (1955): 69–71; "Introduction to a Reading by Robert Frost," *Proceedings,* 2d ser. 6 (1956): 67–68; "A Reading, with Louise Bogan, of Contemporary Poets," *Proceedings,* 2d ser. 6 (1956): 71–72.

18. Maxwell to GW, November 16, 1956, and January 4, 1957, Berg.

19. GW, *Twelve Fables of Aesop: Newly Narrated by Glenway Wescott* (New York: Museum of Modern Art, 1954).

20. Moore to GW, January 4 and January 30, 1955, Berg; William H. Rueckert, *Glenway Wescott* (New York: Twayne Publishers, 1965), 126–28.

21. *Der Wanderfalke,* trans. Wolfgang von Einsiedel (Stuttgart: Verlags-Anstalt, 1952); *Six Great Modern Short Novels* (New York: Dell, 1954); *The Grandmothers* (New York: Harper and Brothers, 1955); "The Sailor," in *Crazy Mixed-Up Kids,* ed. William Hodapp (New York: Berkley, 1955).

22. Malouf, interview by author, April 23, 1990; MW to Porter, January 31, 1955, Beinecke; Sy Myron Kahn, *Glenway Wescott: A Critical and Biographical Study* (Ann Arbor, Mich.: University Microfilms, 1957); Kahn, "Glenway Wescott: A Bibliography," *Bulletin of Bibliography,* September–December 1958, 156–60.

23. GW, *Continual Lessons,* 252–53.

24. GW to Mortimer, November 6, 1951, Beinecke.

25. GW, *Continual Lessons,* 282.

26. GW, journals, January 4, 1952, Beinecke.

27. GW, "Children of This World," manuscript, Berg. The annotation on the cover is dated January 7, 1975. Brief original notes on cards from the 1930s exist at Beinecke. Quotations that follow in this chapter are from drafts of the manuscript at Berg.

28. GW, journals, November 25, 1956, Beinecke.

29. Barbara Wescott to GW, June 25, 1954, Beinecke.

30. Barbara Wescott to GW, April 20, 1957, Beinecke.

31. GW to Mortimer, April 21, 1957, Beinecke.

32. MW to Sitwell, June 16, 1958, Beinecke; Szold to GW, [1957], Beinecke; Toklas to GW, January 19, 1958, Beinecke.

33. Cadmus, interview by author, November 3, 1996; GW, journals, August 1958, Beinecke.

34. GW to Bernadine Szold, September 21, 1958, Beinecke.

35. GW to Josephine Wescott, September 4, 1958, Beinecke; GW to Szold, September 21, 1958, Beinecke; GW to Maxwell, October 30, 1958, Berg; Connolly, interview.

36. *New York Daily News,* July 15, 1959.

37. GW to MW, August 6, 11, 13, 16, 18, 25, 31, 1959, Beinecke.

38. GW, "The Best of All Possible Worlds," *Proceedings of the Academy of Arts and Letters and the National Institute of Arts and Letters,* 2d ser. 9 (1959): 277–89; "The Valley Submerged," *Southern Review* 1, no. 3 (summer 1965), 621–33.

39. GW to Newton, November 6, 1958, Berg; Malouf, interview.

40. The interview took place at the BBC office at Fiftieth Street and Fifth Avenue on March 4, 1959.

41. GW to Rothschild, February 1, 1959, Beinecke; Moore to MW, January 9, 1959, Berg; GW, journals, Beinicke, and conversation, October 22, 1975; GW to Maxwell, May 29, 1959, Berg; Moore to GW, October 30, 1959, Berg.

42. Christopher Isherwood, *Diaries: 1939–1960* (New York: Harper Collins, 1997), 800.

43. GW, "Isak Dinesen Tells a Tale," *Harper's Magazine,* March 1960.

44. Bogan to GW, May 4, 1959, Beinecke.

45. GW to Maxwell, May 29, 1959, Berg; Rothschild to GW, August 2–7, 1959, Beinecke.

46. GW to Newton, September 18 and 25, 1959, Berg; GW to Maxwell, November 3, 1959, Berg.

47. GW, "The Valley Submerged."

CHAPTER 11. THE GREAT DIVIDE AND IMAGES OF TRUTH

1. GW, datebooks, January 4, 1960, Beinecke; Bogan to GW, January 16, 1960, Beinecke.

2. William H. Rueckert, *Glenway Wescott* (New York: Twayne Publishers, 1965), 124.

3. Gerald Clarke, *Capote: A Biography* (New York: Simon and Schuster, 1988), 328.

4. Porter to GW, January 6, 1960, Beinecke.

5. GW journals, September 3, 1960, Beinecke.

6. GW to Knowles, April 5, 1960, Beinecke.

7. GW, "A Succession of Poets," *Partisan Review* 3 (1983): 397.

8. Ibid.

9. John Updike, ed., *A Century of Arts & Letters* (New York: Columbia University Press, 1998), 165–66.

10. Ibid., 166.

11. Ibid., 171.

12. GW, *Images of Truth* (New York: Harper and Row, 1962), 56.

13. GW, "Katherine Anne Porter: The Making of a Novel," *Atlantic Monthly,* April 1962, 43–49; reprinted in *Images of Truth,* 47.

14. "An Open Mind Profile: Katherine Anne Porter Talks with Glenway Wescott and Eric F. Goldman," edited transcript of the May 13, 1962 NBC telecast, ed. E. C. Bufkin, in *Georgia Review* (winter 1987): 769–95, 786.

15. Newton translated Jacob Wassermann's *The Maurizius Case* (New York: Liveright, 1929), and knew Thomas Mann (Robert F. Goheen, ed., *The Letters of Thomas Mann to Caroline Newton* [Princeton, N. J.: Princeton University Press, 1971]).

16. GW to Newton, May 30, 1962, Berg.

17. GW to Newton, June 7, 1962, Berg.

18. *Images of Truth,* 10, 20–21.

19. Ibid., 213, 231; Anthony Heilbut, *Thomas Mann: Eros and Literature* (New York: Knopf, 1996), 556–57.

20. Ibid., 262, 248.

21. Orville Prescott, *New York Times,* September 26, 1962; *Time,* September 28, 1962.

22. Winters to GW, November 19, 1962, Beinecke.

23. Bob Robertson, "Wescott at Berkeley," *San Francisco Chronicle,* November 20, 1962.

24. Moore to GW, December 17, 1962, Berg.

25. GW, interview by John Stevenson, January 28, 1979, author's collection.

26. GW to Gebhard, April 3, 1963, GW's Kinsey letters, author's collection.

27. GW, interview, January 28, 1979.

28. GW, interview by author, December 8, 1982.

29. Malouf, interview by author, April 23, 1990.

30. Connolly, interview by author, July 11, 1998.

31. GW to Bruce Savin, October 23, 1963, Beinecke.

32. GW to MW, March 22, 1962, Beinecke.

33. George Platt Lynes, "Portraits, 1931–1952," Art Institute of Chicago, July–Aug. 1960; GW to Dinesen, December 31, 1960, Beinecke; Moore to MW, December 30, 1960, and January 11, 1961, Berg.

34. GW, interview by author, February 15, 1979.

35. Edith Sitwell to MW, April 6, 1964, Beinecke; GW journals, December 11, 1964, Beinecke; GW to Osbert Sitwell, February 23, 1965, Beinecke.

36. Searle to GW, June 21, 1961, Beinecke; MW to GW, July 20, 1962, Beinecke.

37. Searle to GW, January 27, 1965, Beinecke.

38. GW, "Cremation in Marseilles," journals, Beinecke.

39. Ibid.

40. GW, journals, April 14, 1965, Beinecke.

41. Connolly, interview; Ralph Pomeroy, interview by author, September 21, 1998.

42. GW to Anna Brakke, April 10, 1967, Beinecke.

43. GW, interview by author, August 19, 1982.

44. "Wescotts Give County 72 Acres for Park," *Hunterdon County Democrat,* December 29, 1967; *Newark Sunday News,* September 11, 1967.

45. GW to Bernadine Szold, April 9, 1968, Beinecke; GW, datebooks, April 7–9, 1968, Beinecke.

46. The dates of the television shows were April 17, 1960 ("Paris in the Twenties") and May 8, 1964 ("Personal Report"). The Arlene Francis show was broadcast by radio station WOR-FM on December 14, 1964; the "Paperback" show originated at WBAI and was distributed in December 1964.

47. Wingspread Conference on the Arts, June 8–10, 1962. Now a conference center, Wingspread was originally a spectacular house designed by Frank Lloyd Wright. Wescott commented on the conference in "Professional or Vocational," *Authors Guild Bulletin,* October–November 1962, 1, 3, 4.

48. The "unwelcoming" comment is in GW's letter to Lloyd Wescott, May 11, 1965, Berg; Frank Gado's interview with GW in May 1965 appears in the Union College publication, *Symposium,* spring 1966, and in Frank Gado, ed., *First Person, Conversations on Writers and Writing with Glenway Wescott et al.* (Schenectady, N. Y: Union College Press, 1973), 3–30; Union College awarded Wescott the doctorate of letters degree on May 16, 1968; Wescott presented the commencement address at Rutgers University on June 3, 1963, and was awarded an honorary degree; Wescott's lecture at the MacDowell Colony tribute for Marianne Moore on August 20, 1967, later became the essay "A Succession of Poets."

49. GW, "Not a Proper Gentleman," *New York Herald Tribune,* October 27, 1963; "The Blue Lantern," *New York Herald Tribune,* November 24, 1963; "The Choreographer," *Show,* December 1963.

50. The *Book Week* reviews appeared in the *Herald Tribune* as follows: "A Surpassing Sequel" (Cheever), January 5, 1964; "My Aunt Maxine" (Robertson), June 21, 1964; "All of Us on the Half Shell" (Clark), July 12, 1964; "Subjects before His Predicates" (Connolly), October 4, 1964; "The Journal of Jules Renard, 1887–1910" (Connolly), December 27, 1964; "A Face to Laugh, a Face to Cry" (Sitwell), May 2, 1965.

51. GW, "The Tri-Colored Rainbow," *Book Week,* December 19, 1965; Brenda Wineapple, *Genet, A Biography of Janet Flanner* (New York: Ticknor & Fields, 1989), 275; "A Record of Friendship," *New York Times Book Review,* October 9, 1966.

52. GW, "The Passing of the Old Party," *Life,* January 14, 1966.

53. GW, "The Valley Submerged," *Southern Review* 1, no. 3 (summer 1965), 621–33; "Bernard Perlin," catalog, Catherine Vivano Gallery, May–June 1964.

54. GW, *The Grandmothers* (New York: Atheneum, 1962); GW, *Good-bye, Wisconsin* (New York :New American Library, 1964); GW, "Good-bye, Wisconsin," in *The Personal Voice: A Contemporary Prose Reader,* ed. Albert J Guérard (Philadelphia: Lippincott, 1964).

55. Hawkes to Canfield, September 8, 1966, Beinecke; Sitwell to GW, undated [1966], Beinecke; Jean Stafford,"Paradox of Love," *Vogue,* September 15,1966.

56. GW, interview, August 19, 1982; Howard Moss, "Glenway Wescott: Love Birds of Prey," *New Yorker,* March 11, 1967; reprinted in Howard Moss, *Writing against Time: Critical Essays and Reviews* (New York: Morrow, 1969), 169–78, 169.

57. GW, interview, August 19, 1982.

58. GW, journals, August 1972, Beinecke.

59. GW to Gebhard, January 25, 1963, GW's Kinsey letters, author's collection.

60. GW to Mortimer, February 12, 1961, Beinecke; GW to Gebhard, January 25, 1963.

61. Charles Henri Ford, interview by author, November 3, 1990.

62. GW to Mortimer, September 11, 1964, Beinecke; Perlin to GW, November 14, 1964, Beinecke; GW to Rorem, April 1, 1966, Beinecke.

63. GW miscellaneous, clipping, *New York Times,* September 30, 1966, Beinecke; GW to Hotchner, January 15, 1966, Beinecke; Hotchner to author, February 23, 1998.

64. Felicia Geffen, remarks at Academy-Institute of Arts and Letters, March 11, 1987.

65. GW, journals, April 24, 1964, Beinecke.

66. GW to Capote, not sent, November 16, 1966, Beinecke; Natalia Danasi Murray, ed., *Darlinghissima: Letters to a Friend* (New York: Random House, 1985), 387–88.

67. GW to Wheeler, September, 1962, Beinecke.

68. "Modern Art Museum's Wheeler Recalls Achievements upon Retirement," *Hunterdon County Democrat,* August 10, 1967.

69. GW, journals, October 27, 1957, Beinecke; GW to MW, undated, Beinecke.

70. GW to Barbara Wescott, January 1967 [damaged postcard, date obscured], Beinecke.

71. GW to Butler, October 25, 1967, Beinecke.

72. Brakke to GW, January 4, 1966, Beinecke; GW to Mark Pagano, November 10, 1967, Beinecke.

73. GW to Ford, October 21, 1965, Beinecke; GW, journals, March 2, 1969, Beinecke; Beulah Wescott Hagen to GW, November 15, 1967, Beinecke.

74. GW to Connolly, July 20, 1967, Beinecke.

75. GW to Flanner, October 9, 1967, Beinecke; GW to Szold, April 9, 1968, Beinecke; GW to Deutsch, August 20, 1968, Beinecke.

76. GW, *Continual Lessons* (New York: Farrar Straus Giroux, 1990), 297.

77. GW to Ashby, March 13, 1968, Beinecke.

78. Rothschild to GW, December 24,1968.

79. Ivan Ashby, interview with author, July 11,1998.

80. GW to Ashby, April 14, 1969, Beinecke.

81. Matthew J. Bruccoli and Judith S. Baughman, eds., *Crux: The Letters of James Dickey* (New York: Knopf, 1999), 295–96.

82. 1969 Rockefeller Presidential Mission to Latin America materials, Monroe Wheeler Collection, Beinecke.

83. Ibid.

84. Pomeroy, interview.

85. Moore to GW, September 17, 1969, Beinecke.

86. GW to Maxwell, October 14, 1969, Berg.

CHAPTER 12. "QUAIL AND STRAWBERRIES"

1. GW to Barbara Wescott, January 9, 1970, Beinecke.

2. Bernard Lown, "More Writings by Dr. Lown: The Baroness Pauline Rothschild," Lown Cardiovascular Center, <www.lown.cc/more.html>, 1996.

3. Joan Littlewood, *Baron Philippe* (New York: Crown Publishers, 1984), 327.

4. GW to Connolly, February 22, 1970, Beinecke.

5. Memorial program, Marianne Moore, February 8, 1972, GW miscellaneous, Beinecke.

6. Isherwood to GW, November 19, 1970, Beinecke.

7. GW, "A Dinner, a Talk, a Walk with Forster," *New York Times,* October 10, 1971.

8. GW to MW, February 16, 1970, Beinecke.

9. Leitsch, conversation with author, March 15, 1998.

10. Pohorilenko, interview by author, December 12, 1997.

11. GW, journals, September 4, 1970, Beinecke.

12. GW, scrapbooks, Beinecke.

13. GW, notebook, March 11, 1973, Beinecke.

14. GW to Phelps, December 12–22, 1971, Beinecke.

15. Pomeroy, interview by author, September 21, 1998.

16. GW, journals, September 21, 1970, Beinecke.
17. GW to MW, September 30, 1970, Beinecke.
18. GW, "The Odor of Rosemary," *Prose* 2 (spring 1971): 171–204.
19. Ibid., 203.
20. Anita Loos to GW, May 20, 1971, Beinecke.
21. GW, 'The Emperor Concerto," *Prose,* no. 3 (fall 1971): 163–80.
22. GW, "Memories and Opinions," *Prose* 5 (fall 1972): 177–202.
23. Ibid., 189.
24. Ibid., 194, 202.
25. Ibid., 199, 200.
26. GW, "The Breath of Bulls," *Works in Progress No. 6* (New York: Doubleday 1972), 237–47.
27. Ibid., 240.
28. Sitwell to MW, April 7, 1973, Beinecke.
29. GW to Cowley, May 14, 1971, Beinecke.
30. Canfield to GW, June 25, 1971, Beinecke (referring to *Images of Truth* published by Books of Libraries Press, Freeport, N.Y., which also reprinted *Good-bye, Wisconsin* that year); Cass Canfield, *Up and Down and Around* (New York: Harper's Magazine Press, 1971), 194.
31. James Korges, "Glenway Wescott," in *Contemporary Novelists,* ed. James Vinson (New York: St. Martin's, 1972), 1321–24.
32. Singer to GW, October 24, 1971, Beinecke.
33. GW to MW, September 7, 1972, Beinecke.
34. Campbell to GW, February 29, 1972, Beinecke; MW to GW, [1971], Beinecke.
35. GW to Diamond, September 7, 1971, Beinecke.
36. Hosts of London gatherings for GW and MW were Tony Richardson, on January 17, 1971, and Cecil Beaton, in late January 1972.
37. GW to Meyner, November 8, 1972, Beinecke.
38. Lewis to GW, February 22, 1973, Beinecke.
39. Brenda Wineapple, *Genet, a Biography of Janet Flanner* (New York: Ticknor & Fields, 1989), 288.
40. GW, journal pages, early 1970s, Beinecke.
41. GW, journals, August 17, 1972, Beinecke.
42. Pete Hamill, *New York Post,* November 30, 1973; Michael Lesy, *Wisconsin Death Trip* (New York : Pantheon, 1973); GW, *Images of Truth* (North Stratford, N.H.: Ayer Press, 1977); GW, *Good-bye, Wisconsin* (North Stratford, N.H.: Ayer Press, 1977).
43. Stevenson, interview by author, September 8, 1985.
44. GW to MW, April 7, 1974, Beinecke.
45. Stevenson, interview by author, May 29, 1998.
46. GW to Williams, May 31, 1974, Beinecke.
47. Beulah Wescott to GW, September 12, 1974, Beinecke.
48. GW, datebooks, January 1975.
49. GW to MW, January 22, 1975, Beinecke.
50. GW to Stevenson, May 5, 1975.
51. GW, datebook, May 31, 1975.

52. MW to Raymond Mortimer, [1975], Beinecke.
53. MW to GW, January 21, 1976, Beinecke.
54. GW to Mortimer, February 19, 1976, Beinecke.
55. Littlewood, *Baron Philippe,* 280.
56. GW and MW to Rothschild, March 7, 1976, Beinecke.
57. GW to Rothschild, March 24, 1976, Beinecke.
58. Robert Phelps, *Mademoiselle,* August 1976.
59. GW address, August 1976, John Stevenson papers, and Academy-Institute of Arts and Letters, New York.
60. GW, datebook, November 2, 1976, Beinecke.
61. GW, interview by author, December 8, 1976.
62. Ibid.
63. GW to Barbara Wescott, August 30, 1976, Beinecke.
64. GW, interview by author, July 5, 1981.
65. GW to Szold, September 16, 1976, Beinecke.
66. GW to MW, March 13, 1977, Beinecke; GW, journal, March 13, 1977, Beinecke.
67. GW to Lloyd Wescott, (not sent), March 13, 1977.
68. Ibid.
69. Rothschild to MW and GW, March 20, 1977, Beinecke.
70. "400 Celebrate Memory of Barbara H. Wescott," *Trenton Times,* May 2, 1977.
71. GW spoke at the Anaïs Nin memorial at New York University's Bobst Library, February 22, 1977; GW to MW, May 13, 1977, Beinecke.
72. GW to MW, February 3, 1977, Beinecke.
73. GW to Stevenson, July 15, 1977.
74. GW to Ford, July 16, 1977, Beinecke.
75. GW to Chandlee, November 11, 1977, Beinecke.
76. GW to Stevenson, August 28, 1978, Beinecke.
77. GW, journals, [1979], Beinecke.
78. Valerian Butler-Smith III to author, September 10, 1999.
79. GW, interview, July 5, 1981.
80. MW to GW, November 7, 1978, Beinecke.
81. GW, journals, December 14, 1978, Beinecke.
82. Szold to GW, May 8, 1971 (Duncan), and May 3, 1978 (Flanner).
83. GW to Stevenson, [March 1979], Beinecke; MW to GW, May 1, 1979, Beinecke.
84. GW, journals, March 24, 1979, Beinecke.
85. GW, annotation, materials, November 19, 1979, Berg.

CHAPTER 13. GOLDEN LEAVES AND THE BIRTHDAY BOOK

1. Ford to GW, July 1, 1980, Beinecke.
2. GW, journals, August 8 and September 9, 1980, Beinecke.
3. GW's recollection of Tchelitchew at Earl Butler's apartment, author's journal, March 12, 1981.
4. GW, "Paris 1938," *Grand Street* (autumn 1981): 105–20.

5. GW to author, journal inscription, October 10, 1981.

6. Rockefeller to MW, January 21, 1981, Beinecke; MW greeted Indira Gandhi at MoMA on July 31, 1982.

7. Daniel Diamond, interview by author, January 5, 1981.

8. Jerry Rosco, "Glenway Wescott: The Unfinished Story," *Little Caesar,* no. 12 (spring 1982): 135–40; Ian Young, *Little Caesar,* no. 12 (spring 1982): 3–5, 4.

9. GW, interview by author, August 19, 1982.

10. GW to Roger Straus Jr., March 11, 1983, Beinecke.

11. GW, journals and datebooks, September 1982, Beinecke.

12. Jacques Barzun, "William James, Author," *American Scholar* 52, 1 (winter 1983): 41–48, 41; GW, "A Succession of Poets," *Partisan Review* 50 (fall 1983): 396, 402.

13. "Succession of Poets," 402.

14. Stevenson to author, September 8, 1985, and GW datebook, December 4, 1983.

15. Stevenson to author, August 27, 1983.

16. Phelps, conversation with author, April 15, 1984.

17. Moss, conversation with author, January 25, 1987.

18. MW to GW, April 30, 1985, Beinecke.

19. Lloyd Wescott to MW, September 9, 1985, Beinecke.

20. Jerry Rosco, "Remembering Cocteau: From Conversations with Glenway Wescott," *Sequoia* 29, no. 2 (1985): 54–60.

21. John W. Aldridge, introduction to *The Grandmothers* (New York: Arbor House, 1986), ix–xv.

22. "Glenway Wescott Celebrates 85th," *Lambertville Beacon,* April 23, 1986.

23. MW to author, July 4, 1986.

24. Pohorilenko, interview by author, December 12, 1997.

25. Stevenson's recollections as entered in author's journal, December 7, 1986.

26. Ibid.

27. Edwin McDowell, "Glenway Wescott, 85, Novelist and Essayist," *New York Times,* February 24, 1987.

28. "Mr. Glenway Wescott," *Times* (London), February 27, 1987.

29. Stevenson, interview by author, May 29, 1998.

CHAPTER 14. EPILOGUE

1. Pohorilenko, interview by author, December 12, 1997.

2. Ibid.

3. GW Memorial, American Academy of Arts and Letters, March 11, 1987, audio recording.

4. Pohorilenko, interview.

5. Lloyd Wescott to Stevenson, July 13, 1987.

6. MW to Connolly, November 19, 1987.

7. Lloyd Wescott to MW, October 23, 1987, and subsequent legal correspondence of late 1987, Stevenson papers.

8. Pohorilenko, interview.

9. Ibid.

10. "Monroe Wheeler, a Longtime Trustee of Art Museum, 89," *New York Times,* August 16, 1988.

11. "Robert Phelps, Writer Who Edited Colette and Cocteau," *New York Times,* August 4, 1989.

12. GW, *Continual Lessons* (Farrar Straus Giroux, 1990), 25.

13. Malouf, interview by author, April 23, 1990.

14. Lewis to author, December 16, 1990. See also Janet Lewis, "The Poems of Maurine Smith," *Chicago Review,* winter 1990, 63.

15. Hortense Callisher, "A Heart Laid Bare," *Washington Post Book World,* January 13, 1991, 5; John Litweiler, "Glenway Wescott's Amazing Candor," *Chicago Tribune Books,* April 7, 1991, 6; Stan Leventhal, "Learning from History," *Outweek,* January 30, 1991, 52–53.

16. Edmund White, *The Farewell Symphony* (New York: Knopf, 1997), 188–90; Richard Hall, "Avery Milbanke Day," in *Fidelities* (New York: Viking Penguin, 1994), 266–76; William Burroughs, *Last Words* (New York: Grove, 2000), 61–65.

17. *The Pilgrim Hawk* (New York Review of Books Press, 2001); *The Pilgrim Hawk* (New York: Noonday/Farrar Straus Giroux, 1991); *Der Wander Falke* (Zurik: Ammann Verlag, 1995); *Le faucon pélerin* (Paris: Calmann-Levy, 1997); *The Pilgrim Hawk* (Milan: Adelphi, 2002); Susan Sontag, "The Novel as Self Portrait," *New Yorker,* June 18 and 25, 2001, 152–63; *The Grandmothers* (Madison: University of Wisconsin Press, 1996).

18. Robert Patrick, review of "A Visit to Priapus," *Harvard Gay and Lesbian Review,* fall 1995; Ned Rorem, *Lies: A Diary, 1986–1999* (Washington, D.C.: Counterpoint, 2000), 292.

19. Joseph Campbell, with Bill Moyers, "Masks of Eternity," episode 6 of *The Power of Myth* (Woodbury, Minn.: High Bridge, in association with Parabola, 1988).

Index

Abbott, Berenice, 240
"Adolescence" (GW), 46
Albee, Edward, 92
Aldridge, John W., 256
American Academy-Institute of Arts and Letters, xvi, 118, 119, 123–24, 165, 168, 173, 176–77, 193–95, 208–9, 216, 218, 229, 234, 240, 244, 253, 254, 261–63, 267
Ames, Elizabeth, 119
Anderson, Margaret, xv–xvi, 20, 28
Anderson, Sherwood, 94
Anger, Kenneth, 139–40
Apartment in Athens (GW), 101, 108–14, 117, 207, 232, 259
Apple of the Eye, The (GW), 8, 21, 29–31, 36, 38, 41, 45, 67, 109, 198, 250, 255
Arden, Elsie, 102
Ashby, Ivan, 207, 213, 226, 228, 254, 256, 257, 263
Astor, Brooke, 152, 210, 211, 238, 240
Auden, Wystan Hugh, 118, 136, 140, 177, 208
Auer, Clement, 10, 171
Auriol, Vincent, 153
Authors Guild, 118, 204, 205
Avedon, Richard, 159

Babe's Bed, The (GW), 50–51, 52, 53, 54, 100, 258–59
Bachardy, Don, 159, 160, 229, 239
Bacon, Francis, 119
"Bad Han" (GW), 29–30
Baker, Carlos, 42, 208
Balanchine, George, 62, 76, 162, 205
Barber, Samuel, 78
Barnes, Djuna, 118
Barr, Alfred, 66
Barr, James, 158
Barzun, Jacques, 116, 178, 252
Bawer, Bruce, 62–63
Beach, Sylvia, 40
Beaton, Sir Cecil, 55, 106, 119, 226, 234–35, 245
Bennett, Arnold, 29, 98
Bérard, Christian, 34, 60
Bessie, Connie, 241
"Best of All Possible Worlds, The" (GW), 176
Bianco, Francisco and Pamela, 34
Bird, Bill, 52
Bishop, Isabel, 94
Bitterns, The (GW), 18, 20
Blakeston, Oswell, 37, 249
"Blind Beloved, The" (GW), 58
Bodenheim, Maxwell, 22
Bogan, Louise, 168, 178, 191
Borges, Jorge Luis, 216, 221
Bourgoint, Jean, 35–36, 39, 72, 74
Bourgoint, Jeanne, 35
Bowen, Elizabeth, 117
Bowen, Stella, 24
Boyle, Kay, 27, 37, 205, 240
Bradley, Bill, 242
Brakke, Anna, 70, 130, 156–57, 158, 175, 211, 222, 224
Brando, Marlon, 200
"Breath of Bulls, The" (GW), 223–24
Brice, Fanny, 206
Briggs, William, 56

Britton, Coburn, 221
Brodkey, Harold, 177
Bromfield, Louis, 113
Brown, Al, 73
Brown, William Slater, 205
Browning, Elizabeth Barrett, 35
Bruder, Harold, 203
Bryant, William Cullen, 21, 94
Brynner, Yul, 105, 200
Bryson, Lyman, 116
Buckingham, Bob, 123–25, 219
Bugbee, Virginia, 5–6, 26
Bunshaft, Gordon, 213–14
Burke, Kenneth, 30
Burroughs, William S., 177, 267
Butler, Earl, 199, 200, 207, 211, 228, 229, 230, 245
Butler, Samuel, 249
Butts, Anthony, 27, 60
Butts, Mary, 27, 34, 37, 102, 249
Byrne, Brendan T., 233, 237, 242, 245
Byron, Lord (George Gordon), 66, 164

Cadmus, Fidelma, 69, 119, 121
Cadmus, Paul, 69, 70, 78, 98, 103–4, 119, 121, 124–25, 149, 158, 162–63, 174, 221, 235, 242
"Cain and Abel" (GW), 171
Calder, Alexander, 52, 53, 105, 169
Calendar of Saints for Unbelievers, A (GW), 57–58, 219, 233–34
Callisher, Hortense, 267
Campbell, Joseph, 78, 119, 123–24, 129, 219, 225, 253, 267
Canfield, Cass, 56, 94, 111, 192, 206, 225
Capote, Truman, 122–23, 154, 192, 200, 209–10, 229, 234–35, 241
Carter, Jimmy, 234
Case, Margaret, 113–14
Caskey, William, 123
Cather, Willa, 15, 202
Chagall, Marc, 67, 265
Chandlee, Will, III, 207, 219, 226, 231, 238, 246, 264, 265, 267
Charlton, James, 161
Chateaubriand, François René, 193
Cheever, John, 205
"Children of This World" (GW), 117, 170–72, 173
Churchill, Winston, 201
Chute, Marchette, 177
Clark, Eleanor, 205
Clark, Sir Kenneth, 209, 238
Clark, Thane, 242, 246
Cocteau, Jean, 33–36, 37, 40, 41, 44, 47, 48–49, 66, 67, 72–74, 95, 97, 102, 120, 140, 200–201, 207, 220, 242, 254, 266
Colette, 67, 140–41, 153, 167, 168, 196–97, 201, 205, 212, 266
Colum, Padraic, 116
Connolly, Cyril, 49, 67, 140, 205
Connolly, John, 137–38, 140, 145, 146, 147, 150, 153, 156–57, 161, 165, 166, 167, 175, 199–200, 202–3, 207, 212, 215, 218, 228–29, 231, 242, 254, 256, 257, 263–64
Continual Lessons (and journal materials for) (GW), 68, 76, 220–21, 231, 232, 234, 238, 243, 244, 247–48, 251, 265–67
Cooper, Dennis, 248
Corn, Alfred, 267
Coward, Nöel, 118
Cowley, Malcolm, 205, 224
Crane, Josephine, 99, 111, 116, 139, 158, 160, 167, 174, 201
Crevel, René, 43, 47, 48
Crisp, Quentin, 239–40
Crocker, Virginia, 47
Crosby, Caresse, 205
Cross, Amanda (Carolyn Heilbrun), 224
Crowley, Aleister, 37
Cukor, George, 199
Cummings, E. E., 119, 167, 177, 262
Cunard, Lady Emerald, 97, 100, 116, 209
Cunard, Nancy, 52, 72, 202
Cunninghame Graham, Robert Bontine, 24, 223

Dalí, Salvadore, 74, 99
Daniels, Jimmie, 68, 99
"Dare, The" (GW), 5
Davis, George, 94, 234
"Deadly Friend, The" (GW), 32, 55, 58–59, 63–64, 68, 231
Deane, Peter, 211, 212, 228, 258
De la Mare, Walter, 162
Dellenback, William, 135, 144
Dermit, Eduoard, 120, 140
Desbordes, Jean, 48, 66, 72–74
Desti, Marie, 43
Deutsch, Babette, 27, 213

Diamond, Daniel, 246, 248
Diamond, David, 95, 226
Dickey, James, 214
Dietrich, Marlene, 116
Dinesen, Isak, 167, 175, 177–78, 192, 197, 200
"Dinner, a Talk, a Walk with Forster, A" (GW), 218–19
Dos Passos, John, 57, 96
Doubleday, Nelson, Sr., 99–100, 116
"Dream of Audubon, The" (GW), 78, 95–96
"Dream of Mrs. Cleveland, The" (GW), 49, 53–54, 58
Drew, Robert, 121, 122
Duberman, Martin, 151, 244
Duchamp, Marcel, 205
Duncan, Isadora, 34, 43, 95, 102, 242, 246
"Dust Basket, A" (GW), 170

Eliot, T. S., 18
Elliot, Maxine, 205
Ellison, Ralph, 240
"Emperor Concerto, The" (GW), 222–23
"Example of Suicide, An" (GW), 75–76

Faulkner, William, 165, 170, 198
Fear and Trembling (GW), 55–57, 58
Fenwick, Millicent, 226
Ferber, Edna, 112–13
Ferragut, Paul and Anne, 76
Ferrer, José, 154
Field, W. F., 146
"Fire and Water" (GW), 32, 33
Fire Island, 28, 78, 104, 122, 132, 173–74, 208, 226
Fitzgerald, F. Scott, 42, 46, 53, 56, 96, 117, 122, 167, 254
Flanner, Janet, 37, 53, 66, 72–73, 94, 103, 139–40, 173–74, 177, 204, 205, 208, 209–10, 211, 213, 226, 227, 232, 240, 241, 242
Flaubert, Gustave, 115, 258
Flint, Edith Foster, 8, 21, 29
Forbes-Robertson, Diana, 205
Ford, Charles Henri, 53, 63, 65, 69, 76, 119, 141, 177, 208, 234, 238, 252
Ford, Ford Madox, 24, 31, 33, 42, 44, 59, 70, 94, 100, 167, 205, 223
Ford, Hugh, 212, 258
Ford, Ruth, 65, 99, 177, 208, 238, 244
Forster, E. M., 63, 70, 96, 100, 123–25, 145, 146, 154, 218–19, 258
Forster, Kathleen, 8–9, 14, 22–23, 25, 227, 266
"Fortune in Jewels, A" (GW), 97, 100–102, 108
Francis, Arlene, 204
Frasconi, Antonio, 169
French, Jared, 69, 70, 78, 264
French, Margaret, 69, 78
"Frenchman Six Foot Three, The" (GW), 74, 103
Frost, Robert, 22, 168, 193–94, 252

Gado, Frank, 204
Gandhi, Indira, 248
Garland, Judy, 138
Gathorne-Hardy, Jonathan, 150–51
Gathorne-Hardy, Robert, 74, 151
Gaudreault, Denis, 239
Gaynor, Janet, 120
Gebhard, Paul, 133, 143, 148, 167, 199, 207–8
Geffen, Felicia, 118, 209, 261
Gellhorn, Martha, 206
Genet, Jean, 120, 139, 141,142, 143, 153, 177
George, Stefan, 197
Gerhardt, Elena, 26
Gide, André, 41, 43, 154
Gielgud, Sir John, 146
Gill, Brendan, 165
Ginsberg, Allen, 240–41
Girard, Michel, 74, 103
Goldman, Eric, 195, 204
Goldman, Henry, 26, 103
Good-bye, Wisconsin (GW), xv, 45–46, 53, 54, 56, 206, 214, 227–28
Gordon, Caroline, 34, 95, 133, 195
Gordon, Will, 5, 6
Goudeket, Maurice, 67, 140–41
Goyen, William, 140
Grandmothers, The (GW), xv, 13, 32, 33, 36, 37–40, 45, 46, 50, 53, 54, 56, 58, 63, 117, 169, 198, 206, 224, 225, 238, 250, 252–53, 255–56, 259, 262, 267
Green, Julien, 41, 72, 139
Gregory, Horace, 206
Greuze, Jean-Baptiste, 67
Griffin, Peter, 42
Gris, Juan, 27

Grosz, Georg, 177
Guérin, Jacques, 48–49, 51, 53, 55, 60–61, 66, 72, 120, 139, 153, 222, 231, 238
Guérin, Jean, 47, 48, 153
Gunther, Jane, 241, 261–62, 264
Guy, Reginald, 245

Haeni, Susan, 256
Hagen, Uta, 130, 154, 197
Haley, Alex, 38
Hall, Radclyffe, 63
Hall, Richard, 267
Hamill, Pete, 227–28
Harcourt, Alfred, 41
Harrison, Barbara. *See* Wescott, Barbara Harrison
Harrison, Francis Burton, 47, 51, 125, 203
Harrison, Gilbert, 244
Harrison of Paris, 51–52, 53, 54, 57–58, 59, 60–61, 64, 169, 212, 233, 258
Hartford, Huntington, 149
Hartley, Marsden, 15, 105, 106, 159
Harvey, Katherine, 33
Hawkes, John, 206
Haxton, Gerald, 45, 97, 99–100, 114–15
Haymeadows, 175, 178–79, 192–93, 195, 198, 202–3, 206, 211–12, 220, 227, 228, 229, 238, 242, 246–47, 248, 249–51, 254–58, 259, 260, 263–64, 267
H.D. (Hilda Doolittle), 18, 34
Heap, Jane, 20
Heilbut, Anthony, 197
Hellman, Lillian, 112
Hemingway, Ernest, 6, 40–43, 53, 56, 57, 101, 118, 130, 139, 167, 193, 208–9, 223, 233, 254
Hemingway, Martha. *See* Gellhorn, Martha
Hemingway, Mary, 193, 208–9, 233
Henderson, Alice Corbin, 14
Hobson, Laura Z., 118
Hopkins, Harry L., 118
Horney, Karen, 120; Karen Horney Clinic, 174, 203, 237
Hotchkiss, Bruce, 54, 100, 263
Hotchkiss, Elizabeth. *See* Wescott, Elizabeth
Hotchner, A. E., 208–9
Houseman, A. E., 106
Howard, Chuck, 146, 159
Howard, Richard, 220
Hoyns, Henry, 56, 64
Hugnet, Georges, 34
Humphrey, Hubert H., 118
Humphrey, Paul, 8–9, 172
Hunt, William, 68
Hurd, Clement, 78
"Hurt Feelings" (GW), 58
Huston, John, 106
Huxley, Aldous, 209

Images of Truth (GW), 192, 195–98, 214, 219, 225, 228
"In a Thicket" (GW), 29, 33
Inge, William, 167, 199–200, 227, 228
Institute for Sex Research, xvi, 123–24, 126, 127–28, 130, 131–32, 133–36, 139, 141, 142, 144–45, 146–48, 150–51, 158, 159, 161, 167, 199, 207–8, 229, 238
Invitation to Learning (radio symposium), 116
"Isak Dinesen Tells a Tale" (GW), 178, 192
Isherwood, Christopher, 70, 78, 100, 119, 123, 139, 154, 159, 160, 177, 206, 218–19, 229, 235, 239

Jacob, Max, 34
James, Henry, 64, 95
James, William, 252
Johnson, Ira D., 92, 224
Johnson, Philip, 152, 165
Jones, James H., 150–51
Jones, Leroi (Amiri Baraka), 241
Josephson, Matthew, 205
Jouhandeau, Marcel, 45
Joyce, James, 46, 223

Kahane, Jack, 52
Kahn, Sy M., 37, 159, 170
Kaiser, Charles, 121
Kanin, Garson, 205
"Katherine Anne Porter: The Making of a Novel" (GW), 195
Kennedy, John F., 174, 193–94
Kennedy, Rose, 210
Khill, Marcel, 66, 72–74
"King David and His Court" (GW), 4
Kinsey, Alfred C., xvi, 123–25, 126–28, 130–37, 138, 140, 141–42, 144–51, 157–58, 161, 166–67, 199, 207–8, 219, 220, 235, 244; death of, 150–51
Kinsey, Clara, 126, 132, 150, 208

Kirstein, Fidelma. *See* Cadmus, Fidelma
Kirstein, Lincoln, 43, 62, 65, 69, 95, 119, 121, 136, 139, 152–53, 159, 162, 205, 208, 210
Kissinger, Henry, 257
Knowles, John, 193
Kuelthau, Earl Rix, 4–5, 66, 204
Kushner, Dick, 147

Lane, Katherine, 45
Lansdale, Henry Nelson, 79, 90–91, 93, 98, 102, 105
Lassell, Philip, 34
Lavery, Sir John and Lady, 24
Lawrence, D. H., 249–50
Lawrence, Seymour, 195
Leduc, Violette, 156
Lee, Arthur, 37
Leffert, Henry, 116
"Leider Singer, The" (GW), 170
Leitsch, Dick, 219
Lesemann, Maurice, 9, 11–12, 15–17
Lesy, Michael, 228
"Letters to a Circle of Friends: 1932–1966" (GW and Katherine Anne Porter), 212, 221
Leventhal, Stan, 267
Levin, Gustov, 48
Lewis, Janet, 7, 10, 18, 26, 198, 227, 248, 266
Lewis, Sinclair, 30
"Like a Lover" (GW), 36
Lindsay, Vachel, 15
"Little Ocean Liner, The" (GW), 64
Loos, Anita, 140, 204, 210, 222
Loring, Eugene, 76
"Love of New York, The" (GW), 107
Lowell, Robert, 119
Lown, Bernard, 218
Loy, Mina, 18, 27, 173
Lynes, George Platt, xvi, 38, 43–44, 47–48, 49, 54, 55–56, 59, 60, 61, 62, 64, 65, 67, 68, 69, 70, 76, 77–78, 94, 98, 99, 120–21, 123, 128, 129, 136, 142, 145, 154, 158–63, 173, 212, 246, 251, 264; breakup of relationship with MW, 103–5; death of, 161–63; exhibitions of, 54–55, 68, 99, 103, 162, 200, 238, 245; GW correspondence with, 44, 104–5; health/illness, 49, 105, 159–63; legacy, 160, 162–63, 245
Lynes, Mildred, 65, 162, 206
Lynes, Russell, 65, 158, 159, 160, 162, 178, 212, 213, 262

McAlmon, Robert, 52
McCarthy, Joseph, 147, 220
McCarthy, Mary, 174
McCullers, Carson, 165
MacDowell Colony, 22, 167–68, 193
MacGregor, Frank S., 56
McIlhenny, Henry, 157, 246
MacLeid, Marjorie. *See* Wescott, Marjorie
MacLeish, Archibald, 118, 123
Mailer, Norman, 194
Malanga, Gerard, 208
Malouf, Carl, 113, 122–23, 128, 132, 136–39, 147, 153, 166, 170, 176, 199, 266
Malraux, André, 167
Mann, Klaus, 95, 99, 121
Mann, Thomas, 52, 167, 176, 195–96, 197, 214
Mapplethorpe, Robert, 162
Marais, Jean, 72–73, 140
Martin, Hugh, 138
Masters, Edgar Lee, 15
Matisse, Henri, 69, 153, 200, 211
Maugham, Robin Cecil Romer, 114, 115
Maugham, William Somerset, 44–45, 63, 70, 90, 93, 99–101, 111, 112, 114–16, 119–20, 123, 153–54, 167, 171, 212, 241, 250; death of, 201–2; GW on, 97–98, 141, 168, 170, 202, 205–6, 214, 215–16; on GW's writing, 97–98, 100–101, 109, 113, 115–16, 196, 221; on own writing, 100, 116
Maxwell, William, xv, 153, 168, 175, 177, 178, 179, 207, 215, 262
Meier, Karl, 158
Melas, Alex, 108–9
"Memories and Opinions" (GW), 223
Merman, Ethel, 91
Merrick, Gordon, 105
Merton, Thomas, 74
Meyner, Helen, 226, 237, 242
Meyner, Robert, 174, 203, 226, 237
Miksche, Michael, 132, 134, 136–38, 143–44, 166–67, 198–99
Miller, Arthur, 165
Miller, Charles, 118
Miller, Henry, 131

Miller, William, 121, 136, 151, 199, 219, 227
Mills, Margaret, 261
Mineo, Sal, 200
"Mr. Auerbach in Paris" (GW), 102–3
Mistinguett, 73
Mizener, Arthur, 167
"Monday Classes," 99, 116, 139, 167
Monroe, Harriet, 14, 19, 24
Monroe, Marilyn, 165, 199
Montagu, Lord Edward Baron, 146
Moody, Harriet (Mrs. William Vaugham Moody), 19, 20, 21, 22, 23, 25, 193
Moore, Douglas, 194
Moore, Marianne, 20, 22, 26, 27–28, 34, 64, 72, 119, 120, 146, 153, 154–55, 162, 165, 167–68, 169, 176–77, 200, 204, 209, 215, 221–22, 252; death of, 218; on GW's writing, 57, 169, 198
Moore, Mary Warner, 22, 120
Moore, Warner, 168
"Moral of F. Scott Fitzgerald, The" (GW), 96, 117
Morgan, Ted, 114–15, 241
Morris, Lloyd, 36
Mortimer, Raymond, 24, 44, 74, 155, 160, 170, 173, 208, 210, 211, 215, 232–33, 245
Moss, Howard, 207, 254
Mulhocaway. *See* Stone-blossom
Murphy, Noel, 227
Murray, Natalia Danesi, 173–74, 208, 209–10, 226, 227, 241
Museum of Modern Art, xvi, 62, 66–67, 91, 99, 103, 105, 123, 125, 149, 152, 153, 162, 169, 173, 210, 214–15, 242, 248, 265

National Institute of Arts and Letters. *See* American Academy-Institute of Arts and Letters
Natives of Rock (GW), 32, 34, 223, 267
Naylor, Zena, 43
Neill, Peter, 233
"New Jersey Farm—Christmas Images" (GW), 71
Newton, Caroline, 32–33, 59, 63, 96, 101, 164, 176, 178–79, 195–96, 197
Newton, Jeremiah, 246
Ney, Elly, 25
Nin, Anaïs, 131, 197, 237
Nixon, Richard, 214, 220, 226
North, Sterling, 95
Nyquist, Fredrick, 16–17, 18

"Odor of Rosemary, The" (GW), 221–22, 223–24, 255
O'Gorman, Ned, 244
O'Higgins, Patrick, 121, 140, 227, 245
O'Keeffe Georgia, 234, 262
Oldenburg, Richard, 265
Orlovsky, Peter, 240

Pagano, Mark, 122, 125, 145
"Paris 1938" (GW), 247–48
Parker, Dorothy, 153
"Passing of the Old Party, The" (GW), 206; "Old Party, The" (book project), 212
Patrick, Robert, 267
PEN, 118, 240
Perkins, Maxwell, 40, 41, 56, 250
Perlin, Bernard, 121–22, 145, 150, 157, 158, 159, 160–61, 162, 164, 165, 167, 206, 207, 208, 213, 227, 242
Perlman, S. J., 113
Perry, Troy, 219
Phelps, Robert, xi, 178, 192, 208, 211, 212, 218, 220–21, 223, 230, 231, 232, 233–34, 241, 246, 247, 253, 258, 265–66
Phelps, Rosemarie Beck, xi, 178
Picasso, Pablo, 27, 34, 67, 123, 129, 161, 201, 211, 265
Pilgrim Hawk, The (GW), xv, 79, 89–95, 96, 97–98, 101, 108, 117, 122, 169, 192, 198, 206–7, 221, 224, 237, 249–51, 259, 262, 267
Plimpton, George, 247
Poe, Edgar Allan, 266, 267
Pohorilenko, Anatole, 219–20, 246, 254, 257, 260–61, 263–64, 267
Pomeroy, Ralph, 121, 136–37, 138, 146, 150, 152–53, 155, 156, 160, 161–63, 167, 198, 203, 215, 217, 221, 231, 252, 265
Pomeroy, Wardell, 130, 148, 244
Porter, Alan, 74, 76
Porter, Katherine Anne, 59, 64, 66, 70, 78, 94, 114, 117, 119, 120, 121, 123, 128, 140, 153, 154–55, 160, 162, 170, 177, 195, 201–2, 206, 212, 221, 225, 229, 234; death of, 245; GW on, 70, 125,

148, 165, 195, 196, 214, 218; on GW's writing, 96, 192, 195, 213
"Portrait of Country Life, A" (GW), 117
Posner, David, 114
Potter, Pauline. *See* Rothschild, Baroness Pauline de
Pound, Ezra, 27, 34
Powell, Dawn, 58, 205
Prescott, Orville, 197–98
Prockop, Joanna, 235, 237
Prockop, Leon, 193
Prokosch, Frederic, 78, 154–55
Proust, Marcel, 37, 45, 259

Radiguet, Raymond, 34–35, 74
Rain, Charles, 76
Rascoe, Burton, 38
Ray, Man, 205
Rechy, John, 244–45
Reischenbach, François, 136, 139, 141, 147, 158, 160, 238
Reischenbach, Philippe, 136, 160
Remarque, Erich Maria, 106–7
Renard, Jules, 45, 205
Renoir, Pierre Auguste, 67, 265
"Rescuer, The" (GW), 68
Richardson, Tony, 226, 231
Ridge, Lola, 27
Robbins, Frances Lamont, 31, 37, 54, 66, 76, 95, 105, 241
Roberts, Elizabeth Madox, 7, 53, 248
Robeson, Paul, 28, 34, 37, 244
Robinson, Edwin Arlington, 22, 27
Rockefeller, David, 248, 265
Rockefeller, Nelson, 91, 153, 214–15, 242
Roosevelt, Eleanor, 173–74
Roosevelt, Franklin D., 118
Rorem, Ned, 200, 208, 235, 262, 263, 267
Rosco, Jerry, 230
Rose, Sir Francis, 34, 52, 142
Rothschild, Baroness Pauline de, 55, 129, 139, 158, 176, 210–11, 216, 217–18, 224, 226, 229, 230, 231, 236–37; death of 232–33; on GW's work, 111; relationship with GW, 55, 106, 167, 178, 211, 213, 218, 241
Rothschild, Baron Philippe de, 139, 158, 211, 213, 216, 218, 232–33, 236–37, 238, 242–43, 253
Rueckert, William, 34, 58, 64, 78, 92, 94, 96, 169, 191–92, 224
"Runaways, The" (GW), 33
Rusk, Dean, 148

Sackville-West, Edward, 24, 59, 60
"Sacre de Printemps" (GW), 27
"Sailor, The" (GW), 46, 103, 169–70
Salemme, Betty and Tony, 28, 31
Sandburg, Carl, 15, 20
Sassoon, Sir Victor, 68
Saxton, Eugene, 56, 59, 94; Saxton Fund, 118
Schiff, Nancy Rica, 249
Schlossberg, Leah, 237, 245
Schorer, Mark, 97
Scott, Zachary, 177
Searle, Alan, 100, 115, 116, 119–20, 141, 153–54, 201–2, 231
Selbert, Hubert, 208
Selznick, David, 112
"Sentimental Contribution, A" (GW), 64
Sergeant, Elizabeth Shepley, 15, 202
Shadle, Albert, 133
Shahn, Ben, 119
Shapiro, Karl, 204
Sheldon, Edward, 8, 100–101
"Sight of a Dead Body, The" (GW), 68
Sinatra, Frank, 210
Singer, Isaac Bashevis, 225
Sitwell, Dame Edith, 24, 119, 152, 154–55, 168, 201, 205, 245–46
Sitwell, Sir Osbert, 24, 44, 74, 119, 152, 154–55, 173, 201, 206–7, 214, 241
Sitwell, Sir Sacheverell, 224
Skinner, Cornelia Otis, 130
Smith, Dorothy, 242, 246, 254, 257
Smith, Liz, 239
Smith, Maurine, 8, 10, 12, 26, 171–72
Snow, Carmel, 94
Sohl, Ethel, 175, 211–12, 236, 254
Solano, Solita, 72, 227, 232
"Somerset Maugham and Posterity" (GW), 115–16
Sonnenberg, Benjamin, 247
Sontag, Susan, 212, 267
Spectorsky, A. C., 113
Spender, Stephen, 211, 216, 238, 246, 254
Stafford, Jean, 207
"Stallions, The" (GW), 75, 221, 251
Steegmuller, Francis, 207
Stein, Gertrude, 27, 43, 48, 63, 67, 99, 142, 167, 173, 223

Sterling, Monica, 210
Stevens, Wallace, 18, 164–65
Stevenson, Adlai, 210
Stevenson, John, 228–30, 231–32, 235, 236, 238–39, 239, 242, 244, 245, 246, 251, 253, 254, 255, 256, 257–59, 263–64, 265
Steward, Sam, 134, 142–44, 145, 148, 149, 158, 160, 161
Stone-blossom, 68, 70, 104, 106, 114, 115, 116, 124, 128, 130, 147, 148, 156–58, 174–75, 176, 178–79, 219, 224, 266
Stonewall riots, 215, 227
Straus, Helen, 112, 207
Stravinsky, Igor, 34
Sullivan, Tommy, 122–23, 128, 136
Swanson, Gloria, 161
Symonds, John Addington, 12
Szladits, Lola, 230, 241
Szold, Bernadine, 34, 37, 38, 47, 53, 60, 64–65, 112, 120, 161, 173, 175, 193, 213, 223, 235, 242

Tate, Allen, 34, 95, 133, 244
Tate, Caroline. *See* Gordon, Caroline
Tchelitchew, Pavlik (Pavel), 43, 53, 58, 65, 69, 76, 90, 119, 141, 152, 173, 201, 211, 234, 238, 242, 245
Thomson, Virgil, 139, 140, 205, 210
Tichenor, George, 99, 103–5
Tichenor, Jonathan, 103–5, 120
Toklas, Alice B., 27, 43, 142, 173
Tonny, Kristian, 68–69
Toomer, Jean, 70
"Transatlantic Glance, A" (GW), 168
Trilling, Diana, 113
Turbyfill, Mark, 26
Turgenev, Ivan, 236
Turnbull, Andrew, 167
Twelve Fables of Aesop (GW), 168–69, 233–34, 243
Twysden, Duff, 41
Tyler, Parker, 63

Udall, Stewart, 194
UNESCO, 118
Ustinov, Peter, 141

Valdez, Tito, 73
"Valley Submerged, The" (GW), 176, 179, 206, 229, 238
Vanderlint, Debra, 262
Van Doren, Mark, 78
Van Vechten, Carl, 43, 205
Vidal, Gore, 117–18, 119, 141, 172, 229, 246
"Visit to Priapus, A" (GW), 76–77, 145, 241, 267
Vonnegut, Kurt, Jr., 226
Vreeland, Diana, 78, 106, 119, 197, 233
Vursell, Harold, 122

Warhol, Andy, 208, 211, 246, 258, 261
Wedgwood, C. V., 141
Welles, Orson, 99
Welty, Eudora, 113
Wescott, Barbara Harrison, 47, 49, 51, 53, 54–55, 60, 61, 65–66, 68, 69, 70, 96, 98, 99, 100, 109, 112, 117, 118, 139, 157, 158, 161, 175, 179, 192, 195, 198, 202–3, 206, 222, 238, 241, 263, 267; art collection and patronage, 51, 120, 174, 203, 237; death of, 237; GW's correspondence with, 51, 104, 211, 217, 235; and GW's finances, 51, 170, 172–73, 211, 254; and GW's writing, 89–90, 172–73, 212, 249; health/illness, 61, 119–20, 157, 174, 235–36; and relationship with GW, 51, 65, 104, 106, 119–20, 157, 172–73, 203–4, 215, 229, 231, 241
Wescott, Beulah, 3, 51, 65, 70, 212, 230, 254, 258, 267
Wescott, Bruce, 3, 4, 49–51, 54, 65, 70–71, 125, 157–58, 191, 267
Wescott, Deborah (Debo), 100, 120, 161, 162, 193, 235, 242
Wescott, Elizabeth, 3, 15, 50, 51, 54, 70, 100, 124, 125, 191, 258, 267
Wescott, Glenway: art essays by, 64, 67, 68–69, 77–78, 78–79, 106–7, 116–17, 168, 206; autobiographical notes, 94–95, 171, 206; awards, honors, 6, 40, 118, 176–77, 204, 245; on death, 75, 161, 191, 201, 235; death of, 258–59; education of, 3–8, 26, 48, 94–95; family affairs and relationships, 47–48, 49–51, 54, 55, 59–60, 65–66, 98, 99, 100, 103–5, 157–58, 175–76, 191, 206, 235–37, 246–47; fictionalized by other writers, 58, 67, 224, 234, 267; financial affairs, 13, 31, 40, 50, 54, 112, 114, 158, 170, 172–73, 211, 220, 230, 242, 263; on